The Machinima Reader

The Machinima Reader

edited by Henry Lowood and Michael Nitsche

The MIT Press
Cambridge, Massachusetts
London, England

For information about special quantity discounts, please email special_sales@mitpress.mit.edu

This book was set in Stone Sans and Stone Serif by Toppan Best-set Premedia Limited. Printed and bound in the United States of America.

Library of Congress Cataloging-in-Publication Data

The machinima reader / edited by Henry Lowood and Michael Nitsche.
   p.   cm.
Includes bibliographical references and index.
ISBN 978-0-262-01533-2 (hardcover : alk. paper)
1. Machinima films. 2. Digital cinematography. I. Lowood, Henry. II. Nitsche, Michael, 1968–.
TR897.74.M337   2011
778.5′3—dc22

                                                                                        2010035835

10 9 8 7 6 5 4 3 2 1

Contents

Introduction

Henry Lowood and Michael Nitsche

Machinima is less an enigma than a moving target. It is continuously evolving and morphing—changing shape, makers, markets, and technology. Along the way it has established for itself a vibrant niche in the rapidly developing culture of digital games and play. For several years now it has been on the verge of moving beyond the chaotic mix of artistic, ludic, and technical conceptions that shaped the first decade of machinima production, preparing to jump into a deeper engagement with the established traditions and vocabularies of contemporary media. While the growth and potential of machinima raise many interesting questions, the critical investigation of machinima has not kept up with its technical and artistic development. We believe that, as machinima invents and reinvents itself, its flexibility poses an interesting set of issues for academic writers as well as artists and critics. This reader aims to address these issues as it maps out machinima's journey toward positioning itself in the digital media landscape.

The fundamental goals of this reader are to introduce to a broad readership the various debates that have emerged in the machinima community and to provide a primary resource for the critical study of machinima. Machinima is a prime example of the intermedial nature of digital media. Its study overlaps with that of game and fan studies, film and moving image theory, and various emerging topics in new media, such as game art and digital performance. There is no single answer to the questions that arise when we take machinima seriously as an emerging digital medium. Consequently, instead of a unified view, the reader will find an open discussion in this book, one that includes conflicting perspectives and unsettled debates. The contributing authors range from acclaimed machinima artists to curators and scholars, and they bring expertise from very different fields to support an inclusive view of our subject matter. With their help, we offer this inaugural reader as a foundation for further development and critical discussion of machinima. We hope that this collection will establish a timely point of departure for critical studies by charting the emergence of machinima from its beginnings to the present and projecting possible futures from diverse perspectives.

To Take a Stand

Video games are increasingly recognized by cultural institutions such as museums, libraries, and universities as a legitimate art form. Established venues in the arts include machinima as an example of emergent play, as a new form of real-time animation, and as an art form in itself. In its early days, machinima festivals and awards were organized largely by the community of machinima creators, formalized through organizations such as the Academy of Machinima Arts and Sciences. More recently, film, media, and arts festivals have joined the party by organizing machinima events, programs, and competitions in North America, Europe, and Asia. However, its most productive exchange remains on the Internet. This befits the medium, which arose out of online, multiplayer games and the player and spectator communities, supported by a variety of networking technologies ranging from local area networks to the World Wide Web. Many machinima pieces are global coproductions, influenced and watched by players from many different countries and distributed via Web sites and networked file servers. Thus, even as its roots in the self-referential fan culture of digital games must be acknowledged, the growth and anticipated evolution of machinima are connected to its cultural and technical accessibility beyond game culture.

Over time, machinima has emerged as a game-based cultural practice of digital media. Not only does it span different technologies, it has also formed new communities of practice on the way to a history, an aesthetic, and forms of reception and marketability that it can call its own. Whether it is the rich machinima scene in massively multiplayer online worlds such as *World of Warcraft* or *Second Life* or the more contained worlds of individual modders, hackers, and demo coders, machinima offers a view into the way these subcultures express themselves through networked, interactive digital media and provides an opportunity to explore their evolving practices. Machinima is as much a social as a technological phenomenon, which is why it has entered the digital media catalog as well as figuring in critical studies of games and play. Because machinima grew from the bottom up, driven by enthusiasts and accidental filmmakers, it brings into focus the ways in which player-generated practices and uses of computer technology may be sparked by the use of digital games as a found technology for moviemaking. Players are learning how to deploy technologies from computer games to develop new practices for expressing themselves through game-based performance. In this combination with game play, machinima illuminates modes of digital literacy in ways that are examined in several of the essays in this collection.

Players often learn faster than media industries. In the world of machinima, they realized the new possibilities unlocked by the flexibility of the computer-generated image rendered in real time. As a result, machinima is at the center of efforts to explore potential new directions for digital media. At the same time, its intimate connection to the technology and intellectual property of digital games suggests that the interest of media industries in players' work will intensify, for better or worse. The capacity of a medium based on computer games to venture beyond the self-referential is worth investigating in its own right, but it also raises important issues relevant to technology and to legal, social, and cultural studies. Although the future of machinima remains uncertain, its role in digital media today is exemplary: we can learn quite a bit from machinima about how technology and our use of it are changing the media landscape in which we live.

Exploring these changes, the essays in this reader are assembled along the lines of six main rubrics:

Reflections provides positions for a critical review of machinima's past and future. Henry Lowood looks at machinima as a way to document events in—and by extension the history of—virtual worlds. Focusing on the value of machinima for independent filmmaking, Matt Kelland outlines the development of machinima into a film production tool. In contrast, Katie Salen argues that machinima remains limited in its reach toward professional film production—and that there is nothing wrong with that.

Technology covers various technical elements underlying machinima and related digital film production. Friedrich Kirschner presents his approach to a hands-on solution for real-time machinima production, one that focuses especially on creative access at every level of production. At the other end of the spectrum of digital film production, Lev Manovich discusses the universal capture method used in the *Matrix* films and leverages this discussion to consider possible futures of moving image production. Concentrating more on the technical aspects of controlling virtual characters, Ali Mazalek's essay closes this section with a discussion of virtual puppeteering devices.

Performance continues the thread of digital puppeteering but expands on this theme by applying theory and practice of performance studies to describe machinima as a performative medium. Using performance studies as a jumping-off point, Michael Nitsche outlines key elements of machinima as an independent media format in its own right, pointing to a possible future of a moving image culture. David Cameron and John Carroll position machinima in reference to current discussions of liveness in performance studies. Concentrating on a single platform, *Second Life*, Dan Pinchbeck and Ricard Gras argue for the value of machinima as an element of a given game environment itself. Peter Krapp offers a much wider view as he discusses the role of gestures in the expressive catalog of machinima as moving beyond machinima alone and into our involvement with a computing culture.

Machine Cinema presents critical discussions of machinima in relation to other moving image cultures. Michael Pigott asks what the stylistic conventions of machinima are, concentrating on work done in the *World of Warcraft* game environment. Developing an argument about the role of an underlying game engine for machinima pieces produced using it, Jeffrey Bardzell reveals a spectrum from an instrumental to an immersive view of the relationship between game environment and machinima production, thereby questioning the "reality" of machinima movies. Erik Champion shifts the focus away from a discussion of machinima production, instead asking how machinima can be understood as art.

Pedagogy addresses the operation of machinima as a tool for learning. Pedagogical value can be found in machinima as a storytelling tool, as well as in the ways it offers a learning environment for collaborative digital media practices in the classroom. Matthew Thomas Payne describes the pedagogical value of machinima, using *The Sims 2* as a case study for the development of media literacy through machinima. Daniel Kringiel discusses media literacy in greater detail, touching on its impact, as well as necessity, in video game cultures, and particularly the modding scene.

Context offers a number of different approaches that investigate the social significance of machinima, as well as the cultural and even legal problems raised by the ways in which machinima movies are made and discussed. Robert Terry Jones explores the role of women as machinima artists and draws parallels to the development of early radio usage. Focusing on *Half-Life 2*, Gareth Schott and Bevin Yeatman investigate machinima fan communities on the ground, so to speak, drawing important insights as digital ethnographers operating inside game communities. The in-game work of machinima can often lead to conflicts between player expression in the commercial game world and the ownership of artistic game assets and intellectual property by developers and publishers, a conflict that burdens machinima's independent development and is further investigated by Matteo Bittanti in the closing essay.

This collection of essays is not intended to provide closure on the subject. Machinima is bound to continue changing, entering more arenas of academia, commerce, and art. Technological innovation will continue to alter the practices associated with machinima production, and evolving media literacy will affect its reception. By gathering together the essays presented in this collection, we hope to have provided a useful foundation for a critical discussion of machinima without constraining its ongoing development.

We thank our editors at the MIT Press, especially Doug Sery, Katie Helke, and Mel Goldsipe, and all of the authors for their patience with our seemingly slothful pace as editors. We also thank our colleagues and students at Georgia Tech University (Michael Nitsche's home institution) and Stanford University (Henry Lowood's) for their support, insights, and encouragement. We would be remiss if we did not also acknowledge our admiration for the many players, game developers, and machinima artists who created the medium that made this book relevant. Finally, we especially thank our families for putting up with our obsessions and taking the time to view with us so many machinima videos that we found irresistibly appealing.

I'm Too Busy to Date Your Avatar (PookyMedia/Bernhard Drax, 2009).

1 Video Capture: Machinima, Documentation, and the History of Virtual Worlds

Henry Lowood

In March 2010, Sam Pierce, aka "Sedrin," of the *World of Warcraft*–based machinima group SlashDance, released *Yesterday's News*. This roughly three-minute-long short was created for Blizzard Entertainment's Rise to Power machinima competition, sponsored by Alienware, a high-end personal computer maker acquired by Dell in 2006. The contest was organized to encourage the "best fan-made machinima set in Azeroth, focusing on the rise to power of various characters, heroes and villains from *World of Warcraft*" (Blizzard Entertainment 2010). The competition attracted some of the best-known *World of Warcraft* machinimators, including Baron Soosdon, Olibith, and SlashDance. Pierce's short, however, turned the theme of glorifying heroes on its head, creating instead a nostalgic, sentimental piece in the style of a silent movie about loss and the past. The video opens with the work of a Dwarf miner and stonecrafter who creates the "meeting stones" used by *World of Warcraft* adventurers to port quickly to the "instances" where groups of players would band together to complete quests and gather loot. He reads a newspaper dated patch 3.3, with the headline, "New LFG Tool: Meeting Stones Obsolete?" When he then visits his lovingly created stones, they are all unused, barren, and survive in the game merely as mute vestiges of an inaccessible past. Another crumpled newspaper reveals a similar story about the obsolescence of flight paths, though the miner is at least able now to share his own sense of loss and bewilderment with the former proprietor of that operation.

Yesterday's News points to the possibility of machinima not only as a vehicle for commentary on virtual worlds and the communities of players that inhabit them but also as a source of historical documentation about those worlds and communities as they disappear and fade into memory. It takes its place alongside other projects that explore similar themes having to do with loss in virtual world history, from *Exploration: The Movie* and *Nogg-aholic: The Movie* (Tobias "Dopefish" Lundmark, 2005) about the exploration of normally inaccessible areas in *World of Warcraft*, through Tristan Pope's *For Honor* (2006), a sly reportage about the impact of Battlegrounds instances in *World of Warcraft* on social interaction and activity in the game, to *EA-Land: The Final Countdown* (How They Got Game, 2008), raw video capture of the last few

Figure 1.1
SlashDance, *Yesterday's News*.

minutes of EA-Land before its final shutdown on August 1, 2008. All of these productions underscore the twofold sense in which machinima is at its heart not only about
performance but also about documentation: (1) it is founded on technologies of
capture through which in-game assets and performance are redeployed and reworked,
and (2) it creates historical documentation that captures aspects of the spaces, events,
and activities through the lens of a player's view of the game world. *Yesterday's News*
recalls not just the obsolete activities and artifacts of *World of Warcraft* but also links
its storytelling to the increasingly vestigial medium of the newspaper.

This hint of a linkage between machinima and the recorded chronicle sets the stage
for the central thought of this essay, namely, that the three primary methods for
making machinima during its brief history—code, capture, and compositing—match
up neatly with three ways to document the history of virtual worlds.[1] These linkages
are provocative for thinking about what we can do to save and preserve the history
of virtual worlds in their early days. As it turns out, they also suggest how we might
begin to think about machinima as a documentary medium. It is not really surprising
that we should consider this possibility. Historically, the development of machinima
has been closely tied to the technologies and practices of game replay and screen
capture (Lowood 2007a, 2007b). Machinima is usually produced with the software
used to play games. Seen as a new medium emerging from digital game technology,
it can be described as having been cocreated by developers and players, yet its

Figure 1.2
SlashDance, *Yesterday's News.*

development as a vital part of game culture has been dominated by the innovations, creativity, and participation of players. This rootedness in game culture enhances the value of machinima as a method for capturing footage about events and activities that take place in virtual worlds.

Linking the curation of virtual world history to its "capture" along the lines of production methods established by machinima begs the question of what it is that will be captured and documented. The interactive, immersive, and performative aspects of digital games and virtual worlds take the challenges faced by media archivists and historians beyond software preservation to problems that demand new documentation and preservation strategies. Indeed, the social and performative aspects of online worlds lead us away from thinking about the preservation problem solely in terms of the software and propriety data that support and flow out of these worlds. When we emphasize the *history* of these worlds, our attention turns to events, actions, and activities. Future historians of virtual worlds will want to understand what people—players, residents, users—actually did in early virtual worlds, partly at the level of social and personal experiences, partly in terms of historical events such as political protests or artistic performances, and partly to understand the issues of identity, law, economics, ethnography, and governance that connect the virtual world to real-world activities. Clearly, there is more to the documentation of virtual world history than bit-perfect conservation of software and data.

Machinima and replay both have stimulated cultures of performance and spectator-ship within digital game culture. Players enjoy game-based replay movies as game film for following and learning from superior players and thus improving their own player skills. They watch machinima videos for entertainment but also understand them as a mix of commentary, paratext, and insider-joke referencing of specific games, usually those with which a particular piece of machinima was itself created. As spectators of replays or machinima, players deconstruct what they see as a mix of skills, actions, play, performance, and tricks that go into making these game-based videos. The impor-tance of this indexing of machinima with respect to gameplay is at the heart of its potential application for documenting the history of virtual and game worlds. In other words, the documentary value of machinima is not merely a reflection of its potential use as a neutral capture technology; its value as being rooted in game culture is not at all about the objectivity of capture technologies but derives from machinima being in a sense "tainted" by its intimate connection with game environments and game-play. Efforts to verify and interpret game-based replays and movies have been an integral part of their circulation through player communities since at least the mid-1990s, when games such as id Software's *Doom* and *Quake* offered robust systems for play recording and the emerging Internet provided a foundation for building net-worked player communities and file distribution. Replay and machinima, in short, have been at the historical center of player culture, and the production techniques on which they are based inevitably inform the mix of methods available for documenting that culture.

The use of machinima to produce documentation about game and virtual worlds naturally depends on how these movies are produced. More than that, each of the three primary modes of machinima production—code (demo), screen capture, and compositing of game assets—provides a different take on the recording of events and experiences in virtual worlds, giving us three ways of thinking about methods for their documentation that curators and archivists of virtual world history can use to practical effect.

Take 1. Perfect Capture: Demo Recording and Replay

Demo recording was the first form of widely circulated game replays associated with first-person shooter (FPS) games and remains the primary mode for viewing recorded competitive games in genres such as real-time strategy. Strictly speaking, *Doom* and *Quake* demos or *Warcraft III* replays are not really movies. Rather, they are sequences of commands or scripts that tell the game engine what to do, essentially by repeating the effects of keyboard and mouse input in the same sequence as executed by the player when playing a game. One consequence of the separation of game engine from asset files in John Carmack's canonical solution to the problem of game architecture was that the demo or "intro" movie was stored in a discrete file with its own format, the .lmp (pronounced "lump") file in *Doom* and the .dem (demo) file in *Quake*. This was a game asset viewed when a player started up the game. Players could also record their own game sessions and play them back inside these games by saving, then loading and running, demo files. In Carmack's design architecture, making these movies required no hacking of the game engine, in effect creating a new performance space separate from the game software but one that also allowed for the distribution of archived performance in the form of demo files that could be viewed by players with the identical software configurations. This convention was carried forward from *Doom* to many other games, such as *Quake/Hexen, Half-Life*, and *Unreal Tournament*. Replays captured as demo movies have been circulated as skills demonstrations, as recordings of significant competitive events (i.e., Thresh's defeat of Billox at Quake-delica in 1998, circulated as a recammed highlight reel), as a form of advertisement or recruiting pitch for player clans and tournaments, and for many other purposes. Demonstrating skills through competitive player performance was the primary motivation for creating the first game movies, such as replays and speed runs; learning about gameplay by viewing these movies depended on the development of practices for spectatorship, witnessing, and certification. The result was the full utilization of this new game-based performance space.

Demo recording and editing also became the basis for the first project that we would today recognize as machinima, initially known as *Quake* movies. The Rangers' *Diary of a Camper* resembled the demo movies of *Doom* gameplay, with short bursts of frantic action punctuated by flying blood and bits of body parts. Yet *Diary of a Camper* broke with the *Doom* demo movie in one essential respect: the movie was not seen from the first-person perspective of a player but instead established the independence of the spectator's view from that of any player-actor. It turned out that this *Quake* clan's motto, "Rangers Lead the Way," could be applied to their coding skills as well. They had devised their own programming hacks for editing the *Quake* demo format. The resulting camera view might perhaps be seen as establishing a kind of emancipation from gameplay, perhaps even as a neutral or objective position from which to document gameplay, but this claim hardly squares with the deep dependence of *Quake* movies on game data as well as on programming and player skills, or the fact that *Quake* movies and machinima were often "shot" from a particular player's point of view during an in-game recording session.

Thinking about demos and replays in terms of documenting virtual world history emphasizes another aspect of these recordings as a technique for recording in-game events and actions. A notion that plays into the preservation discussion and is particularly relevant here is the potentially perfect reproduction of digital data. Digital personae, avatars, and player characters are ultimately all bits of data on a machine. If we can acquire and preserve access to these data, should it not be possible to copy the bits forever? Is that how we can solve the problem of preserving the history of virtual worlds? If so, the first step toward this solution is accepting that everything that happens in virtual worlds as software systems is in some sense reducible to data, and the second step asserts that, as a practical matter, it should be possible to capture these data perfectly and preserve them without loss. A paradigm for the perfect capture of activity in the form of data is exactly the recording of in-game activity such as game replay files and demos.

Consider the example of Chris Crosby, aka "NoSkill." He was among the first wave of *Doom* players to be recognized by other players as a "Doomgod," a moniker given to exceptionally skilled players. An active player from about 1994 to 1996, he was killed in a car crash in 2001. His memorial site on the Web, like many others, depicts a young man in the prime of life, with his infant son in his arms. The site also offers a number of demo files for downloading, originally recorded from games he played between May 1995 and April 1996 (NoSkill Memorial Site 2004). After a visitor downloads Chris Crosby's demo files from his memorial site and plays these files inside the correct version of this old game, originally published toward the end of 1993, she in effect is able to see a now-obsolete game through the eyes of a dead player. NoSkill comes back to life as the replay file activates the game engine to carry out the exact sequence of actions performed by the now-dead player. Moreover, because we are using an essentially "dead" game to produce this replay, we are also engaging in an act of software preservation and resurrection. The result is that for this FPS, it is possible to see a historical game as played—and seen—through NoSkill's eyes. The player is dead, but his avatar in some sense lives on through this act of perfect reproduction, accessible to any future historians of the game. Yet we cannot help but contrast the potentially infinite repetition and perfect reproduction of his gameplay to the fading memories of his life, and death. His replays alone are mute with respect to his motivation for playing or his experiences as a player. What we are seeing may represent the perfect reproduction of game states and events, but it is not historical documentation. The perfect capture of gameplay represented by the replay is a remarkable act of software and data preservation. Yet as we begin to conduct early work on preservation of games and virtual worlds, approaching this work in terms of software preservation and the perfect capture mode exemplified by game replays will lead to a barren exercise with respect to the documentation of the events and activities—the history—that have occurred in these worlds.

Let us assume that we are able to capture every bit from a virtual world server, everything from 3D models to account information; that we are able to reverse engineer or disable authentication and log-in controls after the original server is no longer live; and that we have received permission from every rights holder, ranging from game developers to third-party developers and players, to copy, store, and use what they created, to show and even inhabit their avatars, and to reveal their identity and

Figure 1.3
NoSkill replay from *Doom*.

activities. The likelihood of all this actually happening is near zero, of course, but let us assume it can be done. If we then could leap the additional hurdle of synchronizing every state or version of the software with the matching states of the server's databases, it might be possible to run a simulation of the virtual world as an archival time machine, flying around on a magic carpet in spectator mode without interacting with events run by the game engine and player data. This would be an act of perfect capture for a virtual world, much like replay for a digital game or the Internet Archive's Wayback Machine for a historical Web site. This is virtual world history as a demo movie.

Take 2. Screen Capture and Documentation

As tempting as the notion of perfect capture of events in game worlds may be, the dependence of replays on game software hardwires documentation to the vexing problem of software preservation. Demos and replay files consist of saved sequences of instructions from a previously played game that, when executed by the game software, show the same game from the perspective of the original players and, for some games, in-game spectators. Unlike video files captured from the screen or video-card output, demos or replays allow different views and settings as permitted by the game software and produce the best visual quality that the software will produce without degradation or the need to compress files to save storage space. However, all this is possible only when a running version of the game engine is available to view these replays. Not only that, the version used to view the demo or replay nearly always must correspond exactly to the version that was played when it was created. Therefore, any decision about which version of the game will be preserved determines which replay or demo files will be viewable in the future. Likewise, any decision about which demos or replays are historically significant in terms of game culture or history presupposes preservation of the appropriate version of the game software. Treatment of the software artifact affects documentation, and selection of documentation affects treatment of the software artifact. At least in the realm of virtual world or digital game history, the separation of these treatment decisions into specialized areas or departments may lead to disastrous consequences for future archivists and historians. Here we might say that Carmack's separation of game engine from data has turned against the historian, who now needs to preserve and synchronize both in order to make sense of either.

Future historians and others interested in the history of virtual worlds will be intensely curious about the inhabitants of early virtual worlds. They will want to know about the things people were doing in virtual worlds, why they were doing them, and what their activities meant to them. The possibility of perfect event capture with respect to digital data, with the game replay or the demo serving as a paradigm for perfectly reproducing the past, suggests that it will even be possible to track the activities of the earliest virtual world inhabitants by seeing through their eyes. Yet from a historian's point of view, perfect capture is not a perfect solution to the problem of how to document the history of virtual worlds. Besides having to preserve the software and data needed to produce such a replay, the notion of the perfection of this mode of capture is misleading, for it must be placed alongside the very real possibility of "perfect loss" in digital spaces. Even if we save every bit of a virtual world, its software and the data associated with it and stored on its servers, along with a replay of every moment as seen by players, it may still be the case that we have completely lost its history. The essential problem with this approach is that it leaves out the identification and preservation of historical documentation, and these sources are rarely to be found in the data inside game and virtual worlds or on the servers that support them. The same is true for any form of machinima that merely reproduces or replays events.

So, back to machinima. The hybrid nature of this medium as a found or ready-made technology carried important implications as it broke out beyond *Quake* movies and the demo format into a variety of media spaces less closely tied to the hard-core computer game culture of FPS games. This move was determined in part by changes made by id Software to the game software that consequently, if unintentionally, made the demo format less accessible as a means for making machinima. Significantly, those machinima projects that subsequently became popular with larger audiences relied on a mode of production quite different from *Quake's* demo movies. Instead of capture in the game, editing with special tools, recompilation into the demo format, and playback inside the game, these movies followed a path pioneered by Tritin's *Quad God*. They captured what was displayed on the screen (or perhaps more accurately, the graphics card) as video. Machinima based on video capture could no longer be edited as code; it could only be produced by editing video footage using nonlinear video editing software, compressing the edited tracks, then distributing and viewing the resulting movies in digital video formats. Instead of FPS games, popular console games and massively multiplayer online games became the dominant modes of machinima production based on screen capture rather than replay. This was machinima "for the rest of us," no longer tied to hard-core game genres, expert coding of demo files and decoding of game footage, and access to games as playback machines. The breakout title for this mode of production was Rooster Teeth's *Red vs. Blue*, a comedy series based on the Xbox games *Halo* and *Halo 2* that ran for five seasons (one hundred episodes) between 2003 and 2007. During roughly the same period, hundreds if not thousands of game movies and machinima works were produced in massively multiplayer games (*World of Warcraft*), virtual worlds (*Second Life*), or games that exported directly to video (*The Movies*); in each case, the predominant mode of production was direct capture from the screen image.

The essential difference between code and capture for machinima was that the new "orientation of machinima towards the film format came with a price: The game engine lost its value as replay engine and remained only a production tool" (Nitsche 2007). Machinima was thus cut off from its previous dependence on game technology in postproduction and distribution; the game world provided only the production environment. Nitsche underlines a consequence of this separation that has implications for machinima as a documentary medium for virtual worlds: "This is a paradigm shift from the recording of the event (in a demo) to the recording of a viewpoint to the event (in a screen capture)—from a new game-based logging format to the established production of moving images as successive still renderings" (ibid.).

In a post on the Terra Nova blog titled "The History of Virtual Worlds," historian Timothy Burke remarked on the difficulties of carrying out qualitative research on this subject, especially when historians lack personal experiences in these environments. One commenter, Greg Lastowka, responded that "actually, it's far easier to get the data on *everything* happening in virtual worlds and to keep it forever"—essentially, the notion of perfect capture. Burke replied to this comment by noting the limitations of data generated and stored on a server. These "proprietary" data of virtual worlds encompass what is owned, or present on the servers that support that world, but even if historians have access to all of it, their utility for the interpretation of specific events is quite limited. As Burke put it, "I think the one thing that *isn't* in the proprietary data is the history of unusual or defining episodes or events in the life of particular virtual worlds. . . . The narrative history, the event history, of any given virtual world, may in fact be obscured by the kinds of god's-eye view data that developers have. After all, they often don't know what is happening at the subjective level of experience within communities, or have to react to it after it's happened. (Say, when players stage a protest)."[2] Thus, focusing on preservation of what Burke calls proprietary data matches up poorly with the likely needs of future scholars of virtual worlds. The problem for historical research is that a complete set of software with a matching trove of all the data associated with a virtual world's server cannot be interpreted without contextual information. Context and personal perspective are needed to supplement historical documentation in demo mode. For a contemporary participant in this history, such as Burke, personal knowledge or interviews can provide guidance in the selection of events and fill gaps in their interpretation. The essential problem, however, is the identification and preservation of historical documentation, and these sources are rarely to be found inside virtual worlds or on the servers that support them.

Machinima based on screen capture provides a kind of documentary recording of events that take place in virtual worlds. It is also dependent on a personal perspective, not just in the sense that the final piece is carefully edited and produced, but also because unlike demo recordings, the camera view is fixed by the original recording, often corresponding to the view of a particular player (usually the director or an assigned "cameraman"). While any kind of machinima production can be edited to produce a narration of historical events in the sense of a documentary film, machinima based on screen capture removes the temptation introduced by the demo analogy of considering "perfect capture" as the documentation mode for virtual world history. The sifting of historical data is not a bad thing. Nor is the introduction of subjectivity in the creation of documentation about events, as opposed to merely recording the events as data. As Hayden White has argued, "histories gain part of their explanatory effect by their success in making stories out of *mere* chronicles." He calls this process "emplotment" and notes that the task of historians is "to make sense of the historical record, which is fragmentary and always incomplete" (White [1974] 2001, 280). In a sense compatible with this view of documentation and history, machinima as screen capture supplements the demo format not only as a new basis for game-based moviemaking but as a different take on the importance of selectivity and perspective in the use of machinima to produce historical documentation. Collections of virtual world videos, along with other forms of documentation external to virtual worlds, such as blogs, wikis, player-created Web sites, maps, and many other forms of documentation, provide information about player activities that cannot be extracted even from perfectly preserved game software and data.

Douglas Gayeton's *Molotov Alva and His Search for the Creator: A* Second Life *Odyssey* (2007) exemplifies the conflation of documentary film-making and machinima as point-of-view documentation of virtual world history (Au 2007, 2008). Commissioned by the Dutch production company Submarine, it was distributed through a variety of channels, including the Dutch television channel VPRO, mobile phones via Mini-movies, and Cinemax via broadcast rights purchased by the cable channel HBO in the United States. The unprecedented success of *Molotov Alva* as a machinima property belied its mysterious origins as a project. It was originally released as a series of video diaries supposedly created by a *Second Life* character called Molotov Alva. The first of these diaries appeared on YouTube on March 2, 2007. It immediately drew a substantial viewership as an original exploration of virtual worlds set up as this *Second Life* resident's disappearance from "real life" into *Second Life*, followed by his quest to discover the meaning of what he found there. From the beginning, the video desta-bilized boundaries between documentary, chronicle, and fiction. Gayeton steadfastly insisted that he had produced a documentary about Molotov Alva's disappearance and reemergence in *Second Life,* but eventually revealed that he had created the character himself to produce this work. At the same time, many of the scenes were recorded literally as cinema verité; Gayeton, unfamiliar with machinima production tech-niques, simply pointed a high-definition camera at his computer monitor, a technique he eventually called "RumpleVision" after the name of the converted farmhouse in which he set up his "studio." Gayeton was aware that part of his work was to docu-ment history that would otherwise be lost; he realized that he had "documented something that's never gonna exist again" (Au 2008). Indeed, most of the locations captured through his character's Odyssey have since been removed from *Second Life* without a trace other than documents such as Gayeton's video.

Gayeton's unorthodox production technology sets his work against the perfect capture of demo and replay in several revealing and important ways. His high-definition camera, set three feet away from his monitor, is separated in every way from game software and proprietary data. There can be no confusion about the status of these images as personal, selected, and indexical. It is a point of view derived from liter-ally pointing at the screen, not a direct recording from an in-game camera or imagery generated from gameplay data. This separation underscores the potential of machinima as a means for capturing perspective and context, as ethnography, documentary, and history rather than an exact recording of historical events in virtual spaces. In this sense, such point-of-view documentation is exactly, as Burke proposes, about what software and game data cannot deliver, such as motivations, personal accounts, and situated experiences. In short, it is about the meaning of events and activities.

Gayeton's idiosyncratic documentary points the way to machinima as documenta-tion, but hardly as a rigid method for recording the past. Machinima pieces ranging from Tristan Pope's *Not Just Another Love Story* (Lowood 2006) to raw footage such as

Figure 1.4
Douglas Gayeton, dir., *Molotov Alva and His Search for the Creator.*

the *Final Countdown* video that documents the last minutes of EA-Land show us other ways in which personal screen capture provides viewers with thought-provoking documents for interpreting events and activities that take place in virtual worlds. In short, both fictional and nonfictional machinima can contribute to a documentation project by emphasizing point of view rather than perfect data capture.

Take 3. Asset Compositing: Models and Artifacts of Virtual Worlds

Machinima creators do not just use digital games as a production technology. They work inside game spaces and software to scout locations and to build or find sets, artwork, and animation. A third mode of machinima production, neither demo nor screen capture, depends on the direct use of game assets such as models and maps.

Figure 1.5
How They Got Game project, *EA-Land: The Final Countdown.*

This form of machinima production became popular among the many machinima creators who turned to the immensely popular massively multiplayer game *World of Warcraft* as a platform for their work. Server-based games such as *World of Warcraft* deny direct access to code and data outside their use in-game; thus, demo recording is not an option.[3] Initially, *World of Warcraft*–based moviemaking was limited to edited screen captures, as was typical for networked, server-based games. Early *World of Warcraft* movies were created as live performances grabbed via screen capture, then cleverly edited, perhaps with voice-overs or painstakingly lip-synched dialog. These movies rapidly became an essential part of the player culture around the game as it grew in popularity. As the subscriber base grew, so did the demand for new gameplay movies and machinima, which were distributed via sites such as warcraftmovies.com geared to the growing player community. Tristan Pope played on this relationship between machinima and game community in his controversial *Not Just Another Love Story* (Lowood 2006). At the time this movie was created, Pope could only use video capture to produce his work. He called attention to this dependence of *World of Warcraft* machinima on the game itself when he defended his controversial depiction of sexual imagery in this work by arguing that he had only "executed what the Pixels in *WoW* suggest" (Pope 2005). But soon another technique for making machinima emerged that provided its makers with more independence from the pixels on the screen.

By early 2006, new tools such as John (Darjk) Steele's WoW Model Viewer opened up the game's model database to *World of Warcraft* players, giving them direct access to every character and equipment model, particle effect, animation, and other game asset. Initially, players used the viewer to do things like dress up characters or show off items they had received as in-game loot. Before long, machinima creators realized they were able now to composite models and maps (viewed with the appropriately titled Map Viewer), mix them with live in-game performance, and composite these elements to make movies. Some went farther by editing models or creating new animations and added them to the mix. For example, Deeprun Goldwin Michler's *The Man Who Can* (2006) depicts a character who joyfully escapes the limitations imposed by Blizzard's pixels; he proves that he can by dancing with new moves animated by Michler. Machinima projects such as Tristan Pope's own *Switcher* series (2005–2006), Jason Choi's *Edge of Remorse* (2006), Mike Spiff Booth's *Code Monkey* (2006), Myndflame's (Clint and Derek Hackleman's) *Zinwrath: The Movie* (2005), or Nicholas "Snoman" Fetcko's *Wandering Dreamscape* (Snoman 2007a) used new tools such as the Model Viewer or hand-cut elements of game footage to make machinima by compositing scenes and postproduction editing.

One can trace the evolution of techniques from in-game video capture to model editing and compositing most clearly through the progression of specific machinima series and artists, such as Martin Falch's *Tales of the Past* trilogy (2005–2007), Myndflame's body of work, or Joshua Diltz's *Rise of the Living Dead* trilogy (2005–2006). Armed with access to game models, effects, and other assets, *World of Warcraft* movies broke open creative (but not necessarily legal) constraints on the use of online games and their artistic assets. Machinima makers now used these games more freely to make movies that were no longer limited to what they could accomplish with in-game puppeteering. Compositing game assets resembled demo in the sense that it depended on game data, but at the same time this technique primarily called on artistic prowess in realms such as 3D model, animation, or video editing rather than coding (demo) or gameplay and puppeteering (screen capture) skills. Terran Gregory of Rufus Cubed probably expressed a typical attitude when he called the Model Viewer "the 'Key' to unlocking WoW Machinima as a whole." He praised its ability to empower the machinima artist to realize his or her vision; the Model Viewer "was the great virtual socioeconomic equalizer that truly allowed WoW movie makers to experience all of the freedoms that are inherent to Machinima."[4] By 2009, Naughty Dog's *Uncharted 2* acknowledged the use of such tools by releasing its game with a Cinema Mode that included green screen compositing and built-in video editing.

Figure 1.6
The *World of Warcraft* Model Viewer.

Works such as Snoman's *Wandering Dreamscape* and Baron Soosdon's *I'm So Sick* (2007) point to a possible role for asset composition not only as a third path for machinima but also as a model for digital archaeology in virtual worlds. Snoman made *Wandering Dreamscape*, the first in a series of *Dreamscape* pieces, as a "tribute to the Nogg-aholic community" (Snoman 2007a) and its primary video creator, Tobias "Dopefish" Lundmark. The Nogg-aholics guild specialized in an activity that can be described as a combination of spelunking, exploration, excavation, and archaeology in terms appropriate for a digital environment: searching out and documenting unfinished or generally inaccessible locations in *World of Warcraft*. (The name of the guild was derived from an elixir that, when imbibed, causes a game character to undergo one of several random changes or effects.) As explorers, the guild members typically ventured into spaces that Blizzard as developer of the game was not ready to release to its players, such as the alpha versions of upcoming expansion areas. Machinima videos created by members such as Dopefish documented what they found, seeking to provide information to the player community about these spaces. As one commentator put it, these and other *World of Warcraft* explorers tried to "document everything that was suddenly new and uncertain" about the game world (Howgego 2008).

Snoman's tributes to the Nogg-aholic community not only construct an "alternate *Warcraft*" but also explicitly show "what is possible when you have the tools and proper knowledge of the *WoW* data" (Snoman 2007a, 2007b). *Wandering Dreamscape*, for example, deploys over a dozen model changes to transform landscapes into alternative virtual realities, the Model Viewer, FRAPS-based video capture, and Soosdon's own landscape model editing to create the Barrens Biohazard area by mixing in elements from other areas in the game world. Like Snoman, in *I'm So Sick* Soosdon also mixes in elements from other games, such as *Unreal Tournament 2004, Bioshock*, and *Half-Life 2,* and at one point even shows a *World of Warcraft* model playing in front of a poster for another machinima piece, *Edge of Remorse* (Riot Films, 2006). These projects link the activity of exploring and, in a sense, digging out unrevealed spaces to get access to game data, and a project of documenting through machinima what these data reveal.

If with demo and replay we verify functionality and precisely track events in game worlds, and if with video capture we reveal points of view and the meaning associated with these events, then asset capture and editing allow the recreation of environments for the purpose of discovering what was hidden, lost, or inaccessible below the surface. In short, these techniques hint at an archaeology of virtual worlds. What might a resource built on this premise look like as a historical tool? The newfound power realized by *World of Warcraft* machinima makers amounted to pulling assets out of the game and importing them into the artist's workspace. We return again to the assets and content that go into the creation of a virtual world: models, maps, geometries,

Figure 1.7
Baron Soosdon, Barrens Biohazard.

textures, and so on. We do not yet know how future scholars will visualize, analyze, and understand these artifacts in a digital repository consisting of data files and metadata. One way of guessing how future historians might access these materials is suggested by the administrator modes that we have in early examples of digital repositories today, in which the archival collection is presented essentially as a file directory. The use case for access to these materials is that of reconstruction from these data files, such as an installation package or a set of models and textures.

Here is an alternative model for access to the artifacts of a past world: museums. A natural history museum, for example, houses models and suitable spaces for these models. If we go there to see dinosaur skeletons, they are likely to be depicted in front of a diorama that takes the visitor to the prehistoric savannah. The access model in such a museum is based on the visual arrangement of artifacts, and it is reinforced by immersion in a simulation of the historical world of the artifacts. It should be possible to do something similar with 3D artifacts from virtual and game worlds. The importing of models to make machinima provides a clue to how we might go about this project and, in essence, construct digital dioramas about lost virtual worlds.

The first step is to think of objects such as maps and models in virtual worlds as historical artifacts. Historians often distinguish between artifacts and documentation. Both are objects that have survived from the past and can be used by historians as primary sources. According to the *Oxford English Dictionary*, an artifact is an "object made or modified by human workmanship," while a document "furnishes evidence or information."[5] As the practical work of machinima artists described above suggests, tools such as the Model Viewer and Map Viewer make it possible to export 3D models and maps from the software environments in which they support digital games and virtual worlds to another piece of software. The destination for historical software objects of this sort could just as well be another virtual world; this target environment could be a virtual world operated as a library or archive managed by a cultural repository. In this new kind of repository, historical artifacts from virtual worlds would be stored, retrieved, and investigated as 3D objects. This means that just like the machinima maker grabbing models from *World of Warcraft*, a curator would move the original geometry and texture information that defines 3D objects as archival assets from their original environments into such a repository. For example, after the necessary transcoding, an exhibition created on a *Second Life* "island" might be imported into the repository, or perhaps a level from a historical game such as id Software's *Quake* might be created from an original installation. Of course, it would be necessary to validate the authenticity of these objects, if the purpose of this process was to support historical work rather than make machinima.

Maps—also known as levels, zones, and by other names—are among the most important artifacts in game development and player cultures. We have already seen evidence in the work of the Nogg-aholics concerning the importance of documenting the exploration of game worlds. Whereas in the real world, a map is ordinarily a 2D representation of an area, in the design of game and virtual worlds it primarily means the area itself, including the objects and challenges embedded in it. Thus a map is an artifact created by the developers of a game or modified by players. A huge part of player culture encompasses players' efforts to analyze these spaces, recreate them as mods in games other than the ones in which they were originally created, or build viewers and projections to better visualize how to optimize their gameplay in these spaces. As artifacts in a digital repository built with virtual world technology, historical maps would not just be artifacts, they might also provide spaces in which to site other objects and documentation—such as models, screenshots, videos, or documentation—that provide information about what took place in these settings. An interesting quality of virtual and game worlds is that many of them can be navigated by in-world coordinate systems, much like real-world cartography. Two well-known examples are the Second Life URL (SLURL) in *Second Life* and the UI coordinate system in *World of Warcraft*.

Just as we can mash up data by attaching GPS coordinates to real-world maps, photographs, and other media, or a creative player can composite models and maps to create a new machinima piece, these virtual world coordinate systems might make it possible to match documentation we have assembled in our virtual world collections not only with locations in virtual worlds but also with each other. Metadata schemes based on the Dublin Core standard already provide a "coverage" element for individual objects, and as the Dublin Core specification tells us, this element can be applied "for the use of multiple classification schemes to further qualify the incoming information" such as latitude and longitude or other "native coordinate representations" (Becker et al. 1997). In other words, it is possible to "tag" objects such as an island exported from *Second Life* and a group of machinima videos about events that occurred on that island with the SLURL that locates the island in the digital world. Or demo code, replay movies, and machinima created in a particular *Quake* level could be exhibited as documentation in the very space—an artifact created from original game data—in which they were created. Although further development work is necessary to realize this vision, it is certainly possible to export levels (maps) from *Quake* to the open VRML format, from which unaltered geometries and textures can then be moved to other environments, just as Soosdon or Snoman use the Model Viewer or Map Viewer to move a model of an Orc Shaman from *World of Warcraft* into software tools like Milkshape and 3ds Max, so they can edit them. When the pipeline to a virtual repository is completed, it will be possible to drop in and see 3D objects with the same geometries and textures they were given in the original game. In fact, these artifacts will be created from certified copies of original game data used to produce them in the first place.[6] If the Nogg-aholics and their ilk are the spelunkers of virtual worlds, such a resource would be more like an excavation site, where traces of vanished worlds would be revealed and recreated through maps and models.

Conclusion: *Machinima est omnis divisa in partes tres*

Future access environments for digital repositories will need to consider how to provide scholars with access both to data and artifacts from environments such as virtual worlds and to documentation about these artifacts and worlds. Moving artifacts from virtual worlds to historical collections in a manner inspired by asset extraction and compositing in machinima creation is a new way to think about digital repositories as 3D environments filled with 3D objects, rather than simply as bitstreams organized as massive collections of files. Yet it does not replace the "perfect capture" of demo plus replay or documentation that provides context and meaning. Future historians of virtual worlds will not want to be constrained by previous generations' preferences for one form of historical evidence over others; they will want it all. It is our task today to construct a flexible, interdisciplinary approach to virtual world documentation that embraces technical, documentary, and archaeological traditions of work.

I have presented three takes on machinima—demo, screen capture, and asset composition—in parallel with three takes on how to document the history of virtual worlds: replay, POV recording, and asset extraction. As more people spend more time in virtual worlds, the events that take place in those worlds become part of the mixed realities—material and virtual—that the players inhabit and that define who they are. It will not be possible to tell the history of our times without including the history of these places and events. Machinima may well prove to be the documentary medium for recording our experiences, activities, and motivations in virtual worlds. More important for me, however, is that machinima provides compelling evidence of the ability of players to turn digital games into their own creative medium. Historians, curators, and archivists can learn from these examples. Soon it will be our turn to have some fun.

Notes

1. I use the term "virtual worlds" in this essay to mean multiplayer game worlds.

2. Timothy Burke, "The History of Virtual Worlds," post and comment on the blog Terra Nova, December 1, <http://terranova.blogs.com/terra_nova/2006/12/the_history_of_.html> (accessed March 1, 2009).

3. Except, of course, to hackers and enthusiasts, who create private servers from *World of Warcraft* code. This technique has been used for machinima production, despite its murky legal status, as it then returns control of game assets to the production team.

4. Terran Gregory, email to author, December 11, 2006.

5. Oxford English Dictionary online, <http://dictionary.oed.com> (accessed March 2010).

6. At Stanford, we are currently working with a new, open-source virtual world platform called Sirikata to realize this vision.

References

Au, Wagner James. 2008. Making "Molotov": How the Man behind the HBO/Cinemax Special Created His Avatar-Based Documentary, and Why. *New World Notes*, May 15. <http://nwn.blogs.com/nwn/2008/05/making-molotov.html> (accessed March 2010).

Au, Wagner James. 2007. HBO Buys U.S. TV Rights to *Second Life* Machinima Series, Promotes It as Oscar Nominee Contender. *New World Notes*, September 24. <http://nwn.blogs.com/nwn/2007/09/second-life-mac.html> (accessed March 2010).

Becker, Hans, Arthur Chapman, Andrew Daviel, Karen Kaye, Mary Larsgaard, Paul Miller, Doug Nebert, Andrew Prout, and Misha Wolf. 1997. Dublin Core Element: Coverage. September 30. <http://www.alexandria.ucsb.edu/historical/www.alexandria.ucsb.edu/docs/metadata/dc_coverage.html> (accessed October 2009).

Blizzard Entertainment. 2010. *World of Warcraft* Movie Contest: Rise to Power. March 12. <http://www.wow-europe.com/en/contests/alienware-2010/winners.html> (accessed March 2010).

Howgego, Tim. 2008. Exploration Is Dead. Long Live Exploration! August 17. <http://timhowgego.com/exploration-is-dead-long-live-exploration.html> (accessed March 2010).

Lowood, Henry. 2007a. High-Performance Play: The Making of Machinima. In *Videogames and Art: Intersections and Interactions*, ed. Andy Clarke and Grethe Mitchell, 59–79. London: Intellect Books; Chicago: University of Chicago Press.

Lowood, Henry. 2007b. Found Technology: Players as Innovators in the Making of Machinima. In *Digital Youth, Innovation, and the Unexpected*, ed. Tara McPherson, 165–196. Cambridge: MIT Press.

Lowood, Henry. 2006. Storyline, Dance/Music, or PvP? Game Movies and Community Players in *World of Warcraft*. *Games and Culture* 1 (October): 362–382.

Nitsche, Michael. 2007. Claiming Its Space: Machinima. *Dichtung Digital: Journal für digitale Ästhetik* 37. <http://www.brown.edu/Research/dichtung-digital/2007/Nitsche/nitsche.htm> (accessed January 2010).

NoSkill Memorial Site. 2004. <http://www.doom2.net/noskill/index.htm> (accessed December 2004).

Pope, Tristan. 2005. Crafting Worlds Web site. <http://www.craftingworlds.com> (accessed September 2005).

Snoman [Nicholas Fetcko]. 2007a. *Wandering Dreamscape*. Warcraftmovies.com. June 29. <http://www.warcraftmovies.com/movieview.php?id=42529> (accessed March 2009).

Snoman [Nicholas Fetcko]. 2007b. *Ephemeral Dreamscape*. Warcraftmovies.com. August 28. <http://www.warcraftmovies.com/ru/movieview.php?id=45896> (accessed March 2009).

White, Hayden. [1974] 2001. The Historical Text as Literary Artifact. *Clio* 3 (3): 277–303.

2 From Game Mod to Low-Budget Film: The Evolution of Machinima

Matt Kelland

Machinima was, in its first few years, an art form that sprang out of gaming, and was initially regarded as an extreme form of gaming. However, in the last few years, machinima has begun to broaden its appeal from its early base of hardcore game fans to a wider group of both creators and viewers.

"Old-School" Machinima: The Hacking Years (1996–2004)

The history of the early development of machinima has been well reviewed in numerous articles and books, and there is no need to repeat it in detail here (see Kelland, Morris, and Lloyd 2005). However, it is useful to reexamine some aspects of this history in order to understand how the perception of machinima has changed in the last decade and attempt to predict the ways in which it will continue to change.

Machinima was originally an art form created by gamers, for gamers. The first, primitive, machinima films were *Quake* demo films, which began in 1996. These films were more or less sports footage, aimed at audiences that were fanatical about the growing medium of electronic gaming. Whether they were recordings of multiplayer clan matches or displays of individual prowess such as *Quake Done Quick*, they were of little interest to viewers who did not themselves play *Quake*. In fact, without a copy of *Quake* installed on the viewer's computer, it was not even possible to watch these early machinima movies. They relied on *Quake*'s built-in tools, which recorded the players' actions and played them back within the game engine.

Machinima made the first transition from sports to narrative with the 1996 release of the short film *Diary of a Camper*, also filmed in *Quake*. The emergence of the narrative film led people to start exploring the possibilities of *Quake*'s demo mode, captured in the DEM format, and the first machinima tools began to appear. Tools such as Uwe Girlich's LMPC (Little Movie Processing Centre) or KeyGrip allowed filmmakers to move away from the pure first-person view. This advance hugely extended their compositional capabilities and enabled them to do basic postproduction work on their films. However, making films this way demanded a high degree of technical skill, as the tools relied on the filmmaker having a deep understanding of the way games were programmed. The pioneers soon came to realize they had stumbled on a new way of making movies, but were very much aware of the difficulties involved. As Girlich wrote in his DEM specification document, "For people *with too much spare-time* Quake can replace a full 3D modelling system for cartoons or the like" (emphasis mine).

In 2000, the year the term "machinima" was coined, the first feature-length machinima film, *Quad God*, was released. The importance of *Quad God* lay not merely in its length, which at forty-five minutes was considerably longer than anything that had been done before, but in that it broke away from the need for the viewer to have a copy of the game in order to watch it. Director Joe Goss captured the footage by recording the on-screen action directly into a video camera, not into a *Quake III* demo file. He then imported the video into the computer and edited it using standard video editing software, then released it as a video file that anyone could watch, even if the viewer did not play the game, let alone own it.

When *Quad God* was published on numerous magazine cover CDs, the reaction from the machinima community was unexpected. Instead of seeing this as an opportunity for more people to become involved in machinima, many regarded it with something akin to outrage. Access to machinima was no longer restricted to a small, self-selected community of *Quake III* players; *Quad God* could be watched by anyone, even people who weren't gamers. The creators of *Quad God*, Joe and Jeff Goss, were so horrified by the vehemence of some of the comments from other machinima makers that they stopped making machinima altogether.[1]

With the establishment of machinima.com in 2000 as a public platform for disseminating machinima films to a wider audience, the machinima community began to accept that the era of the demo file was coming to an end, and by 2004, very few machinima films required a copy of the game with which they were made in order to watch them. Films made in Matinee, which uses Epic's *Unreal Tournament* engine, were a notable exception. Like *Quake* demos, Matinee films were designed to be viewed in the game engine. *Unreal Tournament* fans maintained, with some justification, that the films could achieve much higher graphical quality when viewed in the game engine than when rendered as video files, but on the other hand, the audience was inevitably limited to those with a copy of the appropriate version of *Unreal Tournament*. Furthermore, if the filmmaker had used any custom assets, the viewers also had to obtain those assets and install them in their game: effectively, both creators and viewers needed not just to own the game but to be sufficiently technically savvy and committed to make the necessary modifications to the game. While making such modifications is normally fairly easy for a committed game player, it can be daunting for casual players, or simply too time-consuming for those who just want to watch a short film. As a result, even Matinee users would normally create a stand-alone video version of their films to attract a wider audience.

Although by 2004, audience members no longer had to be hard-core game fans in order to view machinima films, the vast majority of films were still targeted at gamers. Although visionaries such as Hugh Hancock, Paul Marino, Ken Thain, Friedrich Kirschner, Peter Rasmussen, and Katherine Anna Kang foresaw the potential of using machinima to make many different kinds of film, ranging from music videos to highly original animated series, very few machinimators—machinima creators—followed in their footsteps. Nearly all machinima films continued to be game-related in one form or another. Typical subject matter included characters realizing they were part of a game, or filmmakers extending the backstory from their favorite games. Skills videos in the tradition of *Quake Done Quick* continued to be popular. The massively successful *Red vs. Blue* is a comedy series that can really only be fully understood by fans of the game *Halo*.

The reason for this narrow focus was not simply a lack of creativity or imagination on the part of the machinimators, though that is arguably a contributing factor. The greatest advantage of machinima as a filmmaking tool is that it allows a filmmaker to create a film by recording what happens when one or more people play a game. If the filmmaker is happy to restrict himself to using the assets in the game (i.e., the characters, costumes, props, sets, and animations), creating a film is relatively quick and easy. The corresponding disadvantage is that machinimators are then limited in terms of what they can show on-screen, and thus what stories they can tell. If, for example, the machinimator is using a game set on the Russian front in World War II, it is straightforward to create stories about soldiers fighting for survival in Stalingrad featuring ruined city streets, soldiers in German and Soviet uniforms, and plenty of combat-based action on-screen. If, on the other hand, he (for the overwhelming majority of machinimators at this time were male) is using a game set in the *Star Wars* milieu, then action-based science fiction stories, particularly those with a *Star Wars* theme, become possible, and even inevitable. Such films naturally tend to reflect the game experience: they look and feel very much like the game used to film them, and their appeal is largely to the same people who have enjoyed that game or similar games.

Once the machinimator wants to break free from those restrictions, he must learn a whole new range of skills. To create new settings, the filmmaker needs to create new 3D models and associated animations, and then must find a way to incorporate them into the game. These highly specialized skills, particularly the ability to add new assets to an existing game or change its behavior, are skills that are well established in the game development and game "mod" community but are uncommon outside those small groups.

Game modders—amateurs who like to modify commercial games, either by reprogramming them or by adding new assets—tend to be obsessed with games. Creating a game mod can take hundreds or thousands of hours of work, usually without documentation or support from the game's creators and sometimes having to actively defeat the encryption systems built into the game. This requires considerable dedication. Unsurprisingly, then, most of the machinima content created by modders was also very much focused on game-related themes, and therefore still appealed largely to an audience of gamers. While the modders were able to create a wider variety of settings than other machinimators, the predominant themes were still action stories or gamer humor. Romance, for example, was almost completely absent.

It is therefore reasonable to maintain that by 2004, machinima was practiced by a small subculture within the hardcore gamers' community. With only a few exceptions, machinima films were produced almost exclusively by dedicated gamers and were intended to be seen by gamers. Although a technological change had occurred that made it no longer necessary to be a gamer to watch machinima, the subject matter of these films ensured that the vast majority of machinima viewers were gamers.

"New Wave" Machinima: The Popularization of Home 3D Animation through Games (2004–2006)

The first signs of change came with the release of *The Sims 2* by Electronic Arts (EA) in 2004. This game was the first to be shipped with tools specifically designed to make it easy for users to create films. It was not the first commercial game to include film-making tools; Matinee had been included with *Unreal Tournament* since 2003, but it was cumbersome to use and required some understanding of the underlying principles of 3D animation. *The Sims 2* reduced filming to a single button press. All the user had to do was to press the "V" key to record what was happening on the screen while playing the game as normal. He or she could then edit the video files using a standard video editor such as Windows Movie Maker, supplied free with Windows XP. This single feature simplified the process of creating machinima to the extent that anybody could do it, without needing any technical understanding of how a game worked.

The Sims 2 also simplified the modding procedure by building it into the game. Rather than coming with a set of predefined sets and characters, part of the game involved users creating their own sets and characters. Users could share the sets and characters they had created with other *Sims* users, and to facilitate this, EA provided a Web site that acted as a focal point for this sharing. Adding a character created by someone else was as simple as downloading a file and dropping it into an easily accessible directory. As a result, even novice users could customize their game and create original settings.

The Sims 2 was unique in one other important way: it effectively redefined what it was to be a gamer. Unlike the vast majority of computer games (other than casual or abstract games such as *Tetris* or solitaire), *Sims* players are predominantly female, and the gameplay is creative rather than competitive. When almost every other mainstream computer game was focused on action, violence, and conflict, *The Sims 2* was centered on human social relationships. Characters in *The Sims 2* carry no weapons, and violence is limited to brawls and scuffles. The setting is middle-class suburbia, and the emphasis is on soap-opera-style daily life: cooking, cleaning, talking, parties, and romance. Although its predecessor, *The Sims*, had been very successful, the improved graphics and immense publisher support meant that *The Sims 2* became the most successful PC game franchise of all, outperforming well-known action games such as *Tomb Raider* or *Doom*. Furthermore, *Sims* players, although they obviously did play computer games, tended not to think of themselves as gamers in the same class as the existing, predominantly male community of action game players. *The Sims* was more an electronic doll's house than a game (indeed, its working title had been *The Doll's House*), and it was regarded by its users as more of a toy than a game.

The effect of including filmmaking tools within *The Sims 2* meant that machinima was able to branch out from the action and comedy genres into romance, domestic drama, and other, more feminine styles of filmmaking. The game's emphasis on creativity and storytelling meant that it appealed more to the creative than to the destructive side of its audience, and its subject matter ensured that it was better suited to human drama rather than action. Of note, the majority of people making *Sims* movies are female, which has had the effect of radically changing the demographics of the machinima community. At a stroke, *The Sims 2* simplified the process of creating machinima, expanded its dramatic range, and brought in a vast new pool of creators and viewers.

The explosion of machinima filmmaking resulting from the release of *The Sims 2* is most clearly demonstrated by the number of films produced. When *The Sims 2* was released in autumn 2004, a total of about fifteen hundred machinima films had been released since 1996, using around thirty different game engines. One year later, in November 2005, this total had grown to around five thousand films, of which nearly three thousand had been made with *The Sims 2*.

However, the real accelerant for machinima filmmaking came in November 2005 with the release of Lionhead's *The Movies*. This game was built around the concept that the player is a Hollywood mogul running a movie studio; the player actually creates the movies in-game that the studio is producing. As a result, filmmaking is not just built into the game, it is at the core of the game. *The Movies* takes a very different approach to filmmaking from any previous machinima tool: rather than being given complete freedom, the player is provided with a number of movie clips that he or she can adapt in various ways and then edit together, still within the game environment, to produce a complete film. Within three months, more than fifty thousand machinima films made using *The Movies* had been released, utterly dwarfing the output of everything that had come before. By summer 2006, the number of published films made in *The Movies* had grown to nearly 100,000, compared with about five thousand made in *The Sims 2* and about five thousand made in everything else.

Curiously, neither the *Sims* nor the *Movies* community nor these games' developers thought of what they were creating as machinima. The *Sims* community talked about "*Sims* movies," and Lionhead pointedly refused to use the word "machinima" in any of its marketing material. Simultaneously, in a debate reminiscent of the earlier arguments about demos and videos, many people in the pre-2004 machinima community refused to accept movies made in *The Sims 2* or *The Movies* as real machinima. Many veteran machinimators felt that the essence of machinima was to show prowess at pushing a game engine beyond the limits intended by its developers, and games like *The Sims 2* and *The Movies* simply made it too easy.

From a sociological point of view, this upheaval is symptomatic of any small society or grouping that suddenly becomes mainstream. Community leaders, fearful of losing their dominant position in the group and threatened by newcomers, who offer a different perspective, may cling to whatever set them apart from outsiders, and emphasize those outlying features as core values. While on the one hand they are keen to embrace the benefits of assimilation, particularly if a wider group affiliation brings them enhanced status as leaders, on the other hand they must worry about losing their own identity and privileged position as leaders. In the case of machinima, the rise of the new style of machinima creation led to the formation of many new machinima communities, some considerably larger than the original machinima groups, and the early stars of the machinima world began to be less dominant and less of an authoritative focal point.

"Freeform" Machinima: Breaking Free from the Game (2007 on)

To date, almost all machinima is still produced using commercial games such as *World of Warcraft*, *Halo*, and *Grand Theft Auto*. Another often used machinima platform is the online world *Second Life*; this, however, is not the place to discuss whether *Second Life* is or is not a game. The use of a game engine is so common that the general assumption is that machinima is all about making films in game engines, as it was ten years ago. However, this is not necessarily so. The Academy of Machinima Arts and Sciences defines machinima as "the art of making animated films within a real-time virtual 3D environment." Of course, most real-time virtual 3D environments are games, and so the general assumption is almost always correct, but alternatives are beginning to emerge, and we are beginning to see a new generation of dedicated machinima tools.

Game engines do offer many advantages to machinimators. They are cheap and easily available, and they have familiar, user-friendly control systems. However, they also have a number of drawbacks, and as machinima evolves as an art form, those drawbacks are becoming more noticeable. Although a game engine is a 3D engine, it is a highly specialized type of 3D engine, designed to do a specific task. A 3D engine designed for moviemaking has different requirements, and although machinimators can make do with a game engine, they can achieve much more using dedicated machinima engines.

An extensive review of the different technical and creative requirements of a game engine and a machinima engine would require a full and separate discussion, but the main differences occur in three key areas: graphics, gameplay, and user interface.

Graphics

The primary requirement of a game engine is that it run extremely fast, to give the best possible user experience. As a result, game developers are forced to make compromises with respect to graphics quality. Subtleties such as accurate shadows, reflections, and fine detail are nonessential to a game and are often sacrificed for better performance. Although a machinima engine is also constrained by the need for real-time performance, and so cannot approach the graphical quality of true rendered 3D animation, it can make different compromises, and can focus on the graphical elements required to give a dramatic visual experience rather than a smooth game experience.

A good example of the compromises made by game graphics is the sacrifice of high-quality depictions of human faces or emotions. Most characters in games exist only to be killed as quickly as possible; they rarely occupy more than half the screen height, and frequently they occupy less than a quarter of the screen height, while close-ups are extremely unusual. As a result, game characters are usually unblinking and have unrealistic eye movements, cartoonish breathing, and a very limited repertoire of facial or body gestures to convey emotions. They lack glints in their eyes, their hair and clothing are highly stylized, and there is little variation among individuals. A machinima engine, focusing more on human drama and characterization, has to concentrate more on creating high-quality characters, since these will inevitably occupy most of the screen time and the viewer's attention.

Related to this is the way that game "cameras" work. The camera in a game is designed to allow the player to see what is important to the game experience, and frequently to mimic the head movements of an individual (the "first-person" view, which in machinima is not the same as a POV shot as understood by filmmakers; the latter is a nominal representation of a character's point of view, not an accurate representation of what the character would be seeing). Game engines tend not to have support for multiple "cameras" built in, and the movement paths of the player's viewpoint do not usually replicate real camera movement paths. Film cameras, by contrast, are intended to give a dramatic view of the scene. A film cinematographer uses a variety of lenses, camera positions, and camera movements to tell a story—for the filmmaker, the important thing is not what happens on the set but the way it is framed on the screen and the way the different viewpoints are cut together into a narrative. Alfred Hitchcock allegedly maintained that in a thriller, the audience's sympathies have more to do with where you place the camera than with accepted notions of morality.[2] Film a burglary from the victim's point of view, following him as he walks nervously down the stairs because he's heard an intruder, and the viewer is obviously on the homeowner's side. But if the camera follows that burglar through the window, and then suddenly he hears someone coming down the stairs, the viewer thinks, "Quick, get out!" Filming a character from an angle, or filming the character's spatial position within the frame, implies something about the viewer's relationship to the character or about the character's relationship with other (possibly off-screen) characters. A machinima engine must provide appropriate tools to support cameras in both functions, as filmic and as narrative devices.

Gameplay

Gameplay is an inherent feature of a game. The essence of game design is to create an environment in which the player wants to reach a satisfying goal but has to over-come various challenges to get there. In effect, gameplay is about frustrating players just enough that they don't actually stop playing but feel they have achieved some-thing difficult and earn a reward when they do finally succeed. This frustration can take the form of limiting resources, creating a dangerous or complex environment, mounting attacks from enemies, or simply forcing the player to go through a number of steps to achieve something relatively simple. When players fail, they are penalized in some way, and they may have to attempt the task from the beginning.

This element of frustration is enjoyable when it is part of a game experience, but it is frequently irritating for a machinimator. To make movies, the machinimator needs to have total control over the filming environment, not struggle against it. Cheat codes and game mods can sometimes help, but these aids do not address all eventualities and can introduce problems of their own.

A typical example of gameplay is the way *The Sims 2* controls character behavior rather than giving the user complete control over the character. If the filmmaker wants John to kiss Amy, she has to persuade them to become romantically involved, gradu-ally working through various stages of affection and courtship, and eventually this option will become available. Then, before the characters actually kiss, they have to be in a suitably happy mood, which may involve ensuring they are clean, fed, rested, in a nice room, and not distracted by other elements in the game. This can take several hours of gameplay before the kiss finally takes place. For the gamer, this is part of the fun of the game, and getting to that moment is the experience the gamer is enjoying and the reason she bought the game. For the machinimator, on the other hand, it is a tedious process that gets in the way of achieving the goal, which is to film the kiss and move on to the next part of the scene. A machinima engine simply allows the machinimator to set the moods of the characters as required, and allows characters to kiss on demand. The response of machinimators using *The Sims 2* was to create a number of mods that allowed the player to control the characters and bypass the gameplay. However, it is worth noting that when EA released *The Sims 3* in 2009, the company chose not to provide similar official tools, and even took steps to ensure that unofficial mods were harder to create and install, despite claiming to be keen to support machinima.

Another gameplay feature that can frustrate machinimators is the way characters suffer damage in a game. The script may call for a character to run unscathed through a hail of gunfire before finally being shot and killed at a specific point. The machinimator has to arrange that all bullets fired before that point miss (or cause no damage), but that the crucial bullet hits and causes the requisite amount of damage. This may require considerable skill on the part of the cast and crew and many retakes before they get this right. One group of players using the *Battlefield* games get around this with a system called "five in the foot." A character who is going to die in the next shot is shot five times in the foot with a revolver before the scene starts filming: the cast and crew now know that the next hit, from any weapon, in any part of the body, will kill the character. This enables them to ensure that the character will die at the right time, provided he is not killed by any stray gunfire earlier in the shot. Although this is an adequate workaround, it shows the kind of ingenuity machinimators have to employ when using game engines for their projects.

An important gameplay feature of most game engines is that time almost always runs in one direction only. Part of the element of frustration with this feature is that the player does something in the game, and then has to live with the consequences. Although players can "go back in time" by saving the game and reloading it, they cannot scrub the action backward and forward as would be possible with a traditional animator or video editor, making minor adjustments to get all the actions properly timed and synchronized. A machinima engine recognizes the importance of being able to control time, and provides tools to allow the user to do this easily.

User Interface

The user interface for a machinima engine needs to be redesigned to allow the machinimator to control the engine in a different way than for gameplay. With a game engine, the player chooses an action, and the game engine generates the results. With a machinima engine, the filmmaker needs to be able to control the results of the action as well as the action itself. For example, John shoots Kevin. In a game engine, one player takes the part of John and shoots at Kevin, and then the game engine determines whether Kevin has been hit and what injuries he has sustained. If the screenplay calls for Kevin to be wounded, the player must ensure that he hits

Kevin but does not kill him. This may be impossible to ensure (e.g., if damage is random) or difficult to achieve (e.g., if it is a particularly long shot or if Kevin is moving quickly). In a machinima engine, the filmmaker should be able to determine not only that John shoots at Kevin but that, in response, Kevin is hit and wounded but not killed.

In addition, the audio and video feedback given to a game player needs to be different from the feedback desired by a filmmaker. While a game player is interested in the status of his or her characters, such as ammunition, health, objectives to be achieved, or messages from other players, the machinimator is more concerned with the script, the relative timing of actions, characters hitting marks or cues, or which camera is currently active. In short, what the machinimator needs from a 3D engine is different from what a player needs from a 3D engine in a number of often subtle but important ways.

Several dedicated machinima tools are beginning to appear that have no game heritage at all. Peter Rasmussen's *Killer Robots* was created using a handcrafted 3D engine that incorporated GameStudio, a 3D game authoring package, TrueSpace, an animation tool, and the programming language Python. Fountainhead's Machinimation, based on *Quake III*, showed early promise in 2004 but failed to win widespread acceptance. DakineWave's short-lived VirtualStage, Immersive Education's MediaStage, RealViz's StoryViz, Antics3D, Reallusion's iClone, and Short Fuze's Moviestorm all offer machinima-based 3D animation tools that are completely independent of gameplay and designed purely for creating films.

None of these tools is targeted at a specifically gamer-oriented market. However, research has shown that in the UK, more than 95 percent of people under the age of fifteen play computer games regularly, and even 50 percent of people in the thirty-six- to fifty-year-old age bracket play regularly (Pratchett 2005). The implication of these research results is that most people are familiar with the idioms and controls of computer games, and the term "gamer" is not as descriptive of a social group as it was before games reached such mainstream acceptance. Correspondingly, a key development is that these tools are not being sold or marketed as game products or through the same channels as games. VirtualStage (now defunct) and MediaStage were targeted at the educational sector, with a view to introducing 3D animation skills into the school environment. These software platforms can be used not just to help students develop their understanding of animation and filmmaking but also to help bring drama or literature to life, or to improve storytelling and creative writing skills.

StoryViz and Antics3D are designed as professional previsualization tools for the film and television industry, allowing directors working in traditional media to plan a film in detail before shooting it. While this technique has yet to gain widespread acceptance from the traditional media industries, we are beginning to see signs that previsualization will become an important role for machinima: Steven Spielberg used machinima to assist with previsualization on *AI*, and George Lucas used machinima on the recent *Star Wars* movies. More important, though, the generation of filmmakers currently learning their craft is growing up with machinima and appreciating its benefits. When those film students take on professional roles, they will be in a position to exploit machinima and use it to help them make their films.

Meanwhile, iClone and Moviestorm are aimed at a completely new market, the casual filmmaker. iClone was originally designed to create short clips of animated characters for display on a mobile phone. It is, in the true sense of the word, a machinima tool, but it is a long way from the early *Quake* demo films. Its custom-designed user interface allows novices to generate short 3D animations quickly and easily, and it bears no resemblance at all to a game. In its most recent version, it is rapidly becoming more like a full-fledged entry-level animation tool. Moviestorm continues to show the influences of both *The Sims* and *The Movies*, but with animation-focused extensions that clearly differentiate it from those games.

The growth of user-generated Web content suggests that amateur filmmaking has become a popular pastime. In July 2006, the video site YouTube passed the point of delivering 100 million videos per day, with hundreds of thousands of people creating content for uploading to YouTube and other similar sites. Over the past few years, we have seen that when people are provided with cheap and easy creative tools, they use them, and take-up is often higher than expected. Easy HTML creation tools have transformed the Web from content created by professionals and computer fans to content created by amateurs: to create a home page on a community such as MySpace, the user is not required to understand the underlying technology, only to think of what he or she wants to put on the page. The mass availability of digital photography, fueled by cheap digital cameras and phone cameras, combined with the widespread uptake of broadband Internet connectivity has led to an enormous growth in amateur photography, as demonstrated by sites such as Flickr.

It is therefore reasonable to hypothesize that the availability of easy-to-use machinima tools will have a similar effect on the production of amateur films. There are many barriers to traditional filmmaking, including the cost of equipment and materials, the difficulties of finding locations, sets, and actors, and the time it takes to learn the skills involved. Machinima promises to lower those barriers and enable many more would-be filmmakers to try their hand at creating anything from short clips to full-length epics.

Conclusions

In 1996, machinima began as an art form that could only be produced and viewed by dedicated gamers, and whose subject matter was of interest only to gamers. Since then, three important developments have taken place. First, the new generation of machinima tools is designed to be used without any understanding of the underlying technology. Second, the gamer community has expanded from a small niche to include almost everyone under the age of twenty-five. And third, the assets provided by both games and machinima tools have broadened to include a wide range of non-violent content. The combined effect of these three developments is to extend the scope of machinima. It can now be produced by a wide range of people and viewed by a wide range of people, and it covers a wide range of subjects and themes. Machinima is now being used in educational settings, for corporate training, and in other contexts far removed from the world of games. In addition, several major mainstream film and animation festivals now offer a machinima category, although machinima is still considered separate from other forms of animation.

Nonetheless, the debate as to what is and is not machinima continues. The machinima community has fragmented into several diverse and largely mutually exclusive groups, usually formed around specific games or engines. Many of the game-centered groups are keen to preserve the term solely for game-centered films, while groups based on nongame tools or embracing many different games tend to accept a broader definition of machinima that includes a wide variety of forms of real-time animation. Some have attempted to introduce the term "anymation" to describe animation using a variety of techniques, including machinima, but this term has not been widely adopted. Many filmmakers using traditional animation techniques (insofar as modern computer animation can be called traditional) look down on anything labeled machinima for its comparative low quality and technical and artistic limitations. As a result, there are some filmmakers using nongame creative tools who want to be seen as machinimators and as part of the machinima community, whereas others want to be seen as part of the more mainstream film community and are keen to lose the perceived machinima stigma.

It is my view that the filmmakers who are using techniques for creating low-budget films outside game environments and audiences unconcerned with game-centered content will become less and less concerned with terminology and classification and more interested in the ability to create films quickly, cheaply, and easily. As a result, the term machinima may very well end up being used to refer exclusively to game-based films, while other forms of real-time animation that grew out of game-based filming are simply subsumed into computer animation as a whole.

Arguably, machinima will eventually prove to be a jumping-off point, in that historically it gave rise to a new breed of simple, low-budget animation tools and techniques and provided many filmmakers with their first opportunity to create films, but remained firmly rooted in video games. Future historians of both games and films will decide if this was the case.

Notes

This article is heavily based on unpublished commercial research carried out by the author on behalf of Short Fuze Limited during 2004–2009.

1. Joe and Jess Goss, email to author, 2004.

2. I have been unable to trace the primary source of this statement, but it is widely quoted in film texts.

References

Kelland, Matt, Dave Morris, and Dave Lloyd. 2005. *Machinima: Making Movies in 3D Virtual Environments*. Cambridge: Ilex Press.

Pratchett, Rhianna. 2005. Gamers in the UK: Digital Play, Digital Lifestyles. BBC. <http://open.bbc.co.uk/newmediaresearch/files/BBC_UK_Games_Research_2005.pdf>.

3   Arrested Development: Why Machinima Can't (or Shouldn't) Grow Up

Katie Salen

Applications of any sufficiently new and innovative technology have always been—and will continue to be—applications created by that technology.
—Herbert Kroemer (2001)

Revolution in Disguise

In the beginning, machinima offered itself up as a revolutionary medium, one poised to radically alter the way digital film and computer animation was made, watched, and shared. Early articles written on the topic all pointed to video game engines as harbingers of technological promise, offering a system of production that would change the face of filmic production forever. Whether the focus was on machinima's challenge to traditional production methods ("I think it is safe to say that traditional pre-rendering is increasingly going to come under siege by machinima/real-time rendered filmmaking techniques"[1]), form and style ("If game technology moves forward at the pace I believe it will, machinima will revolutionize animation. . . . We will have CGI, stop motion, claymation, anime, and machinima as the primary styles of creating animated features"[2]), or expression ("Somewhere in the intersection between the code of the game engine, an elegant system of distribution, and the improvisation of game play lies the raw material of a filmic form waiting to explode"[3]), the tone was nothing if not optimistic. A spirit of almost giddy enthusiasm infused the small but growing community of machinima practitioners and, like the mod culture scene that was expanding in leaps and bounds around it, began to slowly attract the attention of those to whom it was most eager to speak: Hollywood.

But like so many young hopefuls, machinima wasn't quite ready for the part. As even Paul Marino, one of the field's strongest advocates, admits, "The promise of filmmaking within a virtual space still needs to be fully realized" (Silverman 2005). While technical advances in game engines have made their real-time rendering power seductive to those looking to cut their bottom line, machinima seemed to offer little else creatively, especially for film aficionados, to whom "FPS" has always meant frames per second. And so the years pass, while the desire for change remains. Writers (including myself) continue to speculate, hoping, perhaps, that machinima will finally make good on all that it seemed to promise. This hopefulness may be more than a little naive, but, as Kevin Kelly has noted, such writing comes not from a fascination with speculations about technology but from a "desire to show the moral and practical consequences" of patterns of behavior (Kelly 2005).

In looking back, it is easy to glimpse such patterns. Machinima mirrored and at times foreshadowed participatory practices in other areas of culture. Part of a larger wave of creative engagements emerging from changes brought on by the rise of digital media, machinima not only defined an innovative form of player production that has become an integral feature of what Henry Jenkins (2005) has termed *convergence culture*—"Convergence involves both a change in the way media is produced and a change in the way media is consumed"—but also predicted the profound impact the ability to produce, post, and share videos online would have on a generation of kids born into games. YouTube today owes a cultural debt to the PlanetQuake of ten years ago. Streaming video technology aside, sites like PlanetQuake or Pysch's Popcorn Jungle sowed the seeds of a community of practice created around the viewing and sharing of game footage. Produced and managed by gamers, these sites set a precedent for user-created content shared freely and without prejudice against movie or maker.

And even though machinima operates outside commercial cultural production, which relies on professionalized, institutionalized, and capitalized systems (Russell et al. n.d.), its development over the past decade was aided in part by a confluence of parallel technologies. For example, where would machinima be without the digital video revolution? Plummeting prices of digital video cameras[4] and desktop editing suites turned what had been a costly and insular process into something mainstream and affordable. Offering a new way of creating, distributing, and screening movies, DV offered a form of movie production that seamlessly aligned itself with film culture's popular and economic imaginations. The birth of machinima and the rise of DV occurred simultaneously with the first wave of blogging (1994–2001). Machinima.com launched at the tail end of this first wave and came to public notice with the first *Quake III: Arena* machinima, which was edited and recorded offline, a point I return to later. Paired with the escalation of mods from illegal (*Doom* wads, 1994) to legit (*Counterstrike*, 1999), it doesn't take much to see that machinima grew up, into, and out of a rich cultural ecology of technology-related practices. When viewed from this perspective, the subsequent popularity of Windows Movie Maker, iMovie, video blogs, and MySpace should have caught no one by surprise.

Framing machinima as a purveyor of change has also helped shape the practice itself. Institutions such as the American Museum of the Moving Image, the Film Society of the Lincoln Center, and Sundance, for example, supported this speculative discourse through inclusion of machinima in "future of" programs, marking machinima as more than a blip on some geeky radar. Universities around the world slowly started to add machinima to film and new media curricula,[5] acknowledging that while they didn't always know what the future would hold for the form, machinima was certainly something worth paying attention to.

Yet beneath the surface of this enthusiastic reception is a sneaking suspicion that machinima doesn't seem to want to grow up, that game boys are still making silly little films about, well, game boys. To most, machinima seems to live in a state of suspended animation, growing in size but not in maturity. How could we have been so wrong about something that felt so right?

Subhistories

The history of machinima might best be told as a series of many possible subhistories. One subhistory, for example, would focus on the status of machinima in the context of real-time animation technology; another would look at the evolution of style, conventions, and aesthetics. A third might locate machinima within a legal discourse around intellectual property rights, file sharing, and the rise of copyleft. Each of these subhistories would probably have a beginning, middle, and end (or at least a "today" marker), and, taken in sum, would show a field that has changed considerably. But my interest is in tracing a subhistory that in some sense has failed to arrive anywhere at all. Instead, it is the history of a medium caught running in place. We look back at a time when, as Dwight D. Eisenhower once put it, "Things are more like they are now than they ever were before."

Prevailing wisdom has long held that an amateurized machinima scene is "something to get beyond" (Russell et al. n.d.). In other words, the endgame for machinima and its cadre of machinimators is in achieving credibility as an alternative to traditional filmmaking techniques. While this focus may highlight where machinima has fallen short in the years since the making of *Devil's Covenant* (1998) or *Father Frags Best* (1999), it might also help us to see that in setting our sights on a revolution in *production*, we might have missed recognizing the one promise machinima has made good on, the promise of *participation*. This promise may in fact be the one promise that truly matters. It is also a promise that has kept machinima from maturing in the conventional sense of the word. Machinima may be showing us that a media form can remain immature and still be meaningful both to its participants and to the culture at large. "Getting beyond" might no longer be the goal (Russell et al. n.d.).

The meaningfulness of machinima can be read in a number of ways. To longtime participants, including dedicated directors such as Paul Marino and Katherine Anna Kang or production studios such as Strange Company and Clan Phantasm, machinima productions are *film* productions. The Academy of Machinima Arts and Sciences, for example, models itself directly after the Academy of Motion Picture Arts and Sciences and presents machinima as an alternative to other digital film and animation techniques. The work of groups like Rooster Teeth and Bong + Dern, on the other hand, takes its cue from television. These machinimators find inspiration in the likes of Homer Simpson or John Stewart, rather than Stone or Scorsese. Despite these differences in inspiration and framing, machinima offers all these producers a rich space in which to experiment with visual storytelling inspired by the games they love.

That is why no discussion of machinima would be complete without considering the countless number of producers posting gamer-made videos to their video blogs or to sites like YouTube who don't necessarily know that what they are doing has an official name. For these producers, making videos is a way of gaining friends in a social network or of simply trying things out. As one YouTube user writes, "[This is] my first film as being the official 'Lost Cause Productions.' I know it's been done before, but i had to give it a try."[6] Their take on Shakira's booty-shaking *Hips Don't Lie* is a shot-for-shot recreation of the popular music video modeled in *The Sims 2*. No actual filmmaking is taking place, by conventional definition; instead, the work simply seeks the transformation of a game avatar into a video pop star.

There is no attempt here either to demonstrate the kind of technical or game mastery that dominated machinima's early demo history. While viewers of *Scourge Done Slick* (1998) or even the more recent *Katamari Damacy* speed run *Make the Moon* (2006) learn a tremendous amount about how to play and even beat those games, the audience for *Hips Don't Lie* learn very little about *The Sims 2,* beyond the game's relative ability to support choreographed gyrations.

Neither is there a desire to write, act, or direct, all activities common to the official machinima scene. Instead, the producer behind the game-made music video uses machinima as a way to signal to others in the YouTube community that he or she is taking part, and that he or she really, really likes this particular Shakira video. Central to the appeal of producing machinima in this context is the fact that posting and sharing the clip makes friendships and social networks visible to others. The affinity groups that cluster at the intersection of Shakira fans and *The Sims 2* revel in a production-oriented dialog expressing an appreciation of the game, the singer, and the community they count themselves part of. Participants therefore use machinima as source material in crafting their online identities. Machinima operates as social currency within a public network, taking over where a user profile leaves off. Perhaps not surprisingly, many of these individuals would be hard-pressed to count themselves as part of a formal machinima community. They just don't see machinima in the same way, if they see it at all.

"I saw the Sex Pistols," said Bernard Sumner of Joy Division. "They were terrible. I thought they were great. I wanted to get up and be terrible too" (Marcus 1989, 7). This is a sentiment shared by a growing number of machinima producers contributing to a machinima-inspired repository of cultural knowledge about their own lives and interests. Knowledge ranges from a player's love of the game of baseball (see Sean Coon's *Mets vs. Red Sox, Game 6 machinima*, a perfect reenactment of the tenth inning of the Buckner game in 1986, reproduced in Nintendo's *RBI Baseball*) to an obsession with snack foods (Myndflame's epic *World of Warcraft* production *Illegal Danish Super Snacks*). When we think about machinima in this way, we see that the history of machinima is more than a history of the maturation of a real-time animation technology. It is also a history of knowledge networks generated through everyday play. Jim Munroe's seminal piece, *My Trip to Liberty City* (2003), can be read as an animated travelogue through *GTA III*, but it is first and foremost a documentary of a day in the life of man, the player.[7]

Gaming Literacy

The story of machinima can be told not only as a subhistory of moving sideways while running in place but also as an account of a medium partly responsible for the rise of an attitude toward digital media and creative production born out of the DNA of games. We might call this attitude a *gaming* attitude, an attitude tied directly to the creative qualities of play. As designed systems, games offer certain terms of engagement, rules of play, that engender stylized forms of interaction. Gaming takes these terms of engagement and elegantly blends them into a practice steeped in transformative play. Players acknowledge rules while pushing against them, testing limits, and causing the system, at times, to change shape. As Mizuko Ito has noted, "The promises and pitfalls of certain technological forms are realized only through active and ongoing struggle over their creation, uptake, and revision" (Ito 2008, 403). When the Rangers recorded *Diary of a Camper* (1996), they were not only taking advantage of the real-time capabilities of the *Quake 1* engine, they were similarly revising their own roles as gamers. Machinima is a story of players who, on occasion, might just be mistaken for filmmakers, too.

Structurally, game engines invite modification along established parameters, a kind of systematized, rule-bound play that is informed by the improvisational play of bits and bytes intrinsic to digital technology. In general, players take apart the game in order to play with it. Instead of accepting the rules, they challenge and modify them. The movies spawned by game engine technology embody both kinds of play. They are systematized objects, bound by the game's interactive structure and underlying code. Yet at the same time they are radically free, offering users a unique space in which to perform and play with both narrative and representational codes. As Paul Virilio writes, "play is not something that brings pleasure; on the contrary, it expresses a shift in reality, an unaccustomed mobility. To play today, in a certain sense, means to choose between two realities" (Virilio and Sans 1996, 96). In machinima, the movement from playing to producing gives place to form in a transient, even momentary, other world; with this movement comes a quaking or stuttering of accepted norms that has provided a point of mobilization for a generation of producers to whom gaming has become second nature.

From Demo to Exploit

Rather than remaining within a speculative space that looks at what machinima *might* offer as technologies and tools evolve, let's instead explore what machinima has *already* contributed to a larger discourse around gaming as a subversive and participatory literacy. Doing so allows us to rethink our assumptions about where machinima was supposed to go and what it was supposed do to. What forms of knowledge, literacy, and social organization are being supported by machinima and related activities? Gaming as a production-oriented literacy moves to the forefront in this discussion, with several styles of participation in evidence. I want to touch on two in particular, demos and exploits, for together with several changes in the way machinima was distributed and edited, they set the stage for a major shift in the way the machinima scene, post 2000, would play out.

Historically, trendsetting first-person shooter games like *Quake* and *Doom* were some of the first to offer an editor to consumers that allowed users to design and program their own maps (environments), skins (character avatars), weapons, and tools for gameplay. This pioneering feature offered users unprecedented power to affect gameplay by altering both the forms and the spaces of designed interaction. Modifications to the game code (known as mods) were written by players (or groups of players known as clans) and posted online in dot-pak4 format for other *Quake* enthusiasts to download and use. Almost instantly, an economy of *Quake* cultural production was born. This economy pushed the edge of technical innovation, fueled as it was by hard-core gamers' desire to explore the absolute limits of the technology: how far could the code be pushed before the system was broken?

Demos, the earliest form of machinima, emerged seamlessly from this established mod economy, and the desire to demonstrate one's mastery of the game and its form dominated. Demos were little more than technical films of gameplay, with players showing off their skills and abilities to an audience eager to emulate them. This same demo form survives today and remains increasingly popular across a diverse group of games and platforms. Two types of demos developed, distinguished by their mode of production. "Real" demos had to be viewed in-engine, maintaining a strict connection to the platform on which they were created, operating as a kind of instruction set for the game engine. These works tended to be produced in machinima-native engines such as *Quake*, *Doom*, and *Unreal Tournament*, and were made by hard-core machinimators. The second type of demos, which developed later—"gameplay recordings"—were made using FRAPS, a free, real-time video capture utility for *DirectX* and *OpenGL* applications released in 1999. FRAPS allowed players to record the gameplay of any game running on a PC, capturing up to one hundred frames per second of footage. The introduction of FRAPS opened up the culture of machinima to a wider range of games and producers,

Films falling into the category of "gameplay" on machinima.com, for example, receive two to three times as many views as do individual films. Hundreds of machinima videos on YouTube are tagged as *compositions* and showcase individual video game characters from fighting games such as *Soul Calibur II* demonstrating stylized fighting techniques. Tira and Sophita have logged the most screen time to date, with a large percentage of the works produced by teenagers, many of them girls.

But demos aren't particularly transgressive, with their focus on technique, and watching one often does little more than challenge one's own confidence in what might already be rather shaky gameplay. Starting with Anthony Bailey and the *Quake Done Quick* (QDQ) crew, however, things were slated to change. Famous for their speed-running demos, the clan was also one of the earliest groups to use machinima to showcase exploits or degenerative game strategies. They refined—on-camera—a running technique known as bunnyhopping, which allowed players to increase the speed at which they could run without cheating. Because there seemed to be no air resistance in *Quake*—the animations for jumping were faster and wider than those for running—it was possible to move more quickly by spending as much time in the air as possible. Designers of the game certainly didn't expect players to discover how to bunnyhop, but once the technique was invented and captured on film, it became a sanctioned if transgressive way to play.

Gameplay recordings focused on the documentation of game exploits serve several functions in the machinima community and in the digital culture more broadly. On the one hand, they offer players a means of recording and transmitting creative cheats, which are picked up and reenacted on what is often a mass scale, altering forever how a game is played. *Warthog Jump* (2002), Randall Glass's tribute to *Halo*'s physics engine, falls into this category, as do many of QDQ's speed runs. A more recent example, however, shows how machinima focused on game exploits can go far beyond technical play. Ubermorgen.com's *machinima No. 0* (2006), by hansbernard, remixes found *World of Warcraft* game footage from video.google.com showing a teleportation hack by Chinese gold farmers. Gold farming refers to an illegal practice in massively multiplayer online games (MMOs) where players known as gold farmers acquire items within the game for the sole purpose of sale to other players in an out-of-game venue, such as eBay. Because there is often significant real-world demand for in-game gold, most modern massively multiplayer online roleplaying games (MMORPGs), including *World of Warcraft*, forbid this kind of activity (*Wikipedia* 2006). While the original footage was probably recorded as a gameplay demo, showcasing a particular farming technique, hansbernard's version remixes the footage to focus specifically on the hack. Here hansbernard uses his film to document and expose illegal activity taking place within the game, in much the same way that a film by Michael Moore might do. Such recordings not only bring to light the existence of exploits within a game, they also point to their ethical dimensions. Machinima takes on new significance for a *World of Warcraft* community that, at last login, counted more than seven million strong (Schiesel 2006).

This complex overlap of in-game and out-of-game activity is one of the most compelling features of games. Both mod and machinima culture take advantage of players' desires to extend their play beyond the formalized period marking the beginning and end of a game session. Many players today spend a great deal of time preparing for the next round of play. This might mean watching machinima demos of gameplay, scouring game guides, writing walkthroughs, trading items, or creating custom skins. This activity is all part of the metagame, or the "game beyond the game." Metagaming refers to the relationship between the game and outside elements, including everything from player attitudes and play styles to social reputations and cultural contexts in which the game is played (Salen and Zimmerman 2003).

The history of machinima is in some sense a story of one particular metagame going, for lack of a better term, meta. While early examples of machinima emerged out of the closed culture of the first-person shooter, it didn't take long before the metagaming practices associated with its production—recording and posting demos, customizing maps and skins, remixing gameplay, authoring tools—spilled over into spaces beyond *Quake*.

Stutter

It is when the language system overstrains itself that it begins to stutter, to murmur, to mumble.
—Gilles Deleuze (1994)

It is easy to forget, in these days of broadband access, T1 lines, and wireless connectivity, that 28k modems were once considered fast. In looking back to the dialog around early machinima production, it is hard to grasp how compelling the ability to distribute film over the Internet was to so many. In a correspondence with Hugh Hancock in 1999, he pointed out that Strange Company's feature *Eschaton: Nightfall* (1999) "took just three hours to download over a normal modem, for 35 minutes of full-screen, DVD-quality footage. The same film would have taken close to a month to download if it had been in any conventional format" (Salen 2002, 540). Patience with a dial-up connection required one to exercise an almost Zen-like disregard for time, in what felt to be cutting-edge production techniques.

There was, however, a moment when everything changed. Prior to 2000 and the release of the *Quake III: Arena* film *Quad God*, watching a piece of machinima meant owning the game it was created in. As in the case of the "real" demos discussed earlier, early forms of machinima relied on the viewer to supply the software that could make sense of the modified lines of code. This requirement, along with a series of unspoken rules intended to maintain the purity of the form by working "in-engine"—no use of *After Effects*, for example, or *Adobe Premiere*—created certain barriers to entry for individuals seeking to join the community. Like members of the demoscene, machinima's hacker-friendly counterpart, early machinima pioneers were programmers themselves. It simply made sense that any code-based forays into procedural animation would maintain roots in the aesthetics of real-time code.

As a result, the early days of machinima were almost entirely hidden from sight. Simply finding ways to watch the work was a major challenge. Nongamers, for example, were unable to view any of the films, unless over the shoulder of a player. If one did succeed in downloading the file and launching it within the appropriate engine, bits of programming might be required to "see" it correctly or to reboot a PC (all early machinima was PC-based) crashed by the film. For a community intent on bringing its work to the attention of a nongamer audience—indie filmmakers, Hollywood—this appeared to be a fatal flaw in the overall game plan.

There is a paradoxical relationship between a game and the play community it generates. In a sense, the play community is an effect of the game, born out of an appreciation of the style of play the game offers. *Doom* generated an intensely loyal and productive community made up of players who not only loved the game but also loved being part of a community that also happened to love *Doom*. At the same time, the game has no life apart from the play that activates it, and it is dependent on the play community for its sustenance. One would simply not exist without the other.

Machinima was most certainly an emergent property of this paradox linking games and play communities, and in the beginning it benefited greatly from the enthusiasm and dedication of its members. But the community was so closed that it lacked any significant exchange with its environment, namely, the thousands of gamers and nongamers growing up in the throes of remix and mashup culture, all of whom owned a laptop and dreamed one day of becoming a famous music video director. At the time, few of these potential machinimators could be bothered to learn KeyGrip or be convinced to drop fifty bucks on a game they didn't really want to play. It was only when the community opened up to the lifestyle of the rest of digital culture that it move off the periphery and onto the screen.

Departure

This opening up happened in two specific ways. First, in January 2000 a group known as Tritin Films released *Quad God* in a variety of streaming formats, which made the film accessible to more people. The audience it reached included hard-core gamers, as had the original machinima community, but it also included individuals who might have been tinkering with DV cameras of their own, or mixing stop-motion footage with newly digitized Super 8. Prior to the release of *Quad God*, only two production companies had experimented with releasing their films in out-of-engine formats. Hugh Hancock of Strange Company was the first to deliver a machinima trailer in RealMedia format (*Eschaton: Darkening Twilight*, 1997), and the ILL Clan experimented with alternative formats with the release of *Apartment Huntin'* (1999) on *Wired* magazine's Animation Express.[8] And while the change to distribution via streaming formats did not diversify the audience overnight, one of the toughest barriers of entry to the scene had been breached from the inside.

Other machinima producers were quick to follow suit, and it wasn't long before the practice of releasing a film in a variety of streaming formats had become common practice. The change did have an impact on two of machinima's strongest technical selling points, however. When saved in dot-pak4 or dot-dem file format, machinima lent itself to quick downloads, as file sizes were small. The conversion from lines of real-time code to what was effectively rendered footage increased file sizes dramatically. An increase in file size mattered less, however, than the loss of machinima's status as pure machine animation. While the films were still produced in real time, viewing them outside the real-time game engine on which they were birthed was a major ideological compromise. The moniker "machinima" lost luster as the films began to be tagged by those outside the hard-core machinima community with the more popular term "video." Even Rooster Teeth Productions, today closely associated with changing the way machinima was conceived and produced, avoided calling its works films, opting instead for the television- and Web-friendly "episode." Machinima had entered popular consciousness at the intersection of DV and mod culture, an identity it couldn't seem to shake. MTV2's machimima-inspired music video show, *VideoMods*, picked up on this shift in lexicon, obscuring further any hoped-for popular definition as film. In hindsight, Hugh Hancock may have killed his own Hollywood dream with the release of Strange Company's work in RealMedia format.

Following closely on the heels of the change in the way machinima was formatted and distributed came a change that occurred so gradually it was nearly imperceptible. As mentioned previously, early machinima productions eschewed the use of commercial editing software in favor of in-game, in-engine production techniques. But many of the people involved in the scene were also starting to play around with programs like *Adobe After Effects* and *Adobe Premiere*. These nonlinear editing tools worked neatly with the imaging programs members of their machinima production teams were using, and it seemed only natural to incorporate them into the postproduction process.

It was most certainly in 2000, with the release of *Quad God*, however, that the floodgates opened and the wave of nonlinear editing techniques swept through. Forced to adopt alternate postproduction techniques in part because of id Software's clamp down on net-code hacking associated with the prerelease of *Quake III: Arena*, *Quad God* was the first to be edited entirely out-of-engine. Id Software believed that demo recording threatened network protocol, as players who deciphered the demo recording would be able to cheat in the game. As a result, the software company refused to release the source code as open source, which they had done traditionally to coincide with the release of the next generation of their engine. Because the makers of *Quad God* were unable to access the engine's source code, they had to resort to the use of video capture if they wanted to work with the engine at all. This decision, along with a parallel in 56k and ISDN connectivity more broadly, set the stage for a transformation in the means of production, leading to an explosion in machinima creativity. In this sense then, while the inclusion of networked play in *Quake III: Arena* was seen initially as counterproductive to the machinima scene, Tritin Film's workaround cast the challenge in an entirely new light.

Examples abound. Rooster Teeth Productions' groundbreaking series *Red vs. Blue: Blood Gulch Chronicles* (2000–) benefited from the efficiency of conventional digital editing tools, as the rigors of a biweekly production schedule made in-engine work impractical. *Grand Theft Halo: Headlong vs. Grand Theft Auto: San Andreas* (2006) relies on a visual style and structure that would have been impossible to produce entirely in-engine. The film uses a split-screen format showing parallel footage from *Halo* and *Grand Theft Auto: San Andreas*. *GTA's New Bad boy = Master Chief* (2006) teleports *Halo's* hero onto the streets of San Andreas, creating a new kind of cultural mashup possible only with off-the-shelf editing tools. Most machinima today relies on a mix of real-time and nonlinear editing; Windows Movie Maker and FRAPS are tools of choice for many budding machinimators, in most cases because this is the platform on which they game.

Both of these changes, the move toward distribution in conventional video formats and the shift from in-engine to out-of-engine editing and special effects dramatically affected who was making machinima and why. As Henry Jenkins writes, "This is what a lot of us had hoped would happen in the digital age: the technology would put low-cost, easy-to-use tools for creative expression into the hands of average people" (Jenkins 2005). Lower the barriers of participation, provide new channels for publicity and distribution, and people would create remarkable things.

Tomorrow

In his 1932 essay, "Theory of Radio," Bertolt Brecht posed the question, "If you should think of this as Utopian, then I would ask you to consider why it is Utopian" (Brecht [1932] 1967, 130). Machinima has long struck many as a media form struggling against its own ideals. While its young history wouldn't be considered turbulent by any stretch of the imagination, it is colored by resistance: resistance to convention, to communities beyond its edges, to compromise. In remaining resistant, machinima could have let the future pass by. Luckily, it only pretended to do so, stepping sideways instead of forward, where we had all been looking. Machinima did this by holding firmly to a set of ideals that lauded a democratic approach to authoring and production, an ease of distribution, and an appreciation for all kinds of stories. Through a unique blending of social structures of consumption and production that made it both personal and safe to fail, machinima blossomed. And in accidentally resisting the push toward maturity desired by so many looking from the outside in, machinima managed to provide the most important thing of all: opportunity. By remaining true to its amateur roots, machinima guarantees anyone a chance to produce work and do it well or badly. People are free to use the medium in whatever way they want; spend time on any of the online sites dedicated to machinima, and revel in the variety.

Some major cultural changes can be seen as directly inspired by new technology, like the change in communication styles ushered in by instant messaging and text messaging, while others occur relatively independently of technology; still others emerge from new "technological metaphors and analogies" that indirectly alter the structures of perceptual life and thought (Sobchak 1994), as in the shift in perception of self explored through online identities in virtual worlds. For a generation fluent in the language of peer-to-peer exchange, player production is a newly realized form of personal agency, affecting both life and thought. What matters a great deal in this model of agency is the network of social creation it offers and the community of collaboration that results. Machinima games this system elegantly, pushing back against a need to codify potential qualities of production. In a space where everything is possible, moving forward means simply staying in place. In the often quoted but still relevant words of Truffaut,

The film of tomorrow appears to me as even more personal than an individual and autobiographical novel, like a confession, or a diary. The young filmmakers will express themselves in the first person and will relate what has happened to them. It may be the story of their first love or their most recent; of their political awakening; the story of a trip, a sickness, their military service, their marriage, their last vacation . . . and it will be enjoyable because it will be true, and new. . . . The film of tomorrow will not be directed by civil servants of the camera, but by artists for whom shooting a film constitutes a wonderful and thrilling adventure. The film of tomorrow will resemble the person who made it, and the number of spectators will be proportional to the number of friends the director has. The film of tomorrow will be an act of love. (Truffaut 1957)

Machinima tells stories, yes, but not in ways we might have originally imagined. The films tell stories of games, players, and most important, of the ways we see ourselves. The view is truly fantastic.

Notes

1. Hugh Hancock of Strange Company, quoted in Salen (2002, 538).

2. Katherine Anna Kang of Fountainhead Entertainment, quoted in Salen (2002, 541).

3. Katie Salen (2002, 539).

4. Digital video was launched as a video format in 1996. DV over FireWire, starting with Sony's VX-1000 and Charles McConathy/Promax's efforts to make it work with the *Adobe Premiere* of the day, paved the way for what we now call the DV revolution.

5. University programs pioneering the study of machinima include the Australian Film Television and Radio School, Georgia Institute of Technology, New York University, Parsons, the New School for Design, and the University of Central Florida.

6. *Shakira Video Sims 2: Hips Don't Lie By Shakira*, Lost Cause Productions (2006).

7. See Monroe's similarly transcendent *Yoga Deathmatch*, made in *Half-Life 2* (<http://www.nomediakings.org/vidz/yoga_deathmatch.html>).

8. The historical information was generously provided by Paul Marino.

References

Brecht, Bertolt. [1932] 1967. Theory of Radio. In *Gesammelte Werke*, vol. 3, 129–134. Frankfurt am Main: Suhrkamp-Verlag.

Deleuze, Gilles. 1994. *Difference and Repetition*, trans. Paul Patton. New York: Columbia University Press.

Ito, Mizuko. 2008. Mobilizing the Imagination in Everyday Play: The Case of Japanese Media Mixes. In *International Handbook of Children, Media, and Culture,* ed. Sonia Livingstone and Kirten Drotner, 397–412. Thousand Oaks, CA: Sage.

Jenkins, Henry. 2005. Welcome to Convergence Culture. *Receiver* 12 (March). <http://www.vodafone.com/flash/receiver/12/articles/pdf/12_01.pdf>.

Kelly, Kevin. 2005. Unto Us the Machine Is Born. *Sydney Morning Herald*, November 15, 2005. <http://www.smh.com.au/news/next/unto-us-the-machine-is-born/2005/11/14/1131816858554.html>.

Kroemer, Herbert. 2001. Nobel Lecture: Quasielectric Fields and Band Offsets: Teaching Electrons New Tricks. *Reviews of Modern Physics* 73 (3): 783–793.

Marcus, Greil. 1989. *Lipstick Traces: A Secret History of the Twentieth Century*. Cambridge: Harvard University Press.

Russell, Adrienne, Mimi Ito, Todd Richmond, and Marc Tuters. n.d. Networked Public Culture. <http://netpublics.annenberg.edu/alternative_media/networked_public_culture>.

Salen, Katie. 2002. The Art of Machinima. In *Future Cinema*. Exhibit catalog, ZKM New Media Institute, 538–542.

Salen, Katie, and Eric Zimmerman. 2003. *Rules of Play: Game Design Fundamentals*. Cambridge: MIT Press.

Schiesel, Seth. 2006. An Online Game, Made in America, Seizes the Globe. *New York Times*, September 5.

Silverman, Jason. 2005. Machinima Marches Toward Amusing. *Wired News*, November 11. <http://www.wired.com/news/culture/0,1284,69550,00.html>.

Sobchack, Vivian. 1994. The Scene of the Screen: Envisioning Cinematic and Electronic Presence. In *Materialities of Communication*, ed. Hans Ulrich Gumbrecht and K. Ludwig Pfeiffer, 83–106. Palo Alto, CA: Stanford University Press.

Truffaut, François. 1957. Vous etes tous temoins dans ce proces: le cinema francais creve sous de fausses legends. In *Arts,* May 15.

Virilio, Paul, and Jerome Sans. 1996. Games of Love and Chance. In *Games of Architecture: Architectural Design*, ed. Maggie Toy. Boston: Wiley.

Gold farming. *Wikipedia*. 2006. Page Version ID: 74734005 (last revised September 9, 2006).

Software References

Adobe After Effects. Adobe Systems. 1995.

Adobe Premiere. Adobe Systems. 1991.

Counter-Strike (modification of *Half-Life*). Minh Le/Jess Cliffe. 1999.

Doom. id Software. 1993.

Final Cut Pro. Apple, Inc. 1999.

Grand Theft Auto III. Rockstar Games. 2001.

Grand Theft Auto: San Andreas. Rockstar Games. 2004.

Halo: Combat Evolved. Bungie Studios. 2001.

iMovie. Apple, Inc. 1999.

Katamari Damacy. Namco. 2004.

Quake. id Software. 1996.

Quake III: *Arena*. 1999. id Software.

RBI Baseball. Namco. 1987.

The Sims 2. Electronic Arts. 2004.

Soul Calibur II. Namco. 2003.

Unreal Tournament. Epic Games. 1999.

Windows Movie Maker. Microsoft. 2000.

World of Warcraft. Blizzard Entertainment. 2004.

II   Technology

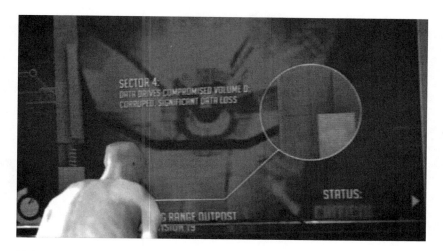

Maintenance Man (Lit Fuse Films, 2007).

4 Toward a Machinima Studio

Friedrich Kirschner

I have been an active machinima creator since 2003, have published on machinima in my own online magazine, machinimag, and directed the 2008 Machinima Film Festival in New York. I see myself as an animated filmmaker, working with real-time animation as a set of tools that allows me to shorten the time it takes to get from idea to finished film.

My own work as a machinima creator evolved from using computer game engines to create movies, such as *Person2184* (2005), to creating tools within those engines to make it easier for myself and others to use the technical possibilities of real-time rendering for filmmaking, to working on an open-source implementation of this new approach in the form of a novel production tool, Moviesandbox, that ties the preproduction and production stages closer together and aims to provide access to all aspects of animated movie production during all stages of the production process. This essay introduces and describes a production approach that moves toward a faster, cheaper, and more accessible method of creating animated movies and reduces the time it takes to illustrate a creative idea in the form of 3D animation. The material is approached from the perspective of machinima film creators and meeting their needs by developing new tools to support machinima as an artistic practice.

Early on, I realized that while the tools that game engines such as *Unreal* Engine 2 provide have great potential, they are not geared toward unconstrained filmmaking or the fast production of linear media. In addition, they cater to a specific visual style, relying on importing low-polygon-count characters and props from third-party programs such as *3D Studio Max* and *Maya* (both by Autodesk). This production model constrained my approach to filmmaking and limited my creative options.

The impetus to use games as a tool to create linear narratives came from multiple sources. One was a desire to create a counterpoint to the prevalent style of real-time computer graphics creation by bringing in more traditional methods such as hand-drawn textures and collages.

In my experience, by abandoning established means of producing content and focusing instead on the creation of a unique visual narrative, a filmmaker can achieve

Figure 4.1
Screenshot from *Person2184*, produced in *Unreal Tournament* (2005).

quite a lot quickly using the real-time possibilities of computer animation not only in the rendering phase but in every part of production.

I believe that a different content pipeline paradigm and tools that provide real-time feedback to creative decisions, whether in the asset creation stage or during production, will reduce movie production time and allow an iterative approach to animated filmmaking. This concept not only proposes new technical approaches and tools, it also has implications for the production timeline and work organization. Ultimately it may even extend to audience participation and novel ways of movie distribution and marketing.

The Machinima Approach

The major distinction between machinima and prerendered animation production is the direct feedback machinima provides to a filmmaker engaged in making creative decisions. It is not so much the fast generation of the final image that is important but the control filmmakers have over aspects such as character movement and camera placement in that final image. That sets and characters react to my user input in real time allows me to sketch out my ideas on the fly and leaves room for improvisation and flexibility in the overall production process. This process, however, hinges on the

Figure 4.2
The Journey, produced in *Unreal Tournament 2004* (2004).

available creative options at hand, and these options are directly related to the number of actions or animations available for the characters to perform, the number of assets available to place and interact with, and the number of sets available to stage the production in.

So far, machinima has shown its strength as a production approach once all assets are in place, but the process of generating assets such as animations or props is still largely similar to the process for creating these same assets in video game or prerendered 3D animation production and is most often accomplished using the same third-party programs that game or animation production companies use. A notable exception is the *Second Life* system (Linden Lab, 2003), which stands out as a toolset with the capability of creating props and characters using its own tools. The complexity of the objects created using the in-game tools is relatively limited, though, as the objects are bound to combinations of predefined primitives or parametrical alterations of an existing base model.

Prerendered 3D Animation Production

To illustrate the differences in the production, it helps to look at an animated movie such as *458nm* (Bitzer, Brunk, and Weber, 2006,Filmakademie Baden-Württemberg, Germany) as an example of a prerendered 3D animated short film. The film won the SIGGRAPH 2006 special jury award and the Golden Nica for Computer Animation at the Ars Electronica Festival in 2007. It was produced in less than one year with a core team of three people and a budget of less than 10,000 euro.

The production time, cost, and team size of *458nm* are comparable to those of many machinima projects, which is why this movie can serve as a good comparison project to real-time filmmaking. In my experience, many machinima movie projects are created on a relatively short production timeline (about one year) by a small team. In addition, *458nm* was praised for its style and "flawless execution,"[1] which lends itself to my investigation of the creative process.

After initial idea and story development, the preproduction process moves on to sketching of the major assets. Characters and sets are iterated through pen-and-paper drawings.

In this stage, the *458nm* team worked with concept artists, who drew sketches of the characters and sets. They cite the fast turnaround times (from idea to visualization) and quick iterations of traditional pen-and-paper sketches as reasons for sticking to traditional tools for early character sketches in their films. Later they used these sketches as the basis for modeling the characters in software programs such as Autodesk's *Softimage* (2000–).

After these initial sketches the storyboard is created. The storyboard is a visual, comic book–like drawing of key scenes and pictures indicating animation and camera motion through a succession of still frames and notes.

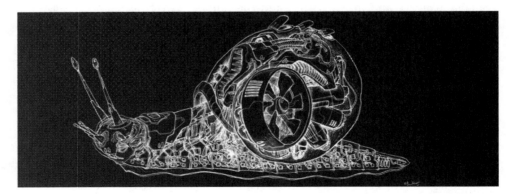

Figure 4.3
458nm character concept.

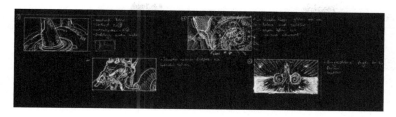

Figure 4.4
458nm storyboard.

After a couple of iterations and rearrangements, the storyboard is often followed by an animatic (or pre-viz) stage. The animatic is either a film consisting of storyboard pictures with added camera motion, editing, and sometimes simple animation or a rough, low-resolution 3D model rendering with minimal animation to get a sense of pacing, to generate asset, animation, and shot lists, and to get an idea of the overall length of the movie. The animatic also often incorporates a rough audio track, including placeholder voice acting and sound effects.

In a film like *458nm*, most major directorial decisions have been made by this point in the process. These decisions have been largely implemented and iterated in a medium that is different from the final outcome, namely, static drawings. They will be implemented in the production phase when the final animation of the images is generated.

Once the final image—the image that represents the end of the production stage and serves as the starting point for the postproduction stage—is generated, a character's actions cannot be modified without rerendering the scene. As a prerendered animated film with rendering times of multiple minutes per final frame on large render farms, a production like *458nm* does not allow much improvisation or flexibility. Many of the decisions that a live-action film director makes on a movie set, for example, when talking with the actors must be approximated in this sort of production through storyboards and animatics, as traditional animation tools do not allow for a comparable real-time implementation. The excessive time it takes to create animations and 3D models is a key reason for the use of storyboards, sketches, and animatics in the production process.

The more concepts and ideas a production team can iterate through, the easier it is to evaluate the implications of each idea for the movie and to experiment with different approaches to find the most desirable result. Drawings, and later storyboards, are a very fast way of implementing ideas but afford a limited basis for qualitative evaluation of the final image, owing to their high level of abstraction and lack of movement.

3D animatics get closer to the final image but take much longer to produce, making it harder to iterate through ideas in a reasonable amount of time. This is where larger productions with bigger teams and budgets often fall back on real-time rendering programs such as Autodesk's *Motionbuilder 10* (2010), or even proprietary software, to cut down on the rendering time and achieve a fluid and rough moving representation of the final scene. Although these additional steps add visual and motion detail, they require significant amounts of additional work and often depend on the export and import of assets from various software packages, creating additional low-polygon models of characters and props and specialized rigging and scene setups that often cannot be implemented in the final scene assembly.

For computer-generated imagery, the typical production process moves from sketching, an abstract but fast way of creative choice evaluation, to rough 3D implementation, to various levels of refinement converging on a final image. The closer one gets to the final image, the easier it is to evaluate one's creative choices but the longer it takes to modify them, owing to their visual and technical complexity. But there is an additional bottleneck in prerendered 3D animation.

The closer one gets to the final image, the more the relation between the time needed to see the final outcome of one's decisions and the time spent modifying the final image shifts to the former.

In other words, changing the camera angle during the preparation of the final scene can be done quickly by adjusting the camera position and rotation. But the rendering time for the now updated scene can stretch from minutes to hours, depending on scene complexity, and stands in no relation to the actual amount of work that was done by the user—the changing of the camera angle. These concepts employ a paradigm of early decision making and an almost linear production process, trading flexibility for image fidelity.

With enough time, personnel, and resources, this trade-off is hardly an argument against prerendered animation. But for projects of similar scope as *458nm*, this way of producing animation results in a strong creative and conceptual emphasis at the beginning of the project, while in later stages the emphasis shifts to execution, making it difficult to correct mistakes in pacing or dramaturgy.

Machinima Production

One could argue that even game-based machinima—with only preexisting game assets used in the final movie—loosely follow the 3D production approach. Game assets are produced through many iterations of storyboarding and design sketches—the production approach that video game companies use for asset generation. Many machinima movies available on portals like machinima.com are produced with these premade assets; others create their own sets, characters, and animations and use the game only to stage their production.

The Ship (Mednis, 2007, Svesas Tehnologijas Ltd., Riga, Latvia), filmed in *Unreal Tournament 2004* (Epic Games, 2004), went through very similar production steps as the ones detailed above. The film received Best Direction and Best Independent Movie awards at the 2008 Machinima Film Festival in New York and was produced with a similarly sized team as *458nm*.

Since none of the in-game character models, sets, or animations were used in creating this film, Mednis had to create them himself using Autodesk's *Maya* and then importing them into *Unreal* Editor. In a process very similar to the one described above for *458nm*, storyboards and character sketches were used to iterate through visual concepts for the assets, making decisions that saved time in the 3D modeling and animation process.

Once characters and textures have been imported into the toolset of the game *Unreal Tournament 2004*, which was used to render this movie, they become available for immediate interactive and real-time access and can be staged without requiring any lengthy processing time. This allowed Mednis to experiment with different creative ideas in real time within the production environment and at the level of the final rendered image. Creative decisions such as camera movement, animation timing, and set design were implemented with direct visual feedback in the 3D engine that represented the final image.

In my own experience from working with *Unreal Tournament 2004*, the real-time approach greatly reduces the time between implementing an idea and evaluating the results in the final image quality. The lack of rendering time between changes to the movie allows more fundamental creative decisions to be made at a later stage in the production process. In addition, the decisions can be evaluated better and faster as they are represented as new final images. This moves the preproduction and production stages much closer together.

The asset creation time is still a limiting factor, given the non-real-time aspect of the *Maya* to *Unreal* production pipeline. While camera decisions can be changed in the final image, the animations and 3D models exported from *Maya* are "final," as they cannot be changed with the *Unreal* toolset and require a tedious exporting and importing process to be usable in the real-time environment. For example, an animator can generate a certain animation in *Maya*, such as a walk cycle; once imported into the game engine it becomes easily accessible, as it is added to the given animation repertoire of the game character. However, it also becomes fixed and cannot be changed in the game engine but only recreated and reimported from the original *Maya* animation program. The time it would take to change these assets bears no relation to the flexibility of changing, for example, the camera's or the character's position.

The visual fidelity and resolution of the final image in *Unreal Tournament 2004* and other game engines are significantly lower than in prerendered animation. Complex lighting calculations, especially shadows, are roughly approximated; textures are compressed and often, for performance and memory reasons, available in much lower

Figure 4.5
Storyboard for *The Ship*, by Egils Mednis.

resolution than their prerendered counterparts. In addition, many other computational compromises are taken to achieve a real-time representation of the final picture.

Ultimately, Mednis's *The Ship* implements a number of aspects of the proposed machinima studio approach—real-time staging of characters and real-time camera control—but lacks the asset-generation possibilities needed to change aspects of the character design or character animation.

The production process of *The Ship* in comparison with that of *458nm* is already more variable owing to the faster turnaround time from idea to implementation, which allows a more iterative approach as it starts to combine the preproduction and production stages. But, as Mednis noted in an interview, he still uses pen-and-paper sketches as his first tool for conceptualizing his movies: "First I made storyboard sketches with pencil on paper. I tried to make it all clear to myself. I basically tried to define the plot-character-environment interaction."[2]

I believe there must be a way to generate useful digital information from the very moment I have an idea in my head. There must be ways of using digital technologies that replace these first pen-and-paper sketches, or at least play a role in the very early stages of production and leave all aspects of the production process open to modification within a reasonable amount of time until the moment the film is deemed finished. The goal should be to shift the process from a linear model with "final" components, such as Mednis's Maya characters and animations, that are relatively time-consuming to change to a completely open approach that allows creative decisions to affect every part in the production process up to the finished film.

What Is a Machinima Studio?

The ideal machinima studio would apply the real-time approach of machinima filmmaking in all other aspects of 3D animation production. This would create a workflow for rapid, collaborative development of asset building, story development, animation, and editing that would better parallel the iterative design approach found in video game design, allowing different tasks, such as character directing, camera placement and editing, dialog writing and improvisation, and animation, to work together simultaneously.

My exemplary implementation of this process is the 3D real-time animation software Moviesandbox. It provides new tools and dedicated interfaces for many aspects of machinima production, such as prop and character generation, camera movement and editing, animation and puppeteering, scene scripting, and color grading, with real-time or close to real-time feedback. This allows a seamless flow of the preproduction, production, and postproduction stages.

In the next section I illustrate this new approach by comparing it to different 3D animation productions and discussing relevant aspects of their production process.

Changing the Workflow with Moviesandbox

During my endeavors as a filmmaker with *Unreal Tournament 2004*, starting with my film *The Journey* (2003, 2004), I quickly realized that creative choices depended directly on technological adjustments in the game engine. Some simple coding could go a long way toward making filmmaking easier for me and others. What started as a small set of predefined objects for the built-in editor of *Unreal Tournament 2004*, UnrealEd, using the Scriptcomposer, quickly became a complete modification of the underlying game, called Moviesandbox.[3] In this early stage of developing a real-time filmmaking tool, I was mostly interested in optimizing ways of creating all the assets needed to make an animated film in one program, and to make the asset creation process simple and intuitive. As my work was initially focused on game-based machinima, the first incarnations of the tool were developed as modifications of the *Unreal* game engine. After two years of its existence as a modification for *Unreal Tournament 2004*, I created a stand-alone open-source application using the ideas and workflows outlined above.

Moviesandbox is not a complete filmmaking tool but an investigation into the process of quickly and intuitively creating animated movies. I tried to implement the real-time approach in as many aspects of the film creation process as possible, starting from the way characters are created, then moving on to how they can be animated and how they should be directed and staged, all informed by machinima filmmaking practice.

Moviesandbox is meant to be a tool that enables the production of animated movies in a very quick and intuitive way, allowing the sketching and implementation of ideas in short periods of time and providing a wide variety of visual styles to overcome the technical limitations of real-time rendering, all the while keeping the creative process simple and modifiable up to the final rendered image. My concepts and reasoning for the paradigms are detailed below and show how it changes real-time animated filmmaking from a linear process of refinement to a dynamic process of iteration, enabling more high-impact creative decisions regardless of stage in the production process.

Machinima Studio: The Real-Time Approach for All Departments

The core idea of a machinima studio is to combine the sketching and conceptual stage of animation production with the actual directing and staging of the movie. In other words, instead of a linear progression from one stage of production—concept drawings, then storyboards, then animatics, followed by increasingly detailed final image rendering—I suggest an iterative approach in which asset design can be woven into the directing process, which in turn can start at a much earlier stage. The creative decision

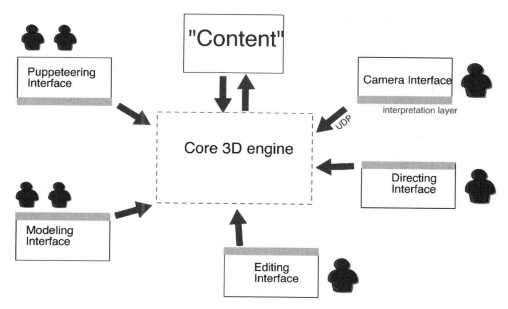

Figure 4.6
Machinima studio diagram.

process becomes more flexible and production times will be reduced significantly when rooted in a production environment that treats all aspects of animated filmmaking equally and encourages collaboration at a very early stage.

This is achieved by allowing more creative decisions to be made at all stages of production through software that allows all departments to start the creative process immediately, using interfaces that are streamlined for flexibility in the decision-making process of each department. In addition, in a highly team-based field such as filmmaking (both animation and live action), the decisions made in one area of production, such as animation, often have massive consequences for other departments, such as camera placement or scene staging, and vice versa. The ability to evaluate individual decisions faster should greatly enhance team productivity. The creative process is a constant back-and-forth of ideas that flow into an animated movie.

I often start with a rough outline indicating where I want the movie to go, and develop the visual style in accordance with the path the evolving movie takes in my experimentation. Decisions regarding pacing and character development often come out of the fast iteration of ideas, and my process ultimately relies on flexibility rather than on final visual fidelity. Because creative decisions are easier to evaluate when the time between the decision making and the review of the outcome is short, the ideal processing time would obviously be real time.

This is where real-time animation and real-time or near real-time asset generation interfaces such as the puppet control and the sketching interface mentioned earlier prove their value. The artist can sketch camera positions and directorial choices with rudimentary character designs in place directly within the final render engine and streamline the production effort. Visual styles, plot decisions, and camera angles can all be quickly experimented with.

Because any content element can be modified at any point in time and can be changed through a multitude of interfaces that are optimized for the type of modification the filmmaker wants to make (e.g., a 3D tracking GameTrak device for camera control, a puppet interface for animation, or a graphics tablet for asset creation), rapid iterations of the production can start much earlier than is possible with traditional toolsets and production approaches. The goal is to, quite literally, start with stick figures and already iterate staging, camera decisions, and animations.

The Technical Approach: Intuitive Tools for Faster Production

Drawings can be produced in a variety of forms and styles, using expressive illustration techniques to overcome the lack of detail. To integrate this conceptual stage of sketching better into the final production process, I took a different approach to the way we create character models in traditional 3D animation software. Moviesandbox incorporates the idea of drawing and illustration in its asset creation process. Instead of a traditional vertex-based 3D modeling approach, it converts image files into 3D particle-based objects, using added depth information for every pixel of the image.

This allows characters, props, and sets to be literally sketched in real time within the render engine. It also means that modifications or refinements can be applied in the same manner during all the following stages of production. The preproduction phase of 2D sketching turns into a 3D form of painting, not unlike the concepts seen in projects like rhonda 3D[4] or ILoveSketch (Bae, Balakrishnan, and Singh 2008). It keeps the simplicity of the toolset, which is already familiar and established, and adds functionality that allows animators to create movement for these same sketches by applying skeletons and animations directly onto the character sketches. Artists are able to sketch basic characters into the stage and apply default skeletons for further animation.

Another important and time-consuming aspect of production is the generation of animations for characters and moving props. A way to speed up the animation process is to use interfaces and methods that allow the movement to be performed directly. Motion-Capturing (Moeslund and Granum 2001) or, more recently, Performance-Capturing (De Aguiar et al. 2008) are tools that move toward that goal. These options require training, proprietary software, expensive technical equipment, and space. In addition, these solutions focus on the detailed capture of movement more than on their quick implementation in existing scenes, requiring additional cleanup and importing steps before the animations operate in the real-time engine.

Ideally, the character animations should be generated in real time, much like the above-mentioned Motion-Capture solutions. However, in animated movies, characters are often nonhumanoid, or move in ways that are not easy to perform by actors. A practical reference in the industry is the Jim Henson Company's tool to capture performances for their TV series *Sid the Science Kid*, which comes close to this ideal (Strike 2008). Their highly specific setup also illustrates how tedious and resource-intensive this kind of setup is. Within the aforementioned limitations of budget and crew in a typical machinima production, these kinds of interface remain unfeasible.

There are affordable solutions for such a virtual puppeteering control, however, that can speed up the time it takes to create character animation and thus evaluate a character's behavior and movement within an animated scene very quickly.

Examples are simple and cheap interfaces that resemble puppets, such as the work done by Mazalek, Nitsche, and colleagues. at the emBodied Digital Creativity project at Georgia Tech; an open-source, by-hand motion-capture tool such as Character Recorder, as used in the production of *Verion* (Kahn, Kirschner, and Sugrue, 2009, We Need More Data Bureau, Trondheim, Norway); or an implementation of a puppet interface using GameTrak controllers, as demonstrated in my work at Eyebeam Center for Art and Technology in 2007 and 2008 (Kirschner 2007).

These interfaces and tools allow the rapid production of animations. With the ability to incorporate these animations in real time directly into the final rendered image, animation sequences can be quickly iterated and creative options explored in very little time.

To achieve this functionality and be open for various tools and interfaces, *Moviesandbox* implements a simple network protocol built on top of the Open-Sound Control protocol. It allows outside applications to send data that can be bound to any asset's properties. This capability in turn allows the data from puppet interfaces, like the ones mentioned above, to be directly connected to a character's bone movements, allowing real-time puppeteering of characters within the toolset (Mazalek et al. 2009). A similar concept is used to move virtual cameras in real time in 3D space, using either an AR marker or a GameTrak input device. The use of game-specific interfaces also illustrates the combination of game-based approaches that are driving the development of real-time engines and more traditional animation tools.

The architecture allows any form of input device to be connected to Moviesandbox, so long as it sends data in the specified format. This enables users to create arbitrary input devices for their production and allows complex types of movement (or other data) measuring and adaptability to existing capture systems. One such device is Mika Satomi and Hannah Perner-Wilson's puppeteer suite, created for the *Ein kleines Puppenspiel* performance.[5]

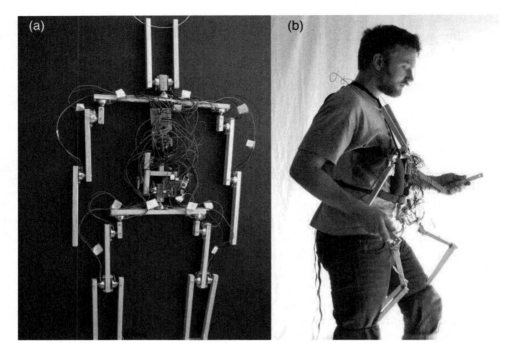

Figure 4.7
Georgia Tech puppet interface.

The inclusion of real-time feedback for animation production and sketching of assets greatly reduces the time that elapses between creative decisions and their implementation in the animation environment. In addition, using real-time network transfer protocols allows the use of new tools and interfaces. Together with real-time rendering, it allows a real-time or almost real-time evaluation of creative choice and intuitive ways of creating assets.

From Theory to Practice

Moviesandbox allows the real-time generation of animation and rapid sketching of content, thereby enriching existing production pipelines. However, the claim was that such a change in production method through a new tool would allow new forms of real-time animation production. The possibility of creating content in real time at any stage of production not only significantly reduces production time, it also enables puppeteering performances, such as real-time computer-rendered talk shows with audience interaction,[6] which are significantly changing the way we understand the

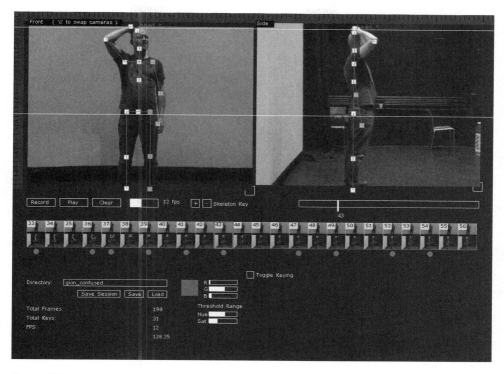

Figure 4.8
Character recorder.

medium of animation today. The following examples are practical sample scenarios of this new pipeline.

Ein kleines Puppenspiel (Kirschner, 2007, Dresden, Germany, 2007)[7] was created using a prototype of Moviesandbox built within the *Unreal Tournament 2004* game engine. The ten-minute film was produced in three weeks and was performed live at the CyNetArt Festival in Dresden 2007 and at the International Trickfilm Festival in Stuttgart in 2008. It uses a variety of input devices to create character and camera animation in real time.

This project exemplifies how intuitive tools and open architectures lend themselves to fast production times. All of the movie's assets were created from simple 2D base images, and all animation was performed live. In addition, the interfaces used for the performance were custom-made using Moviesandbox. The final visual style and live puppet show were iterated in the limited time to match the style of animation we wanted to generate. As proof of the accessibility of the toolset, audience members had the chance to puppeteer the characters themselves after the first performance and

Figure 4.9
Screenshot from *Ein kleines Puppenspiel.*

successfully reenacted the first scene of the movie with no prior knowledge of the toolset used.

Verion is a Norwegian theater production based on the same toolset for real-time creation. It combines 3D stereoscopic rendering and projection in real time with two live actors on-stage. The sixty-minute performance was produced in three months and performed in 2009 in the Avant-Garden theater in Trondheim, Norway.

Again, mixing animation and live action greatly benefited from fast iteration and real-time rendering. Staging and camera movement had to be performed in accordance with the actors' movements and the directorial decisions for each specific scene. In addition, prerecorded voices had to be triggered in response to spoken dialog, with real-time feedback in the form of mouth movements for the virtual actors. Even though no real-time animation input was used, the timing of the animations and actions of the virtual characters had to be variable during every performance to match the real-life actors' pacing.

These examples illustrate ways in which a full new production pipeline based on real-time principles can unlock new animation processes for rendering and content creation. Both works were created by small teams in very limited time and would not have been possible without the intuitive, fast, and inexpensive creative iteration of ideas. To me, they also suggest new fields that computer animation can be applied to, notably live staging and the mixing of virtual and real performances in a narrative way.

Figure 4.10
Verion actress Martha Standal.

Conclusion

The workflow I have described changes the production process from a mostly linear progression from initial idea to finished production to an iterative approach in which decisions can be quickly evaluated and altered at any point in the process, thanks to an interconnected pipeline of shared assets. The ability to modify assets at any stage of production does not necessarily end with the completion of the movie. Changes to the image can be made even after the production process is completed, enabling live performances in the medium of animated movie production, as in *Ein kleines Puppenspiel*, or enabling the mixing of real-life performances such as theater performances with virtual characters and sets, as exemplified by *Verion*. A technique of continually renewed iteration as fresh ideas are incorporated also allows a more experimental approach to narrative and visual expression, assisted by a newly empowering and accessible toolset.

In a workshop at the Games Convention 2007 in Leipzig, visitors were able to create their own characters, sets, and short movies quickly using the sketching tool in the

Unreal Tournament 2004 implementation of Moviesandbox. With limited instruction, users were able to create highly individual assets and animate them with little effort, using a GameTrak controller for live puppeteering. This outlines a spontaneous way of generating computer animation that is at the same time highly personalized and intuitive to use. It allows new ways of expression that are closer to the older technologies of sketching and drawing than to computer algorithms.

Animated filmmaking extends beyond the narrative structures of live-action movies and facilitates creative endeavors based on more visual and graphical structures. The freedom of experimentation afforded by this technique only makes sense, however, if the final outcome is not predetermined by early concepts fashioned largely in the imagination. Instead, we should aim for the continual iteration of new ideas as they are generated through the creative process while production is under way.

This new way of animation through iteration, addition, and subtraction of ideas and concepts requires that tools be easy and intuitive to use and the production environment be open to change at any point in the creative process.

Significantly lowering the level of entry for computer animation and enabling spontaneous creation are key possibilities of this new paradigm of real-time animation. This opens new ways of collaboration and interacting with audiences that can reshape the way we look at and understand animation today.

Notes

1. Rick Sayre on the official movie Web site, <http://www.polynoid.org/polynoid_458nm.html>.

2. Mednis on the Submarine Channel Web site, <http://mmbase.submarinechannel.com/video/index.jsp?video=33903>, 2008.

3. See <http://www.moviesandbox.net>.

4. By Amit Pitaru; see also <http://rhondaforever.com>.

5. See also "Puppeteer" (<http://www.kobakant.at/index.php?menu=2&work=3>), by Satomi and Perner-Wilson.

6. For example, Bob Block, created in 2006 by Neumann, Scholz, and Kirschner; see <http://www.blockspot.net>.

7. See also <http://puppenspiel.moviesandbox.net>.

References

Bae, Seok-Hyung, Ravin Balakrishnan, and Karan Singh. 2008. ILoveSketch: As-Natural-as-Possible Sketching System for Creating 3D Curve Models. Presented at the ACM Symposium on User Interface Software and Technology 2008, Monterey, CA, October 19–22.

De Aguiar, Edilson, Carsten Stoll, Christian Theobalt, Naveed Ahmed, Hans P. Seidel, and Sebastian Thrun. 2008. Performance Capture from Sparse Multi-view Video. *ACM Transactions on Graphics* 27 (3): 1–10.

Kirschner, Friedrich. 2007. A Guerilla Guide to Real-Time Animation. Diplomate thesis, Hochschule der Medien, Stuttgart.

Mazalek, Ali, Sanjay Chandrasekharan, Michael Nitsche, Tim Welsh, Geoffrey Thomas, Tandav Sanka, and Paul Clifton. 2009. Giving Your Self to the Game: Transferring a Player's Own Movements to Avatars Using Tangible Interfaces. In *Proceedings of Sandbox SIGGRAPH '09*, ed. Stephen N. Spencer, 161–168. New York: Association for Computing Machinery.

Moeslund, Thomas, and Erik Granum. 2001. A Survey of Computer Vision-based Human Motion Capture. *Computer Vision and Image Understanding* 81 (3): 231–268.

Strike, Joe. 2008. *Sid the Science Kid*: Henson Uses Mocap Smartly. <http://www.awn.com/articles/production/isid-science-kidi-henson-uses-mocap-smartly/>.

Software References

3D Studio Max. Autodesk. 1995–.

Maya. Autodesk. 1998–.

Motionbuilder 10. Autodesk. 2010.

Second Life. Linden Lab. 2003.

Softimage. Autodesk. 2000–.

Unreal Tournament 2004. Atari. 2004.

5   Image Future

Lev Manovich

For the greater part of the twentieth century, different areas of commercial moving image culture maintained their distinct production methods and distinct aesthetics. Films and cartoons were produced completely differently, and it was easy to tell their visual languages apart. Today the situation is different. Softwarization of all areas of moving image production created a common pool of techniques that can be used regardless of whether one is creating motion graphics for television, a narrative feature, an animated feature, or a music video. The abilities to composite many layers of imagery with varied transparency, to place 2D and 3D visual elements within a shared 3D virtual space and then move a virtual camera through this space, to apply simulated motion blur and depth-of-field effect, and to change over time any visual parameter of a frame are equally available to the creators of all forms of moving images.

The existence of this common vocabulary of software-based techniques does not mean that all films now look the same. It does mean, however, that while most live-action films, animated features, and motion graphics do look quite different, this is the result of deliberate choices rather than the inevitable consequence of differences in production methods and technology. Given that all techniques of previously distinct media are now available in a single software-based production environment, what is the meaning of the terms that were used to refer to these media in the twentieth century—such as "animation"? From the industry point of view, the answer is simple. Animation not only continues to exist as a distinct area of media industry but is also very successful, in no small part owing to the new efficiency of software-based global production workflow. 2D and 3D animated features, shorts, and series are being produced today in larger numbers than ever before; students can pursue careers in animation; Japanese anime and animated features continue to grow in popularity; China is building whole cities around megasize animation and rendering studios and production facilities.

Certainly, the aesthetics of many contemporary feature-length 3D animated features largely rely on the visual language of twentieth-century commercial animation. So, while everything may be modeled and animated in 3D computer animation programs, the appearance of the characters, their movements, and the staging of scenes conceptually owe more to mid-twentieth-century Disney than to twenty-first-century Autodesk (producer of industry-standard *Maya* software). Similarly, hybrid-looking short-form films (exemplified by but not limited to motion graphics) also often feature sequences or layers that look very much like the character animation we know from the twentieth century.

The examples I have cited illustrate just one, more obvious, role of animation in the contemporary postdigital visual landscape. In this essay I explore its other role: as a generalized toolset that can be applied to any images, including film and video. Here, animation functions not as a medium but as a set of general-purpose techniques, to be used together with other techniques in the common pool of options available to a filmmaker or designer. Put differently, what has been "animation" has become a part of the computer metamedium.

I have chosen for discussion a particular example that illustrate wells this new role of animation. It is an especially intricate method of combining live action and computer graphics (CG). Called "universal capture" (U-cap) by its creators, it was first systematically used on a large scale by ESC Entertainment in *The Matrix 2* (Andy Wachowski/Lana Wachowski, 2003) and *The Matrix 3* (Andy Wachowski/Lana Wachowski, 2003) films from *The Matrix* trilogy. This method differs in particular ways from the now standard and older techniques of integrating live-action and CG elements. The use of universal capture also leads to visual hybrids—but they are quite distinct from the hybrids found in motion graphics and other short-form moving image productions being created today. With universal capture, different types of imagery are "fused" together to create a new kind of image. This image combines the best qualities of two types of imagery that we normally understand as ontological opposites: live-action recording and 3D computer animation. Such image hybrids, however, are likely to play a large role in future visual culture, while "pure" images that are not fused or mixed with anything are likely to gradually diminish.

Uneven Development

What kinds of images will dominate visual culture several decades from now? Will they be similar to the typical images that surround us today—photographs that are digitally manipulated and often combined with various graphical elements and type? Or will future images be completely different? Will the photographic code give way to something else?

There are good reasons to assume that the images of the future will be photograph-like. The photograph turned out to be an incredibly resilient representational code: it survived waves of technological change, including computerization of all stages of cultural production and distribution. One reason for this persistence of the photographic code lies in its technological flexibility: photographs can be easily mixed with all other visual forms, including drawings, 2D and 3D designs, line diagrams, and type. As a result, while photographs continue to dominate contemporary visual culture, most of them are not pure photographs but various mutations and hybrids: photographs that have been put through different filters and manual adjustments to achieve a more stylized look, a flatter, graphic look, or more saturated color; photographs mixed with design and type elements; photographs not limited to the part of the spectrum visible to a human eye (infrared, x-ray); simulated photographs created with 3D CG; and many other combinations. Therefore, while we can say that today we live in a photographic culture, we also need to start reading the word "photographic" in a new way. "Photographic" today is really photo-GRAPHIC, the photograph itself providing only an initial layer for the overall graphical mix. In the area of moving images, the term "motion graphics" captures perfectly the same development: the subordination of live-action cinematography to the graphic code.

One way in which change happens in nature, society, and culture is from the inside out. The internal structure changes first, and this change affects the visible skin only later. For instance, according to Marxist theory of historical development, the infrastructure (i.e., the mode of production in a given society—also called the base) changes well before the superstructure (i.e., the ideology and culture of this society). A different kind of example comes from the history of technology in the twentieth century. Typically, a new kind of machine was at first fitted within an old, familiar skin: for instance, early twentieth-century cars emulated horse carriages in form. The popular idea usually ascribed to Marshall McLuhan, that new media first emulate old media, is another example of this type of change. In this case, a new mode of media production, so to speak, is first used to support old structure of media organization, before the new structure emerges. As examples, typeset books were initially designed to emulate handwritten books, cinema first emulated theater, and so on.

This concept of uneven development can be useful in thinking about the changes in contemporary visual culture. Since the process started in the middle of the 1950s, the computerization of photography (and cinematography) has completely changed the internal structure of a photographic image. Yet its "skin," that is, the way a typical photograph looks, still largely remains the same. It is therefore possible that at some point in the future the skin of a photographic image will also become completely different, but this has not happened yet. So we can say that at present, our visual culture is characterized by a new computer base and an old photographic superstructure.

The *Matrix* films provide us with a very rich set of examples perfect for thinking further about these issues. The trilogy is an allegory about how its visual universe is constructed. That is, the films tell us about *The Matrix*, the virtual universe that is maintained by computers—and, of course, the images of *The Matrix* trilogy that we, the viewers, see in the films were all indeed assembled with the help of software. (The animators sometimes used *Maya* but mostly relied on custom-written programs). So there is a perfect symmetry between us, the viewers of a film, and the people who live inside *The Matrix*—except that whereas the computers running *The Matrix* are capable of doing it in real time, most scenes in each of the *Matrix* films took months and even years to put together. So *The Matrix* can also be interpreted as the vision of computer games in the future, when it might become possible to render *Matrix*-style visual effects in real time.

The key to the visual universe of *The Matrix* is the new set of CG techniques that were developed over the years by Paul Debevec, Georgi Borshukov, John Gaeta, and a number of other people both in academia and in the special effects industry.[1] Their inventors coined various names for these techniques: "virtual cinema," "virtual human," "virtual cinematography," "universal capture." Together, these techniques represent a true milestone in the history of computer-driven special effects. They take to their logical conclusion the developments of the 1990s, such as motion capture, and simultaneously open a new stage. We can say that with *The Matrix*, the old photographic base has finally been completely replaced by a new computer-driven one. What remains to be seen is how the superstructure of a photographic image—what it represents and how—will change to accommodate this base.

Reality Simulation versus Reality Sampling

Before proceeding, I should note that not all of the special effects in *The Matrix* rely on universal capture. Also, since *The Matrix* appeared, other Hollywood films and video games (such as *Tiger Woods PGA Tour* [EA Sports, 2007]) have already used some of the same strategies. However, in this essay I decided to focus on the use of this process in the second and third films of *The Matrix*, for which the method of universal capture was originally developed. And while the complete credits for everybody involved in developing universal capture would run for the length of a page, here I will identify it with John Gaeta. The reason is not because, as a senior special effects supervisor for *The Matrix Reloaded* and *The Matrix Revolutions*, he got the most publicity. More important, in contrast to many others in the special effects industry, Gaeta has extensively reflected on the techniques he and his colleagues developed, presenting them as a new paradigm for cinema and entertainment and coining useful terms and concepts for understanding them.

To understand better the significance of Gaeta's method, let us briefly run through the history of 3D photorealistic image synthesis and its use in the film industry. In 1963 Lawrence G. Roberts (who later in the 1960s became one of the key people behind the development of Arpanet but at the time was a graduate student at MIT) published a description of a computer algorithm to construct images in linear perspective. These images represented the objects' edges as lines; in the contemporary language of CG they would be called wire frames. Approximately ten years later computer scientists designed algorithms that allowed the creation of shaded images (called Gouraud shading and Phong shading, after the computer scientists who created the corresponding algorithms). From the middle of the 1970s to the end of the 1980s the field of 3D CG went through rapid development. Every year new fundamental techniques were created: transparency, shadows, image mapping, bump texturing, particle system, compositing, ray tracing, radiosity, and so on.[2] By the end of this creative and fruitful period in the history of the field, it was possible to use combinations of these techniques to synthesize images of almost every subject that often were not easily distinguishable from traditional cinematography. "Almost" is important here, since the creation of photorealistic moving images of human faces remained a hard-to-reach goal—and this is in part what the total capture method was designed to address.

All this research was based on one fundamental assumption: to recreate an image of visible reality identical to the one captured by a film camera, it is necessary to systematically simulate the actual physics involved in constructing of this image. This means simulating the complex interactions between and among light sources, the properties of different materials (cloth, metal, glass), and the properties of physical film cameras, including all their limitations, such as limited depth of field and motion blur. Since it was obvious to computer scientists that if they exactly simulated all the physics, a computer would take forever to calculate even a single image, they put their energy into inventing various shortcuts that would result in sufficiently realistic images while involving fewer calculation steps. As a consequence, each of the techniques for image synthesis I mentioned in the previous paragraph is one such "hack," a particular approximation of a particular subset of all possible interactions among light sources, materials, and cameras.

This assumption also meant that a filmmaker recreates reality step by step, starting from a blank canvas (or, more precisely, an empty 3D space). Every time a filmmaker makes a still image or an animation of some object or a scene, the biblical story of creation is replayed.

Imagine God creating the universe by going through the numerous menus of a professional 3D modeling, animation, and rendering program such as *Maya*. First he has to make all the geometry: manipulating splines, extruding contours, adding bevels. Next, for every object and creature he has to choose the material properties: specular color, transparency level, image, bump and reflexion maps, and so on. He finishes one set of parameters, wipes his forehead, and starts working on the next set. Now, on to defining the lights: again, dozens of menu options need to be selected. He renders the scene, looks at the result, and admires his creation. But he is far from being done: the universe he has in mind is not a still image but an animation, which means that the water has to flow, the grass and leaves have to move under a blowing wind, and all the creatures have to move. He sighs and opens another set of menus, where he has to define the parameters of algorithms that simulate the physics of motion. Finally, the world is finished, and it looks good; but now God wants to create man so he can admire his creation. God sighs again, and takes from the shelf a particular *Maya* manual from the complete set that occupies the whole shelf.

Of course, God was creating everything for the first time, so he could not borrow things from anywhere; everything had to be built and defined from scratch. But we are not creating a new universe but instead visually simulating a universe that already exists—physical reality. Computer scientists working on 3D CG techniques realized early on that in addition to approximating the physics involved they could also sometimes take another shortcut. Instead of defining something from scratch through algorithms, they could simply *sample* existing reality and incorporate these samples in the construction process.

The examples of the application of this idea are the techniques of texture mapping and bump mapping that were introduced in the second part of the 1970s. With texture mapping, any 2D digital image—which can be a close-up of some textures such as wood grain or bricks, but can be also anything else, such as a logo or a photograph of a face or of clouds—is wrapped around a 3D model. This is a very effective way to add the visual richness of the real world to a virtual scene. Bump texturing works similarly, but in this case the 2D image is used as a way to quickly add complexity to the geometry itself. For instance, instead of having to manually model all the little cracks and indentations that make up the 3D texture of a concrete wall, an artist can simply take a photograph of an existing wall, convert it into a gray-scale image, and then feed this image to the rendering algorithm. The algorithm treats the gray-scale image as a depth map, that is, the value of every pixel is interpreted as the relative height of the surface. In this example, light pixels become points on the wall that are a little in front, while dark pixels become points that are a little behind. The result is an enormous saving in the amount of time necessary to recreate a particular but very important aspect of our physical reality: a slight and usually regular 3D texture found in most natural and many human-made surfaces, from the bark of a tree to a woven cloth.

Other 3D CG techniques based on the idea of sampling existing reality include reflection mapping and 3D digitizing. Even though all these techniques have always been widely used as soon as they were invented, many people in the CG field felt they were cheating. Why? I think it was because the overall conceptual paradigm for creating photorealistic CG was to simulate everything from scratch through algorithms. If moviemakers had to use the techniques based on directly sampling reality, they somehow felt that this was just temporary, either because the appropriate algorithms were not yet developed or because the machines were too slow. They also had that feeling because once they started to manually sample reality and then tried to include these samples in a perfect algorithmically defined image, things rarely would fit exactly right, and painstaking manual adjustments were required. For instance, texture mapping would work perfectly if applied to a flat surface, but if the surface was curved, distortion was inevitable.

Throughout the 1970s and 1980s the reality simulation paradigm and reality sampling paradigms coexisted side by side. More precisely, the sampling paradigm was embedded in the reality simulation paradigm. It was common sense that the right way to create photorealistic images of a physical world was by simulating its physics as precisely as possible. Sampling existing reality and then adding these samples to a virtual scene was a trick, a shortcut in the otherwise honest game of mathematically simulating reality with a computer.

Building *The Matrix*

So far we have looked at the paradigms of the 3D CG field without considering the uses of 3D images. What happens if an artist wants to incorporate photorealistic images produced with CG into a film? This introduces a new constraint. Not only must every simulated image be consistent internally, with the cast shadows corresponding to the light sources, for example, but now it must also be consistent with the cinematography of a film. The simulated universe and live-action universe have to match perfectly.[3] In retrospect, this new constraint eventually changed the relationship between the two paradigms in favor of the sampling paradigm. But this change is only visible now, after films such as *The Matrix* made the sampling paradigm the basis of their visual universe.[4]

At first, when filmmakers started to incorporate synthetic 3D images in films, this did not have any effect on how computer scientists thought about CG. 3D CG briefly appeared in a feature film for the first time in 1981 (*Looker*, Michael Crichton). Throughout the 1980s a number of films were made that used computer images, but only as a small element in the overall film narrative. (One exception was *Tron* (Steven Lisberger, 1982), which can be compared to *The Matrix,* since its narrative universe is situated inside the computer and created through CG, but this was an exception.) For instance, one of the *Star Trek* movies has a scene of a planet coming to life that was created using CG. In fact, the now commonly used particle systems were invented to create this effect. But this is a single scene, and it does not interact with all the other scenes in the movie.

In the early 1990s the situation started to change. With pioneering films such as *The Abyss* (James Cameron, 1989), *Terminator 2* (James Cameron, 1991), and *Jurassic Park* (Steven Spielberg, 1993), computer-generated characters became the key protagonists of feature films. This meant they would appear in dozens or even hundreds of shots throughout a film, and in most of these shots computer characters would have to be integrated with real environments and human actors captured via live-action photography (such shots are called in the business "live plates"). Examples are the

T-1000 cyborg character in *Terminator 2: Judgment Day* or the dinosaurs in *Jurassic Park*. These computer-generated characters are situated inside the live-action universe that is the result of capturing physical reality via the lens of a film camera. The simulated world is located inside the captured world, and the two have to match perfectly.

As I pointed out in *The Language of New Media* (Manovich 2001) in the discussion of compositing, perfectly aligning elements that come from different sources is one of the fundamental challenges of computer-based realism. Throughout the 1990s film-makers and special effects artists dealt with this challenge using a variety of techniques and methods. What Gaeta realized earlier than others is that the best way to align the two universes of live action and 3D CG was to build a single new universe.[5]

Rather than treating sampling reality as just one technique to be used along with many other "proper" algorithmic techniques of image synthesis, Gaeta and his colleagues turned it into the key foundation of the universal capture process. The process systematically takes physical reality apart and then systematically reassembles the elements to create a new software-based representation. The result is a new kind of image that has a photographic or cinematographic appearance and level of detail yet internally is structured in a completely different way.

Universal capture was developed and refined over a three-year period from 2000 to 2003 (Borshukov 2004). How does the process work? There are actually more stages and details involved, but the basic procedure is the following (Borshukov et al. 2003). An actor's performance is recorded using five synchronized high-resolution video cameras. "Performance" in this case includes everything an actor will say in a film and all possible facial expressions.[6] During the production the studio was capturing over 5 terabytes of data each day. Next, special algorithms are used to track each pixel's movement over time in every frame. This information is combined with a 3D model of a neutral expression of the actor captured via a 3D scanner. The result is an animated 3D shape that accurately represents the geometry of the actor's head as it changes during a particular performance. The shape is mapped with color information extracted from the captured video sequences. A separate very high-resolution scan of the actor's face is used to create the map of small-scale surface details such as pores and wrinkles, and this map is also added to the model. How's that for hybridity?

After all the data have been extracted, aligned, and combined, the result is what Gaeta calls a "virtual human"—a highly accurate reconstruction of the captured performance, now available as 3D CG data, with all the advantages that come from having such representation. For instance, because the actor's performance now exists as a 3D object in virtual space, the filmmaker can animate the virtual camera and "play" the reconstructed performance from an arbitrary angle. Similarly, the virtual head can be lighted in any way desired. It can be also attached to a separately constructed CG body (Borshukov et al. 2003). For example, all the characters that appeared in the Burly Brawl scene in *The Matrix 2* were created by combining the heads constructed via the universal capture process done on the leading actors with CG bodies, which used motion capture data from a different set of performers. Because all the characters along with the set were computer generated, the directors of the scene could choreograph the virtual camera and have it fly around the scene in a way not possible with real cameras on a real physical set.

The process was appropriately named total capture because it captures all the possible information from an object or a scene using a number of recording methods—or at least, whatever can be captured using current technologies. Different dimensions— color, 3D geometry, reflectivity, and texture—are captured separately and then reassembled to create a more detailed and realistic representation.

Total capture is significantly different from the commonly accepted methods used to create computer-based special effects such as keyframe animation and physically based modeling. In the first method, an animator specifies the key positions of a 3D model, and the computer calculates in-between frames. In the second method, all the animation is automatically created by software that simulates the physics underlying the movement. This method thus represents a particular instance of the reality simulation paradigm. For instance, to create a realistic animation of a moving creature, the programmers model its skeleton, muscles, and skin, and specify the algorithms that simulate the actual physics involved. Often the two methods are combined. For instance, physically based modeling can be used to animate a running dinosaur while manual animation can be used for shots in which the dinosaur interacts with human characters.

When the third *Matrix* film was released, the most impressive achievement in physically based modeling was the battle in *The Lord of the Rings: Return of the King* (Peter Jackson, 2003), which involved tens of thousands of virtual soldiers, all driven by *Massive* software.[7] Similar to the nonhuman characters (NPCs or bots) in computer games, each virtual soldier was given the ability to "see" the terrain and other soldiers, a set of priorities, and an independent "brain," that is, an artificial intelligence (AI) program that directs a character's actions based on the perceptual inputs and priorities. But in contrast to game AI, *Massive* software does not have to run in real time. Therefore it can create scenes with tens and even hundreds of thousands of realistically behaving agents (one commercial created with the help of *Massive* software featured 146,000 virtual characters).

The universal capture method uses neither manual animation nor simulation of the underlying physics. Instead, it directly samples physical reality, including color, texture, and the movement of the actors. Short sequences of an actor's performances are encoded as 3D computer animations, and these animations form a library from which the filmmakers can draw as they compose a scene. (The analogy with music sampling is obvious.) As Gaeta pointed out, his team never used manual animation to try to tweak the motion of character's face; however, just as a musician may do, they would often "hold" a particular expression before going to the next one.[8] This suggests another analogy, analog video editing. But this is second-degree editing, so to speak: instead of simply capturing segments of reality on video and then joining them together, Gaeta's method produces complete virtual recreations of particular phenomena—self-contained microworlds—that can be then further edited and embedded in a larger 3D simulated space.

Animation as an Idea

The brief overview of CG methods presented above to explain universal capture offers good examples of the multiplicity of ways in which animation is used in contemporary moving image culture. If we consider this multiplicity, it is possible to conclude that animation as a separate medium hardly exists anymore. At the same time, the general principles and techniques of putting objects and images into motion developed in nineteenth- and twentieth-century animation are used much more frequently now than before computerization. But they are hardly ever used by themselves. Usually they are combined with other techniques drawn from live-action cinematography and CG.

In light of these developments, where does animation start and end today? When you see a Disney or a Pixar animated feature or many graphics shorts, it is obvious that you are seeing animation. Regardless of whether the process involves drawing images by hand or using 3D software, the principle is the same: somebody created the drawings or 3D objects, set key frames, and then created in-between positions.[9] The objects can be created in multiple ways, and in-betweening can be done manually or automatically by the software, but this does not change the basic logic. The movement, or any other change over time, is defined manually—usually via key frames (but not always). In retrospect, the definition of movement via keys probably was the essence of twentieth-century animation. It was used in traditional cell animation by Disney and others, for stop-motion animation by Starevich and Trnka, and for the 3D animated shorts by Pixar, and it continues to be used today in animated features that combine traditional cell method and 3D computer animation. And while experimental animators such as Norman McLaren refused keys-and-in-betweens system in favor of drawing each frame on film by hand without explicitly defining the keys, this approach did not change the overall logic: the movement was created by hand. Not surprisingly, most animation artists exploited this key feature of animation in different ways, turning it into aesthetics, for instance the exaggerated squash and stretch in Disney, or the discontinuous jumps between frames in McLaren.

It is also true that images and objects can be set in motion in other ways. We need only consider the methods developed in CG: physically based modeling, particle systems, formal grammars, artificial life, and behavioral animation. In all these methods the animator does not directly create the movement. Instead, it is created by the software, which uses some kind of mathematical model. For instance, in the case of physically based modeling the animator may set the parameters of a computer model that simulates a physical force such as wind that will deform a piece of cloth over a number of frames. Or she may instruct the ball to drop onto the floor, and let the physics model control how the ball bounces after it hits the floor. In the case of particle systems, which are used to model everything from fireworks, explosions, water, and gas to animal flocks and swarms, the animator has only to define the initial conditions: the number of particles, their speed, their life span, and so on

In contrast to live-action cinema, these CG methods do not capture real physical movement. Does it mean that they belong to animation? If we accept that the defining feature of traditional animation was the manual creation of movement, the answer is no. But things are not so simple. With all these methods, the animator sets the initial parameters, runs the model, adjusts the parameters, and repeats this production loop until she is satisfied with the result. So, even though the actual movement is produced not by hand but by a mathematical model, the animator maintains significant control. In a way, the animator acts as a film director, only in this case she is directing not the actors but the computer model until it produces a satisfactory performance. We could also compare her to a film editor who selects among the best performances of the computer model.

James Blinn, a computer scientist responsible for creating many fundamental CG techniques, once developed an interesting analogy to explain the difference between the manual keyframing method and physically based modeling. He told the audience at a SIGGRAPH panel that the difference between the two methods is like the difference between painting and photography. In Blinn's terms, an animator who creates movement by manually defining key frames and drawing in-between frames is like a painter who observes the world and then makes a painting of it. The painting's resemblance to the world depends on the painter's skills, imagination, and intentions. By contrast, an animator who uses physically based modeling is like a photographer who captures the world as it actually is. Blinn wanted to emphasize that mathematical techniques can create a realistic simulation of movement in the physical world, and an animator need only capture what is created by the simulation.

Although this analogy is useful, it may not be completely accurate. Obviously, the traditional photographer whom Blinn had in mind (i.e., before Photoshop) chooses composition, contrast, depth of field, and many other parameters. Similarly, an animator using physically based modeling also has control over a large number of parameters, and it depends on her skills and perseverance to make the model produce a satisfying animation. An example from the related area of software art that uses some of the same mathematical methods illustrates my point. Casey Reas, an artist well known both for his own still images and animations and for the Processing graphics programming environment he helped develop, told me he may spend only a couple of hours writing a software program to create a new work—and then another two years working with the different parameters of the same program and producing endless test images until he is satisfied with the results.[10] So, whereas at first, physically based modeling appears to be the opposite of traditional animation in that the movement is created by a computer, it is better understood as a hybrid cross of animation and computer simulation. Although the animator no longer directly draws each phase of movement, she is working with the parameters of the mathematical model that "draws" the actual movement.

And what about universal capture methods as used in *The Matrix*? Gaeta and his colleagues also banished keyframing animation, but they did not use any mathematical modes to automatically generate motion either. As we saw, their solution was to capture the actual performance of an actor (e.g., the movements of the actor's face) and then reconstruct it as a 3D sequence. Together, these reconstructed sequences form a library of facial expressions. The filmmaker can then draw from this library, editing together a sequence of expressions (but not interfering with any parameters of separate sequences). It is important to stress that a 3D model has no muscles or other controls traditionally used in animating CG faces. It is used "as is."

As is the case when an animator employs mathematical models, this method avoids drawing individual movements by hand. And yet its logic is that of animation rather than of cinema. The filmmaker chooses individual sequences of actors' performances, edits them, blends them, and places them in a particular order to create a scene. In this way the scene is actually constructed by hand, even though its components are not. In contrast to traditional animation, in which the animator draws each frame to create a short sequence (e.g., a character turning his head), here the filmmaker "draws" at a higher level, manipulating whole sequences rather than individual frames.

To create final movie scenes, the universal capture method is combined with virtual cinematography to stage the lighting and the positions and movement of a virtual camera that is "filming" the virtual performances. What makes this virtual cinematography as opposed to simply computer animation as we already know it? The world as seen by a virtual camera is different from a normal CG world. It consists of reconstructions of the actual set and the actual performers created via the universal capture process. The aim is to avoid manual processes usually used to create 3D models and sets. Instead, the data about the physical world are captured and then used to create a precise virtual replica.

Ultimately, ESC's production method as used in *The Matrix* is neither pure animation nor cinematography nor traditional special effects nor traditional CG. Instead, it is a pure example of hybridity in general and of "deep remixability" in particular. With its complex blend of the variety of media techniques and media formats, it is also typical of the moving image culture today. When the techniques drawn from these different media traditions are brought together in a software environment, the result is not a sum of separate components but a variety of hybrid methods—such as universal capture. I think this is how different moving image techniques function now in general. After computerization virtualized them, "extracting" them from their particular physical media to turn them into algorithms, they started interacting and creating hybrids. While we have already encountered various examples of hybrid techniques, universal capture and virtual cinematography illustrate how creative industries today develop whole production workflows based on hybridity.

Gaeta is very clear that what he and his colleagues created is a new hybrid. In a 2004 interview he said, "If I had to define virtual cinema, I would say it is somewhere between a live-action film and a computer-generated animated film. It is computer generated, but it is derived from real world people, places and things" (Feeny 2004). Although universal capture offers a particularly striking example of such "somewhere between," most forms of moving image created today are similarly "somewhere between," with animation being one of the coordinate axes of this new space of hybridity.

Universal Capture: Reality Reassembled

The process that came to be called universal capture combines the best of two worlds: visible reality as captured by lens-based cameras and synthetic 3D CG. Although it is possible to recreate the richness of the visible world through manual painting and animation, as well as through various CG techniques (texture mapping, bump mapping, physical modeling), it is expensive in terms of the labor involved. Even with physically based modeling techniques endless parameters have to be tweaked before the animation looks right. In contrast, capturing visible reality via lens-based recording (the process that in the twentieth century was called filming) is cheap: just point the camera and press the record button.

The disadvantage of such lens-based recordings is that they lack the flexibility demanded by contemporary remix culture. Remix culture requires not self-contained aesthetic objects or self-contained records of reality but smaller units, parts that can be easily changed and combined with other parts in endless combinations. However, the lens-based recording process flattens the semantic structure of reality. Instead of a set of unique objects that occupy distinct areas of a 3D physical space we end up with a flat field made from pixels (or film grains, in the case of film-based capture) that do not carry any information about where they came from—that is, which objects they correspond to. Therefore, any kind of spatial editing operation—deleting objects, adding new ones, compositing, and so forth—becomes quite difficult. Before anything can be done with an object in the image, it has to be manually separated from the rest of the image by creating a mask. And unless an image shows an object that is properly lit and shot against a special blue or green background, it is practically impossible to mask the object precisely.

In contrast, 3D computer-generated worlds have the exact flexibility one would expect from media in the information age. It is not accidental that 3D CG representation, along with hypertext and other new computer-based data representation methods, was conceptualized in the same decade when the transformation of advanced industrialized societies into information societies became visible. In a 3D computer-generated world, everything is discrete. The world consists of a number of separate objects. Objects are defined by points described by their coordinates in a 3D space; other properties of objects, such as color, transparency, and reflectivity, are similarly described in terms of discrete numbers. As a result, although a 3D CG representation may not have the richness of a lens-based recording, it does contain a semantic structure of the world. This structure is easily accessible at any time. A designer can directly select any object (or any object part) in the scene. Thus, to duplicate an object one hundred times requires only a few mouse clicks or typing a short command, and all other properties of a world can similarly be easily changed. And since each object itself consists of discrete components (flat polygons or surface patches defined by splines), it is equally easy to change its 3D form by selecting and manipulating its components. In addition, just as a sequence of genes contains the code that is expanded into a complex organism, a compact description of a 3D world that contains only the coordinates of the objects can be quickly transmitted through the network, with the client computer reconstructing the full world (this is how online multiplayer computer games and simulators work).

Universal capture brings together the complementary advantages of lens-based capture and CG representation in an ingenious way. Beginning in the late 1970s, when James Blinn introduced the CG technique of texture mapping, computer scientists, designers, and animators have been gradually expanding the range of information that can be recorded in the real world and then incorporated into a computer model. Until the early 1990s this information mostly involved the appearance of the objects: color, texture, light effects. The next significant step was the development of motion capture. During the first half of the 1990s it was quickly adopted in the movie and game industries. Now, computer-synthesized worlds relied not only on sampling of the visual appearance of the real world but also on sampling of movements of animals and humans in this world. Building on all these techniques, Gaeta's method takes them to a new stage: capturing just about everything that at present can be captured and then reassembling the samples to create a digital—and thus completely malleable—recreation. Put in a larger context, the resulting 2D/3D hybrid representation perfectly fits with the most progressive trends in contemporary culture, which are all based on the idea of a hybrid.

The New Hybrid

It is my strong feeling that the emerging information aesthetics (i.e., the new cultural features specific to the information society) already have or will have a very different logic from modernism. The latter was driven by a strong desire to erase the old, a desire visible as much in the avant-garde artists' (particularly the futurists') statements that museums should be burned as in the dramatic destruction of all social and spiritual realities of many people in Russia after the 1917 Revolution, and in other countries after they became Soviet satellites after 1945. Culturally and ideologically, modernists wanted to start with a tabula rasa, radically distancing themselves from the past. It was only in the 1960s that this move started to feel inappropriate, as manifested both in a loosening of ideology in communist countries and the beginnings of a new postmodern sensibility in the West. To reference the title of a famous book by Robert Venturi, Denise Scott Brown, and Steven Izenour (published in 1972, it was the first systematic manifestation of the new sensibility), "learning from Las Vegas" meant admitting that the organic development of vernacular cultures involves bricolage and hybridity, rather than purity as seen, for instance, in the international style, which was still practiced by architects the world over at that time. Driven less by the desire to imitate vernacular cultures and more by the new availability of previous cultural artifacts stored on magnetic and eventually digital media, in the 1980s commercial culture in the West systematically replaced purity with stylistic heterogeneity. Finally, when the Soviet empire collapsed, postmodernism had won the world over.

Today we face the very real danger of being imprisoned by a new international style, something we can call the new "global style." The cultural globalization, of which cheap airline flights, the Web, and billions of mobile phones are three most visible manifestations, erases some dimensions of the cultural specificity with an energy and speed impossible for modernism. Yet we also see today a different logic at work: the desire to creatively combine old and new, local and transnational, in various configurations. It is this logic, for instance, that made cities such as Barcelona (where I spoke with John Gaeta in the context of the Art Futura 2003 festival that informed this writing) such "hip" and "in" places at the turn of the twenty-first century. All over Barcelona, architectural styles of many past centuries coexist with the new, "cool" spaces of bars, lounges, hotels, new museums. Medieval meets multinational, Gaudy meets Dolce & Gabana, Mediterranean time meets global time. The result is an invigorating sense of energy that one feels physically just walking along the street. It is this hybrid energy that in my view characterizes the most interesting cultural phenomena today.[11] The hybrid 2D/3D image of *The Matrix* is one such example.

The historians of cinema often draw a contrast between the Lumières and Marey. Along with a number of inventors in other countries, all working independently of each other, the Lumières created what we now know as cinema, with its visual effect of continuous motion based on the perceptual synthesis of discrete images. Earlier, Eadweard Muybridge had already developed a way to take successive photographs of a moving object such as a horse; eventually the Lumières and others figured out how to take enough samples so that when projected, the images perceptually fused into continuous motion. A scientist, Marey was driven by an opposite desire: not to create a seamless illusion of the visible world but to be able to understand its structure by keeping subsequent samples discrete. Since he wanted to be able to easily compare these samples, he perfected a method whereby the subsequent images of moving objects were superimposed in a single image, thus making the changes clearly visible.

The hybrid image of *The Matrix* in some ways can be understand as the synthesis of these two approaches, which remained in opposition for a hundred years. Like the Lumières, Gaeta has as a goal to create a seamless illusion of continuous motion. At the same time, like Marey, he also wants to be able to edit and sequence the individual recordings of reality.

At the beginning of this essay I invoked the notion of uneven development, pointing out that often the structure inside (infrastructure) completely changes before the surface (superstructure) catches up. What does this idea imply for the future of images, and in particular for 2D/3D hybrids as developed by Gaeta and others? As Gaeta pointed out in 2003, while his method could be used to make all kinds of images, so far it had been used in the service of realism as it was defined in cinema: anything the viewer saw had to obey the laws of physics.[12] In the case of *The Matrix,* its images still have a traditional "realistic" appearance while internally they are structured in a completely new way. In short, we see the old superstructure, which stills sits on top of the old infrastructure. What kinds of images might we expect to see when the superstructure finally catches up with the infrastructure?

While the images of Hollywood special effects movies so far follow the constraint of realism, obeying the laws of physics, they are also continuously expanding the boundaries of what realism means. To sell movie tickets, DVDs, and all the other merchandise, each new special effects film tries to top the previous one, showing something that nobody has seen before. In *The Matrix 1* it was "bullet time"; in *The Matrix 2* it was the Burly Brawl scene in which dozens of identical clones fight Neo; in *The Matrix 3* it was the Superpunch (Borshukov 2004). The fact that the image is constructed differently internally does allow for all kinds of new effects; listening to Gaeta, it is clear that for him the key advantage of such imagery is the possibility it offers for virtual cinematography. That is, if before, camera movement was limited to a small and well-defined set of moves—pan, dolly, roll—now it can move in any trajectory imaginable for as long as the director wants. Gaeta discusses the Burly Brawl scene in terms of *virtual choreography*: both choreographing the intricate and long camera moves impossible in the real word and also all the bodies participating in the fight (all of which are digital recreations assembled using the total capture method). According to Gaeta, creating this one scene took about three years. So, whereas in principle, total capture represents one of the most flexible ways to recreate visible reality in a computer to date, it will be years before this method is streamlined and standardized enough for these advantages to become obvious. But when that happens, artists will have an extremely flexible hybrid medium at their disposal: completely virtualized cinema. Rather than expecting that any of the present pure forms will dominate the future of visual culture, I think this future belongs to such hybrids. In other words, future images will probably still be photographic—although only on the surface.

And what about animation? What will be its future? In addition to animated films proper and animated sequences used as part of other moving image projects, animation has become a set of principles and techniques that animators, filmmakers, and designers employ today to create new techniques, new production methods, and new visual aesthetics. Therefore, I think it is not worthwhile to ask if this or that visual style or method for creating moving images that emerged after computerization is animation or not. It is more productive to say that most of these methods were born from animation and have animation DNA, mixed with DNA from other media. Such a perspective, which considers "animation in an extended field," is a more productive way to think about animation today, and it also applies to other modern media fields that provided genetic material for a computer metamedium.

Notes

1. For technical details of the method, see the publications of Georgi Borshukov at <http://www.virtualcinematography.org/publications.html>.

2. Although not everybody would agree with this analysis, I feel that after the end of the 1980s the field significantly slowed: on the one hand, all key techniques that can be used to create photorealistic 3D images had been discovered; on the other hand, the rapid development of computer hardware in the 1990s meant that computer scientists no longer had to develop new techniques to speed up the rendering, since the algorithms already developed would now run fast enough.

3. I refer here to the "normal" use of CG in narrative films and not to the hybrid aesthetics of TV graphics, music videos, and the like, which deliberately juxtapose different visual codes.

4. The terms "reality simulation" and "reality sampling" are my confections; the terms "virtual cinema," "virtual human," "universal capture," and "virtual cinematography" are John Gaeta's. The term "image-based rendering" appeared in the 1990s. See the publications list at <http://www.debevec.org/Publications>.

5. Therefore, while the article in *Wired* that positioned Gaeta as a groundbreaking pioneer and a rebel working outside Hollywood contained the typical journalistic exaggeration, it was not far from the truth (Silberman 2003).

6. The method captures only the geometry and images of an actor's head. The body movements are recorded separately using motion capture.

7. See <http://www.massivesoftware.com>.

8. John Gaeta, presentation during a workshop on the making of *The Matrix*, Art Futura 2003 festival, Barcelona, October 12, 2003.

9. Of course, in the production of commercial films, this is not one person but large teams.

10. Casey Reas, personal communication, April 2005.

11. From this perspective, my earlier book, *The Language of New Media* (2001), can be seen as a systematic investigation of a particular slice of contemporary culture driven by this hybrid aesthetics: the slice where the logic of the digital networked computer intersects the numerous logics of already established cultural forms.

12. John Gaeta during a making of *Matrix* workshop.

References

Blinn, James. 1978. Simulation of Wrinkled Surfaces. *Computer Graphics* 12 (3): 286–292.

Borshukov, Georgi. 2004. Making of *The Superpunch*. Presentation at Imagina 2004. <www .virtualcinematography.org/publications/acrobat/Superpunch.pdf>.

Borshukov, George, Dan Piponi, and Oystein Larsen, J. P. Lewis, and Christina Tempelaar-Lietz. 2003. Universal Capture: Image-based Facial Animation for *The Matrix Reloaded*. In *SIGGRAPH 2003 Sketches and Applications Program*. <http://www.virtualcinematography.org/publications/ acrobat/UCap- s2003.pdf>.

Feeny, Catherine. 2004. *The Matrix* Revealed: An Interview with John Gaeta. *VFXPro*, May 9.. <www.uemedia.net/CPC/vfxpro/article_7062.shtml>.

Manovich, Lev. 2001. *The Language of New Media*. Cambridge: MIT Press.

Silberman, Steve. 2003. *Matrix 2*. *Wired* 11.05 (May). <http://www.wired.com/wired/archive/11.05/ matrix2.html>.

Venturi, Robert, Denise Scott Brown, and Steven Izenour. 1972. *Learning from Las Vegas*. Cambridge: MIT Press.

Software References

Maya. Autodesk. 1998–.

Tiger Woods PGA Tour. EA Sports. 2007.

Photoshop. Adobe Systems. 1990–.

Processing. Casey Raes and Ben Fry. 2001-.

6 Tangible Narratives: Emerging Interfaces for Digital Storytelling and Machinima

Ali Mazalek

The machinima art form incorporates elements of both live performance and cinematic production. Machinima artists puppeteer their characters inside real-time 3D game engines and edit the captured sequences into linear digital films. For the most part, existing machinima groups have used standard off-the-shelf PC input devices, such as mice, keyboards, and joysticks, for real-time control in the virtual world. However, these tools are limited in terms of their expressive potential. Emerging fields such as tangible interfaces and physical computing can provide new alternatives for machinimakers of the future. This essay examines these emerging areas of interface research and relates them to the production of digital stories in different formats, with a particular view to how they could be applied in machinima production. The essay concludes with a discussion of novel research focused on the design and development of physical puppet interfaces for real-time control in 3D game engines.

How do we convey our intentions to a computer? How can we seamlessly express ourselves in a digital space? Although these questions may seem simple, providing satisfactory answers is not easy. For nearly half a century, the expressive potential of the digital medium has been growing with incredible speed. Computers now offer a vast variety of media applications and environments to explore and enjoy, providing increasingly impressive real-time visuals that can be viewed on ever crisper, bigger, and cheaper digital displays. But despite this progress on the output side, the input interfaces used to navigate these information spaces have changed very little: two-axis pointing devices and arrays of on/off switches providing low-bandwidth single-channel streams of input data. While this might not be so bad if one is simply composing an email message, writing an essay, or even browsing the Web, the question of how to get one's intent into the machine becomes far more critical when related to expressive forms of interaction. The particular case examined in this essay is the area of dramatic expression, where the goal is real-time control of virtual characters and environments in an unfolding narrative piece.

The human body is a powerful expressive machine. In physical performance such as live theater, performers move their bodies around the stage, their movements enacting a narrative in real time. Not only can humans perform many kinds of physical actions and convey a broad range of emotions, they can also switch seamlessly from one action or expression to the next. This fluidity extends naturally to the art of puppeteering, where the actions of human puppeteers are mapped onto physical puppets and integrated into an unfolding narrative performance in real time. Puppeteering also opens up a space for expressive exaggeration, since puppets can be made to perform actions that would be unachievable with the human body alone.

In cinematic storytelling, on the other hand, the actors express themselves in real time in front of a camera, but the effects of their physical actions and performances are not immediately seen in their final narrative form. The editing phase imposes a delay on the narrative experience since the bits of recorded footage have to be cut and assembled together into a final piece that can be screened for an audience. Through this editing process, space and time are (re)constructed for storytelling purposes, yielding on-film narrative worlds that do not correspond directly to the physical spaces in which the story pieces were executed. Nevertheless, as the actors perform their scenes, they exist inside the narrative world, taking on the roles of the fictional characters and acting them out in real time with their bodies. Of course, digital effects can also complicate the filmmaking process, since any given scene might be assembled from a mix of both real and virtual elements. In this case, the separate digital and physical pieces are brought together in the rendering of the final cinematic scene.

The emerging storytelling art form of machinima incorporates elements of both live performance and cinematic production. Machinimakers control the characters in a 3D virtual world in real time, much as puppeteers control their physical puppets in the real world, generally following some kind of narrative script. Sequences captured from these digital performances by virtual cameras are later edited together to create a final machinima piece. The tools for editing and assembling the video sequences may be similar to those used in regular digital moviemaking. The question addressed here is, what are the tools that machinima puppeteers use (or could use) to control their digital characters in real time as the virtual cameras roll? For the most part, existing machinima groups have used standard off-the-shelf PC input devices for this purpose, such as mice, keyboards, and joysticks. However, these tools are very limited in terms of the expressive potential they offer. This is where the emerging field of tangible interfaces and physical computing might provide some new alternatives for the machinimakers of the future.

This essay examines evolving areas of interface research, such as tangible interfaces and responsive spaces, as they relate to new media and expressive dramatic formats such as digital storytelling and performance. Particular attention is given to research on interfaces for the control of 3D virtual characters and spaces, and how these might inform the emerging art form of machinima. The essay concludes by presenting novel research on physical puppet controllers for machinima production.

A Question of Interface: Bridging the Physical-Digital Divide

The use of computer technologies continues to spread across different areas of our everyday lives in both work and leisure activities. Because of the limited form factor of existing human-computer interfaces, application designers and researchers are exploring new ways to better integrate the physical and digital spaces in which we exist. These efforts have resulted in emerging areas of digital interaction research, such as ubiquitous computing and tangible user interfaces, or TUIs, which are discussed briefly here.

Ubiquitous computing researchers envision a world in which computers become invisible and move off the desktop into everyday physical devices and spaces that provide computational services through embedded sensors, displays, and networking capabilities (Weiser 1991). Central to this vision is the expectation that these computing technologies should be able to understand human contexts and adapt their services or interfaces based on the user's preferences or needs in specific situations. This functionality requires sensing, actuation, networking, and computation to be transparently embedded in the everyday objects and spaces that surround us. Once this environmental network is established, an explicit interface that users must learn to operate is no longer always needed. The tool seems to disappear, allowing users to focus on the task at hand.

In contrast to ubiquitous computing, TUIs aim to extend our means of input and output into the digital space beyond a primarily audiovisual mode to interactions that can make better use of the natural skills that humans have with their hands (Ishii and Ullmer 1997). This approach involves coupling digital information with physical artifacts that can act as both controls and representations for the underlying systems they embody. In the case of TUIs, there is typically an explicit interface that must be manipulated with the hands by one or more people at a time. These interfaces take advantage of our manual dexterity and capitalize on the well-understood affordances and metaphors of the physical objects we use in our daily lives.

Like traditional filmmaking, machinima is a creative art form that involves a variety of different tools at different stages of the process. In contrast, however, machinima actors must map their expressions onto characters that exist inside a virtual world rather than assume the roles of the characters with their own entire bodies. Similarly, machinima camera operators must manipulate their cameras in a virtual space rather than on a physical set. The controllers used in these activities should allow the actors and filmmakers to focus on the task at hand, allowing them to develop the piece according to a scripted or mental vision without significantly detracting from the creative flow. Since current game controllers (mostly gamepads, joysticks, keyboards, and mice) have limited expressive capabilities, certain concepts from ubiquitous and tangible computing can be useful in the context of machinima production. From ubiquitous computing research, machinima can derive the importance of providing transparent technological tools, where the interface disappears in the face of the task performed by its user. Machinima can also benefit from interfaces that make use of human manual dexterity to provide expression in a virtual space and that offer immediate feedback to our actions, two central notions of tangible computing.

A number of efforts have been made to describe and classify the different technological approaches and interaction styles used for tangible interface systems (see Mazalek and Hoven 2009 for a summary). Some of the more common approaches are spatial systems, where the users' body parts or other physical objects are tracked in real time and computationally interpreted within a spatial reference frame, such as an interactive surface (e.g., floor, wall, tabletop). The large flat surfaces often used in these cases allow the display of computer-generated graphics that are coincident with the tracked objects. This provides an easy and fluid means of coupling the physical and virtual elements of the interactive system. Another approach to TUIs involves constructive assemblies, where physical objects (e.g., modular tiles or blocks) can be attached together to form larger constructions. Frequently, the individual pieces of the construction kit can store certain kinds of data or have specific meanings, which can be communicated with other pieces when they are connected together. The digital meaning and functionality created through the assembly of individual pieces are typically reflected in the physical form of the overall construction. Finally, many tangible interfaces take the form of custom-designed or specialized physical controllers, where the physical design of the artifact reflects both its method of use and its functionality in the digital space. The following sections discuss how some of these approaches could be applied in the creation of machinima pieces. I consider first past works in which emerging digital interaction technologies were used for expressive and dramatic purposes.

Dramatic Expression: Evolving Forms and Interactions

Technological progress continuously pushes the bounds of media communication and entertainment forms. As new platforms emerge, artists are able to explore new modes of creative expression and storytelling, all the while drawing on their knowledge and understanding of past traditions. Machinima is an example of an art form that draws from a number of earlier traditions, such as cinematic storytelling, live performance, and puppeteering, and also makes use of new computer game and real-time 3D graphics technologies for the creation of narrative works. Related forms of narrative expression include digital systems for interactive storytelling, live theater, and virtual agents. Some of the work in these areas has made use of tangible interfaces and physical computing technologies, demonstrating how technologies such as computer-vision-based full-body interaction, tabletop object tracking, and radio frequency identification (RFID) can be used to an expressive end.

Interactive Storytelling

Digital interactive storytelling systems allow users to influence the path of an unfolding narrative. Unlike machinima pieces, which provide a single linear story experience, interactive stories typically offer a multitude of possible paths and often require users to interact to keep the story moving forward. The narrative approaches vary widely and offer different levels or means of dramatic agency to users. A discussion of interactive story forms is outside the scope of this essay; a good overview of the theories and techniques can be found in Meadows (2002).

In addition to the many kinds of narrative structure used, interactive stories can be designed for and played out on a variety of different interaction platforms. These range from screen-based graphical user interfaces (GUIs) or immersive virtual reality systems to mobile platforms or real-world responsive spaces. While the goals and experience of interactive stories differ notably from machinima pieces, some of the interfaces through which users gain dramatic agency could inform the design of new input devices and interaction tools for machinima creation. Following are some examples of physical interfaces that have been used for character control or spatial navigation in interactive stories.

The *Romeo & Juliet in Hades* piece created at the ATR Media Integration and Communication Research Labs in Japan was an interactive story system in which players could control on-screen avatars (either Romeo or Juliet) to move through the story (Tosa 1998). The system used a motion capture system based on magnetic sensors attached to each player's body, and their movements were thus reflected in those of their avatars. An important aspect of this work was to provide an immersive experience in which participants could actually feel they were contributing to the story development. Since the story itself was played out in virtual space, participants could engage in the experience from remote physical locations. This type of setup demonstrated how participants can take on the role of characters in an unfolding story through full-body interaction, and how that interaction could translate to the control of game characters by machinima actors. The setup was cumbersome and costly, however, and such resources are most likely beyond the means of most machinimakers. The puppet interfaces discussed later could provide lower-cost alternatives for virtual character control.

The Tangible Spatial Narratives project carried out at the MIT Media Laboratory used a tangible media interaction table as a shared interface for navigating multithreaded and spatially structured stories (Mazalek and Davenport 2003). A map of the story setting was displayed on the surface of the table, and audience members could browse the database of story clips using tangible interaction objects, such as pawns and a clock tool (figure 6.1). These interactions would cause the story to unfold, gradually revealing the different pieces of a complex spatially structured story. The

Figure 6.1
Tangible character pawn and clock tool used for navigation in the Tangible Spatial Narratives tabletop storytelling application.

application was used to document a large group event in which sixty-five participants distributed across a variety of physical spaces on the campus of an arts school contributed to the construction of the story. The tangible media table acted as a shared meeting place where participants could view and discuss the pieces of their growing story. This kind of tangible spatial navigation could be useful in the creation of machinima pieces, perhaps in the form of a stage manager toolset, as discussed later.

Theater and Performance
Although both the above examples involved real-world actors mapped into virtual performance spaces, some artists and researchers have also reversed this mapping, incorporating virtual puppets into a live performance unfolding on a physical stage. For example, Jørgen Callesen (2005) describes an artistic experiment in which virtual puppets were used on a real-world live performance stage. The play was called *The Family Factory* and was realized in a collaboration among the Aarhus University Multimedia Department, the Department of Puppet Theater at the Ernst Busch Theater School, Berlin, and the Danish Film School Department of Animation. The creators originally envisioned a combination of human-controlled and autonomous virtual puppets but, because of technical complexities, eventually settled on human-controlled virtual puppets alone. Performers were instrumented with magnetic sensors that mapped to various parts of the animated characters in a one-to-one relationship;

for example, the hair of the Mother character was controlled by a sensor attached to the performer's foot.

Other examples of virtual puppets on a physical stage exist in the context of the Interactive Virtual Environment (IVE) stage created at the MIT Media Laboratory in the 1990s (Sparacino, Davenport, and Pentland 2000). The IVE stage was a room-sized area in which real-time computer vision techniques were used to interpret a performer's movements, including posture, gestures, and identity. A projected backdrop served to integrate the virtual imagery into the unfolding performance. A microphone on the stage was used to pick up audio for speech processing. Together, these technologies enable an improvisational form of performance in which both human and virtual actors work together to generate a story. For example, several IVE performances involved a human actor interacting with her alter ego, which took the form of expressive animated text displayed on the projection screen. This improvisational form of story-play presents a different model for virtual character interaction. Rather than being directly controlled like puppets, the virtual characters are endowed with some basic artificial intelligence (AI) that allows them to respond to human actors. Although this diverges from the scripted form of machinima, in certain cases intelligent virtual agents could be used to enhance an unfolding machinima piece. Nowadays, some movie production companies make use of computer-generated characters endowed with AI for scenes in which it would be too costly or too time-consuming to create and script each character individually. For example, in the Battle of Helm's Deep scene in *The Lord of the Rings: The Two Towers* (2002), virtual Orcs are generated by the *Massive* software program (<http://massivesoftware.com>) and endowed with a digital brain to enable them to act and fight independently. The following section looks briefly at research in the area of intelligent virtual agents, particularly as it relates to new interface technologies or puppetry.

Intelligent Virtual Agents

Intelligent virtual agents (IVAs) are autonomous and graphically embodied agents that exist in an interactive 2D or 3D virtual environment. They are generally able to interact intelligently with the environment, with other IVAs, and with human users within certain application contexts. IVAs could be used to support machinima production by providing characters that do not require direct fine-grained player control but could instead be either completely autonomous or else loosely controlled by human players, for example at the level of tasks performed.

For scripted machinima, the idea of supervisory or task-level control is perhaps the most interesting. This functionality could leave a certain amount of character direction in the hands of the machinima actor while still reducing the cognitive load required to control the virtual character enough to allow him or her to perform other tasks at the same time. Some IVA researchers have placed human actors into the virtual environment where the characters reside to enable interaction. For example, the ALIVE (Artificial Interactive Video Environment) system placed the user in a virtual space using computer vision and a "magic mirror" concept; there, users could interact with software agents that took the form of virtual characters, such as a dog or hamster (Maes et al. 1997).

Other researchers have also explored control through novel physical-digital interfaces. For example, Johnson's work on "sympathetic interfaces" used a plush toy (a stuffed chicken) to manipulate and control an interactive story character in a 3D virtual world (Johnson et al. 1999). In a similar form factor and equipped with a variety of sensors in its hands, feet, and eye, the ActiMates Barney plush doll acted as a play partner for children, either in a freestanding mode or wirelessly linked to a PC or TV (Alexander and Strommen 1998). In the latter case, Barney would communicate with the PC or TV wirelessly and help to encourage the participation or direct the attention of the child. In a different vein, researchers at Oregon State University have demonstrated a tabletop tangible interface to provide a high level of animated character control in specifying the movements of many characters during the simulation of moves in a sports game (Metoyer, Xu, and Srinivasan 2003). More recently, our research lab at Georgia Tech has been exploring how wearable RFID technology can be used to control virtual avatars (Medyniskiy et al. 2007). The Real-Life Sims project looks at how a user's everyday activities can be mapped onto corresponding avatars in a virtual space to provide a sense of presence to distant friends and family or to control characters in online game spaces like *The Sims* (2000).

Tangible Puppeteers: Emerging Platforms for Machinimakers

Most machinima groups to date have used standard devices for character control, such as mice, keyboards, gamepads, and joysticks. The ILL Clan has also used nonstandard devices, such as Belkin's Nostromo Speedpad N52 (figure 6.2), which can allow a greater level of customized control during live performances. However, even these nonstandard devices do not support intuitive mappings between a performer's physical actions and their effects in the virtual space, and they can be difficult to learn and use.

As the machinima art form continues to grow in popularity, machinima creators will seek more intuitive control mechanisms to enable both a broader range of expression and finer-grained control in the virtual environment. The field of TUI design can offer a natural solution by providing control devices that can more easily be mapped to the interactive elements in the virtual space. It is possible to imagine a suite of tangible tools that would provide control not only of the virtual characters but also of the other elements in the virtual set, such as props, lights, or cameras. Existing research on new interfaces for the manipulation of 3D characters or spaces is inspiring in this regard.

Figure 6.2
Belkin's Nostromo Speedpad N52 controller used by the ILL Clan group for live machinima performances.

Manipulation of 3D Characters

Complex characters have too many degrees of freedom to easily control. One possible solution is to provide task-level control using IVAs, as described above, which enables the abstraction of many low-level motions into a few high-level tasks, giving the animator supervisory control over the motion. Different kinds of devices have also been used to directly and interactively control the posture of 3D character models on computer screens, but control of multiple degrees of freedom at once remains difficult. In GUI systems, control typically happens sequentially. Some portion of the character's body is selected with the mouse and is then interactively dragged around the screen following the mouse movements, as far as the relevant joint limits will allow it to move, based on an inverse kinematics system. One of the core problems with this method of character manipulation is that most input devices, like the mouse, provide only two degrees of freedom, while the desired manipulations are in 3D.

Jacob and Sibert (1992) describe this as a mismatch between the perceptual structures of the manipulator and the perceptual structure of the manipulation task. They have demonstrated that for tasks that require manipulating several integrally related quantities (e.g., a 3D position), a device that naturally generates the same number of integrally related values as required by the task (e.g., a Polhemus tracker) is better than a 2D positioning device (e.g., a mouse). For this reason, a number of production and research endeavors have centered on the creation of new interfaces for control in 3D virtual spaces. These approaches have generally been costly and have not focused on the integration with existing commercial gaming platforms, making them beyond the reach of most machinima creators today.

Over the past decades, production companies have increasingly turned to various forms of puppetry and body or motion tracking to inject life into 3D character animation. Putting a performer in direct control of a character, as in puppetry, or capturing body motion for real-time or postprocessed application to an animated character, can translate the nuances of natural motion to computer characters, making them seem much more alive and greatly increasing their expressive potential. The Character Shop's trademark Waldo devices are telemetric input devices for controlling puppets and animatronics that are designed to fit a puppeteer's or performer's body. They allow single puppeteers or performers to control multiple axes of movement on a virtual character at once. Waldos are a great improvement over the older lever-based systems, which required a team of operators to control all the different parts of a single puppet. Lever-based systems thus required precise timing and coordination among the operators in order to present a unified performance (Robertson 1993). For example, many of Jim Henson's puppets are Waldo-controlled. In the late 1980s, Pacific Data Images developed a real-time computer graphic puppet named Waldo C. Graphic for the TV show *The Jim Henson Hour*. This digital puppet's motion could be performed in real time together with conventional puppets using a simple armature that controlled its position, orientation, and jaw movements (Walters 1989). During the performance, the puppeteer watched a simplified graphical representation of the character superimposed over live video of the physical puppets. The movement data captured during this performance with the armature were later cleaned and applied to a more complex representation of the character in a non-real-time mode, with dynamic features such as dangling legs and a floppy body added. A similar approach is used in the "Elmo's World" segment at the end of *Sesame Street* episodes, in which traditional Muppets and a virtual set of animated characters consisting of animated furniture (chairs, tables, doors) perform together in real time. While the need to clean sensor data during post-processing (typical for most motion capture and puppetry systems) is not practical for real-time machinima performance, and the price of these controllers far exceeds the budget of every machinima production house, it is still possible to draw inspiration from these techniques in the design of specialized controllers for machinima performance and production.

Another example of digital animated character control in the production realm is the Dinosaur Input Device (DID) digital stop-motion armature created by Stan Winston Studio and Industrial Light and Magic for the movie *Jurassic Park* (1993) (Shay and Duncan 1993). In this case, a miniature dinosaur armature was instrumented with encoders at key joints. Stop-motion animators could manipulate the model while keyframe data were sent to the animation system. Also, the French video and computer graphics production company Videosystem developed a real-time computer animation system that used a variety of input devices, such as DataGloves, MIDI drum pedals, joysticks, and Polhemus trackers, to control an animated character named Mat the Ghost (Tardif 1991). Typically, Mat was controlled by several puppeteers or actors working together. Two puppeteers would control facial expressions, lip synch, and special effects such as shape transformations using joysticks and other controllers, while an actor wearing a suit equipped with electromagnetic Polhemus trackers would control Mat's body motions. The character was then chroma-keyed with previously shot footage of live actors, and there was no post-rendering involved.

In the 1990s, glove-based interactions became popular for certain digital applications and were explored for both computer animation and video games. For example, the DataGlove system developed by VPL Research was used with virtual reality environments. At MIT, Dave Sturman (Sturman and Zeltzer 1993) created an expressive finger-walking puppet that was controlled by a DataGlove and used it to evaluate his "whole-hand" input method for controlling the walking character in comparison with conventional input devices. The Mattel toy company developed a low-cost glove called the Power Glove as a controller for Nintendo video games. The Nintendo Wii console also includes new kinds of input devices for video games, such as the Wii Remote, a wireless controller that can be used as a handheld pointing device, and can also detect motion and rotation in three dimensions.

Another notable research effort that has centered on new physical interfaces for character control and animation is the Monkey Input Device, an eighteen-inch-tall monkey skeleton that is equipped with sensors at its joints to provide 32 degrees of freedom from head to toe for real-time character manipulation (Esposito and Paley 1995). Other possible direct manipulation interfaces include products like Measurand's ShapeTape, a fiber-optic-based 3D bend-and-twist sensor that provides continuous position and orientation information. Researchers at the University of Toronto have explored using ShapeTape to facilitate direct manipulation of curves and surfaces in 3D (Balakrishnan et al. 1999). Puppeteer Brain Windsor has also done some preliminary tests with ShapeTape to explore the potential of attaching it to a physical puppet. Another puppeteering project is Virpet Theater, from Carnegie Mellon University's Entertainment Technology Center. Geared toward live performance, it makes use of puppeteering techniques based on a variety of input devices (joysticks, MIDI controllers) for manipulating virtual characters in a 3D environment in real time. More recently, researchers at Georgia Tech have used a paper hand puppet tracked by computer vision to control a character in the *Unreal* game engine (Hunt et al. 2006). This project in particular has been used for machinima creation and is the predecessor of the TUI3D project discussed later.

Manipulation of 3D Space

In addition to animated characters, controlling 3D virtual environments includes manipulating a variety of other elements in the virtual space, such as objects (furniture, props), lights, and cameras. For machinima production, one could imagine a set of tangible stage manager tools to enable real-time control of these different spatial elements. Research on both 3D modeling and manipulation using TUI techniques provides a preliminary idea of what such a set of tools might look like.

As early as 1980, John Frazer and his colleagues developed working prototypes of 3D input devices for architectural design (Frazer 1982). He called these machine readable models or intelligent modeling systems, since the models were able to communicate their geometry to design software running on a host computer. This software was able to provide interactive insights and advice to the designer, such as pointing out flaws or alternative design solutions. One example of Frazer's tools is the Segal model, which was developed to support the architect Walter Segal's timber-frame technique for self-homebuilders. The Segal model featured a large flat grid onto which electronically identified physical pieces such as colored plastic panels could be attached to construct home plans. Frazer and his colleagues were not alone in their work on tangible 3D modeling systems for architectural design, as similar methods were also developed by Aish and Noakes (1984) around the same time.

In recent years, researchers at the University of Calgary, working together with Frazer, have revived the Segal model tangible interface for 3D building layouts and connected it to the *Half-Life* graphical engine (Sutphen et al. 2000). With this approach, the building models can be rendered as fully active 3D worlds and populated with virtual characters. Also, researchers at Mitsubishi Electric Research Labs have explored the use of clay and blocks to create easy-to-use tangible modeling systems (Anderson et al. 2000). These interfaces are combined with graphical interpretation techniques to enhance the digital models created. If the physical model is built from rigidly connected building blocks of known size and shape, then it is possible to determine the 3D geometry of the blocks if they communicate their identity and connectivity information to a host computer. The computer can graphically interpret the structure by identifying walls, floors, doors, and other features. The 3D virtual model can then be enhanced or detailed, for example by texturing its surface in various styles. A different approach for tangible 3D modeling is seen in the DO-IT (Deformable Objects as Input Tools) system, which uses a custom-designed cubic shape made of electrically conductive polyurethane foam as an input tool for 3D shape deformation (Murakami et al. 1995). Manipulation of the virtual shape is achieved through intuitive operations on the input tool, such as pressing, bending and twisting.

A tangible interface simulation approach for urban environments is demonstrated in Urp, which lets multiple users work together to specify the layout of an urban environment by placing and arranging building models on a horizontal sensing surface (Underkoffler and Ishii 1999). When the buildings are detected on the table, virtual information is graphically projected directly onto them, such as shadows cast at a specific time of day or flowing lines to indicate wind speed and direction. The immediate graphical feedback that is colocated with the physical building models is a powerful feature and could easily translate to the layout of scenes and settings in a machinima piece. Moreover, multi-user tabletop platforms could provide a means for simultaneously and easily adjusting multiple parameters of a setting or scene during the creation of a machinima piece. For example, several machinimakers could work together to quickly adjust position and properties of characters, props, or settings, either beforehand or in real time during the recording process. A single machinimaker could also do the same adjustments alone, using both hands at once to do multiple tasks in parallel, such as adjusting one of the lights while repositioning a camera. This approach could also be combined with mobile devices for 3D navigation. For example, Hachet's camera-based interface allows two-handed interaction to navigate information spaces, such as 3D objects, large maps or 3D scenes, on a mobile display (Hachet, Pouderoux, and Guitton 2005). One hand holds the mobile device while the other holds a target behind the device, which is observed using the device's built-in camera. The approach provides three degrees of freedom interaction: by moving the target around with respect to the device, users can translate, rotate, or zoom 3D objects or scenes.

Tangible User Interfaces for 3D Spaces Research Project

Thus far, I have presented an overview of research on emerging TUI technologies for applications in narrative arts and entertainment, with particular attention to how these technologies could be used to support machinima production. This section presents the Tangible User Interfaces for 3D Spaces (TUI3D) project, a joint research effort of the Synaesthetic Media Lab, the Experimental Game Lab, and the Digital World and Image Group at Georgia Tech. The project specifically seeks to address the production and performative challenges of machinima creation and real-time interaction with commercial game environments (Mazalek and Nitsche 2007). Not unlike the stage manager and character control toolsets suggested above, the goal of the project is to design a suite of tangible interface tools that can be used to control three core aspects of 3D virtual space: character, camera, and the space itself. To be immediately useful for machinima creators today, these controls need to be easily connected to a commercial game engine. TUI3D thus makes use of the *Moviesandbox* tool created by Freidrich Kirschner, allowing the tangible interface tools to connect to Epic's *Unreal Tournament 2004*. Although the *Moviesandbox* game modification was originally intended for better control of scene scripting in *Unreal* to improve the production process of prestaged machinima pieces, it can easily be further modified for experiments that, like TUI3D, focus on live performances. The tool is available as a free download.

The first phase of the project has focused on the character aspect of real-time 3D environments, using a puppeteering approach for real-time character control in *Unreal*. The theme of the work draws inspiration from classic children's adventure radio shows, such as *The Cinnamon Bear* and *Tom Mix*. The virtual stage reproduces a young girl's room in 1940 London. Although she has been evacuated to the countryside, her toys remain behind and come to life as the main protagonists of the piece.

Cactus Jack

The first TUI3D interface prototype takes the form of a cactus-shaped marionette that is used to control a virtual cactus toy character named Cactus Jack. Marionettes are a form of puppet that is indirectly controlled by strings attached to a control frame above (e.g., a paddle or cross). In the case of the cactus puppet, the head and arms are attached to the paddle with nylon strings. By moving the paddle, the user can control the body movement of the puppet (tilting side-to-side and back-to-front) and raise or lower its arms. The cactus puppet is sewn from cloth and filled with a soft foam material, which gives it the feeling of a plush toy. It stands on a rigid base that houses a hardware I/O board used to communicate sensor data to a standard consumer-level PC that runs *Unreal*. The puppet is equipped with three two-axis accelerometers, one mounted on each arm and one inside the paddle at its center. This configuration allows us to get the up/down movement of the arms, as well as the body movement of the puppet with respect to its base. The flexible nature of the strings used in marionettes allows easy and fluid control of the puppet's movements, which maps well to a real-time 3D space. Marionettes also support multihanded or even multiperson interactions, since multiple hands or people can help control the different strings at once. In contrast, hand puppets can be implemented with glove controllers, but their expressions and actions are limited by the shape and affordances of the human hand.

The data from the puppet sensors are transmitted to a Java applet running on a PC via the HID (Human Interface Device) standard. The applet cleans and interprets the data and sends it via the UDP protocol to the *Moviesandbox* tools running within the *Unreal* game engine. The data are processed in real time, and the virtual character can be seen moving on-screen as users manipulate the physical puppet (figure 6.3). Key frames for the poses of the cactus character are set in Maya and exported as single-frame animations to *Unreal*. These poses define the furthest points of possible character animation available to the virtual puppet. The TUI3D system builds on the basic animation principles used in the *Unreal* engine by blending between poses based on incoming data from the tangible puppet controller. With the exception of head movements, animation in *Unreal* is triggered and can only be blended, but not interrupted. TUI3D extends the higher granularity of control to the whole character to raise its expressive range.

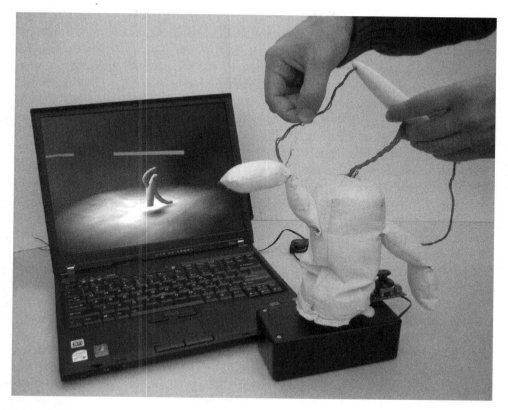

Figure 6.3
As a user manipulates the cactus puppet, the Cactus Jack virtual character dances on-screen.

Universal Character Control
A strong benefit of the cactus puppet interface is that the mappings to the virtual Cactus Jack's skeleton structure can be immediately and easily understood. The virtual character behaves just as the user expects when he or she manipulates the physical puppet, and users are able to perform a range of expressive gestures that would take considerable practice with a less intuitive or less obviously mapped interface, such as making the cactus puppet dance in a way that synchronizes specific movements of the arms and the body at once.

Although providing intuitive interfaces with clear mappings is an important goal for TUI3D, real machinima production can require the control of many different virtual characters, possibly with vastly different skeleton structures. In this respect, the cactus puppet leaves open some important questions. What happens if the user wants to take control of a different character than a cactus, such as a virtual dragon with a body, four legs, a head, and two wings? Does the user need to switch to a different physical puppet controller? Or can the same puppet be mapped to the different bone structure? In the cactus-to-dragon example, it is not clear how the skeletal structure should translate, and the mappings between the two could be arranged in different ways. With this in mind, we settled on another phase of TUI3D character-control research with the goal of creating a universal puppet controller. Such an interface should provide a level of abstraction and adjustability that more easily maps to a variety of different virtual skeleton structures, while still retaining the physical resemblance in form and motion that increases its usability.

Our universal character controller takes the form of a puppet we call the Uniball, a large plush ball to which the user can attach up to ten limbs at fixed locations on its surface. By attaching limbs at different locations, users are able to configure the physical puppet to resemble the virtual character they wish to control. In this way the interface can be easily repurposed to control different virtual skeleton structures, and the mappings from physical to virtual body or limbs can be done automatically.

Unlike the cactus puppet, the Uniball is not a marionette with strings and does not stand on a fixed base. Instead, users hold the body of the puppet and move its limbs with their hands (figure 6.4, left). Strings could be attached to the limbs to allow the user to control the puppet in different ways—for example, with their feet. Currently the limbs of the Uniball are jointed (like a human arm or leg), but single-part limbs (e.g., a head) could be created as well. As with the cactus marionette, accelerometers are used to detect the movement of each limb. Uniball limbs also contain bend sensors to detect the angle of the joint (figure 6.4, right). A gyrometer inside the body of the puppet is used to detect its orientation. Although this work is still preliminary, we

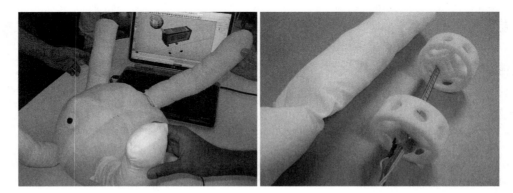

Figure 6.4
The Uniball puppet with four limbs attached is used to control a four-legged creature (left). The inside of each Uniball limb contains an accelerometer and a bend sensor to detect the movement of the limb and the angle of the joint (right).

hope that further experimentation with physical sensors and configurations for the Uniball will lead to a versatile interface for machinima character control.

Conclusion

As the machinima art form gains in popularity among amateur filmmakers, professional production companies are beginning to take notice. In the professional realm, machinima can be used as a fast and inexpensive method for real-time previsualization, and game engines have already been used to this end in productions such as Steven Spielberg's *A.I.* (2001). However, for amateur and professional filmmakers alike, the question of how to achieve intuitive, fine-grained, expressive control inside the game engine remains an issue. In this respect, early research efforts such as the TUI3D project have already raised interest among machinima artists, CGI professionals, and researchers in both academia and industry.

Although intuitive, commercially available controllers for use with real-time game engines have until now been quite limited, novel interface and interaction methods like those described here promise to lead the way to a whole new realm of real-time expressive control inside 3D virtual worlds. At this stage, the key to moving forward is to seed collaborations and bring together people from traditionally separate domains, such as 3D gaming, film and video production, animation, and physical interface design. In this respect, I hope that this essay, as well as research efforts like TUI3D, can serve as a source of inspiration and information for others.

Acknowledgments

I would like to thank my collaborator on the TUI3D project, Michael Nitsche, as well as the excellent group of undergraduate and graduate students we have had the pleasure to work with: Nils Beck, Nicholas Bowman, Katie Fletcher, Will Hankinson, Shanks Krishnan, Mike Lee, and Matthew Miller. We are also grateful to Friedrich Kirschner for his *Moviesandbox* tools and his practical help on the TUI3D project.

References

Aish, R., and P. Noakes. 1984. Architecture without Numbers: CAAD Based on a 3D Modeling System. *Computer Aided Design* 16 (6): 321–328.

Alexander, K., and E. Strommen. 1998. Evolution of the Talking Dinosaur: The (Not So) Natural History of a New Interface for Children. In *CHI 98 Conference Summary on Human Factors in Computing Systems*, 7–8. New York: Association of Computing Machinery.

Anderson, D., J. Frankel, J. Marks, A. Agarwala, P. Beardsley, J. Hodgins, D. Leigh, K. Ryall, E. Sullivan, and J. Yedida. 2000. Tangible Interaction + Graphical Interpretation: A New Approach to 3D Modeling. In *Proceedings of the 27th Annual Conference on Computer Graphics and interactive Techniques*, 393–402. New York: ACM/Addison-Wesley Publishing Co.

Balakrishnan, R., G. Fitzmaurice, G. Kurtenbach, and K. Singh. 1999. Exploring Interactive Curve and Surface Manipulation Using a Bend and Twist Sensitive Input Strip. In *Proceedings of the 1999 Symposium on Interactive 3D Graphics*, 111–118. New York: Association of Computing Machinery.

Callesen, J. 2005. Virtual Puppets in Performance. In *Proceedings of Marionette: Metaphysics, Mechanics, Modernity*. International Symposium, Copenhagen, 28 March–1 April 2001.

Esposito, C., and W. B. Paley. 1995. Of Mice and Monkeys: A Specialized Input Device for Virtual Body Animation. In *Proceedings of the 1995 Symposium on Interactive 3D Graphics*, 109–114. New York: Association of Computing Machinery.

Frazer, J. H. 1982. Use of Simplified Three-Dimensional Computer Input Devices to Encourage Public Participation in Design. In *Proceedings of Computer Aided Design'82*, 143–151. Boston: Butterworth Scientific.

Hachet, M., J. Pouderoux, and P. Guitton. 2005. A Camera-based Interface for Interaction with Mobile Handheld Computers. In *Proceedings of the 2005 Symposium on Interactive 3D Graphics and Games*, 65–72. New York: Association of Computing Machinery.

Hunt, D., J. Moore, A. West, and M. Nitsche. 2006. Puppet Show: Intuitive Puppet Interfaces for Expressive Character Control. In *Medi@terra* 2006: Gaming Realities: A Challenge for Digital Culture, 159–167. Athens, October 4–8.

Ishii, H., and B. Ullmer. 1997. Tangible Bits: Towards Seamless Interfaces Between People, Bits and Atoms. In *Proceedings of a Conference on Human Factors in Computing System*s, 234–241. New York: Association of Computing Machinery.

Jacob, R., and L. Sibert. 1992. *Proceedings of the SIGCHI Conference, Human Factors in Computing Systems: The Perceptual Structure of Multidimensional Input Device Selection*, 211–218. New York: Association of Computing Machinery.

Johnson, M. P., A. Wilson, B. Blumberg, C. Kline, and A. Bobick. 1999. Using a Plush Toy to Direct Synthetic Characters. In *Proceedings of the SIGCHI Conference, Human Factors in Computing Systems: Sympathetic Interfaces*, 152–158. New York: Association of Computing Machinery.

Maes, P., T. Darrell, B. Blumberg, and A. Pentland. 1997. The ALIVE System: Wireless, Full-Body Interaction with Autonomous Agents. *Multimedia Systems* 5 (2): 105–112.

Mazalek, A., and G. Davenport. 2003. A Tangible Platform for Documenting Experiences and Sharing Multimedia Stories. In *Proceedings of the 2003 ACM SIGMM Workshop on Experiential Telepresenc*e, 105–109. New York: Association of Computing Machinery.

Mazalek, A., and E. v. d. Hoven. August 2009. Framing Tangible Interaction Frameworks. *Artificial Intelligence for Engineering Design, Analysis and Manufacturing* 23 (3): 225–235.

Mazalek, A., and M. Nitsche. 2007. Tangible Interfaces for Real-time 3D Virtual Environments. In *Proceedings of the International Conference on Advances in Computer Entertainment Technology*, vol. 203, 155–162. New York: Association of Computing Machinery.

Meadows, Mark S. 2002. *Pause & Effect: The Art of Interactive Narrative*. Indianapolis: New Riders Press.

Medynskiy, Y., S. Gov, A. Mazalek, and D. Minnen. 2007. Wearable RFID for Play. Paper presented at the Tangible Play Workshop, Intelligent User Interfaces Conference, Honolulu, January 28, 2007.

Metoyer, R., L. Xu, and M. Srinivasan. 2003. A Tangible Interface for High-Level Direction of Multiple Animated Characters. In *Proceedings of Graphics Interface 2003*, 167–176. Halifax, Nova Scotia, Canada.

Murakami, T., K. Hayashi, K. Oikawa, and N. Nakajima. 1995. DO-IT: Deformable Objects as Input Tools. In *Conference Companion on Human Factors in Computing System*s, 87–88. New York: Association of Computing Machinery.

Robertson, B. 1993. Motion Capture Meets 3D Animation. In *On the Cutting Edge of Technology*, ed. T. Ringo, 1–14. Indianapolis: Sams Publishing.

Shay, D., and J. Duncan. 1993. *The Making of Jurassic Park*. New York: Ballantine Books.

Sparacino, F., G. Davenport, and A. Pentland. 2000. Media in Performance: Interactive Spaces for Dance, Theater, Circus, and Museum Exhibits. *IBM Systems Journal* 39 (3–4): 479–510.

Sturman, D. J., and D. Zeltzer. 1993. A Design Method for "Whole-Hand" Human-Computer Interaction. *ACM Transactions on Information Systems* 11 (3): 219–238.

Sutphen, S., E. Sharlin, B. Watson, and J. Frazer. 2000. Reviving a Tangible Interface Affording 3D Spatial Interaction. In *Proceedings of the 11th Western Canadian Computer Graphics Symposium*, 155–166.

Tardif, H. 1991. Panel: Applications of Virtual Reality I: Reports from the Field. In *ACM SIGGRAPH Panel Proceedings: Character Animation in Real Time*.

Tosa, N. 1998. Theater, Movie with A-Life: *Romeo & Juliet in Hades* as A-Life Based Cinema. In *Proceedings of the Sixth ACM International Conference on Multimed*ia, 17–21. New York: Association of Computing Machinery.

Underkoffler, J., and H. Ishii. 1999. Urp: A Luminous-Tangible Workbench for Urban Planning and Design. In *Proceedings of the SIGCHI Conference on Human Factors in Computing System*s, 386–393. New York: Association of Computing Machinery..

Virpet Theater Project, Entertainment Technology Center, Carnegie Mellon University. <http://www.etc.cmu.edu/projects/virpets/spring03>.

Walters, G. 1989. The Story of Waldo C. Graphic. In *3D Character Animation by Computer*. ACM SIGGRAPH '89, Course Notes 4 (July 1989), 65–79.

Weiser, Mark. 1991. The Computer for the Twenty-First Century. *Scientific American* 265 (3): 94–104.

Software References

Half-Life. Sierra. 1998.

Maya. Autodesk. 1998–.

The Sims. Electronic Arts. 2000.

Unreal. GT Interactive. 1999.

Unreal Tournament 2004. Atari. 2004.

III Performance

Tristan Pope, dir., *Not Just Another Love Story* (2005).

7 Machinima as Media

Michael Nitsche

Why is machinima important? The answer to this question varies, depending on the context and audience. Is machinima the digital natives' way to document and comment on events in virtual worlds? Is it a new form of play? Is it an animation technique for film and television? Is it a footnote in the history of game development? Or is it something new altogether? In this essay I propose that there is a revolutionary element of machinima that is not primarily about faster production cycles or grass-roots computer-generated imagery. Neither does it presume machinima's connection to game engines or gaming communities as a defining basis. Instead, it reflects on machinima as media defined by a specific format that is based on real-time image and event production, on the one hand, and performative forms of replay on the other. Limiting the value of machinima to either replay or (more often) production is not only an unnecessary restriction, it threatens the identity of machinima as a media format.

To identify machinima as a media format in its own right, we need to specify what machinima does that other media such as video games or traditional animated film technologies do not do. Only once its media attributes have been characterized can its potential be outlined, exemplified, and developed. As a caveat, it should be noted that some key points mentioned in this essay point back to the seemingly lost origins of machinima and run counter to the dominant conditions in contemporary machinima practice. They seem almost archaic, if such a term could apply to a media format of such recent vintage, but a return to the roots seems at place. In light of the disconnect between current practice and an understanding of machinima as a media format, this essay concludes with a brief look at the promise of machinima as an moving image format.

Machinima has been usefully described as "animated filmmaking within a real-time virtual 3D environment" (Marino 2004, 1) and as the "technique of making films inside virtual realities [. . .] the technique of taking a viewpoint on a virtual world, and recording that, editing it, and showing it to other people as a film" (Hancock and Ingram 2007, 10). These definitions help situate machinima in the media landscape.

They claim a stake and suggest entry points for discussing how machinima as media format differs from other media formats. But they are also limited in their scope.

With respect to technological invention, the level of procedurality in machinima was higher earlier in its history, and some of that original technical prowess has since been lost. To recapture the original strength of machinima, we must turn back the clock to the days when machinima movies were still demo files that were reprocessed in real time in the game engine. The live-rendered image technically places machinima in the same digital procedural media family as video games, but machinima differs from games in the way the image is controlled. To describe this difference, I first turn to performance studies as a stepping stone on the path to a media-specific definition of machinima. Following that, I return to a discussion of procedurality and the image.

In regard to media specifics, we can attempt a description of machinima based purely on its technological condition. However, the initial connection to gaming is shrinking, as is readily apparent in machinima creation packages such as *Moviestorm* (Moviestorm, 2007–) and *iClone* (Reallusion, 2003–), which launched without any gaming functionality. Artists have separated animation tasks and game functionality and often disregard the latter to optimize the former, which is why award-winning machinima artist Tom Jantol used the term "anymation" instead of "machinima." Anymation does not distinguish different forms of possible animation techniques and is entirely goal-oriented, to optimize the expression of the outcome. To achieve their expressive ends, animators remain rather uncommitted to any single engine or production technique. Machinima is not as inclusive, but as artistic practice it is no longer tied to gaming. It remains an offspring of the larger digital revolution, though. If we look for reference points other than gaming, we can conceive of machinima in terms of performance in the world of moving images.

Performing the Image

Others have considered machinima through the lens of performance studies for players (Cameron and Carroll 2009) and camera operators (Nitsche and Thomas 2004). From this perspective, the players controlling the avatars and the camera operators controlling the point of view are regarded as performers in the dramatic tradition. A focus on image production similarly prevails in work on machinima as media (Berkeley 2006). But production covers only half of machinima; replay is not covered by these approaches. To cover both conditions of machinima as media, we expand this view further as we apply concepts of performance studies outlined by Jon McKenzie (2001). The goal is to view machinima as a media format based on procedural image production and reproduction instead of a form of emergent play or a subcategory of traditional animation.

McKenzie starts by differentiating three kinds of performances: *organizational performance*, or the performance of workers in some form of production or service for a company; *cultural performance*, or "the living, embodied expression of cultural traditions and transformations" (ibid., 8), found most often in traditional performance media such as theater, film, or TV; and *technological performance*, or the performance of machines. From this point McKenzie unfolds a general theory of performance, a journey this essay will not follow in greater detail to remain focused on machinima. Machinima incorporates all three of McKenzie's forms and, through its specific combination of these forms, can be more clearly defined on its own terms and differentiated from like media by means of its performative qualities.

The demoscene community consists of coders and artists that optimize usually self-developed code to showcase technical as well as artistic computer animation skills. The technical achievements of the demoscene that are showcased at sites such as pouet.net or scene.org are good examples of McKenzie's technological performance in action. The quality of the demos is measured in the sheer number of visual extravaganzas that can be fitted into the smallest possible code base to deliver the most impressive visuals in real time. Farbrausch's *debris* demo, for example, packs a seven-minute 3D animation full of effects, massive urban-scale levels, textures, and music into a 179 kb file—smaller than most single textures used in commercial video games. Demoscene artists optimize the procedural generation of audiovisuals, and the expression of the final image is accompanied by the artistry of the code. To experience both in their original conjunction, a user can download and execute the program, for only in the execution can one truly recognize the artistry at work. Pieces such as Brody Condon's *3 Modifications* or Cory Archangel's *Super Mario Clouds* might operate on the more conceptual end of this spectrum but likewise depend on the performance of code and image. Both are driven less by spectacular effects than by careful accentuation. But, not unlike the Farbrausch demos, they come to life only in the ongoing rendering of the image. Both are modifications of game engines that infinitely loop a live-rendered moving image that cannot be changed by the audience. Like most of the demoscene examples, these pieces do not hide but show the technicality of how the images were created; the live creation is part of their artistic statement. Watching a video recording of any of these pieces reduces them to an alienating linearity and conserves them in a form that disrespects their original artistic concept, which depends on the technological performance activity of the computer throughout.

Machinima may also concentrate on the performance of the virtual puppeteer, thus shifting the focus to McKenzie's cultural performance. Here the connection to gaming is clearer, as the performances are often framed by a given game context. Very often machinima serves as a documentation of expert play, as seen in the original *Quake Done Quick* demos, which served as proof of the performers' (runners') outstanding mastery not of the rendering code but of the overall game. The same applies to the plethora of bragging videos posted by players for other players to display their playing skills. These are documents of cultural play or performances that are clearly embedded in gaming's sociohistorical context. At times these game references can be subverted, as seen in the *Leeroy Jenkins* video in *World of Warcraft* (Blizzard Entertainment, 2004), which presents a staged performance meaningful only as part of the *World of Warcraft* universe, or in Chris Brandt's *Dance Voldo Dance* music video performed in *Soul Calibur* (Namco, 1999). *Dance Voldo Dance* is an ingenious fight-as-dance choreography rehearsed, performed, and screen-captured by two players over the course of seven days in 2002. *Dance Voldo Dance* plays with the intertextual references throughout: from the sexualized virtual identity of the dancer-fighter character Voldo to the pop song used in the original version (Nelly's "Hot in Here"). Players have started to utilize the game engine either as the cultural ground itself (creating machinima about their gameplay experience with the system) or as a basis for a cultural statement beyond the game (creating machinima with the help of the game engine but subverting its functionality in order to express issues that lie outside the original game's frame). Both are statements of cultural performance.

Finally, machinima also provides for specific "organizational performance." Part of the digital revolution is the much-discussed shift in the author-reader relationship and the increasing "authorship" of digital media audiences. Those new readers and writers can be active—from blogs to Twitter to modding *Quake* (id Software, 1996) to the birth of machinima itself, or seemingly "passive"—from the automatic suggestions generated by Amazon.com based on one's search interests to Pandora's musical genome project to Google's customized advertising. Machinima's qualities as animation production tool are not debated here. But in addition to such active forms of player participation, a machinima film can include customization and adjustment of the piece through a more passive involvement of the audience. For example, Erik Champion has experimented with modifying the rendering and game events based on player biofeedback (Dekker and Champion 2007; see also "Undefining Machinima," chap. 13, this volume).

Machinima can also adjust to more direct user profiling, as exemplified in Kuma Games' Leaving the Game project, developed for the AFI Digital Content Lab. Leaving the Game offers a typical TV action series setting with the difference that it uses the Source game engine to render each episode on a local Xbox 360 console. Because the final image remains variable, the system is able to adjust the content of a pre-scripted episode to the profile of the user logged in to that specific console. Leaving the Game can adjust details of the imagery including blood or revealing costumes to fit a certain rating if a minor is logged in, and can provide dynamic product placement in the 3D world depicted, depending on the gender, age, or preferences of the player. Both example projects use audience information—biofeedback in the former and user profiles in the latter—to dynamically adjust the content and presentation of the moving image produced in real time in a game engine. Audiences thus indirectly influence the image generation, which poses an interesting shift in authorship in the areas of image production and organizational performance that McKenzie outlines.

Machinima thus permits audiences to affect the event and text creation not only in an active way, via modding and guerrilla film production, but also passively during playback. In the tradition of the new authorship lies a form of new organization of media production and consumption. The responsiveness of machinima makes it a good example of how this new organization is manifested in new artifacts of moving image media. The performative character of machinima can be realized in a game engine (technologically), in a player's performance (culturally), or in different forms of player involvement with the production of the final moving image (organization-ally). This threefold performance capability and machinima's ability to move seam-lessly from one quality to another stand out as media-defining features. Machinima thus differs from other media formats in its unique navigation of McKenzie's three categories of performance.

In distinguishing machinima from other media, we face the generalized observation by some scholars that all moving images share to some degree in performance, even traditional TV images. For instance, Phil Auslander, basing himself on Cubitt as well as on Heath and Skirrow, suggests that any broadcast TV image might be read as perfor-mance, as "its production as a televisual image occurs only in the present moment" (Auslander 2008, 49). Because the TV image is constantly in the making, it can be affected and altered. However, the nature and form of these alterations remain extremely limited during this "occurrence." The process remains closed unless the viewer interacts physically with the image generation, as Nam June Paik did in *Magnet TV* and other installation pieces. The kind of material image manipulation applied by Paik certainly remains available in the digital image production. Screens can be altered, cables manip-ulated, interfaces and graphic cards modified. But, as Lev Manovich rightly argues, the digitalization and transformation of information through code offers an entirely new level of flexibility (Manovich 2001). We can influence the TV cable, the game cartridge, the rendering chip, or the monitor by applying physical force, but digital media offer a different and additional access point to any kind of image manipulation and genera-tion. Because each image is processed from a set of data, we can interfere on this level of image data. This underscores the particular condition that distinguishes machinima from film and television: machinima as a form of media is defined not only by the means of production, the content assembly, or its recording but also by the means of playback in the live-rendered image that remain variable because of this code.

Procedural Images

Technically, machinima does not feature the same procedural qualities found in video games. It is a media format that is in between, and in need of some positioning in the digital landscape. Traditional cinema is based on the recording of an image. The digital revolution might have shifted this base farther into the digital format but the result remains an image recording. In contrast, games operate through image production. Virtual cameras render viewpoints of virtual worlds in real time to allow the player immediate access to events in the game world. At the heart of this concept is not the image but the event, which functions as part of the interface with the player.

Where is machinima in this dichotomy of event production and image production? Is it on the side of the image-shaping film technologies, with innovations in camera and recording technology, or on the side of the event-producing technologies, with game engines? The answer is to be found in the original relationship of machinima and games, and how machinima evolved into a closer love affair with cinema.

The birth of machinima as an offspring of video games can be located in the practice of demo recording. A demo recording is a log file of events in or inputs into a game world. Depending on the specific game engine, a demo recording can contain different kinds of information. For example, *Doom* (id Software, 1993) recorded only the player input data, while demos recorded in *Quake* store the movement of objects in the game environment itself. Thus, different demo formats can serve different and specialized purposes. The introduction of advanced physics added yet another level of complexity to these recordings. Owing to the development of game engines over time and the availability of competing engine architectures, no unified standard for demo recording using different game engines exists. As a result, a demo file can be played back only in the same game engine in which it was produced. Because demos use existing game assets as their active ingredients, any additional material, such as new 3D models, sound files, or animations, have to be installed to a flawless playback. This means that only audiences with the exact game configurations are able to play back a demo file the way it was intended to be played. The ability to render the image in real time comes at a price.

Historically, there are two main origins for today's demos: commercial game development and the user-driven demoscene. The demoscene itself—a worldwide group of players, programmers, and artists—can be traced back to the late 1970s, as it evolved in parallel with the availability of home computers. It grew out of the hacker community; however, it was fueled by a drive for expression and reputation. The first signs can be traced back to hackers cracking the copy protection of commercial video games and distributing them for free or for personal gain—but also to gain more recognition for their hacking skills in the rapidly growing community of players. In this competitive setting hacking, not playing, became the aim. To celebrate themselves and their craft, hackers started to include so-called crack intros to the game programs, little programs delivering short graphical sequences that identified the hacker, not unlike film credits. In this way, crack intros spread the names of famous hackers or hacker groups through the player community. Soon the intros themselves attracted attention, and the competition was on not only to hack the best, most recent, and most advanced games but also to present oneself in the most impressive way in the intro. As a result, the intros acquired a fan base, with the consequence that "often intros outshone the games they preceded in terms of technical and esthetic brilliance" (Tasajärvi 2004, 15). The reason for the increasing value attached to intros was the interest among a growing number of players to use the computer not only as a gaming machine but to create their own moving image works. The challenge evolved into a display of technical prowess, a demonstration of computer mastery on every possible level, not the hacking of a game or two. The goal was to dive into the specific computer system and get the most graphic quality out of it. Coding a demo like Farbrausch's *debris* is a technical and artistic challenge, and the workload is often divided up among visual artist, musician, and coder. Intros became acknowledged and collected pieces of digital art. Their creators sought greater recognition of the art of demo creation, and in this way gradually separated themselves from the illegal hacker scene to form their own communities.

The origin of the demo as retold above is interwoven with the growth of independent social networks of players and users, and underground communities forming around the more official and commercial world of game production. It is a social as well as a technical phenomenon, and the player-driven face of machinima remains an important part of it today.

At the same time, there is a parallel and as yet unwritten history of the demo and of machinima in which corporations take center stage. Arcade games often included sections of gameplay that would run as noninteractive show reels attracting the attention and ultimately the quarters of interested teenagers and passers-by. Company logos, animated high-score lists, prerecorded gameplay, loading screens, level interludes—all relied on the same procedural techniques used by the demoscene, although generated with the professional tools of the company. These corporate examples of machinima could form early narratives, as seen in the intermissions of the original *Pac-Man* (Atari, 1981). They retell the game's chase in short sequences between different boards. The sequences play with the nature and character of the ghost, Blinky, versus the hero, Pac-Man. Though very basic, the narrative of this chase between hero and antagonist differs significantly from the later *Ms. Pac-Man* (Atari, 1982) scenes, in which Ms. Pac-Man chases Pac-Man to end up with a family of smaller Pac-Mans in the last sequence. Even in this early form, the machinima interludes are tinged by small stories reflecting conventional ideologies and procedures. The arcade games and *Pac-Man* show an early form of machinima and underscore the major role played by commercial developers in its development. The *Pac-Man* pieces, for example, were released some sixteen years before the release of *Diary of a Camper* by the Rangers, a work that is often cited as the first narrative machinima piece. And more than a decade before the Rangers' milestone production, Enix's *Portopia Renzoku Satsujin Jiken*, aka

The Portopia Murder (Enix, 1983), is considered to be the first game to use elaborate cut-scenes, another important technique in the evolution of machinima. Over time, developers created new tools to generate these in-between cut-scenes. When those tools were released by the game developer to the player community, they often proved to be technical milestones for the independent scene as well. Whether it was the release of the various editors by id Software, Epic's UnrealEd, or Valve's Source SDK with its Faceposer tool, all helped and empowered the machinima makers, commercial as well as independent.

They became the artistic tools for mainstream machinima and demo production. But here I want to advance an understanding of machinima as a media-specific form, not only as a production method heading toward a cinematic ideal but also as a playback method in the form of the real-time-rendered image. The constellation of performances available during the production phase might be obvious, but each playback reflects not only the cultural aspects (e.g., the player's original moves in the game world) but also the technological (e.g., the rendering speed of the reproducing computer and its software set up) and organizational (e.g., the camera angles can be altered by the user playing back the demo file) aspects. At this point the performative and the procedural faces of machinima merge, and machinima's difference from established 3D tools such as *Maya* (Autodesk, 1998–) or *3D Studio Max* (Autodesk, 1995–) become clear. While the latter tools offer better control over content generation, namely, 3D model creation, texturing, and animation, they lack the possibility of real-time playback and the procedural-performative nature of the image. Game engines provide this real-time rendering as well as other features, including levels of interactivity, that allow dynamic replay of a data file on the local machine of the player audience. 3D modeling programs do not offer such a game-based feature and thus lack the media possibilities associated with it.

However, while machinima is part of the same procedural media family as video games, it differs in functionality. Machinima can much more easily switch between its performative modes or levels. The procedurality of a video game is primarily dependent on the player. Aarseth established the idea of a textual machine for video games that works only with the help of a participating player (Aarseth 1997). The persuasive power of video games rests with the player's embracing and enactment of the given games. Without player participation, this performance is reduced to that of an active reader—such as an engaged film audience—and does not hold for video games in particular. In contrast to video games, machinima's expression rests in a much stronger focus on cinematic presentation. The telling (narrating) of the event is equal to or more important than the creation of the event itself (the action or fabula). The telling becomes the event in the playback of a machinima demo. As a result, the procedural involvement is far less concentrated on a single performing entity. A machinima piece can easily and completely switch among McKenzie's three categories as realized in media, from the machine as performing entity to the performance of the virtual pup-peteer to the performance of the player. In this combination of procedurality based on gaming technology and performance capability, machinima can lay claim to a unique "change of scale or pace or pattern that it introduces into human affairs" (Marshall McLuhan quoted in Wardrip-Fruin and Harrigan 2004, 203). In other words, it begins to take its place as a fully emancipated media form.

Battling Media

We are now in position to define machinima as a media format: machinima is digital performance that controls procedurally animated moving images.

This is a definition of machinima as a media format, not technique or artistic prac-tice. Machinima—like film, television, radio, theater, or other media forms—can also be understood in different terms, for example, as communities of practice, or in his-torical context. Thus, such a new definition is always only partial. However, the focus on the media specifics of machinima suggested here might provide a useful differentia-tion for future discussions even in these related areas. This does not mean that such a definition simplifies the challenges posed by machinima. For one, it clashes with the current practice of machinima production and distribution. Because the image must be procedurally animated, the current practice of machinima as rendered movies is seen as a step away from the core of what machinima constitutes. The path sug-gested here also breaks with a strong tradition in the development of machinima from an in-game niche format to more commercial productions that continually adjust to the media channels to which they cater. Popular machinima practice clearly did not follow the strengths of its own media specifics. It gave up on the procedural image when it relied on the practice of screen capturing of gameplay and entered existing mainstream distribution channels. Because these channels were already established and used widespread technology, such as YouTube uses Adobe's Flash player, machin-ima's presence grew exponentially, because watching a machinima piece no longer depended on preinstalling a specific rendering engine. However, the newfound success came at a price, as the very same channels reduced machinima to a production tech-nique that fed into traditional media formats.

There are few indications that machinima is ready to follow through with the revo-lution it once promised. Technically, it offers all the necessary ingredients to answer Enzensberger's call for a revolution that "must make everyone a manipulator" of "shooting, cutting, synchronization, dubbing, right up to distribution" (Enzensberger [1970] 1974, 104)—in machinima this applies on every level. Like other digital media channels before it, machinima stands ready to revolutionize the way we originate, distribute, and actively participate in the moving image, breaking the preventive stance of predominantly unidirectional media such as film and television. But instead of bringing these traits to full fruition and continuing the tradition of the procedurally generated playback image, it hesitates, abandons the real-time playback origins, and falls back onto a distinction between producers and consumers. Admittedly, this view of machinima opens up new possibilities to new producers, but it still reduces the audience to a mass of consumers. Why?

One reason for this hesitation might be the connection of the format to existing game engines as clearly commercialized birthplaces. All of the dominant machinima production environments are defined by games, which is why portals such as machinima.com are not structured along genres, but game engines and many successful machinima sites such as warcraftmovies.com concentrate on single game engines. A most telling example might be Lionhead's *The Movies* (Activision, 2005), which offered a streamlined production and publishing experience—as long as one remained within the preset channels provided by the publisher. With these kinds of structures or the help of end-user license agreements, publishers try to maintain control over the potential that is at work in machinima. A number of former engines became freely available to players and machinima artists, but with the exception of a few examples, such as Kirschner's Moviesandbox, such availability is provided after that specific engine has had its heyday and its relevance as a platform for cultural performance has diminished.

Engines also pose inherent technological challenges to the continuous development of machinima. These challenges can be simple limitations to the underlying code, such as the lock that id Software put on the demo format of *Quake III: Arena* (Activision, 1999) to stabilize online play. But they also manifest in the stream of ever-improving cutting-edge game engines that fragment the basis. Any artist who tries to stay at the forefront of what is possible in technology and design of machinima faces the dilemma of short life circles in the engine developments. Every new system can provide some unique element in the arms race of game engines. Added to this challenge is the fact that older, freely available game systems might become nearly impossible to maintain in the wake of ever-improving hardware and software. The original demo files for a specific *Quake* speed run might be still available, but reproducing the necessary precise configuration of game assets and engine version on a modern computer system is daunting. It becomes increasingly difficult to run outdated game software on more recent computers given new operating systems, graphic cards, drivers, and processing speeds.

A third reason might be the aspirations of artists themselves. The portmanteau word *machinima* implies a focus on cinema as the ultimate output format. There might be a preconceived idea about what machinima should be: one of this word's inventors, Hugh Hancock, marketed his coauthored book with the tag line, "Just what you need to make animated movies" (Hancock and Ingram 2007). Pioneers of the community have often supported such a view, and many machinima artists find themselves employed by cinematics departments of game studios (e.g., Paul Marino, Tristan Pope). Others enter the machinima world already having a background in film and animation (e.g., Jun Falkenstein) and look for new production methods, not necessarily new media outlets. Success in machinima is still mainly measured along the lines of traditional media outlets (e.g., the DVD collections offered by Rooster Teeth for *Red vs. Blue* or the hits on YouTube for *Leeroy*). It is at the margins of the machinima community, in the works of artists such as Brody Condon, Eddo Stern, or Cory Archangel, that some of machinima's media specifics remain active. All of these creators live more in the world of fine art, which is used to breaking boundaries and making a living from it.

My comments are by no means a critique of the outstanding work that machinima artists do using screen capture and postproduction techniques. Insinuating machinima into existing media formats is a valid and clearly successful approach. But it is also dangerous for the identity of machinima as its own format. It might be too early to say that machinima's media specifics are lost, but they have certainly become subordinated to other practices. Instead, we find signs of these media specifics in new video games such as *Heavy Rain* (Sony, 2010) or in forms of interactive television. Is machinima as an independent media form obsolete before it ever reached its full potential?

I would like to suggest a different, more positive view, namely, that machinima is part of a larger media movement that grew out of the digital revolution. This revolution does not stop at the home video, the game engine, or the TV screen but instead it is part of a redefinition of the moving image as such. Manovich (2001) has outlined many elements for the production side of this redefinition, but machinima adds some missing parts to this puzzle with its real-time image generation during playback.

Thus, the specific importance of machinima might be that it shines a new and focused light on how the revolution unfolds before our eyes. It offers a preliminary window into the future of customized moving images and provides a haven for the ideal of interactive cinema as long as it supports its own media specifics.

Machinima remains an important media laboratory for the moving image. With the help of machinima we can prototype and sketch out the possible development of new media formats to come. Machinima is a Petri dish, an electronic crystal ball that reveals a future when our movies and TV shows will be rendered individually on-screen in our living rooms and adapted to our viewing, shopping, and aesthetic preferences, as well as our profile on Xbox Live, PlayStation Network, or our Google search history. In that way, machinima is not only an example of new forms of authorship and media production but also a stepping-stone toward a larger new vision of the interactive moving image. We cannot know whether this potential will be realized with machinima itself, or whether machinima will fade away, replaced or absorbed by some other procedural moving image format. But it remains a guiding light and a torchbearer that, at this moment in time, might have decided to leave its own path too early and adjust to given channels. Even if machinima never completely fulfills the promise it has carried since its inception, it affords a priceless laboratory for future developments in the moving image.

References

Aarseth, Espen J. 1997. *Cybertext: Perspectives on Ergodic Literature*. Baltimore, MD: Johns Hopkins University Press.

Auslander, Phil. 2008. *Liveness: Performance in a Mediatized Culture*, 2nd ed. London: Routledge.

Berkeley, Leo. 2006. Situating Machinima in the New Mediascape. *Australian Journal of Emerging Technologies and Society* 4 (2):65–80.

Cameron, David, and John Carroll. 2009. Encoding Liveness: Performance and Real-Time Rendering in Machinima. In *Breaking New Ground: Innovation in Games, Play, Practice and Theory. Proceedings of DiGRA 2009*. London: DiGRA.

Dekker, Andrew, and Erik Champion. 2007. Please Biofeed the Zombies: Enhancing the Gameplay and Display of a Horror Game Using Biofeedback. In *Situated Play: Proceedings of DiGRA 2007*, 550–558. Tokyo: The University of Tokyo.

Enzensberger, Hans Magnus. [1970] 1974. Constituents of a Theory of the Media. In *The Consciousness Industry*, 95–129. New York: Seabury Press.

Hancock, Hugh, and Johnnie Ingram. 2007. *Machinima for Dummies*. Hoboken, NJ: Wiley.

Manovich, Lev. 2001. *The Language of New Media*. Cambridge: MIT Press.

Marino, Paul. 2004. *3D Game-Based Filmmaking: The Art of Machinima*. Scottsdale, AZ: Paraglyph Press.

McKenzie, Jon. 2001. *Perform or Else: From Discipline to Performance*. New York: Routledge.

Nitsche, Michael, and Maureen Thomas. 2004. Play It Again: Film Performance, Virtual Environments and Game Engines. In *New Visions in Performance: The Impact of Digital Technologies*, ed. C. Beardon and G. Carver, 121–139. Lisse, The Netherlands: Swets & Zeitlinger.

Tasajärvi, Lassi. 2004. *Demoscene: The Art of Real-Time*. Helsinki: Even Lake Studios.

Wardrip-Fruin, Noah, and Pat Harrigan. 2004. *First Person: New Media as Story, Performance, and Game*. Cambridge: MIT Press.

Software References

3D Studio Max. Autodesk. 1995–.

Doom. id Software. 1993.

Heavy Rain. Sony. 2010.

iClone. Reallusion. 2003–.

Maya. Autodesk. 1998–.

The Movies. Activision. 2005.

Moviestorm. Moviestorm. 2007–.

Ms. Pac-Man. Atari. 1982.

Pac-Man. Atari. 1981.

Portopia Renzoku Satsujin Jiken, aka *The Portopia Murder.* Enix. 1983.

Quake. id Software. 1996.

Quake III: Arena. Activision. 1999.

Soul Calibur. Namco. 1999.

World of Warcraft. Blizzard Entertainment. 2004.

8 Encoding Liveness: Performance and Real-Time Rendering in Machinima

David Cameron and John Carroll

By replacing the graphics with their own cartoon-like 3-D graphics, and reprogramming the game technology to allow for character lip-synching and a virtual camera, the ILL Clan has transformed a fast paced game with marines and rocket launchers into a live, animated comedy show with talking lumberjacks. (ILL Clan 2004)

The core of machinima as a form of digital performance is the use of a 3D software engine to generate the on-screen content in real time. Whether it is an off-the-shelf commercial game title like *The Movies*, a game engine modified expressly for machinima production such as the altered *Quake* used by ILL Clan, or a virtual world environment like *Second Life*, the software renders both the performance space and the performances taking place in it on the fly. More problematic for those wishing to discuss performance techniques, as a body of work machinima embraces recorded gameplay, puppetlike avatar control for live or "on-camera" performance, and coded animation sequences. The trend toward heavily postproduced stand-alone machinima video clips rather than game-specific demo files has further blurred these performance approaches from the audience perspective. Most current machinima audiences know the product only as produced video clips, not as files requiring specific game software for playback. Unlike traditional animation, the cinematic and televisual form with which it is commonly compared, machinima inherently generates an ambiguity for audiences concerning the status of the performer: to what extent is the human player/actor/coder or the real-time software engine responsible for the performances seen on the screen?

The Mass Reproduction of Performance?

If Auslander's (1999) reading of liveness is brought into play, then the discussion can be reframed as one about the ontology of the performer rather than the nature of the performance (Auslander 2002). Auslander argues that "as historical and technological conditions have changed, so has the definition of liveness" (2000). For example, radio broadcast technology gave rise to the concept of "live" as a means to distinguish between a recorded performance and a performance broadcast in the moment of its execution. Prior to radio, audiences clearly understood the contextual differences between listening to a gramophone recording or experiencing a concert in person. However, the technology of radio created an interface that effectively hid the nature of the performance. Similarly, the production and distribution technology of machinima tends to obscure the nature of the performer, provoking consideration of a definition of liveness that can accommodate the real-time rendering of screen content by game software in response to human input or—at the extreme—*as if* there were human input in accordance with performance parameters coded by humans. Auslander notes that an online conversation with real-time artificial intelligence software "undermines the idea that live performance is a specifically human activity; it subverts the centrality of the live, organic presence of human beings to the experience of live performance" (Auslander 2002, 21).

A key difference between machinima and other mediated performance outlets such as radio is that machinima generates its own content as part of the interaction with the performer, whereas a radio broadcast does not. The use of bots, agents, or artificial characters in video games and machinima is perhaps the ultimate mediatization of performance possible with contemporary technology. It is now not uncommon to see these agents interacting within game worlds, and it is technically possible for two bots to engage in a chat session. For example, nonplayer characters (NPCs) in the game *Elder Scrolls IV: Oblivion* (Bethesda Softworks, 2007) go about their daily "lives" according to assigned goals and personal characteristics. They seek food when hungry, shop at their favorite merchants, and fight other NPCs to achieve a goal or pursue quests independently of interaction with the player character. If a player never encounters these NPCs during the course of a game, then their roles have perhaps been played out entirely as data calculations within the game engine rather than as on-screen performances. When the player's character is within earshot, NPC's can engage in limited conversations with each other, drawing from a set of prerecorded phrases often based on major events within the *Oblivion* world. For those like Phelan who wish to assert the traditional dichotomy of live versus mediated performance, the argument becomes one of presence and reproduction:

Performance's only life is in the present. Performance cannot be saved, recorded, documented or otherwise participate in the circulation of representations of representations: once it does so, it becomes something other than performance. (Phelan 1993, 146)

In particular, performance is seen as something that occurs before a limited audience (because of the limited physical capacity of the performance space) and that disappears and cannot be repeated once enacted. In many respects this is similar to video game play, which, if viewed as a form of performance, could meet those criteria. Performance theorist Richard Schechner (2003) proposes that the difference between "ordinary behavior" and "acting" is one of reflexivity, where professional actors are always aware that they are acting. McGonigal (2003) feels that video game play is often a role-based strategic activity in which reflexive performance is part of a conscious, deliberately assumed belief. In the improvised role-based performance form known as process drama, this convention is characterized as the assumption of a role persona. O'Neill (1995) describes process drama being used to explore a problem, situation, theme, or series of related ideas or themes through the use of the artistic medium of unscripted drama; process drama's strategies for improvised role-play would seem closely related to some of the role conventions emerging in video games and virtual spaces (Cameron and Carroll 2009). Blau argues that although some theatrical performances can appear so "thoroughly coded and familiar" as to give equal status to mediated or virtual performers, a proper sense of liveness stems from human "liabilities":

stage fright, lapses of memory, a stomach ache on stage, a coughing fit, unscripted laughter—that give a local habitation, in the body, to the succinct and apposite admission of imperfection that no bot will move us by—"We are all frail"—no less the myriad inflections of a performance that, intended or unintended, really make it live. (Blau 2002, 23)

Machinima's origins in live video gameplay, and more particularly the capture (digital recording of data in real time) and replay elements of elite gameplay, suggest the possibility of a revised interpretation of liveness that takes into account more recent technological and production developments. Is there, for example, a difference between recording human interaction with a computer game and recording on-camera performance in front of a video camera? Machinima production has recently turned toward recording of the on-screen output of the performance in a more traditional filmic approach, rather than recording gameplay data such as keystrokes and mouse moves for later replay within the game engine. Certainly, the process of capturing performance suggests consideration has been given to what parameters are required to provide reasonable fidelity of liveness when reproduced for an audience. In the game environment, capturing of performance means recording not only the on-screen (on-camera) appearance of the scene and the characters' actions in it but also metadata about the characters' variable states (e.g., health levels, scores, inventories, experience points) that can affect a character's abilities and appearance.

In a virtual world, these are perhaps the "liabilities" that lend the subtle variations that virtual performances are often assumed to lack. For instance, producers choosing to use *The Sims 2* (Electronic Arts, 2004) for machinima development must continually confront the difficulties in dealing with software "actors" prone to mood swings and relationship problems. Unlike Heinrich von Kleist's (1810) nineteenth-century view of puppets, which understands performance as achieved through the elimination of self-awareness, the interaction in the digital world of a reflexive performer and a software responsive avatar produces a sense of empathy that simulates much of the "liveness" Blau proposes.

One of the earliest forms of machinima, the game demo, challenges the notion that performance cannot be saved, recorded, and shared. Here, the player's in-game performance is captured—digitally recorded—as sequences of interface input (e.g., keyboard and mouse commands) and stored as binary data. If the player moves a character forward and shoots a weapon, the character's changing coordinates in the 3D space and the player's command actions are recorded and stored as data in the demo file. It is capturing the player's input to the virtual world and defining the virtual world's responses. When the demo file is replayed, the software engine can replicate the same input over and over, feeding the data to the game world and characters. An analog equivalent is the old pianola or player piano, where holes punched in a roll of paper captured a pianist's "input"—essentially key and pedal press sequences over time—which could then can be fed into the piano to mechanically reproduce the song.

A digital game demo file can be shared among other players and replayed at will with the appropriate game software. The experience of viewing a demo file is functionally akin to watching a film or TV program. While some formats allow control over camera or point-of-view positions during replay, the viewer has no control over the captured scenes and action being rendered in real time by the game software. Yet there is a contextual and experiential sense in which the viewer is aware that this is not an animated film. As Lowood (2007) describes, it can be eerily like inhabiting "the shell of the ghosts of players"—seeing the game experience through their eyes. As technically precise as many of these virtuoso demos are, there is still a sense that you are watching a human-generated performance. Online archives collect and store these past performances of game players, in the same way pianola rolls are collected by musicologists for the performances of the musicians they contain.

These demos are grounded in fan-based cultural practice. What better way to learn from another player's experiences in a first-person perspective game than to step into that person's shoes and relive the experience through his or her eyes? But in a society culturally attuned to the televisual, this "ghost in the shell" experience can only go so far. Lowood (2009, 419) notes that archival production to document gameplay has preceded textual or storyline projects in the history of machinima across different game genres, though he is careful not to present this path as a "necessary progression from lower to higher forms of narrative—say, from chronicles to histories." The development of tools to turn these demo files into movie files—viewable without the need for proprietary game software—or to allow postrecording production decisions such as alternative and external camera positions (recamming) illustrates a move from merely recording gameplay to creating narrative forms aesthetically closer to TV or cinema. Despite this shift, all machinima inherently requires real-time rendering within the 3D game software of the original source content, including the original performance, whatever the level of postproduction detail included in the final product.

The degree of liveness and direct human player input is most evident in forms of machinima designed for live performance, either within a persistent virtual game world or in front of a live audience. For example, there are performers such as New York's ILL Clan that work in the area of live improvisational performance, generating real-time shows using the game engine as the virtual strings for their puppet show. These performances, enacted before live audiences, strengthen the sense that this is a more traditional performance, if one entirely mediated through virtual environments and characters. Unlike a real-world stage performance, the software creates the lighting, sets, and characters on the fly in real time; but the action, plot, and performances unfold at a human pace. Other live performances may be enacted in virtual worlds, where characters come together and act out a scenario in real time, while the audience members view the performance through the eyes of their own characters or avatars. Examples of this form of live performance include the trend of music video–style dance routines enacted in *World of Warcraft* (Blizzard Entertainment, 2004) or the virtual rock concerts in *Second Life* (Linden Lab, 2003).

The machinima performance style in which liveness is perhaps most questionable involves the use of precoded scripts to trigger events. The scenario design tools used to create game levels also allow machinima producers to script elements such as the performance of NPC characters (bots) and environmental factors such as lighting, sound effects, and camera positions. These machinima productions are technically the closest to the computer-generated imagery (CGI) animation process that renders a sequence frame by frame. The critical distinction is that the machinima production relies on the game software to render the precoded sequence in real time. While human-controlled characters may participate in the scene at the same time as it is being rendered, some producers prefer to produce entirely automated sequences of custom animation. One of the key criteria for differentiating, and thus examining, different forms of machinima therefore becomes the real-time involvement of the player-performer.

Two of the prize categories for one of the major machinima contests, the annual Machinima Festival (Academy of Machinima Arts and Sciences 2008), or "Mackies," reflect some of machinima's basic performance styles: Best Virtual Performance and Best Voice-Acting. Neither of these categories is necessarily privileged over the others by the machinima community. Virtual performance presumably encompasses both real-time avatar manipulation using player controls and custom animation (i.e., scripted or coded sequences, or modification of game content), and both demonstrate a level of technical expertise beyond mere gameplay. Thus, customization of the game environment is seen as worthy of recognition as a form of virtual performance, along with the real-time or (live or encoded) puppetry of on-screen characters, or voice acting, which may occur in real time or in postproduction. Interestingly, although machinima production often requires a high level of gameplay skill to create the desired on-screen performance, this aspect is not recognized in the award categories. The award categories illustrate the growth of machinima from a means of sharing the accomplishments of skilled gameplayers to a means of generating virtual performances for a wider audience. These awards represent more traditional filmmaking skills, such as scriptwriting, directing, editing, visual design, and cinematography, underscoring the point that regardless of the emphasis placed on a particular technique, machinima generally aims for on-screen performances that meet a TV or cinematic aesthetic.

Machinima Forms and the Performance Ecology

Although machinima performances may ultimately be captured and edited and distributed as movie files, they often start with live gameplay and a desire to test the possibilities of storytelling allowed by the game world. Nonetheless, producers use the resources available in the game, and draw on or expand the game world in a fashion typical of much fan fiction, as described by Jenkins: "Fandom generates its own genres and develops alternative institutions of production, distribution, exhibition, and consumption. The aesthetic of fan art celebrates creative use of already circulating discourses and images" (1992, 279).

Game engines are generally not designed for moviemaking, although some incorporate the tools that make it possible. Machinima films often pay homage to or build on the existing storylines and characters presented in the game titles. Machinima makers are typically fans of the games they use to create their works. Even if a machinima maker chooses to buy a particular game title to use as a production platform rather than as a game per se, a certain amount of gameplay is inevitably required to develop an understanding of the game's machinima capabilities. The different affordances of the game engines adopted for machinima are reflected in the different types of performances possible, and therefore evident in machinima archives. Some games allow relatively easy, puppetlike control over on-screen performances (*Halo: Combat Evolved* [Bungie Studios, 2001], *Half-Life 2* [Valve Corp., 2004], *World of Warcraft*), some are preferred for the combinations of scripted bot performances and human-controlled avatars they allow (*Unreal* [Epic Games, 1998], *Half-Life 2*), and others deliberately include machinima-like capture and playback tools as part of the game experience (*The Sims 2*, *The Movies* [Lionhead Studios, 2005]).

These performative approaches signal a change in the ecologies of performance operating in the online world. This concept proposed by Kershaw (2001) includes the complicated and unavoidable interdependencies between every element of a performance and its environment. In the online world, the change includes the even more complicated digital interdependencies between every element of a digital performance and its mediated environment. These interdependencies mean that a change in one element will produce changes in all the rest, including approaches to dramatic role, characterization, and the meanings and the mobility of those approaches in the cultural context of the particular performance style (Auslander 1999). In the case of machinima, perhaps what we are seeing, in Auslander's terms, "is not so much the incursion of media-derived 'technics' and techniques into the context of live performance but, rather live performance's absorption of a media derived epistemology" (ibid., 33).

This interdependency has led to the development of a range of very different performance forms, all often lumped under the rubric of machinima. Taking a cue from Guattari (1995), who suggests that ecological concerns must address the interactions of both the natural world and the "incorporeal species" of human culture such as arts, music and cinema, it may be possible to reframe the concept of machinima into an ecology of interconnected performance forms that exist in the digital environment. In this way the relationship between the different levels of liveness within the variations of machinima can be differentiated and described. This performance ecology of incorporeal digital forms includes live puppetry for real-world or virtual audiences, game demos for replay in a software engine, and scripted character and camera interactions. Currently the most familiar form of machinima takes on a strongly televisual or cinematic production aesthetic, with multiple avatar interactions captured as video files and edited in postproduction. The use of nonlinear video editing packages such as *Adobe Premiere* (Adobe Systems, 1991) or *Final Cut Pro* (Apple, 1999) to produce machinima films is now part of a very large community of practice in which techniques and knowledge are developed and shared among people joined in a common interest. The machinima community blends with other learning communities, such as those based on short film production, and even film schools, where machinima is increasingly seen as a means of experimenting with film forms. The Australian Film, Television and Radio School, for example, maintains a virtual island in the *Second Life* environment for use by students as a machinima production and screening space. This cinematic leaning of the machinima production community is often reflected in the language used in online support forums and discussion groups. For example, in 2009 the following forum names on machinima.com provided a key to this favored approach: Filmmaking Tips & Tutorials; Gameplay Recording & Capturing; and Video Editing, Audio Recording, & Other Post-production and Director Tools.

The language of cinema dominates the machinima production world, with these products often referred to as films when more accurately they are commonly produced and distributed as digital media files. As the form evolves, new terms to describe the output of this process may become generally accepted, but for now, "film" and "film-making" remain common descriptions of the product and process of machinima.

The discussion of performance techniques is not so clearly discretized. Getting on-screen characters to do what you want, when you want, is often seen as a technical filmmaking problem to be overcome rather than a question of dramatic or theatrical direction. Typical of the computer community, these techniques are often framed as "hacks" or "workarounds"—techniques for circumventing the perceived limitations of the game engines being used. The artistic or dramatic aspects of performance tend to be subsumed by the technical aspects, for example, how to go about wrangling emotionally unstable *Sims* characters, or how to add distinctive character traits to otherwise identical on-screen avatars in *Halo*.

In this strongly cinematic approach, the content is still created in real-time by the game software, but it is the audiovisual (on-screen) element that is captured and edited in postproduction. In this sense, for the performers it is very similar to performing for a camera. The use of multiplayer environments allows for ensemble scenes. In many cases, a player-performer may even take on the role of the camera, using the first-person perspective of a player to see the action through the lens. Again, this is a technical workaround to produce the content in a cinematic form, rather than a performative decision. Material is then captured using in-game tools or specialized software, which records the screen action as a video format file. This file can then be imported into editing software and postproduced using the same techniques as video and cinema. It is not surprising that this approach has resulted in some of the most popular and best-known machinima, as it lends itself to traditional storytelling genres and techniques. There are feature and short films, drama, talk shows, documentaries, and sitcoms. This type of production can make use of pre-scripted game elements, or producers may modify characters or sets to produce a suitable milieu for their piece. Remixing content is an important element here, resulting in a proliferation of crossover projects. These projects attempt to shortcut the production process by relying on established franchises, story worlds, and even the direct use of plots and scenes from movies.

Machinima as a Community of Practice

Although regularly touted as a form of cheap and easy CGI animation, making machinima can be a time-consuming and technically difficult exercise, primarily because most game software is not designed to accommodate this repurposing. Those titles that do support in-game recording and exporting (*The Sims 2*, *The Movies*) or that are complemented by accessible and powerful content modification tools (*Quake* [id Software, 1996], *Second Life*, *Neverwinter Nights* [Bioware, 2002], *Unreal*, *Half-Life 2*) are clearly favored by producers. Not all machinima is simply about extending what Sutton (2009) describes as the existing "dramatic property," with extensive modification of in-game characters, environments, props, music, and effects becoming almost a technical production subgenre in itself. However, most games are not easy to work with as filmmaking tools, and many producers find it difficult to create projects beyond the game world. From a review of current online machinima archives it appears that individual producers tend to become familiar with one or two game platforms and stick to them to develop their films. This decision may also be driven in part by the game fan mentality, and by the complementary game modification industries that accompany some titles. A range of game genres underlies the practice of machinima, but despite these variations the continuum of machinima production points to the formation and development of a community of practice that may provide a methodological framework for further exploration of liveness in machinima performance.

A community of practice, of which machinima is a good example, is a specific group with a local culture, operating through shared practices, linked together through a shared repertoire of resources. They are what James Gee (2005, 1) describes as a way of "seeing, valuing, and being in the world." These communities of practice, as outlined by Wenger and Lave (1991), provide participants with a focused repertoire of knowledge about, and ways of addressing, shared problems and purposes. One of the interesting shifts in interpersonal communication that also applies to machinima was that in the past, communities of practice were bounded by spatial boundaries and proximity: the workplace, the studio, the office. With the advent of the online world, digital communities of practice sprang up based on shared interest, not shared location. They have now developed in such a way that even a relatively specialized form of machinima most likely has an online community of practice formed around it.

Focusing on communities of practice has emerged as a research interest, allowing examination of the range of practices that make up the continuum of the machinima subgenres. Benzie et al. (2005) propose that Wenger and Lave's ideas about communities of practice can be used as a theoretical framework for research, and refer to the case studies of Brown, Collins, and Duguid (1989) to support this position. Machinima, which according to Wenger and Lave is a relatively young community of practice, probably falls into the early coalescing stage, characterized by a significant growth in membership as greater awareness of the form brings together previously isolated practitioners or attracts new members to the group. As such, machinima is useful for researching the evolving connection between live and mediated performance. The boundaries of the community are still forming and being tested, but there is a buzz of excitement over machinima's potential as a new creative visual art form. Among the commonalities being discovered and developed into shared practices are the elements of in-role performance articulated in the different styles of machinima production.

Improvised Performance in Machinima and Process Drama

Communities of practice do not exist in isolation. They share edges with other communities, or they include members who move between communities, sharing knowledge and information. Digital performance methods emerging from video games and machinima production exhibit influences from a range of other communities, most obviously the game-playing, game-modifying CGI animation and filmmaking communities. From a dramatic viewpoint, the performers in a machinima production are also operating in much the same way as in-role improvisation occurs in the community of practice associated with process drama—a strongly framed environment defined by a digital pre-text (Carroll 2006; Carroll and Cameron 2009), which is the common digital environment that provides the agreed fictional context for the dramatic action to unfold in. Some machinima performers are forced to interact with the real-time-rendered world of the game engine in a way that is partly improvised because the game environment is partly autonomous. If machine-generated bot characters appear on the screen or if physical features of the rendered environment change during the performance, then the performers may have no choice but to respond dramatically to their changed circumstances. In some performances the game interface cannot be completely avoided and must be integrated or accepted as part of the production process; an example is a gun crosshair icon on-screen in a first-person or camera point of view. A key factor in most machinima production is that the game environment is not a passive performance space; the game engine may react to the actions of the player-performer in ways that hinder the machinima production but that are consistent with game-oriented behavior.

Although the performance of the actors has a fluid interactive and improvised nature that mirrors the improvisational strategies of process drama, it is not the whole story. Most machinima genres also incorporate some element of postproduction. In this way the producer acts more like a film documentarist or an actor or producer or director than happens in the production model and work divisions that occur in TV or cinema production. Consequently, there are as yet no widely recognized machinima "actors," although there are recognized and respected producers and performers. Often the respect recognizes good gameplay and technical understanding of the software rather than acting ability. The producers of machinima often see the performance element of their productions in a technical light: getting the machinima characters to perform is difficult enough without attempting to direct the performers in a way that produces an emotional engagement of empathic acting for the audience. An example of this line of thought is the machinima content produced for an episode of the animated TV series *South Park*. The animators used real-time gameplay in the *World of Warcraft* online multiplayer environment to generate some of the content, but not without some of the problems inherent in using a live game space and game players, as animator Eric Strough describes:

The tough part was trying to get the in game characters to "act." They are limited and stiff. For example, it was hard to get them to stop on their mark. . . . As for goofing around, the game players would have to wait awhile in between takes so they would challenge each other to duels and tell each other to go screw off by using game chat. They would break into dance and balance themselves on top of fences. ("Make Love" 2006)

Perhaps the most appropriate model of performance is to see machinima as a filmed and edited version of an improvised performance, in much the same mold as process drama that has been recorded and edited for broadcast. A well-known early example is *Three Looms Waiting*, a BBC Panorama production of Dorothy Heathcote's work in process drama. However, it must be noted that unlike process drama, machinima performances are enacted within the limitations of the on-screen role persona. Unless they have the skills to alter the game representations of character appearances, props, and sets, machinima performers are working with preconstructed elements. Also, the game world may not allow unfettered subversion of the environment and game goals, and producer or performers may be forced to work with or around the game's responses to their actions. There are also the improvisational films, such as Mike Leigh's *Secrets and Lies*, which attempt, as Leigh explains, "to get the actors involved from the word go to create a world that really does exist, whether we point a camera at it or not. . . . [F]ilm should aspire, in a sense, to the condition of documentary." Leigh's vision is to depict ordinary life, "real life," unfolding under extenuating circumstances. In *Secrets and Lies*, for example, although Leigh is credited with writing the screenplay, most of the performances were actually improvised, with Leigh providing each of the actors with his or her role and requiring them to make up their own lines (Miller 1997).

When presented in this way, machinima, improvised film, and process drama have a feeling of immediacy and ease with performance conventions, which provides the spontaneity and freshness of the forms. Of course, machinima is a continuum of evolving performance conventions, and the level at which the performers are scripted varies from improvised speech to written scripts, mirroring the performance conventions of process drama and improvised cinema. The performance connections are even stronger when considered in terms of the semiotic production of meaning. Eco (1989) uses the term "open text" to describe a characteristic of contemporary communication that allows multiple interpretations of a text by readers, rather than a closed single meaning intended by the author. Machinima, improvised film, and process drama exhibit this multimodal open text as they are all oriented toward the production of improvised original texts that respond reflexively to the environment in which they are set. In machinima terms, this response requires, technically and performatively, that the performers accept they are in the same virtual space at the same time, responding to the same digital pretext. This could be in the form of a computer network or a simulated world, for example *Second Life* or *World of Warcraft*, where machinima productions occur without a physical meeting of participants.

Role Protection and Role Distance

The concept of the dramatic frame is at work in machinima. In a dramatic frame, the player or performer engages "as if" the situation were real (Goffman 1974). But there exists a range of dramatic conventions and levels of improvisation, and these in turn afford different levels of protection for the performer. A performer can choose a close identification with his or character or an observer's perspective that is more distant from the action. A protective distance from role identification allows performers to experiment at extreme levels of behavior in order to discover how to operate in the performance environment. This is a clear extension of the risk-taking and learning behaviors exhibited as part of gameplay. Novice players of a video game are often allowed, even encouraged, by the designers to experiment in the early stages of the game before moving on to more challenging tasks or levels.

This penalty-free behavior reflects what psychologist Eric Erikson (1968) has called a psychosocial moratorium, which James Gee (2003) succinctly sums up as "a learning space in which the learner can take risks where real world consequences are lowered." In game studies the concept is widely known in terms of Huizinga's "magic circle" (1955), which describes how game spaces are segmented from the real world with respect to rules and outcomes. In process drama this concept has come to be known independently as "role protection," where the personal "role distance" from the consequences of actually being in the event have been elaborated and structured for different learning outcomes.

The player or performer in a machinima piece always has the option to select from a range of distance and protection conventions (Carroll 2006). The most obvious position is immersion in the action of unstructured first-person participation. This full role, while providing high levels of involvement and activity, provides little emotional protection for the participants. For example, in video game terms the first-person shooter (FPS) position provides full role participation with least protection, as the player experiences the world through the eyes of the character. In video games, FPS game forms are often based on reflex action and physical controller skills and depend on an ever-growing body count of increasingly ferocious adversaries for success. As gameplay gives way to machinima production, the FPS mode is more often used as a camera position to record the up-close action occurring in the dramatic frame. Thus the performer in machinima has a greater sense of role protection than does a player in the game.

In process drama, first-person full role participation and immersion in the event is usually the culmination rather than the starting point of any improvisational drama. First-person "in-the-event" drama requires a background understanding of the context and high levels of group trust to operate in a situation with minimal role protection. In machinima, this type of performance is most likely to occur in live performance, in a situation requiring improvisational skills before a live audience. Each performer is directly responsible for the unfolding narrative. The minimal role distance in such a setting can often prove overly confrontational or challenging for performers in both drama and machinima. If so, the participant or player may choose a greater role distance and stand back from the action by assuming a signed or attitudinal role. The performer can become a central character without assuming a full role by "signing" the role she adopted through costume, name, career path, or some other attribute. This is the level of role protection evident in much current machinima, where the role performances are often shaped by familiarity with the characters or character types from gameplay or game backstory. To move even farther away requires only the agreement of the player to take on an attitude of a character in the drama for it to operate—to act "like" a certain character would be expected to behave. In machinima, this extreme distance may take the form of pre-scripted actions for NPCs to act out under the control of the software engine.

Within these incorporeal species that make up the evolving ecology of machinima there exists a continuum of performance conventions that mirrors the conventions of process drama, on the one hand, and those of improvised cinema on the other, with each grade in the range connected to a specific level of liveness as outlined by Auslander. Although all variations ultimately depend on the game engines for their dramatic frame, they occupy different niches, and different communities of practice have developed around them. The machinima performance range includes the following:

• Live puppet machinima operating for a physically present audience, or a virtual audience in a shared game space
• Demos and "speed runs" working as game engine replay
• "Recamming" of demo data files using software to alter game engine replay
• Scripted bot and camera interactions, possibly combined with live puppet machinima
• Multiple avatar interactions captured as video files and edited in postproduction.

It would be useful if research into the range of machinima subgenres in this developing typology of performance could be categorized in more detail. As the communities of practice in machinima evolve into more extensive and differentiated forms, it would also be valuable if discussion within the field were precise enough to categorize discrete performance genres in the same range of technical conventions. Machinima currently covers an evolving and complex range of contemporary technological performance forms that requires a concomitant level of sophistication in its analysis. Underlying the energetic ongoing development of machinima as a performance form there remains the inherent ambiguity of its nature as the product of real-time software rendering that allows differing interpretations of liveness.

References

Academy of Machinima Arts and Sciences. 2008. <http://festival.machinima.org>.

Auslander, P. 2002. Live from Cyberspace: Or, I Was Sitting at My Computer This Guy He Appeared He Thought I Was a Bot. *PAJ 70* 24 (1): 16–21.

Auslander, P. 2000. Response to Roundtable on Liveness. <http://www.athe.org/FG/tc/AuslanderResponse.html>.

Auslander, P. 1999. *Liveness: Performance in a Mediatized Culture*. New York: Routledge.

Benzie, D., D. Mavers, B. Somekh, and E. J. Cisneros-Cohernour. 2005. Communities of Practice. In *Research Methods in the Social Sciences*, ed. B. Somekh and C. Lewin, 180–187. London: Sage.

Blau, H. 2002. The Human Nature of the Bot: A Response to Philip Auslander. *Performing Arts Journal* 70:22–24.

Brown, J., A. Collins, and P. Duguid. 1989. Situated Cognition and the Culture of Learning. *Educational Researcher* 18 (1): 32–42.

Cameron, D., and J. Carroll. 2009. Lessons from Applied Drama: Conventions to Help Serious Games Developers. In *Serious Games on the Move*, ed. O. Petrovic and A. Brand, 27–41. Vienna: Springer-Verlag.

Carroll, J. 2006. Digital Natives and Virtual Literacy: Process Drama and Online Learning. *International Journal of Learning* 11, 1211–1217.

Carroll, J., and Cameron, D. 2009. Drama, Digital Pre-Text, and Social Media. *Research in Drama Education* 14 (2): 295–312.

Eco, U. 1989. *The Open Work*, trans. A. Cancogni. Cambridge: Harvard University Press.

Erikson, E. 1968. *Identity, Youth and Crisis*. New York: Norton.

Gee, J. P. 2005. What Would a State of the Art Instructional Video Game Look Like? *Innovate* (online) 1 (6). <http://www.innovateonline.info/index.php?view=article&id=80>.

Gee, J. P. 2003. *What Video Games Have to Teach Us about Learning and Literacy*. New York: Palgrave.

Goffman, E. 1974. *Frame Analysis*. Norwich, UK: Peregrine.

Guattari, F. 1995. *Chaosmosis: An Ethno-Aesthetic Paradigm*, trans. P. Bains and J. Pefanis. Sydney, Australia: Power.

Huizinga, J. 1955. *Homo Ludens: A Study of the Play Element in Culture*. Boston: Beacon Press.

ILL Clan. 2004. NY Based Studio to Perform Live-Animated Comedy Show at Cinema Classics Aug 28th. News release, ILL Clan, August 8. <http://www.illclan.com/liveshowcinemaclassics2004-pr.htm>.

Jenkins, H. 1992. *Textual Poachers: Television Fans and Participant Culture*. New York: Routledge.

Kershaw, B. 2001. Oh for Unruly Audiences! Or, Patterns of Participation in Twentieth-Century Theatre. *Modern Drama* 42 (2): 133–154.

Kleist, H. v. 1810. On the Marionette Theater. *Drama Review* 16 (3): 26.

Lowood, H. 2009. Warcraft Adventures: Texts, Replay, and Machinima in a Game-Based Storyworld. In *Third Person: Authoring and Exploring Vast Narratives*, ed. P. Harrigan and N. Wardrip-Fruin, 407–427. Cambridge: MIT Press.

Lowood, H. 2007. High-Performance Play: The Making of Machinima. In *Videogames and Art: Intersections and Interactions*, ed. A. Clarke and G. Mitchell, 59–79. London: Intellect Books.

Machinima.com. 2009. Forums. <http://www.machinima.com/forums>.

Make Love, Not Warcraft: Q&A with Frank Agnone, J. J. Franzen, and Eric Stough. 2006. Machinima.com. <http://www.machinima.com/article/view&id=459>.

McGonigal, J. 2003. A Real Little Game: The Performance of Belief in Pervasive Play. Paper presented at the DiGRA "Level Up" conference, Utrecht, November 4–6.

Miller, L. 1997. Listening to the World: An Interview with Mike Leigh. Salon.com. <http://www.salon.com/weekly/interview2960916.html>.

O'Neill, C. 1995. *Drama Worlds: A Framework for Process Drama*. London: Heinemann.

Phelan, P. 1993. *Unmarked: The Politics of Performance*. New York: Routledge.

Schechner, R. 2003. *Performance Theory*. London: Routledge.

Sutton, P. 2009. Lip Sync: Performative Placebos in the Digital Age. In *Drama Education with Digital Technology*, ed. J. Carroll, M. Anderson, and D. Cameron, 38–51. London: Continuum.

Wenger, E., and J. Lave. 1991. *Situated Learning: Legitimate Peripheral Participation*. Cambridge, UK: Cambridge University Press.

Software References

Adobe Premiere. Adobe Systems. 1991.

The Elder Scrolls IV: Oblivion. Bethesda Softworks. 2007.

Final Cut Pro. Apple, Inc. 1999.

Halo: Combat Evolved. Bungie Studios. 2001.

Half-Life 2. Valve Corporation. 2004.

The Movies. Lionhead Studios. 2005.

Neverwinter Nights. BioWare. 2002.

Quake. id Software. 1996.

Second Life. Linden Lab. 2003.

The Sims 2. Electronic Arts. 2004.

Unreal. Epic Games. 1998.

World of Warcraft. Blizzard Entertainment. 2004.

9　Machinima: From Art Object to Cultural Practice

Dan Pinchbeck and Ricard Gras

From Game to World: "Traditional" and *Second Life* Machinima

Second Life, the online virtual world launched by Linden Lab in 2003, provides immense opportunities for the creation of new cultural artifacts. The virtual world itself is rich in collaborative creative projects, with media streaming in and out of its confines, along with internally realized, self-enclosed cultural works. In this essay we identify some key factors differentiating *Second Life* machinima and explore the emergent production methods of this increasingly popular medium. *Second Life* has been selected for investigation because of its rapid expansion and increasing dominance as a cultural space, as well as the inherent difference of *Second Life* machinima in terms of products and practice.

It is important at the outset to distinguish between *Second Life* and every other machinima platform. *Second Life* is not a game in the traditional sense. That is, it is not goal-orientated or rule-based (low-level procedural rules excepted, of course), and, most important, it relies almost totally on user-generated content. Unlike other virtual worlds, such as *EverQuest* or *World of Warcraft*, it contains neither mythos nor structured frameworks for system-generated narrative. It comes with no predetermined relationships, expectations, or priming material, and this in itself necessitates an entirely different psychological and creative relationship of the user to the world. A parallel may perhaps be drawn to the transition from the early *Dungeons & Dragons*–oriented MUDs (multiuser dungeons) to more open-ended MOO (MUD, object oriented) environments that, while often thematically attached to preexisting media artifacts, either reduced the goal orientation or did away with it altogether. Similarly, *Second Life* is not inherently competitive, and it lacks a stable contextual environment on which new narratives could be built.

Machinima has a number of traditional content genres. For example, disregarding documentaries of speed-runs or other demonstrations of prowess, the classic first-person shooter (FPS) machinima, typified by the *Red vs. Blue* series (Rooster Teeth, 2003–2006) or *Die Waltons Raeumen Auf* (Olmos and Schmidt, 2001), is a satirical reaction to title and genre. This is perhaps a result of the self-referentiality that comes from utilizing strongly themed and defined preexisting media elements in a production, such as *Halo*'s Master Chief avatar. Episodic comedy also features heavily, as do promotional or spoof advertisements and music videos with varying degrees of abstraction and interpretation. Finally, most machinima is short, perhaps because of the lone machinimator or small team behind the production, and it should be no surprise that those genres and structures that best fit this production limitation are commonplace.

Developing machinima is a matter of negotiating between content and system capabilities as a matter of course. When strong thematic avatars, textures, and environments are available, the end product would be expected to reflect the implicit content of the system. Put another way, it is not just the action of *Halo*, for example, that transmits the game's themes; they are distributed throughout the visual experience. Contemporary games are sophisticated multimodal delivery systems. Machinima lends itself to satire and comedy because it requires little additional work to stamp individuality on a given set of resources, often just by layering an audio file over standardized objects and animations. *Second Life*, by contrast, has a degree of visual identity but no theming. A *Second Life* avatar generally looks and certainly moves like a *Second Life* avatar, but there is none of the associative depth of a Master Chief or a Barney. Thus, subversion of the original context is not an option for the machinimator in *Second Life*, although, as we shall see, self- and system-referentiality still form a backbone for some of the movies being made.

Second, *Second Life* is inherently communal. The attraction of *Second Life* is the sharing of experience within *Second Life*, and it is no surprise to find in-world communal media experiences: galleries, nightclubs, radio stations, cinemas. Alt-Zoom, one of the key machinima promoters, organizes the monthly Take 5 festival, screening movies in-world. By contrast, even though a multiplayer FPS may provide a powerful tool for creating machinima, it does not provide a communal, persistent virtual world where the product can be consumed. That is, the presentation space for machinima is not usually coexistent with the production space. It is worth noting that most *Second Life* machinima is still consumed via a mediating technology, such as a Web browser, but at least the potential is there for a more diegetic consumption.

One can look at this another way: Machinima is the process of rendering a linear artifact from a nonlinear system, of reducing the field of affordances within this system to an individualized stream. Not only does *Second Life* massively expand this field of affordances, which brings its own challenges to the machinimator, but its very nature suggests that the linear output should be fed back into the nonlinear system for consumption. Let us consider this arrangement in more detail. A machinima piece created using an FPS engine, such as *Red vs. Blue*, uses a small number of existing elements (objects and animations) to create a new sequence. Additional media may be added to this sequence, but it is inherently centered on the constraints of the engine. As any gamer is aware, even with the relatively tiny number of affordances and actions allowed by an FPS engine, a complex and substantial set of sequences can be produced—games, although based around a common sequence, do vary in nonsignificant ways, in terms of their affective outcome. However, games are, as Eskelinen (2003) has noted, configurative spaces, and FPS games in particular tend to operate according to the principle of simplicity—that is, a player configures the space to optimum simplicity by removing objects (soldiers, demons, aliens, or what-have-you) from the environment and then progresses in the game. Games are closed systems and do not generally offer the means to represent action, though the ability to record, edit, and replay sequences of action (such as in Reflections' [2000] PlayStation title *Driver*) have been embedded in engines for some time and may be seen as a logical precursor to machinima. *Second Life*, on the other hand, is both inherently and explicitly an open system, where configuration has no end-point but is its own reward. Increasing system complexity is the goal of the producer in *Second Life*, and increasing the available resources is part of this goal. *Second Life* does not reduce through experience; it expands, and invites an exploration of system capabilities, including creation and representation, within the presented environment. In other words, whereas the world of *Halo* is presented as more or less complete, existing as a resource for production, *Second Life* is its own production; it is never finalized or closed. Outputs have the capacity to feed back into the system as well as to be represented within it. Under these circumstances we would expect to find producers seeking to exploit this very different relationship between media product and originating system.

So, two things are happening here. First, the division between spaces is reduced or removed altogether. Second, the production space itself is fundamentally communal, as reflected inthe production methodology of *Second Life* machinima. It moves beyond the supply of vocal talent to an animator toward virtual acting, or at the least puppetry, in which both avatar and operator may become part of a production *as themselves*. Avatars or costumes and custom gestures may be provided, and the direction and editing remain the province of a small team or individual, but there is the opportunity to literally act in the movie, while retaining a relatively high degree of control over one's contribution during the shoot. An example of this capability is Eric Call's *Silver Bells and Golden Spurs* (2006), with its opening track along a Western street replete with a high number of extras or its crowded saloon forming the central scene. Similarly, *Ijttihad* (Gras, 2006) combines a predefined bespoke set of gestural responses with expressive freedom on the part of the avatar operator. This collaborative potential also means one can teach machinima from within the system itself, during the production process—an unprecedented practice-based learning opportunity for this new medium. This is also evidenced by the growing number of companies and individuals offering machinima "services" in-world, from training to production.[1]

Figure 9.1
Eric Call, dir., *Silver Bells and Golden Spurs* (2006).

Second Life machinima is thus essentially different from traditional models in several key ways: its lack of thematic context to be used as a base for inspiration, priming, subversion, or satire; the ability to present the product in the production environment; and the ability to distribute responsibility for the work among a team of collaborators in real time. These differences mark a profound shift from other animated media formats and should yield machinima products and practices that push the medium in new and interesting directions.

Thematic, Referential, and Internally Supportive Content

To the comic, satirical, and system-referential content that has dominated machinima is slowly being added the gravity of serious, self-contained works. Thuygen Nguyen's *An Unfair War* (2006), for example, references no games and demands attention purely as a work of short moving image. Visually, it is extremely simple: a man sits at his computer composing a potentially final email about the titular war while the bombs and troops move ever closer to his position. The film is carried by the narrative, delivered primarily through a voice-over. A medium that has begun to cease operating only self-referentially may be said to be in maturation. The lack of context to anchor *Second Life* machinima too may actually be seen as a blessing in disguise: although it makes the process more difficult technically, it forces machinimators to consider content other than reactionary satire. This is not to downplay the narrative and comic sophistication of some referential machinima, merely to recognize that, as *Doom* was to shooters, *Red vs. Blue* is an easy format to ape but a tough act to follow.

While *Second Life* has no content-based identity, it nevertheless has a clear system identity, and it is no surprise to find some pieces using this identity as a springboard. *Lip Flap* (directed by Kronos Kirkorian, 2006) features extensive and elaborate costumes (visual customization being a key feature of the system) and makes its central joke the lack of avatar speech animations. This is effective enough, but it remains a one-trick pony and offers little in the way of development. By contrast, *Better Life* (directed by Robin Wright, 2006), though somewhat obvious in terms of its narrative of a wheelchair user escaping into a virtual world that offers him bodily freedom, makes use of *Second Life*'s sense of scale in its skydiving sequences, creating a palpable sense of a world to discover. Given its inception as a social space, it is as a convincing and dramatic environment, unlimited in scope, that *Second Life* is really defined. *Better Life* offers a convincing emotional vision, all the more so because of its relatively self-reliant context. Essentially, it reiterates the old mantra of virtual reality that originated with Lanier, Rheingold, and the other early enthusiasts, namely, that a computer-mediated existence could function as a comparably real-enough experience to transcend either system or psychological extension and become a reality on a par with the "natural" world. However, Wright does evade the naiveté of this vision by returning to the user at the end of the piece, slumped over the console asleep, an image that reinforces the temporal nature of any virtual fantasy and the inescapable supremacy of the real. Another of Wright's works, *Stage* (2006), dispenses with any notion of location at all and takes place in what resembles a studio set, with only a piano, a children's train set, and spotlights for props. *Stage* is more successful in its emotional and narrative delivery, perhaps as a result of this simplicity, relying more on its storytelling prowess, and particularly on the relationship between the visual elements and the score. In fact, it could be argued that Wright's work is successful exactly because it evades system referentiality; it exhibits no need to show off the engine used to build it, unlike the plethora of *Second Life* machinima works that operate primarily as a showcase for the object-building skills of the developers.

Both Gras and Call have commented that they view machinima as an opportunity for creative production, not a technical showcase, and further, that storytelling is often the weakest link in machinima productions. It should be remembered, however, that storytelling in virtual worlds is never limited to either simply theming or vocal acting and extends to both elements distributed throughout the multimodal space and to the catalog of animations and gestures utilized. Just as *Red vs. Blue* relies primarily on spoken rather than visual comedy to succeed, so *Second Life* machinima pieces often overemphasize superficial visuals, perhaps as a means of diverting attention from the current limitations in gestural and facial animation. It should also be noted that these limitations are likely to be temporary and are high on Linden Lab's priority list for future developments for the system. Indeed, *Silver Bells* was initiated as a proof-of-concept project that would, in particular, begin to examine speech emulation and gestural sophistication.[2]

Linden Lab has not only produced a machinima starter-pack but has also made a large variety of objects available to users that, it could be argued, may eventually support a strong norm-seeking tendency. Similarly, one of the aims of Alt-Zoom studios is to help create a bank of usable props and sets for machinima. BuhBuhCuh Fairchild, Alt-Zoom's coordinator, states,

I had the idea that a shared group inventory of assets would work like a Hollywood studio's backlot. You might notice in the background of Back to the Future 2 that one of the cars is a spinner from Blade Runner, etc. If we could share sets, scripts, animations, etc, as time went on, it would make it that much easier to make movies.[3]

A more recent development is Tube2SL, which also offers screenings, purchasable televisions with which to watch machinima in-world, and viewing booths.[4] Although this assembling of standard scripts and objects for generic use will no doubt make life easier, *Second Life* is first and foremost an environment for building, a system in which the creation of new forms rather than the utilization of existing ones is paramount, and it is unlikely to blunt the inventiveness demonstrated by the best machinima being produced. Inherent to *Second Life* are not just the capacity and flexibility to build bespoke, highly individual objects, environments, and avatars but also the culture of doing so. In fact, the only factors that could dissuade potential users may be *Second Life*'s drive toward linearity and noninteractivity, and the availability of more exciting possibilities for world builders than moviemakers. But, true to *Second Life*'s aspirations as an open system (that is to say, a largely deregulated one) that enables the formation of communities, and therefore potentially of internal cultures, one might argue that such modern communities and cultures necessitate media, and machinima fits the bill perfectly for such a medium.

Second Life already has a burgeoning economy, with ramifications outside the system itself, and the skinning and modding culture has developed into a serious pocket industry. *Second Life*'s user demographics extend far beyond builders, and users will always demand high-quality creative goods in any culture, virtual or otherwise. Thus, the fact that production economy exists in architecture, clothing, skins, objects, and even gestures, and that this economy exists in both virtual and real worlds, adds considerable adaptability to machinima. When Call built *Silver Bells,* he researched the period extensively and handed his findings to a designer-cum-"wardrobe manager," who created the buildings, furniture, and population of the movie. These obects were then imported back into *Second Life* for use.

For *Ijttihad,* Gras recruited graphic designers and visual artists outside *Second Life* to work with a team of programmers to create the machinima's unique visual identity. Although the avatars do retain some characteristics of *Second Life,* primarily in their basic movement animation, and the camera work retains the imprint of the system, *Ijttihad,* like *An Unfair War,* demands to be viewed as a moving image work independent of any engine. Indeed, its visual style has more in common with anime than with traditional machinima. In other words, it seeks to escape the look of a game and hew to an entirely separate style.[5]

A Singular Space for Production and Presentation

Bringing media into *Second Life* is straightforward. By means of existing streaming technologies, moving image feeds from URLs can be delivered directly into devices in-world. The ability to do so is already being utilized as a means of showing movies and establishing radio channels in the system, alongside more specific events such as concerts, album launches, and so on. At the time of writing, a genuine feedback loop of production and presentation has yet to emerge, but it can only be a matter of time. *Second Life* will demand its own television stations, its own homegrown cinema. and other media forms.

Alt-Zoom regularly streamed media developed in world back into the world for consumption via the Take5 monthly festival. Although also available through more conventional, Web-based platforms, the presentation of work in a virtual world adds a hitherto unexplored aspect of media consumption to the machinima experience: the social. With the exception of specialist festivals and conferences, machinima deviates from conventional cinema not just in scale but in its inevitable isolation of the consumer. Cinema is a social experience that brings viewers into proximity to one another; the movies are viewed in a shared space. By routing machinima back into *Second Life,* where avatars can group, Alt-Zoom, Tube2SL, and other cinemas in the world create a form of social media experience that is vitally different from a social presentation in the real world as the mediation of embodiment is, of course, central to the viewer's experience.

Take5 was presented in a custom-built cinema with a capacity of sixty avatars. Feedback on the films could be given in real time via instant messaging, which, in addition to the other social aspects of the event, is encouraged. BuhBuhCuh Fairchild has remarked that the third-person perspective of *Second Life* helps establish a sense of social presence further, as it enables users to place their avatars visually in a crowd.

The experience is tailored specifically to highlight the social nature of cinema.[6] That is, the mediation of the avatar makes one aware of one's presence socially in the act of watching. Unlike traditional notions of presence in relation to cinema, consumption of the medium is not an opportunity for escapism or relocation of the psychological center, so to speak. Instead, the focus, or channel, is the avatar and its relation to its surroundings. To see this in another way, we can consider the ergonomics of modern cinemas. With their ever-expanding screen size, surround-sound, and large, isolating furniture, they work to downplay the physical act of watching and prompt a greater immersion in the presented content. The system itself aims for optimum transparency, as do most virtual reality technologies. For the controller of the avatar viewing film in *Second Life*, however, the system is geared toward increasing the visibility of the mediating technology, and the act of watching. The system presents a re-embodied user sharing the watching with other re-embodied users, and it is through this act that it shares significance with the presented media. The capacity to interact is therefore seen not as a problem but as potential. Talking, moving around—those actions that are discouraged in the cinema house become exciting opportunities to reaffirm the shared experience in an interactive world.

The importance of this ability to present work socially in the same environment it was produced in may perhaps be better illuminated by discussing media schema theory. Based on Bartlett's (1932) notion of generic mental architectures that can be applied to specific occurrences within a wider contextual set, media schema theory proposes that individuals develop distinct means of engagement with various media forms. One could also consider Marshall McLuhan's (1964) concept of hot and cold media, that is, media typified by extensive stimulation and requiring little user effort (hot), or the opposite (cold). Between the classic schemata, which exist as virtual machines for reducing the cognitive load needed to assess new instances of familiar stimuli, and McLuhan's typology, we can form clear distinctions between not the content but the context of machinima productions. The medium is the message, indeed! Media schemata have been extended to virtual environments through the concept of presence, or the subjective projection of the user's sense of locative reality, by IJsselsteijn and Riva (2003), and the idea that a distinct schema may be formed within a virtual environment suggests that media consumed in this setting would pass through an additional filter. Put more prosaically, watching machinima in *Second Life* is a different mental experience than watching it in a cinema or alone via a Web browser.

The idea that watching machinima may activate schemata for cinema, schemata for virtual reality, and schemata for games suggests that *Second Life* machinima is a new and very different experience. Just as *Red vs. Blue* or other FPS satires operate primarily by insinuating a community "in the know," that is, those who have played *Halo* extensively and understand its world, thereby making the subversion comic, so a group of avatars watching films made in their world is singular. Further, as we have seen, this does not relate inevitably to the content of the work: it does not have to be about the *Second Life* experience in order to represent it. At this early stage of the world's, and the medium's, development, perhaps a certain pride is instilled: "Look what we can do here!" This is certainly the case in *Happy Birthday to Pierce P* (Portacarrero, 2006), a message to the titular avatar/producer's mother about this strange viral world that he has spent so much time in. Interestingly, a work that is so heavily system-referential has much in common visually with the format of an FPS machinima. In other words, it is relatively static and relies primarily on voice-over for narrative delivery. Call sees a direct parallel between the development of machinima and the development of early cinema, in that currently machinima exists somewhere around the stage of the very early talkies, and, as with that part of cinema history, a substantial degree of amazement and pride in the capabilities of the medium is common. At the same time, however, Call sees a shift from "vaudeville to serious, interesting things," evident in work such as *An Unfair War* or *Stage*.[7]

The collapse of production and presentation into a singular place has ramifications for the wider conceptualization of *Second Life* machinima. For instance, the user and producer demographic expands considerably. This is, once again, not simply limited to the content of the work but occurs in the approach of consumers to the product. In other words, traditionally, one must actively seek out machinima in niche sites. By contrast, in *Second Life*, going to the movies is a standard social activity limited only by one's knowledge of the existing cinemas, social grouping, and so on. If one is bored with virtual parties, dances, and the like, why not try another social media experience? The nonludic nature of *Second Life* imposes an entirely different temporal framework on in-system activity that potentially allows new forms of content to develop. Although machinima is often episodic owing to production constraints, *Second Life* at least offers a space where consumption can occur at a reasonable pace.

The social consumption of machinima within the system it is produced in also permits a very different kind of feedback system to emerge. One can watch the audience for reactions, talk to audience members afterward, involve them in the production process, and retest shoots and sections, all without the need for further rendering. A cycle of production and presentation is therefore implied by the system's context, rather than the segmented processes of building, shooting, editing, and distribution one finds in traditional machinima.

This brings us full circle, to the idea of ongoing and persistent media stations in *Second Life*—or any other virtual world, for that matter. Machinima is generally discussed in the context of short or animated film. Television is another matter altogether. This is not to discount machinima productions that are based on existing television genres, sitcoms such as *The Strangerhood* (Rooster Teeth, 2004–2006) or chat shows such as *Select-Start* (Select-Start, 2006). *Second Life* machinima, however, offers a persistent world in which to anchor episodes in an ongoing media environment. It also enables the replication of that staple of contemporary television, the phone-in, via instant messaging channels, and that other, more historical, expectation, the studio audience. The collapsed distinction between production and presentation space not only helps a culture of production to emerge in *Second Life* that has the potential to transform a medium into a virtual industry, it also paves the way for a self-sufficient broadcast environment to emerge. In light of the existing cultures of periodic events, clubs and groups, and specifically located media already in place in *Second Life*, it is only a matter of time before this extends to the regular presentation of media developed within the system to established points of distribution. And this does not stop at public displays, such as cinemas or open-air screens. Fundamentally, *Second Life* is about the creation of personalized spaces, including media distribution outlets. There will undoubtedly come a time when avatars gather in their houses or the houses of their friends to watch in-world television, with a fully realized celebrity system, developed in the virtual world and available only in it. At this point, machinima will have evolved from singular artifacts into a mass-market communications medium.

Collaborative Production and Virtual Puppetry

The idea of a celebrity system in machinima pieces leads to the third differentiating factor, collaboration. There is no question that the sophistication of gestural animations and the ability to customize and control in real time the set of behavioral responses available to avatars will increase dramatically in a relatively short period of time. As this happens, the skills required to puppeteer machinima characters will also develop in scope, and it is not unreasonable to assume that some users will be more adept at conveying the requisite depth and complexity of response better than others. When the product (and production) is anchored in a persistent world, such as *Second Life*, we can expect the development of an internal industry. Alongside highly skilled designers and technicians, performers and "emotioneers," to borrow David Freeman's (2004) term, will begin to establish themselves and, given *Second Life*'s propensity to collapse the distinction between in-world and real-world economics, start to make a real living working as actors in virtual media.

Let us quickly examine the production process once more to place this in context, before moving on to consider *Second Life* as a learning environment for would-be machinimators. Roughly, machinima developed in *Second Life* can be divided into two forms, singular and collaborative. Singular works, such as *Better Life* or *Happy Birthday Peirce P*, utilize a lone avatar or a small number of avatars and can be produced by an individual without the need for further production staff. Collaborative works, typified by titles such as *Silver Bells* and *Ijttihad*, use large numbers of avatars and potentially require an equally large number of operators. In these cases, "collaborative" may be a slightly misleading description, as it in no way implies a lack of authorial control or vision: both Gras and Call remain the authors and directors of their work. However, the manner in which the work is produced shifts significantly and requires a new type of working relationship to be established with contributors.

In addition to custom props and avatars, both *Silver Bells* and *Ijttihad* use custom gestural animations attached to avatars. In *Silver Bells*, the custom animations take the form of a standard set of gestural animations that operators can spontaneously trigger. Thus, within the limited framework of actions that we preattached to the avatars, operators can respond in real time to the action of the scene to help establish a compelling context for the action. *Ijttihad* binds facial animations to keys, enabling operators to explore a more complex vocabulary of emotional response than has been previously available in *Second Life* machinima (though other forms of machinima have taken advantage of this capability for some time). Operators, or avatar puppeteers, can then be recruited in-world, through open calls or emerging groups such as the Guild of Machinima Actors or via the Machinimators' group. Operators are given a specific time and location for a shooting, and then log in to avatars provided to them in order to take part. Once again, it seems only a matter of time—and necessity, in the case of machinima television—before a form of virtual casting emerges, replacing custom-built avatars, and it will become a question of supplying costumes to existing avatars who present themselves with a strong gestural and emotive set. At the time of writing, Linden Lab is developing inverse kinetic-based additions to the engine that will massively expand the potential for expressive performance. Users will be able to manipulate avatars in real time via a set of "handles" attached to avatar limbs. Custom gestures can then be stored and recalled at later points. This capability will open up the market for expression designers. As a result, individual gestural puppetry will be as defining a factor in successful virtual acting as the less dynamic design of costumes, hair, and face.[8] Thus, the balance between degree of control and ability to outsource workload has yet to become an issue for machinima, but it cannot be avoided as the medium becomes more complex.

If more responsibility gradually shifts to puppeteers, along with set, prop, and costume producers, then the role of the machinimator will also evolve, from animator to something more closely resembling a real-world movie director. This shift is fundamental to machinima's maturation as a medium, for it suggests that other aspects of production can also be farmed out to subcontractors. Perhaps one of the more important aspects of this shift toward real-world relationships is the division between director and writer, a separation that is generally accepted as vital in media industries from comic books to movies, including the video games that gave birth to machinima in the first place. It is unsurprising that Gras and Call place similar emphasis on the importance of storytelling in machinima. Gras considers himself first and foremost a media producer who happens to use machinima as a tool. Indeed, *Ijttihad* is the output of a larger project, Collaborative Narratives, which is primarily about the transformation of user-generated narrative input, via text messaging and a Web interface, into a stable, consistent media product. For Gras, machinima is the best means for achieving this goal, as it potentially enables the production process to be laid bare on completion of the project. To create *Ijttihad*, his group purchased a block of land in *Second Life* and sculpted an entire island that functions as the set for the piece. He has discussed the possibility of making this set, complete with props and avatars, available for public exploration following the completion of the machinima itself. Users who generated the content would be able to explore its transformation from text to moving image in an unprecedented way, by tracking the filtration, editing, and implementation of content originated and communicated through text as both interactive objects and then linear product. It is this ability to expose the mechanics of production, this transformative process, that interests Gras. The technical advances being made during the production of *Ijttihad* are solutions to creative problems—How does one increase the degree of emotional sophistication? How can abstract themes and narrative elements be effectively embedded in a machinima piece?—rather than a pursuit of a more technically impressive work. Likewise, the technical progressions made by Call in *Silver Bells*, although serving its remit as a proof of concept, are driven by the desire to, essentially, tell better stories. For example, an early problem was providing feedback to operators, as they had no sense of how the 3D, interactive experience they were involved in would translate back into a linear, 2D product. To address this issue, Call set up a large screen on-set and streamed the daily rushes back into *Second Life* for performers to watch. Operators were then able to understand better how their actions translated, and adjust where necessary. This innovative solution took advantage of the potential for virtually instantaneous feedback inherent in *Second Life* to provide an international cast of operators with group responses to their work.

Alt-Zoom operates training courses in addition to the monthly Take5 festival. Describing themselves as "less in the Hollywood model of a movie studio, more in the model of a cooperative artists' studio," Alt-Zoom designers act as an in-world agency for machinima development. There are several aspects to this model of practice that, once again, point to *Second Life* as the primary environment for the transformation of machinima from a product-by-product practice to a cultural industry. The training courses themselves operate within *Second Life*. This allows a far greater degree of flexibility by placing learner and educators face-to-face and thus creating the first genuine, non-classroom-based machinima training environment. A far richer and more effective learning experience is therefore possible. It also extends the type of learning beyond the technical, as it enables group discussion to occur during sessions, a flexibility to respond to unexpected directions the session may take in real time, the ability to relate as a group to media being created as the pieces are created, and a deeper relationship between tutor and tutee. Further, this approach binds the production space explicitly to the virtual world rather than simply seeing the world as an engine to be negotiated with; it makes the creation of machinima occur from within a system. This shift of perspective from exterior to interior may be expected to affect the network of relationships between and among camera, director, set, character, narrative, location, temporal sequencing, voice, focus, and so on. It also allows the production experience to be shared in a new way, with avatars not only collaborating within a framework to act scenes out but also collaborating in real time to define and manage this framework. Multiple camera operators join puppeteers in real-time manipulation and recording of the action, and the implicit trend toward collaboration also makes possible a far greater sophistication and diversity of both animated and, critically, reactive elements within the mise-en-scène, *in real time*. Making movies shifts from being primarily a case of capturing raw material and applying extensive postproduction effects to increasing the potential for spontaneous contributions to the final work in the production phase. Thus, we begin to see the shift from individual, satirical, system-based machinima toward collaborative, content-driven machinima that, crucially, has the capacity to be self-contained, that is, consumed within the producing system without relying on it for context. This not only has the inevitable effect of widening audience demographics but also signals a move out of the ghetto in terms of production as well as consumption and toward a new form of social and cultural expression.

From Art Object to Collaborative Experience

Any survey of digital media that anchors itself to the technology utilized will inevitably date badly, unless recognizing itself as essentially a historical snapshot of the current state of play. There is general agreement that a greater degree of synchronicity between voice and expression is the next major developmental step for *Second Life* machinima, although some practitioners have chosen, on aesthetic grounds, to visually represent speech. Reducing the postproduction element seems a likely subsequent concern, with manipulating media feeds from cameras and editing, even real-time editing, being moved to within *Second Life* itself. Live streaming across the virtual world seems equally inevitable, effectively creating the kind of live machinima production currently appearing as highlight events at conferences and festivals.[9]

These shifts in technological capability are inevitable primarily because the cultural and creative development of *Second Life* machinima demands them. If Gras and Call are correct in drawing parallels between machinima's development and early cinema, then it is not unreasonable to suggest that in addition to evolving genres and cinematographic sophistication, machinima's development as a cultural object, as a distributive medium, is also occurring. Anyone can own a cinema in *Second Life* and, rights permitting, anyone can bring media into or across the world. This trend enables a personalization of the broadcast channel, which demands choice, which in turn demands an increase in production. Add this to *Second Life*'s stable, persistent, self-enclosed culture and we would expect to see an increase in the widespread development of *Second Life*–built machinima on a massively expanded number of distribution devices.

The generation of a substantial amount of complex content requires a supporting industry where collaboration and eventually competition will thrive. There is already plenty of evidence demonstrating the inherent respect for individual specializations and team-orientation within *Second Life* machinima; this can only increase as the sophistication and complexity of gestural (and vocal) puppetry develop and skilled operators begin to offer their services to serious, professional producers. This is not to downplay or disregard the work of the lone machinimator; as with any other art form, single visions are critical. But in a persistent creative industry, as will doubtless emerge from *Second Life*'s machinima, complex content requires complex teams. The nature of the machinimator begins to shift toward something resembling a traditional director: part visionary, part manager, all pragmatist, defining the next necessary technological progression by the aspirations for its output. Without descending into hyperbole, this early stage of the medium offers unparalleled opportunities for creative practitioners to define the direction and momentum of its affordances. It is not just a case of negotiating with the engine to create work but of creating adaptations of the engine in response to the demands of the work. Call notes that his analogy of the early days of cinema extends to this technological experimentation, even going so far as to suggest that the invention of tools to fit aspirational techniques is suggestive of aspects of *Citizen Kane*.[10]

In *Second Life*, we see the early stages of the maturation of a new medium: no longer a cheap means of creating animations as rough cuts or films in themselves, no longer a channel for satirical comment on a mass-market medium, no longer a place for artists and filmmakers to bypass the production and distribution demands of traditional, offline broadcast media. It is no longer about streaming media or viral comedy. There is an inherent distinction in the process of making machinima in *Second Life* that branches off from traditional game-based production, a trend toward social production, toward virtual shared learning experiences. This trend in turn invokes a burgeoning industry of specialist designers and operators and ultimately will shape the turn away from "cinema envy"—Eskelinen's ludologic term—toward a much smaller yet far more ubiquitous type of screen within a screen.

If the development of activities in *Second Life* holds true to form, we speculate that the production of moving images in-world will eventually solidify into an industry. As a final point, it is worth reiterating those aspects of *Second Life* machinima that set it apart from other forms. It has the capacity to be displayed diegetically—that is, within the world of its production—and this display can foreground the social act of media consumption. It has the capacity, with *Second Life*, to move from the niche into a conventionally conceptualized and recognizable activity: going to the cinema, going to a friend's house to watch a film. In other words, the media can be brought directly to the community via established schematic channels. The provision of feedback between product and producing system is markedly increased, which introduces the capacity for reportage of events within the system rather than just critique of the system. The world itself is expanding rapidly in scale and complexity, which offers the opportunity to develop means of mass communication of significant events, from album launches to riots. As with mass communication capabilities, the potential for creative production and user-generated events is necessarily vastly greater in an open system like *Second Life* than in a game engine, and machinima can be separated from the production to primary content to a secondary or representational role. These developments necessitate a supporting industry populated by specialists who can move from project to project according to an internally managed labor market, rather than small teams or individuals motivated by direct creative interest. Such a market is likely to diversify according to ability, potentially falling into patterns of supply and demand not unlike real-world celebrity systems. Similarly, repeated transmissions from recognized producers targeting specific consumer markets in the world of *Second Life* will likely start to coalesce into something resembling the scramble of deregulated cable channels. Indeed, projects such as Tube2SL and Treet.TV[11] certainly suggest this is beginning to occur.

Social watching, mass remote transmission, reference to the events of the world in a short temporal response period, both primary and secondary production and representation, a complex supporting industry with teams assembling according to recognized masters and stars, niche programming and high degrees of choice of simultaneous transmission—it all sounds very familiar. One day, *Second Life* machinima will, we predict, produce virtual television.

Notes

1. See <http://wiki.secondlife.com/wiki/Machinima_Content_Companies> (accessed October 9, 2009).

2. Eric Call, personal communication, July 27, 2006.

3. BuhBuhCuh Fairchild, personal communication, August 7, 2006. See also *Alt-Zoom*, <http://www.alt-zoom.com>.

4. See <http://www.tube2sl.com/index.php?name=Cinema&name=Cinema> (accessed August 9, 2009).

5. Though the relationship between anime and game graphics in some genres is long established, as with the Final Fantasy or even Metal Gear franchises.

6. BuhBuhCuh Fairchild, personal communication, August 7, 2006.

7. Eric Call, personal communication, July 27, 2006.

8. Eric Call, personal communication, August 1, 2006. Linden Lab's official press release was released the same day.

9. ILL Clan, *Introducing Will and Ma* (from the Tra5h Ta1k with ILL Will series), dir: the ILL Clan. Presented at the Machinima Film Festival 2005, New York, November 13, 2005.

10. Eric Call, personal communication, August 7, 2006.

11. See <http://www.treet.tv> (accessed September 8, 2009).

References

Bartlett, Frederic C. 1932. *Remembering: A Study in Experimental and Social Psychology*. Cambridge, UK: Cambridge University Press.

Eskelinen, M. 2003. Towards Computer Game Studies. In *First Person: New Media as Story, Performance and Game*, ed. Noah Wardrip-Fruin and Pat Harrigan, 36–43. Cambridge: MIT Press.

Freeman, David. 2004. *Creating Emotion in Games: The Craft and Art of Emotioneering*. Berkeley, CA: New Riders.

IJsselsteijn, Wijnand, and Guiseppe Riva. 2003. Being There: The Experience of Presence in Mediated Environments. In *Being There: Concepts, Effects and Measurements of User Presence in Synthetic Environments*, ed. Guiseppe Riva, Fabrizio Davide, and Wijnand IJsselsteijn, 4–16. Amsterdam: IOS Press.

McLuhan, Marshall. 1964. *Understanding Media*. Cambridge: MIT Press.

Machinima References

Better Life. Robin Wright. 2006.

Die Waltons Raeumen Auf. Rodrigo Olmos and Axel Schmidt. 2001.

Happy Birthday to Pierce P. Pierce Portacarrero. 2006.

Ijttihad. Ricard Gras. 2006.

Lip Flap. Kronos Kirkorian. 2006.

Red vs. Blue. Rooster Teeth Productions. 2003–2006.

Select-Start Episode 1. Select-Start. 2006.

Silver Bells and Golden Spurs. Eric Call. 2006.

Stage. Robin Wright. 2006.

The Strangerhood. Rooster Teeth Productions. 2004–2006.

An Unfair War. Thuygen Nguyen. 2006.

10   Of Games and Gestures: Machinima and the Suspension of Animation

Peter Krapp

Semantic aspects of communication are irrelevant to the engineering problem. (Shannon and Weaver 1962, 31)

Technology is making gestures precise and brutal, and with them men. It expels from movements all hesitation, deliberation, civility. It subjects them to the implacable, as it were ahistorical demands of objects. (Adorno 1978, 30)

Machinima is to computer gaming what Brechtian epic theater was to dramatic and cinematic conventions a century ago. Moments and sequences of gameplay are interrupted and time-shifted into a different context, in adjustments that allow them to be recorded as significant, interesting, or entertaining, independently of the immediate context of their production. This momentary halting of fluid technical as well as semiotic relations can make visible, rather than merely felt, what is at stake in machinima. This essay proposes there are at least two reasons to look at machinima from the vantage point of gestures. On the one hand, gestures and their citability mark the performative space of theater or cinema that is cited by machinima. On the other hand, precisely calibrated in-game gestures remain particularly difficult, even for highly accomplished examples of machinima such as Paul Marino's *I'm Still Seing Breen* (2005). Many of the digital assets that come with a particular game tend not to allow certain simple character movements, such as nodding, facial expressions, turning one's head, or pointing without a weapon in hand—as one can quickly glean, for instance, from episodes of the long-running machinima sitcom series, *Red vs. Blue* (2003–2007) (Delaney 2004).[1] The difficulty of emulating a range of affective expression through gesture and facial controls is among the constraints of making machinima without modifying the game engine or the digital assets (Kelland, Morris, and Lloyd 2005; Hancock and Ingram 2007). In machinima, there is a dual register of gestures: the trained motions of the player determine the in-game images of expressive motion. In this sense, machinima is not simply the recording of consumer-generated content in computer games, any more than speech is merely the consumer-generated movement of air through the larynx. Machinima consists of controlled gestures in a collective frame of reference in the history of technology and entertainment. Instead of reducing machinima to fan culture or to contributions to an oral history of video games, this essay seeks to show how machinima's gestures may grant access to gaming's historical conditions of possibility, and how it offers links to a comparative horizon that informs, changes, and fully participates in video game culture.[2]

Gestures are neither necessary nor natural. They are acquired wherever specific cultural tasks are to be performed, and the process of accommodation or acculturation creates the kinetic body (Mauss 1935; Leroi-Gourhan 1993).[3] A gesture is a manner of carrying the body, a controlled motion used to express attitude or emotion. Gestures communicate: each gesture is a bodily motion, but not all bodily motions can be understood as gesture. Involuntary movement (including posture, facial expressions, or even a mere reaction of the pupil of the eye) does not constitute a gesture: to the extent that gestures are taken as expressions of an intention, we assume significance, and constantly read or interpret gestures.[4] We also know that gestures are readily imitated or cited, and if they seem derivative or kitschy, then they are less expressive. When it comes to the gestures of machinima, beyond the twitchy hand-eye coordination video games require there is the motion of the camera itself inside game-space. As recorded from the point of view of one player, who thereby acts as the camera, game action may feature high jumps, teleporting, and seemingly impossible positions and angles, yet apart from (or indeed by dint of) such reminders of the technical capacity of virtual cinematography, the player tends to disappear from screen. Even as cut-scenes, in-game footage, and ad campaigns for blockbuster gaming products such as *The Sims*, *Halo*, or *Grand Theft Auto* must interpolate a player, that player herself is absent from the screen, which seeks to impress instead with the promise of spectacle (Atkins 2006). This disappearance of the player offsets some of the advantages of real-time rendering that make machinima a new chapter in motion graphics.[5] Here, what Agamben says of early cinema applies to the interruption of motion graphics that is machinima: "In the cinema, a society that had lost its gestures tries at once to reclaim what it has lost and to record its loss"(Agamben 2000, 53). For, arguably, machinima recoups the gestures of play, compensating for a loss of theatrical and cinematic gestures that seem difficult or impossible in videogames. In terms of this effect of alienation and distancing, Walter Benjamin observed that "the more an acting subject is interrupted, the more gestures we have" (Benjamin 1977). Benjamin read the Brechtian epic theater as a systematic interruption of the frame, of narrative representation and context, of myth and plot—of the things that since Aristotle had been considered pivotal for the dramatic genre. Samuel Weber argues that Benjamin's writing can be read as an instantiation of what he is writing about, "perhaps because the citability of gesture already entails a mode of writing" (Weber 2008, 97). Without customized game engines and video capture tools, machinima moves in jerks and jolts; rather than seeking to overcome this limitation, machinimators tend to accept it as something to toy with, something to be mobilized for aesthetic effect. Experimental animators working with game engines "have created a form of animation that exemplifies some of the possibilities for production and distribution that are unique to digital animation" (Crawford 2003, 120; cf. Nitsche and Thomas 2004). As motion-capture animation and inverse kinesthetics approximate our idea of human movement and gesture ever more closely, computer-generated imagery becomes legible as related to theater and cinema; just how these relationships are negotiated is something that may become clearer through a closer look at machinima.

The first decades of cinema raised the expectation that this new medium would extend and refine the expressive tradition of gesture from pantomime. Insofar as silent film was comparable to pantomime in its wordless expression, it did foreground a stylistic limitation that was a consequence of a typology of gestures, as a schematic reduction of affective communication. But on the other hand, if mimodrama chose silence as a means of expression, early film did not: it was less an artistic abstraction than a technical constraint. Just as silent film used writing, with intertitles and subtitles guiding the viewer through the moving images, the expanding menu of in-game communications, particularly in networked gaming, pushes the possibilities of drama and interaction in game space. By the same token, if an emphasis on action as movement in space (in sound film as in many computer games) came at the expense of an expressive ballet of gestures, one might surmise that machinima is also a way of injecting the complexity of miming and gestures into the kinds of games that tend to reduce their elementary setup to something as easily summarized as a pantomime or puppet theater handout. Thus, machinima can reintroduce some of the narrative potential that tends to be eliminated from the compressed standard plot that marks many first-person shooter (FPS), adventure, or strategy games, and it can elaborate on the rudimentary narratives that introduce open systems for gaming, such as *Second Life* or *The Sims*. Nonetheless, it is too narrow to define machinima as an exploration of modes of play as modes of production, since some games are already "designed to be manipulated and modified by the people who purchase and play them" (Salen and Zimmerman 2003, 539; see also Lowood 2009). This is not to deny that machinima has opened up unforeseen avenues for creative expression using computer games. It is rash to claim, as some game critics are wont to do, that "film theory fails in the face of such tweaked-out technology," for if the digital animation made possible by computer games is used for short films, series, or even feature-length movies, then clearly the legacy of moving image forms may retain some relevance, especially if it includes traditions from theater and puppeteering (Salen 2003, 540). On the other hand, it is equally valid to assert the fundamental departure from cinema in computer space, for instance the simple fact that the computer image, now omnipresent in the production and editing of all manner of visual media, derives its point-and-click addressability from radar screens. Too often, anecdotal attempts to string together a history and typology of computer games fail to take into account the basic technical dispositive and its influence on the body—from Jacquard looms to Zuse's film, from oscilloscopes to Sutherland's Sketchpad, and indeed from the lurking style of early machinima like *Diary of a Camper* (1996) to machinima clips pushing the limits of in-game dance like *The Man Who Can* (2006) (Sutherland 1980).[6] Furthermore, while film theorists emphasize the immobilizing of their audience, the gamer's gaze is perhaps fixed on a screen or display, but in terms of their twitchy virtuosity with a mouse, keyboard, joystick, or other input device, gamers are hardly immobilized. Yet Salen is right to associate machinima with a kind of déjà vu, for it cites not only gameplay but many other media discourses as well. Conceiving cinema in terms of the reception of an event, Bellour (1976) had called film an "unattainable" text, but today, loops of repetition and mashups of moving images on TV, video, DVD, and computers have become commonplace and make film easily citable as still image or clip. Similarly, earlier video games took place only as real-time graphics and were hard to stop, interrupt, cite, and archive; machinima is possible only because this is no longer the case. This situation in turn raises questions about the status of repetition and remixing, ranging from remakes and parodies to citations, allusions, video responses, and more. For instance, when machinimators such as Kendra Flemons remodel singer R Kelly's *Trapped in the Closet,* is that a video remix via *The Sims* or consumer-generated censorship that replaces steamy scenes with innocuous ones? When the physics experiments of Randall Glass's remarkable *Halo* machinima *Warthog Jump* cite the seventies' arcade game *Cannonball* and are in turn cited by a flash game on the Web (*Warthog Launch*), is it sufficient to celebrate a mass mediation of user-generated content?[7] Here, pseudo-stabilities are upset in an entirely different way, as machines are placed under the control of a new kind of subjectivity that is aligned not just with a technical setup but with its historical possibilities and impossibilities (Guattari 1992, 29; Mehigan 1993). This underscores the point that cutting off video games, arcades, and consoles from their conceptual and technical history across several media dispositives risks losing sight of what precisely makes machinima's cut-and-paste montages fascinating and worthy of popular appraisal (and academic attention).

Of course, reading machinima as cinematic is not to ignore its ludic aspects: interrupting, citing, and reassembling the game, machinima is a way of playing with the game; by the same token, it plays with cinematic conventions (Kinder 2002). While "on the one hand, images are the reification and obliteration of a gesture," as Agamben puts it, "on the other hand, they preserve the *dynamis* intact (as in Muybridge's snapshots or in any sports photograph)" (Agamben 2000, 55). By analogy, since the collective memory of digital culture is hampered by the impracticability of anything like a museum of hardware and software, machinima in the form of captured replays or as video of tournament games serves as one way of preserving (interrupting and fixating) the experience of gameplay—something that is otherwise irretrievably lost once a platform has become outdated (Hagen 2005). As Agamben surmises,

In cinema, a society that has lost its gestures tries at once to reclaim what it has lost and to record its loss. An era that had lost its gestures is, for that very reason, obsessed with them; for people who are bereft of all that is natural to them, every gesture becomes a fate. And the more the ease of these gestures was lost under the influence of invisible powers, the more life became indecipherable. It is at this stage that the bourgeoisie—which, only a few decades earlier, had been firmly in possession of its symbols—falls victim to interiority and entrusts itself to psychology.[8] (Agamben 2000, 53)

Drawing a parallel between Tourette's proto-cinematographic study of human motor coordination and Muybridge's photographic motion studies, Agamben asserts that "the element of cinema is gesture and not image" (ibid., 55). Citing Gilles Deleuze's argument that sought to erase the fallacy of a distinction between image as psychic reality and movement as physical reality, Agamben developed his ethics and aesthetics of "gestural cinema." Deleuze held that cinematography consists of movement-images; and Agamben extended this argument to show how "cinema leads images back to the homeland of gesture" (Crary 1990, 110). It is not too much to infer here that reading machinima by its gestures may lead video game studies back to the conditions for a possibility of computing culture—to the triple setup of computer graphics, interface ergonomics, and database form.

To an extent, these three aspects correspond with experiences of embodiment as distinguished by phenomenology: from motor control and perceptive self-awareness, to the socially and culturally constructed body, to technological embodiment as it is observed, for instance, in film and computer games (Ihde 2002, xi et passim). What this means for reading machinima through gestures is that there is no clear distinction between the controlling manipulation of gaming interfaces and the controlled in-game motions of avatars. The necessary but ultimately impossible distinctions among controller syntax, avatar performance, and embodied player are collapsed once one asserts that the technological premise of video gaming's audiovisual setup is indeed programmed by what makes the relation between rapid finger twitches and 3D illusion possible, namely, that they mean each other, point to each other, supplement each other. This is observed not only in media history and film theory but also in the applied motion studies that underlie the discipline of scientific management and ergonomics.

Despite Deleuze's (1987, 56–57) dismissal of phenomenology in considering cinema, it is perhaps worth mentioning that Maurice Merleau-Ponty's approach to cinema outlined a "sign language of gesture and gaze" (Merleau-Ponty 1962, 68; 1964, 58). While Deleuze considered the phenomenological account of media experience as merely derivative in relation to natural visual perception, Merleau-Ponty saw that the structures of cinema were refined and perceived in the cinematic experience: "The meaning of a film is incorporated into its rhythm just as the meaning of a gesture may immediately be read in a gesture: the film does not mean anything but itself" (Merleau-Ponty 1964, 57). And parallel to the phenomenological analysis of modes of embodiment via technology, applications of moving image technology also allowed much more exacting study of bodily motion. A scientific attitude to efficiency was already evident in the historical roots of film, for instance in Marey's "stoppages at the moment of pose," and it inevitably became crucial for usability engineering, whether for work or for play.[9] For computer games to avoid the programmatic and inevitable fatigue of repetitive strain, behaviorist or Taylorist assumptions about efficiency of motion have to be complemented by a consideration of motivation. If one asks what allows games to continue for hours, and what entices repeated play, then one has to ask also what enticed gamers, accomplished as they are in the interactive mode of interfacing with video games, to switch into the archival mode of performance that is machinima (Lowood 2007, 2008).[10] Once one adapts to computing culture—graphics, interface devices, and data space—one finds a way of communicating with others about computing culture. What congeals in gaming and in machinima is a set of gestures that may be read as the epistemic program of gaming culture's technologies, institutions, and machines: from management science, performance training for ever-improving reaction times, hand-eye coordination, speedy and ergonomic efficiency; from army mental tests, problem solving in mazes and puzzles, scenario planning; and from computer science, metonymic routing and database access (Pias 2002a).

While machinima can be made with the aid of just about any computer game, its early development owed not just to recordings of speed runs and other in-game performances but also to the increasing possibility and popularity of modifying game maps, skins, and tools for games like *Quake* and *Doom*. Salen and Zimmerman argue that "the player-as-producer paradigm takes the modification of a game so far that the invented activity no longer resembles the play of the game at all. Such is the case with machinima"(Salen and Zimmerman 2003, 550; see also Salen 2002). However, whether one takes the earliest examples, such as speed runs, or the many clips surfacing each day on the Web and in digital film festivals, the fact remains that these are mostly dilettantish efforts at harnessing the power of a game engine, and few attain a level of visual and conceptual sophistication that rivals the more costly productions of the imaginary counterpart, the professional animation or movie studio experts. It is ironic how readily academics in cultural studies have revived the eighteenth-century discourse of dilettantism as a direct challenge to the increasing specialization of knowledge and its organization into disciplines and professions; interviews with machinima pioneers such as Hugh Hancock and Paul Marino portray them as zero-budget challengers to Disney and Pixar.[11] Meanwhile, in late 2008 machinima.com, seeking to position itself as an entertainment network, announced a $3.85 million investment from MK Capital and other private investors to help fund expansion. With the proceeds, machinima.com commissioned fifteen television writers to create game-based comedy shows for the online site, a talent pool that includes former writers of such shows as *The Simpsons, Futurama,* and *Family Guy.*[12]

Yet more than half a decade ago, as students in my first machinima seminar grappled with the vicissitudes of producing and editing their first clips, they were unanimously struck by the Strange Company clip *Ozymandias,* since the Shelley sonnet concerns a series of framed acts of reading: a sculptor reading a royal's face, a traveler discovering the statue, a narrative "I" listening to the report, and a reader encountering the sonnet.[13] To be sure, the sonnet contains the act of reporting an ancient inscription that commands the reader to be in awe of a grand (yet fallen) ruler, but it is quite evident that the sculptor's reading of the "hand that mocked them" and the royal visage already was no mere copy but also an act of ridicule and distancing, long before the statue falls into ruin. This seems lost on the lonely walker in the sand as represented in the machinima clip; Strange Company seems to suggest that low-budget machinimation will be alive and moving on in the face of the ruined omnipotence and arrogance of Hollywood, without acknowledging that the machinima clip and the poem consist in a series of gestures pivoting around an imitation of that powerful point of reference. Shelley offered a reading that is both faithful and resistant, both subservient and subversive; its transfer and transformation of (gestures and poses associated with) power is not a succession or eclipse. The ruin's hold over the "traveller from an ancient land" persists, while his contemporary scene is a vast wasteland.

More recently, amateur production has come to be seen in opposition less to professionalism than to its side effects, as it were. Yet to oppose the managed process of a large, established animation outfit to the ingenious inventions of the end-user amateur means to ignore the very structures and strictures of the computer in the production of audiovisual culture. The overly hyped paradigm of user-generated content, so often associated with machinima in particular and with game modifications and fan art in general, is unsatisfying precisely because its concept of "content" is so resolutely divorced from the technical and historical conditions of computers, networks, and media industries. As Hans Magnus Enzensberger pointed out decades ago, what is new about the new media is the fact that they are no longer dependent on programs (in the sense of content scheduling) (Enzensberger [1970] 2003). It would be better, perhaps, to regard the impact of electronic mass media in terms of programming in the computer science sense, for in a very real sense what is generated by the technical setup of computer graphics, interface devices, and database structures is first and foremost the idea of the computer user. Instead of opposing a natural organic body to one conditioned by technology, we see that all bodies produce culture by interfacing with prosthetic devices: "the body never springs forth fully realized but is instead shaped and constructed by the gestures that machines impose upon it"(Noland 2006, 220; see also Keep 1999). As the small motor motions required by human-computer interactions can become inscribed as automatisms or habits, they accentuate the body's originary articulation. Michel Foucault had already documented how handwriting, for instance, "presupposes a gymnastics—a whole routine whose rigorous code invests the body in its entirety, from the points of the feet to the tip of the index finger" (Foucault 1979, 152). As machinima cites the gestures of gaming, it foregrounds and exhibits the timing and motion patterns acquired and necessary for advanced skills in *Max Payne* or *Counterstrike*, including, for the purpose of gameplay and concurrent recording, the ability to manipulate several game controllers simultaneously with hands and feet. While PlayStation sports characters are not programmed to do anything but play their sport, a helpful glitch in *Halo* that makes a game character's head pop up when the gun is lowered all the way allows for a puppeteering index of talk. Thus, what animation pioneer Alexandre Alexeieff observed still holds true for recamming and screen captures in game environments: "For movie animators, the movement which happens on the screen for the first time is the one which makes the original work: contrary to the photo-film, which is satisfied with a photomechanical analysis of the real events that the synthesis of the screen recreates as déjà vu" (Alexeieff 1996, xxi).

In this way, computer games, and the explorative or emergent play that includes the making and distribution of digital videos (or of code that would render, in the right engine, as a video sequence), are simply a way of learning to interface with computers—a way of coping with technology. Accommodation to repetitive tasks is a question of timing and motion patterns. Certainly the definition of computer workspace and of human-computer interaction is deeply influenced by "desktop" logistics that normalize the motions of hands and tools, with drawers, folders, files, pens, rulers, and so forth all in their predetermined and standardized relation to each other. Two-dimensional document processing anticipates the screen metaphors implemented in the computer; data processing is the application of standardized tools according to industrial norms in prescribed sequences of motions and calculations (Fairthorne 1956; Pias 2002b). Time-motion study of repetitive labor, using film cameras and stopwatches, also laid the foundation for ergonomics and scientific management: measuring efficiency in such activities as bricklaying, Frank and Lilian Gilbreth found a different set of motions used for faster work than for slower work, and accordingly developed the laws of a human motion economy.[14] Of course, it was Taylor's parsimonious charge that work resembled childish play, and management was going to eliminate invisible waste by establishing firm rules. Inversely, one may suggest, machinima is a form of emergent play in that it toys with the game, and in that it records its own kind of time-motion study of the gamer: whether in speed runs or in quasi-documentary footage of other in-game performances—even as brought to light by the humor of Jim Munroe's walking tour of *Grand Theft Auto* in his magnificent (and deceptively simple) machinima clip, *My Trip to Liberty City*.

As popular machinima examples such as the restaging of episodes of the TV show *Friends* on a *Quake Arena* server or the in-game talk show *This Spartan Life* amply illustrate, machinimators can borrow from the self-reflection of established formats while at the same time arousing curiosity among peers, fans, and academics.[15] Not all machinima needs to function as self-conscious commentary on the stereotypes about computer games, as is too often said of *Red vs. Blue*. Most popular examples follow the rather narrowly circumscribed conventions of established entertainment media.[16] This is the problem I see with a game like *The Movies*, which has been called "machinima in a box": precisely because here, gameplay and the recording, editing, scoring. and distributing of digital clips coincide, the bulk are rather kitschy after-images of Hollywood fantasies and generic sets. Machinima is at its best where it is not merely *recording* a media setup but reconfiguring its parameters, for instance in juxtaposing immersion and reflection, as April Hoffmann's *The Awakening* or Rooster Teeth's *The Strangerhood* do. Real-time animation such as the live puppeteering performances by the ILL Clan (e.g., *Common Sense Cooking*, 2003) is far from being truly improvisational, considering the highly constrained and circumscribed dispositives of networked gaming that is required even before any camera angles or shot sequences are hashed out. This is all the more readily recognized in approaches to machinima that interfere with the digital assets of a game, modify a game engine, or heavily edit and postprocess recorded game action.[17] Clearly, the player is both subject and object of play, and may herself be played; machinima brings this to the fore, as does the work of Beijing artist Feng Mengbo, who replaced all *Quake 3* characters with his own likeness, holding a video camera instead of a weapon in machinima clips and canvas displays, and in installations that invite gallery viewers to shoot at him.[18]

Thus it becomes clear that gestures are not improvisational or loosely user generated; rather, they are highly scripted. To understand the preparation necessary for machinima clips like *Dance Voldo Dance*, one might consider the dance notations that emerged around the same time as the time-motion study of manual labor: surely they do not constitute the invention of choreography, but they established a regulation of motion that is not merely descriptive but openly prescriptive. Distilling elementary gestures and simple bodily actions from the sequences he observed, Laban sought to establish a holistic system of bodies in time and space. (Brandstetter 1995, 46f) This kind of kinetographic script (or "Labanotation") is not dissimilar from the way computer games make the hands of the gamer dance on the keyboard or game controls; like dance notation, a computer program can prescribe the gestures of its user, testing in terms of advances in game space whether they are precisely timed and executed in order. Interestingly, successful machinima music videos like *Rebel vs. Thug* for Chuck

D (2002) or *In the Waiting Line* for Zero 7 (2003) face the constraints as artistically productive, rather than seeking to overcome them in elaborate modding; a concise index of increased capability might be the elaborately choreographed *Cantina Crawl* machinima dance series that is the result of multiplayer collaboration in *Star Wars Galaxies*.[19] What Agamben observed as a loss of meaning of certain gestures under the influence of mechanization also establishes new possibilities of social inscription by the technologies that make motion visible and "scriptable," with consequences for sports, theater, work, and everyday life. Just as telegraph operators had to practice until the encoding and decoding had become fully automatic, computer games train the player to acquire certain motor skills—after which, one need only continue the analogy, the transmission of communications has become possible. The mimetic dimension of playing "as if" is complicated by the dark compulsion to repeat over and over again, which tilts gaming and machinima beyond creative mimicry and into a performance that is as much a (dis)play as it is a test—a controlled exhibition that is training humans in the apperceptions and reactions required by living with technology. (Of course, Theodor Adorno scoffed that "art that seeks to redeem itself from semblance through play becomes sport" (Adorno 1997, 100; see also Huizinga 1955, 470f). Machinima, the dance of gaming gestures, is both a test of games and of gamers, a performance in the context of art as in the context of sport. But beyond that, what machinima demonstrates is that computer games are ultimately not about adventure, strategy, speed, or violence so much as they are about usability as a precondition to communication. The required motor skills, hand-eye coordination, and reaction speeds apply equally to radar operation, flight simulation, word processing, Web surfing, and playing (with) games.

The point of looking at computing culture from the vantage point of gestures is not to introduce some kind of humanism through the back door of technological determinism. Certainly it is true that adaptation to the simplest tool already commences a tendency toward the machine. The increasing interpenetration of bodies and machines raises a question about the essential quality of gesture. Stelarc's *Movatar* exhibits the many ways in which the body can be constrained and programmed by the machine.[20] What is at stake in playing with game technology is much more than consumer entitlement: to believe so would be to forget media history. For too long, definitions of games and play have emphasized an exercise of freedom, following early romanticism (Huizinga 1955; Ehrmann 1968, Callois 1979). I doubt that what makes machinima interesting, and what allowed it to grow so substantially over the past decade, is simply the consumer's carefree explorative play, in ways more or less condoned by the programmers and marketers of computer and console games. After a certain shelf-life, many games have been re-released with a relaxed license that encourages modification; as user-generated content is observed to enhance brands, this time-span is shrinking—another reason to debunk claims to a subversive or counter-marketing ethic of machinima. Copyright law and contemporary culture converge in the conundrum of end-user license agreements for game engines, in-game assets, and computer programming as a kind of writing. (Irvin 2005) [21] What is intriguing about machinima, I would argue, is precisely a way of citing, reclaiming, and incorporating the gestures of disparate discourses of mediation, gestures of communication and information, of repetition and citation, of embodiment and accommodation in handling technologies that are increasingly pervasive.

Vilem Flusser's information theory of gestures holds that the less a gesture informs, the more it communicates, and the more information it contains, the more difficult it is to read it as a mere gesture. Inversely, the more kitschy a gesture is, the less information it contains; empty gestures are pleasing insofar as they require no effort to be decoded (Flusser 1994). Indeed, a theory of gesture should strip out any surmise as to a gesture's potential intentions, whether this is argued with phenomenology or with Taylorist motion studies, for to define gestures as expressions of an intention raises difficult matters of freedom and subjectivity. Avoiding the ontological trap, a better (if still rough) definition might be that gestures are those bodily motions that betray no direct cause—that is, they are not reflexes or involuntary motions, they are part and parcel of our expressive, semantic culture. Our ideas about acting as representation of human motion continue to change with each technological step, from sound to color to television, and from postprocessing to computer-generated imagery to the affordances of game engines. A formalized vocabulary of gestures was transferred from theater and puppeteering to early film, and now, in any cursory study of the computer history of gaming, one can discern the legacy not only of media discourses of communication and the rituals of art forms but also the legacy of Taylorism and usability engineering, of army testing and flight simulation. Flusser warned that conjectures about a general theory of gestures may tempt one to see it as a metatheory of communication, of art criticism, of a future theory of the absurd, and in fact as a metatheory of magic and of ritual—validity claims that are surely too broad and insufficiently deep. Nonetheless Flusser went on to suggest that we try to distinguish communicative gestures that are directed toward someone else, gestures of labor that directed toward material, phatic, disinterested gestures that tend to be directed toward nothing in particular, and self-reflexive gestures that ritually refer to themselves. Gameplay tends to include all four types, juxtaposed and commingled to different degrees, and they are certainly inscribed in the genealogy of the technologies used in any computer and gaming setup: but it is in the last sense in particular that a gesture is "the exhibition of a mediality: it is the process of making a means visible as such," as Agamben writes. Precisely in this sense, machinima is a way of observing, commenting on, and archiving the mediality of our setup—citing the gestures of gaming as the gestures of computing culture.

Notes

1. See <http://rvb.roosterteeth.com>.

2. Two eloquent appeals for a historically and conceptually rigorous study of gaming are Ian Bogost, "Comparative Videogame Criticism," *Games and Culture* 1, no. 1 (January 2006): 41–46, and Alex Galloway, *Gaming: Essays on Algorithmic Culture* (Minneapolis: University of Minnesota Press, 2006).

3. It is worth noting that like Pierre Lévy, André Leroi-Gourhan refers more to the Catholic teleology of Teilhard de Chardin than to Darwin or archeology or anthropology for support for his history of technology.

4. For a gesture's socioeconomic and cultural context, see Radan Martinec, "Gestures That Co-Occur with Speech as a Systematic Resource," *Social Semiotics* 14, no. 2 (2004): 193–213. Compare Adam Kendon, *Gesture: Visible Action as Utterance* (Cambridge: MIT Press, 2004), especially chapter 4.

5. PlayStation Home, an online environment built by Sony, offers machinima-ready tools in its Stage Set, and machinima tools are also being built into new games, including, for instance, *Left 4 Dead* (2008) and *Uncharted 2: Among Thieves* (2009). The *Unreal* engine was used by George Lucas for previsualization, and The History Channel used the engine for *Rome: Total War* to stage televisual battles. Other examples include the machinima Volvo ad *Game On*, by NYU-CADA students, a series of machinima "Video Mods" on MTV2, produced by Alex Coletti and Tony Shiff, as well as the UPN show *Game Over* and the Canadian children's show *ZIXX* on YTV.

6. For all machinima examples mentioned in this text, see <http://www.machinima.com> and <http://www.archive.org/details/machinima>.

7. See <http://rkellyscloset.com/the-sims-machinima-in-the-closet-chapters-1-5> and <http://www.warthog-jump.com>, respectively.

8. Discarding all reference to consciousness, American experimental behaviorism tried to discount mental activity and experience by focusing exclusively on observable interactions in environments. As John B. Watson wrote, "Psychology as the behaviorist views it is a purely objective experimental branch of natural science. Its theoretical goal is the prediction and control of behavior. Introspection forms no essential part of its methods, nor is the scientific value of its data dependent upon [. . .] interpretation in terms of consciousness" (Watson 1913). Consequently, mental labor would have nothing to do with the mind, consisting instead in the spatiotemporal organization of motion; education would aim not for comprehension but rather would constitute training to optimize certain functions according to a rule-oriented process.

9. Regarding Etienne-Jules Marey, chronophotography, and gesture, see Sekula (1999), Braun (1984, 1997), and Marey (1878).

10. The inroads machinima makes into the art world can be seen, most recently, in the Laguna Beach Art Museum's exhibit, "WoW: Emergent Media Phenomenon" (2009), in the work of the

Second Life Machinima Artists Guild, at <http://slmachinimaarts.ning.com>, in the entries to the Bitfilm Festival 2009 (Hamburg and Tel Aviv) or in the MachiniCast Machinima Award Show, at <http://www.MachiniCast.com>.

11. See <http://www.strangecompany.org/page.php?id=26> for information on Hugh Hancock and <http://blog.machinima.org> for information on Paul Marino. Marino, for example, proposes the equation "Hollywood + Moore's Law = Machinima" (Marino 2004, 11).

12. *BusinessWire*, November 9, 2008. As of summer 2010, Machinima.com claims $14 million in venture capital. See Ben Fritz, "Machinima Directors Step Up Their Game," *LA Times* (August 29, 2010), <http://www.latimes.com/entertainment/news/la-ca-machinima-20100829,0,6035173 .story>.

13. See <http://www.strangecompany.org/Ozymandias>.

14. The Taylorist use of the camera became itself the object of cinematic observation in the 1950 movie *Cheaper by the Dozen*, based on the Gilbreth family. See Frank B and Lilian M Gilbreth, "Application of Motion Study," in *Management and Administration*, September 1924, n.p.

15. See <http://www.unr.edu/art/DELAPPE/Gaming/Quake%20Friends> and <http://www .thisspartanlife.com>, respectively.

16. This includes many documentary and archival approaches to game worlds, as well as clips mimicking TV, remaking film scenes (often using the original sound track), and so forth. Also worth mentioning in this conjunction is the convergence of game-themed comics, or "gamics" (see <http://www.gamics.com>); see "Games + Comics = Gamics," *Globe and Mail* (Toronto), April 5, 2009, <http://www.theglobeandmail.com/news/technology/games-comics-gamics/ article812003>. There are also some literary efforts regarding machinima, for instance, "Moving Pictures," by Mike Hoefflinger (<http://packetswitched.blogspot.com/MovingPicturesPSP2005f/ MovingPicturesv09HTML.htm>) and "Give the Dog a Bone," by Patrick Kolan (<http:// jumpbuttonmag.com/?p=21>).

17. See <http://www.atlas-enterprises.net> and again <http://sh.roosterteeth.com>.

18. See <http://www.thingsasian.com/goto_article/article.2950.html> and <http://q4u1.uchicago .edu>.

19. See <http://www.furplay.com>.

20. See Stelarc, "Movatar: Inverse Motion-Capture System," on his Web site, <http://www.stelarc .ca.com.au/movatar/index.html>. Compare Andy Clarke's discussion of Stelarc (Clarke 2003, 115). A company called GestureTek recently announced that Microsoft will license its video gesture control technology for use with the Xbox Live network: using networked cameras, gamers can manipulate real-time visuals using full-body gestures, for instance moving left or right to steer a snowboard down a simulated mountain (Project Natal).

21. Compare also the presentations at the Play Machinima Law Conference at Stanford University, April 2009 (<http://kotaku.com/5293190/watch-the-play-machinima-law-conference>).

References

Adorno, Theodor. 1997. *Aesthetic Theory*. Minneapolis: University of Minnesota Press.

Adorno, Theodor. 1978. *Minima Moralia: Reflections on a Damaged Life*. London: Verso.

Agamben, Giorgio. 2000. Notes on Gesture. In *Means Without End: Notes on Politics*, 49–60. Minneapolis: University of Minnesota Press.

Alexeieff, Alexandre. 1996. Praise of Animated Film. In *Giannalberto Bendazzi, Cartoons: One Hundred Years of Cinema Animation*. Bloomington: Indiana University Press.

Atkins, Barry. 2006. What Are We Really Looking At? The Future-Orientation of Video Game Play. *Games and Culture* 1 (April): 127–140.

Bellour, Raymond. 1975. The Unattainable Text. *Screen* 16 (3): 19–28.

Benjamin, Walter. 1977. What Is Epic Theater? In *Illuminations*, ed. Hannah Arendt, 147–154. New York: Schocken.

Brandstetter, Gabriele. 1995. *Tanz-Lektüren: Körperbilder und Raumfiguren der Avantgarde*. Frankfurt am Main: Suhrkamp.

Braun, Marta. 1997. The Expanded Present: Photographing Movement. In *Beauty of Another Order: Photography in Science*, ed. Ann Thomas, 150–184. New Haven, CT: Yale University Press.

Braun, Marta. 1984. Muybridge's Scientific Fictions. *Studies in Visual Communication* 10 (1): 2–22.

Caillois, Roger. 1979. *Man, Play, and Games*. New York: Schocken.

Clarke, Andy. 2003. *Natural Born Cyborgs: Minds, Technologies, and the Future of Human Intelligence*. Oxford: Oxford University Press.

Crary, Jonathan. 1990. *Techniques of the Observer: On Vision and Modernity in the 19th Century*. Cambridge: MIT Press.

Crawford, Alice. 2003. The Digital Turn: Animation in the Age of Information Technologies. In *Prime Time Animation*, ed. Carol Stabile and Mark Harrison, 110–130. New York: Routledge.

Delaney, Kevin. 2004. When Art Imitates Videogames, You Have "Red vs Blue." *Wall Street Journal*, April 9.

Deleuze, Gilles. 1987. *Cinema 1: The Movement-Image*. Minneapolis: University of Minnesota Press.

Ehrmann, Jacques. 1968. *Homo ludens* Revisited. *Yale French Studies* 41:31–57.

Enzensberger, Hans Magnus. [1970] 2003. Constituents of a Theory of the Media. In *The New Media Reader*, ed. Noah Wardrip-Fruin and Nick Monfort, 261–275. Cambridge: MIT Press.

Fairthorne, R. A. 1956. Some Clerical Operations and Languages. In *Information Theory*, 111–120. London: Butterworth.

Flusser, Vilem. 1994. *Gesten: Versuch einer Phänomenologie.* Frankfurt: Fischer.

Foucault, Michel. 1979. *Discipline and Punish: The Birth of the Prison.* New York: Viking.

Guattari, Felix. 1992. Regimes, Pathways, Subjects. In *Incorporation,* ed. Jonathan Crary and Sanford Kwinter *(Zone 6)* New York: Urzone.

Hagen, Wolfgang. 2005. The Style of Sources. In *New Media, Old Media: A History and Theory Reader,* ed. Thomas Keenan and Wendy K. H. Chun, 157–175. New York: Routledge.

Hancock, Hugh, and Johnnie Ingram. 2007. *Machinima for Dummies.* New York: Wiley.

Huizinga, Johan. 1955. *Homo ludens.* Boston: Beacon Press.

Ihde, Don. 2002. *Bodies in Technology.* Minneapolis: University of Minnesota Press.

Irvin, Sherri. 2005. Appropriation and Authorship in Contemporary Art. *British Journal of Aesthetics* 45 (2) (April): 123–137.

Keep, Christopher J. 1999. The Disturbing Liveliness of Machines: Rethinking the Body in Hypertext Theory and Fiction. In *Cyberspace Textuality: Computer Technology and Literary Theory,* ed. Marie-Laure Ryan, 164–181. Bloomington: Indiana University Press.

Kelland, Matt, Dave Morris, and Dave Lloyd. 2005. *Machinima: Making Animated Movies in 3D Virtual Environments.* Boston: Thomson.

Kinder, Marsha. 2002. Narrative Equivocations between Movies and Games. In *The New Media Book,* ed. Dan Harries, 119–132. London: British Film Institute.

Leroi-Gourhan, André. 1993. *Gesture and Speech.* Cambridge: MIT Press.

Lowood, Henry. 2009. Warcraft Adventures: Texts, Relay and Machinima in a Game-Based Story World. In *Third Person. Authoring and Exploring Vast Narratives,* ed. Pat Harrigan and Noah Wardrip-Fruin, 407–428. Cambridge: MIT Press.

Lowood, Henry. 2008. High-Performance Play: The Making of Machinima. In *Videogames and Art: Intersections and Interactions,* ed. Andy Clarke and Grethe Mitchell. London: Intellect Books.

Lowood, Henry. 2007. Shall We Play a Game: Thoughts on the Computer Game Archive of the Future. <http://www.stanford.edu/~lowood/Texts/shall_game.pdf>.

Marey, Etienne-Jules. 1878. *La méthode graphique dans les sciences expérimentales et principalement en physiologie et en médecine.* Paris: Masson.

Marino, Paul. 2004. *3D Game-Based Filmmaking: The Art of Machinima.* Sebastopol: Paraglyph.

Mauss, Marcel. 1935. Les techniques du corps. *Journal für Psychologie* 32:3–4.

Mehigan, Tim. 1993. Brecht and Gestus: The Place of the Subject. *Faultline* 2:73–95.

Merleau-Ponty, Maurice. 1964. Film and the New Psychology. In *Sense and Non-Sense,* 48–59. Evanston, IL: Northwestern University Press.

Merleau-Ponty, Maurice. 1962. *Phenomenology of Perception*. Atlantic Highlands, NJ: Humanities Press.

Nitsche, Michael, and Maureen Thomas. 2004. Play It Again, Sam: Film Performance, Virtual Environments, and Game Engines. In *New Visions in Performance: The Impact of Digital Technologies*, ed. Gavin Carver and Colin Beardon, 121–138. Abingdon, UK: Swets & Zeitlinger.

Noland, Carrie. 2006. Digital Gestures. In *New Media Poetics*, ed. Thomas Swiss and Adalaide Morris, 217–243. Cambridge: MIT Press.

Pias, Claus. 2002a. Digitale Sekretäre: 1968, 1978, 1998. In *Europa: Kultur der Sekretäre*, ed. Joseph Vogl and Bernhard Siegert, 235–251. Zurich: Sequenzia/Diaphanes.

Pias, Claus. 2002b. *Computer Spiel Welten*. Munich: Sequenzia-Verlag.

Salen, Katie. 2003. Strange Universe: The Art of Machinima. In *Future Cinema: The Cinematic Imaginary after Film*, ed. Jeffrey Shaw and Peter Weibel, 538–541. Cambridge: MIT Press.

Salen, Katie. 2002. Telefragging Monster Movies. In *Game On: The History and Culture of Video Game*, ed. Lucien King, 98–111. London: Laurence King.

Salen, Katie, and Eric Zimmerman. 2003. *Rules of Play*. Cambridge: MIT Press.

Sekula, Alan. 1999. The Body and the Archive. In *The Contest of Meaning: Critical Histories of Photography*, ed. R. Bolton, 343–349. Cambridge: MIT Press.

Shannon, Claude E., and Warren Weaver. 1962. *The Mathematical Theory of Communication*. Urbana: University of Illinois Press.

Sutherland, Ivan E. 1980. *Sketchpad: A Man-Machine Graphical Communication System*. New York: Garland.

Watson, John B. 1913. Psychology as the Behaviorist Views It. *Philosophical Review* 20:158–177.

Weber, Samuel. 2000. Between a Human Life and a Word: Benjamin's Excitable Gestures. In *Mediatized Drama, Dramatized Media*, ed. Eckart Voigts-Virchow. Vol. 7, *Contemporary Drama in English*, 15–30. Trier, Germany: Wissenschaftlicher Verlag.

Weber, Samuel. 2008. *Benjamin's -abilities*. Cambridge: Harvard University Press.

IV Machine Cinema

Douglas Gayeton, dir., *Molotov Alva and His Search for the Creator* (2007)

11 How Do You Solve a Problem Like Machinima?

Michael Pigott

Machinima often appears to adopt the stylistic articulations of other forms, such as traditional cinema and the music video. This borrowing of style occurs either as a subconscious defaulting of the creator's conception of style or as a conscious appropriation, arising from a desire to acquire authenticity through identification with an established form. This desire is often tempered by a concurrent urge to play with and subvert those forms. Nevertheless, one of the driving factors in the adoption of cinematic style is the need to prove that machinima can be as good, and as worthy, as more prestigious and accepted art forms. It often seems that the measure of success for machinima creators is how much like a "real" film their work is. This, I suggest, can result in the integration of all the clichés of cinema, TV, and the music video as proof of mastery over the technical aspects of machinima production.

However, showcasing the technical possibilities of machinima is not the only reason a machinima maker might seek comfort in the familiarity of the cinematic form. Those concerned more with the content, with genuine artistic expression, or even just burdened with the simple desire to tell a story also adopt the conventions of cinematic narrative and visual style. These conventions constitute a contemporary language of visual storytelling that crosses many art forms, though its roots are in the great art of the twentieth-century: cinema. For the vast majority of machinima viewers the touchstones of their visual culture are cinema, TV, and video games, and it is arguably still predominantly from the first two that they gain their experience of visual narrative. Therefore it seems only natural that they should provide the initial point of reference for the first machinima storytellers. As the form evolves and matures, the audience will evolve along with it (assuming it diverges from the path of traditional film, rather than being absorbed into it), and a new "form language," as the Hungarian film theorist Béla Balázs (1970, 30) called it, will slowly develop.

Essentially, the question I want to ask here is, what are the stylistic conventions of machinima?—a question that admittedly might seem a little premature at this early stage in the form's evolution. The machinima corpus is fractured, unwieldy, and rapidly growing, in both quantity and quality. To tie a definition to this loose and mutable amalgam would seem foolish, so in this essay I will strive only to describe what I see as two broadly defined movements in machinima. The first evolutionary trajectory is that of machinima oriented toward a cinematic ideal, the second is an unguided and almost careless movement toward an individuated, self-sufficient, and ultimately new form language. I use the word "careless" not to imply error but in the sense that many of the most innovative machinima works seem to lack a desire for recognition as "real art," or an abiding concern with artistic merit. Movies of this kind are most frequently produced within game worlds like that of *World of Warcraft* (Blizzard Entertainment 2004), where the rules of the world are set and unalterable owing to the game's online nature, as opposed to works produced within user-created worlds built using offline game engines such as *Half-Life 2* (Valve 2004). They often contain references that make sense only to those who have already played the game and are familiar with the places, quirks, and famous events of its particular world and surrounding community. Indeed, the whole point of some of these works is often missed entirely by casual viewers if they are not involved in the game themselves. Yet this phenomenon points only to an originality and specificity of content, and my concern here is with style. Therefore, in looking at these two movements I will try to identify, with the aid of some specific examples, elements of style that are borrowed and elements that are newly emergent.

To limit the possible breadth of this research, I have chosen to confine my case studies to examples of machinima made in *World of Warcraft*. This choice is not meant to imply the inferiority or unimportance of machinima made outside *World of Warcraft* (many would claim that this is where the true testing ground, focus, and future of machinima lie) but should be seen rather as an attempt to somewhat narrow the field, and to maintain clarity in comparison. *World of Warcraft* machinima contains examples of practically every kind of machinima—story, dance and music, gameplay recordings, other forms—and, more important in this context, clear examples of both movements within machinima, the movement toward a cinematic ideal and the movement away from cinema and into the unknown. I have also chosen *World of Warcraft* because of its currently booming movie industry and its vibrance, innovation, and variety of player-produced films. Moreover, the tremendous popularity of *World of Warcraft* machinima makes it impossible to ignore.[1] Even though my study is constrained in this way, I hope any conclusions will apply to the larger field of machinima. The decision to make machinima in the *World of Warcraft* environment necessarily entails an acceptance of greater limitations than those afforded other game engines—the camera is not entirely free to roam, and the landscape itself is fixed, the mise-en-scéne for any movie unalterable (except through postproduction techniques). However, such limitations can serve to emphasize the style and content of the film itself over the creative technical use of the game engine.

The Problem of Analogy

Writing about the emergence of film as an art form, Béla Balázs once asked, "What is the difference between photographed theatre and film art?" (1970, 30). Technically, one medium is very much like the other, especially when one considers films produced in the early years of cinema's history. The admission that film is *like* a play on-screen tends to stick in the throats of only film academics and makers, and the analogy temptingly offers a simple reduction of a varied and sometimes contradictory amalgam of styles and forms for a public that isn't all that worried about rigorously accurate definition. That difference, however, is what sets film apart and makes it a once new, now established art form.

Balázs answers his own question with a list of the technical abilities of film that theater lacks. The list seems only to describe new and more flexible ways of showing, of telling stories visually, with the fundamental content, the "what is being shown," remaining constant. However, it is the way of showing, and of storytelling, peculiar to an art form that constitutes a "form-language" for Balázs. The means of articulating and communicating the content both produce and limit the aesthetic potential of the art form, and essentially *are* the art form.

This idea of a form language is something that I return to later. For now I would like to dwell for a moment on a tendency that is hinted at in Balázs's question, a tendency that is not necessarily a bad thing but that can sometimes prove to be a limiting factor. Balázs proposes an opposition between two types of film, one type that is nothing more than theater plus the recording technology of film, and another type, the newly minted and essentially different art of cinema. But why bring theater into the discussion at all? The strategy of analogy is a useful tool for explaining and theorizing, but, like any tool, what it can do is limited by its shape and original purpose. The insight and understanding that it offers are often equaled by a reciprocally narrowed horizon.

This is why I find the idea of a form language so useful. It emphasizes the specificity and uniqueness of a form's mode of communication and implies a two-way transaction between the work and its audience, as well as an obligation on the part of the audience to "know" the language for the transaction to occur at all. A form language is a set of habits (rather than rules) that arise through use. Its origin lies as much in the desire and appetite of the audience as in the innovative force of the artist. And it never just pops into existence. It always occurs as a negotiation between those two entities, a settling of chaotic possibility in the interest of understanding. The interesting thing about some machinima (and especially some *World of Warcraft* machinima) is that it assumes a very specialized knowledge and set of expectations on the part of the audience. The more it can assume, the more fully it can lay claim to a specialized territory.

Bolter and Grusin's (1999) work on remediation adds credence to the idea that machinima might function predominantly as a resetting of old texts or traits in new contexts, but it also suggests that new art forms need not depart radically from the forms that preceded them. It may suffice, rather, for a new form to use, alter, abuse, and transform elements of what came before.

One of the obstacles in machinima's path toward establishing itself as an art form in its own right is the assumption that if a work doesn't abide by the rules of visual narrative as outlined by the many guides to film editing available online and in book form, it won't make any sense to the viewer, and will find itself swiftly dismissed as amateur or even childish (the secret fear at the heart of many machinima makers). What is necessary for this obstacle to be removed is the willingness to take a chance, an attribute that is becoming increasingly apparent in many recently released works (the work of Tristan Pope, for instance). The fortuitous circumstance of *World of Warcraft* machinima is that the films are by default community-based, and so assume a degree of viewer knowledge. The great proliferation of *World of Warcraft* movies in the game's relatively short history has meant that certain conventions from the days of pure gameplay videos have seeped into the style of story-based works. The *World of Warcraft* machinima community has developed its own set of internal conventions because its target audience is itself. This statement, however, is not definitive, as an increasing number of machinima works made in *World of Warcraft* are aimed at non-players, even nongamers, as are the majority of machinima pieces made outside *World of Warcraft*. Movies such as *Return* (Rufus Cubed Productions, 2005) and *Rise of the Living Dead III* (Sleeping Dogs Productions, 2006) display this aspiration.

To describe machinima as analogous to film or animation also limits the possibilities of the new form. Machinima creators should be encouraged to ask not how their films can become more like real cinema but what machinima can do that traditional cinema cannot. The real advantage of machinima over traditional cinema or animation is that it offers the ability to create fantastic, ambitious spectacles and narratives without the same cost (in money, time, or manpower), therefore placing fewer constrictions on expression, creativity, and stylistic flexibility. In a perverse kind of payoff, this freedom is again constricted by the built-in limitations on camera movement and mise-en-scène of a product never intended to provide artistic freedom. This is explicitly the case for *World of Warcraft* machinima, though more and more, games come packaged with built-in game-editing applications (sometimes even machinima-creation applications, as is the case with *The Sims 2* [Electronic Arts, 2004]). The availability of freedom, however, does not always ensure its enjoyment, as many machinima makers consciously choose to style their works after popular cinema and animation.

This is not necessarily a bad thing. A perfectly viable future for machinima lies in its incorporation into the Hollywood studio machine as a technique complementary to traditional computer-generated imagery. Indeed, should the technique evolve to a point of near photorealism, parallel with improved 3D game engines, its obvious time- and money-saving aspects would make it impossible to ignore as a possible replacement for many entrenched studio processes.

Before taking up a close study of some selected works I would like to consider some of the entrenched stylistic principles of visual narrative—the kind from which escape is practically inconceivable at this stage—and also to look more closely at Balázs's concept of a form language.

Lev Manovich, in *The Language of New Media* (2001), observes that the conventions of cinema permeate almost all forms of emergent media technology, not just those that fit the term "visual narrative." He writes, "A hundred years after cinema's birth, cinematic ways of seeing the world, of structuring time, of narrating a story, of linking one experience to the next, have become the basic means by which computer users access and interact with all cultural data" (ibid., 78–79). When graphical interfaces for computer systems developed, the ready-made language of cinema was adopted by default. With the advent of windows and the progressive spatialization of data into virtual 2D and 3D environments, we came to navigate those spaces using the articulations of the cinematic camera: "zoom, tilt, pan, and track" (ibid., 80). The imaginary camera is embedded in most multimedia applications and artworks. With this in mind, it is not surprising that machinima makers would choose to use a conventional cinematic viewpoint in their movies. For one thing, the game engines they use are all already infected. So the machinima movie often is, by virtue of the tools available, already in a cinematic mode, even before it is shot. Escape from this convention is difficult to conceive, yet it might not be too much of a stretch to suggest that any attempt at reconfiguring the viewpoint might very well occur in the world of machinima.

The concept of a form language accounts for both the technical capabilities of the medium and the evolved conventions of its use. Balázs makes it clear that a form language is constituted not just by its technical abilities but also by how they are used—the agreed language that arises between the artwork and the audience. A medium has both a mechanics (the physical and conceptual properties of production and presentation) and a grammar (the agreed rules of usage of those properties). Both of these aspects contribute to the creation of a range of expressions for the artist. However, while one of these aspects (mechanics) is concrete, and surmountable only through technological innovation, the other (grammar) is self-imposed and can conceivably be overcome at any time through sheer force of will.

Balázs claims that the new art form cinema was not born simultaneously with its technology but several years later, with D.W. Griffith's inauguration of the rules by which stories would be told visually for the remainder of the century.[2] The great strength of Balázs's work, though, lies in his admission that the state of an art form owes as much to its audience as to its innovators. The two evolve together, each one taking turns to push the other forward. From here arises the difficulty in distinguishing the bad from the new, the mistake from the merely different. As difficult as it is for the artist to conceive of a truly new form, or a new use of a form, it is perhaps even more difficult for an audience to accept the unfamiliar. However, this parallel evolution permits the audience influence through a process of selection, and the form itself to slowly open up new areas of perception for the viewer.

And so we come to machinima, an art form that, if we take the history of cinema as a guide, should soon reach its point of self-determination. The question this prompts is whether any formal innovation will gain the requisite momentum to steer a course for the form as a whole, thereby defining its own form language, or whether it will take its place within a future family of visual media, all finding their formal roots in cinema. The influence of mainstream cinema on the emergent form seems not to present a problem for most, as introductions and guides to cinematography and film editing are regularly recommended on machinima Web sites and blogs; for instance, Jennifer Van Sijll's *Cinematic Storytelling: The 100 Most Powerful Film Conventions Every Filmmaker Must Know* (2005) is, among several similar works, recommended on the machinima LIVE! Web site, machinimalive.com.[3]

Rise of the Living Dead III and *Return*

The *Rise of the Living Dead* series, produced by Sleeping Dogs Productions, provides microcosmic evidence, within its three episodes, of a desire to create increasingly cinematic machinima. With each new episode the production values and technical skill in shooting, editing, and acting (voice and virtual) increase dramatically. One of the most obvious progressions is from the text dialog of the first episode to the true voice acting of the second and third episodes. The first episode is characterized by its many rough edges, a distinctly lo-fi atmosphere, and a lack of refinement in its approach to editing and shooting. The second episode improves on all these aspects, but it is with the third episode, released a full year after the first, that the series gains a professional sheen and the possibility of comparison with commercial animation becomes startlingly real. The most important thing to note is that the story, and the style of its communication, make sense to the average viewer who has never played *World of Warcraft*.

At this stage, I would like to point out some of the specific editing and shooting articulations of *Rise of the Living Dead III* that can be identified as originating in traditional cinema techniques. The episode begins with the cleverly reset genre staple of a reporter being awoken by a call from his boss and given orders to cover a breaking story, the kind of story he has "dreamt of covering ever since I got in the news business." In this case the reporter is a gnome, and the breaking news is the swarm of undead threatening the population of the in-game world of Azeroth (the buildup to this point having been described in the first two episodes). Tellingly, the creators have chosen to begin this sequel by introducing a new character in a pre-credits sequence, who will proceed to discover the situation as it now stands (having progressed slightly from the last episode) along with the viewer, before we eventually end up back with the characters we already know—a very Hollywood-sequel thing to do, and a regular setup from the horror genre, to boot.

In this first scene the conversation between Bannon (the gnome) and his girlfriend is conveyed through a shot-reverse-shot structure. The 180-degree rule is respected, and the cuts are not jarring or disorienting—they *flow*. This is all good continuity editing. Moreover, not only is the movie displaying Hollywood style, it might also be classified as *stylish*. The (imaginary) camera, rather than remaining still, glides smoothly in and out; coupled with the ominous yet restrained music,[4] this movement creates a feeling of impending doom. One of these slow zooms on Bannon achieves a selective focus, blurring his girlfriend's head in the foreground right (figure 11.1), and when he leaves at the end of the scene he actually walks into the foreground and out of focus, a move that focuses the viewer's attention on his anxious girlfriend in the background. All of these shots are framed artfully, not just efficiently.

The action moves to Gnomevision headquarters, where Bannon is briefed on the situation and then begins a news report, gravely informing the viewers of the danger

Figure 11.1
Selective focus in *Rise of the Living Dead III* (2006)

that lies before them. What follows is an amalgam of familiar horror tropes: interrupted communication, glimpses of the monster, the realization that it is close by, and finally the blood-splattered screen.

Later on there are more examples of a skillfully deployed use of focus, and throughout the movie the shooting and editing comply with mainstream cinematic conventions, as well as displaying a determined use of those conventions for dramatic effect. Watching this film, I feel as though the director and editor J. Joshua Diltz is stretching *World of Warcraft* machinima as far as it will go toward becoming like what is conventionally understood as cinema. The movie draws from two genetic pools, horror and the fantasy epic (in the mode of *The Lord of the Rings* [New Line Cinema, 2001, 2002, 2003] specifically). The movement between sites of action, between fronts in the great battle against evil, and the tone established through those movements are especially indicative of the influence of this type of film on the creator.

Another characteristic that the movie shares with a film like *The Lord of the Rings*, and with a great number of contemporary blockbusters, is the use of digital effects during the editing stage to create much of the content. Several shots in the movie seem to have been made using a program called Model Viewer (WoW Model Viewer 2005–10), which allows the user to isolate a *World of Warcraft* character and record his movements in front of a monochrome background. This permits the relatively seamless superimposition of a character into another shot, in a similar way to green screen technology in the film industry. This technique presents a wide spectrum of possible uses, yet the director of *Rise of the Living Dead III* chose to use it to approximate the kinds of shots one finds in cinema, and particularly in animated features and on TV shows.

Return, a simple tale of a soldier returning after many years at war to find his home destroyed and significant other dead, is a much-lauded, critically acclaimed (taking an award at the 2005 Machinima Awards and the Blizzcon Movie Contest 2005), and enormously popular feature from Rufus Cubed Productions. It too exhibits a studio sleekness and polish absent from most machinima. Like *Rise of the Living Dead III*, it displays a desire to model itself after traditional cinema. This comes across not only in the formal style of the movie but also in a few telling details inserted by the creators, perhaps as sly indulgences or perhaps as statements of this movie's intent to be taken seriously as a type of cinema rather than as frivolous fan art. The end credits proclaim "*Return*—A *Warcraft* Motion Picture," and "Shot on Location in Frostwolf." The intent, it seems, was to produce a fantasy epic film in *World of Warcraft* that would be perceived as being just like a "real" film.

From the opening sequence's smoothly gliding vistas, it is clear that this machinima work will be of a different caliber from most. We are soon presented with a man, Voldigar, staring out across the sea from the side of a ship, his back to us. The voiceover begins, and we view a rapidly edited flashback to his past, describing his departure

Figure 11.2
Use of depth and framing in *Return.*

from his home and his "sweet Gwyneth." The stillness of the shots on the ship stands in contrast to the constant movement of the camera in the flashback sequence. A series of fades string together images of sadness, determination, and nostalgia. The framing of these shots reveals an understanding of classic cinematic organizations of mise-en-scène. In one we see Gwyneth in the foreground, kneeling on a bed and crying, her face hidden in her hands, as in the background Voldigar stares into the corner, again with his back to us (figure 11.2). The low plane of the bed and the vertical bedpost create a framing structure in the foreground, endowing the background with great depth and making Voldigar appearing small and distant. A shot of this sort imparts a great deal of information and emotional resonance in a very short time; it is an effective deployment of a tested cinematic device. In all of the shots the camera glides smoothly, matching its speed to the violence of feeling attached to the action. In one scene the camera retreats, tracking backward down a stairway and away from Gwyneth. An exterior shot of Voldigard's home shows him exiting and walking quickly, not looking back, through the foreground left and out of the shot, a typically cinematic articulation of determination. The flashback ends with the camera hurtling toward the pair, who sit, backs turned, staring into their fireplace. As the camera view passes between their heads and meets the flames, the image flashes and fades back to Voldigar on the ship, again a stylistically familiar articulation, ending the flashback with a flare of light that fades to return us to the present, and tying that flare logically to an on-screen light source.

Later on, once Voldigar has returned and found his home in ruins and Gwyneth gone, we are treated to an emotive scene change. Another character, Liadov, has just confirmed that she knows where Gwyneth is when the screen turns black, and remains so for several seconds. An image slowly returns. It is slightly blurry at first, and then appears to be manually focused, whereupon we find Voldigar kneeling at a grave, with Liadov in the background. Again the shot is framed cinematically, with good presentation of depth, the characters in a diagonal relationship, one in the foreground, the other in the back right. The apparently manual focusing is a stylistic touch inserted by the creator in the postproduction stage. Additionally, the decision to withhold the image for a few moments suggests a confident grasp of this storytelling grammar.

The success of this movie is overshadowed only by the promise of the sequel, the trailer for which evinces an even greater command of cinematic technique on the part of the cinematographer and editor, Terran Gregory. It looks like a theatrical trailer one might see in any Cineplex. It is tightly edited, mixing the loud moments of action and excitement with moments of quiet character development, the music soaring and dipping in time, suggesting that this movie will have an epic sweep, and an element of everything the viewer could want—action, romance, drama. It showcases many of the stylistic techniques already seen in the first film but makes it clear that the process has advanced, and that an entirely new level of near cinematic quality has been achieved. Its purpose is unashamedly to entice, to awe, and to tease. For most of the machinima-viewing public (especially those who follow the *World of Warcraft* movie production) it cannot but impress, ironically achieving a greater awe-inducing effect than most Hollywood trailers. The cinema audience has, to a large degree, become immune to epic scale and elaborate special effects, simply because there is nothing surprising about them anymore: we expect as much from Hollywood. However, for the machinima audience, innovation and technical advancements are still very much capable of taking one's breath away. Which brings me to my concluding point in relation to the machinima that wants to be cinema—the technical spectacle.

In an essay on *Half-Life* (Sierra, 1998) and other technologically impressive games, Andrew Mactavish identifies a tendency among academics to "ask questions within the context of narratives: are computer games narratives?" (2002, 33). This approach, as Mactavish makes clear, ignores not only the sensory stimulation provided by visuals, sound, and interactive gameplay but also the element of technological spectacle: the degree to which the player is thrilled by the sophistication of the graphics, sound, and underlying artificial intelligence effects. Narrative certainly plays an element in most games but is by no means the primary interest for either developer or player. However, a large amount of the player's satisfaction with a game may stem solely from the perceived quality of the game engine and graphics; its representation of the cutting edge in current game technology.

I would like to suggest that machinima viewers derive a similar satisfaction. Much of the surprise and pleasure produced by these two movies comes from their technological and technical sophistication. They evince both a mastery over the technology of machinima and a technical adeptness (the creator's ability to use the technology skillfully, in the sense of impressive cinematography and editing). The ability to use a game engine to create something that resembles a real film constitutes much of the attraction of machinima for both the creator and the audience.

Leeroy!!

The infamous *Leeroy Jenkins*[5] sketch, perpetrated by the Pals4Life *World of Warcraft* guild, is a deceptively simple, even flippant, gameplay recording. It is by far the most widely viewed *World of Warcraft* movie, and its popularity extends well beyond the confines of the *World of Warcraft* gaming culture. It purports to be a recording of a genuine period of gameplay, featuring the player's group huddled and discussing their strategy before entering a particularly difficult room. The viewpoint remains continuous throughout—it is the ordinary player interface (rather than a clean interface—minus buttons, chat-box, and statistics—as is usually the case for story-driven machinima movies). We hear the voices of the actual players as they communicate through the *Teamspeak* program. All of the technical aspects of the movie can be attributed to real gameplay, but the action that occurs, the comedy that plays out, can only be attributed to clever staging.

The group stands in a circle around the leader (figure 11.3), who is giving the pre-battle pep talk. During actual gameplay, however, there would be no real reason to form such a perfect circle around someone in this way, as the players' game avatars and voices are not connected in a way that can be perceived by other players, nor is a player's line of sight directly linked to that of his or her avatar (we do not see through the avatar's eyes). The real reason for this formation is more likely a concern to make it clear to those watching the movie that the person speaking is the one in the middle of the circle—to allow the viewer to attribute the voice to the avatar and, more important, to create a spectacle. It is spectacle that creates story, telling us, "before the raid the team gathered in a circle and discussed their plans." The leader turns around as he talks, as if looking at the members of his group. This is not just recorded gameplay but performance, and what's more it is theatrical performance. The virtual camera rolls as the Pals4Life guild performs a work of guerrilla theater in the world of *World of Warcraft*.

Leeroy, who has been sitting off to the side of the circle (clearly distinguished for the viewer by this fact) and is marked as being AFK (away from keyboard), has missed the strategy meeting. He suddenly awakes and charges into the room, yelling his own name. The surprised group follows, and its members are quickly killed. However, because this is gameplay and not staged story, the group's in-game death does not preclude the posthumous expression of the members' anger. And so the piece is brought to an end with the players' recriminations and Leeroy's statement that "at

Figure 11.3
Staging gameplay in *Leeroy!!*

least I got chicken." Throughout the slaughter the camera remains tied to just one character, in the default "following" camera position of *World of Warcraft* gameplay. Nevertheless, we are undoubtedly being "told" a story; no matter how authentic the footage feels, it bears the hallmarks of a certain amount of staging. This is evident in the position and framing of the group during its strategy meeting, and most notably in the way the camera is made to preemptively swing around in order to capture Leeroy's headlong charge into the dragon room.

The movie takes the form of one long take. There is no editing aside from the decision of where to begin and end the piece (but even this displays signs of authorship), and there is no postproduction work in evidence. This surface absence of authorial intent and interference, however, should not eliminate the possibility that this is a piece of genuine community art.

What is interesting about the piece is that the narrative straddles the virtual world of the game and the real world of the player, rather than just creating a narrative within an enclosed fictional world. It is a story about playing the game, set both within and without, yet taking the *World of Warcraft* landscape as its site.

World of Warcraft movies somewhat negate part of the drive toward the display of technical mastery because many of the rules are set (e.g., the game's physics, graphics, and virtual geography), as a result of the online nature of the game. Machinima makers are not permitted control of these parameters, so in a curious way the *World of Warcraft* movie industry functions in what is theoretically closer to a model of real-world film-making, in comparison to machinima pieces made using fully manipulable game engines. This might seem to contradict my earlier statement that the conditions of production within online worlds catalyze the movement away from traditional cinema, but if we look closely at those conditions, then perhaps the relationship will become clear.

The machinima maker uses a virtual camera (screen capture software or demo recording), coupled with the already cinematically modeled viewpoint of the game, to capture events within the game, having perhaps already scripted and choreographed the event. The action occurs within a constant and virtually concrete online world, running temporally parallel to that of the player. The original, creative element of the process occurs when the director decides what to shoot, where, and from what angle, and how to frame it.[6] This produces the raw material for editing and sound tracking, at which point the movie is born. This all sounds a lot like filmmaking in the real world, although with an altogether different origin for the raw material.

We might go so far as to say that gameplay movies produced in an online world invoke the ideal of filmic realism. This obviously cannot apply literally to machinima, but it might prove a useful concept if we consider that, at one phenomenological remove, the computer screen presents a world for the player, a world that is perceptually constant and interactive, like the world outside it. And so a simple gameplay movie might be considered the equivalent of a home video. Therefore, in the *World of Warcraft* movie industry we theoretically have the possibility of a perverted sort of cinéma vérité, a kind in which every aspect is constructed.

My contention here is not, however, that all new machinima works should fit the mold of *Leeroy!!*, only that this movie represents quite clearly the side of machinima that is not concerned with comparisons with traditional cinema, and which illustrates one possible approach to fashioning an original and fresh form of visual narrative.

Illegal Danish—Super Snacks

Illegal Danish—Super Snacks (Dementia Myndflame, 2006) is, like *Return*, a wildly popular movie, this fact evinced not only by download figures but also by the rabid uptake of the trailer for the sequel. It is also held in high regard, having taken the Best Picture award (along with several other bests) at the first Xfire/Blizzard *World of Warcraft* Machinima Contest. For me, it represents a synthesis of the evolved language of traditional cinema and animation with the freedom of form and content offered by machinima. This work uses Hollywood style, but it also *abuses* it, recklessly toying with conventions, creating a rapid, colorful montage that is both dazzling and slightly confusing on initial viewing. The story is too complicated to elaborate here, so I will describe just a few of the movie's characteristics, and encourage readers wholeheartedly to seek it out and watch it for themselves, have they not already done so. That said, I should mention that while the story is not unintelligible to those without knowledge of the game and its culture, it certainly helps to have played it, especially in relation to some of the game-specific jokes and visual gags.

The movie presents a frenetic and slightly madcap tour through a specific dimension of the *World of Warcraft*, one in which the real-world player is not acknowledged as an extragame entity but in which characters ask each other to join their guilds and talk about their in-game powers and abilities. It draws freely from the realms of fantasy, comedy, and sci-fi. Its humor is scatological and infectious.

The director and editor, D. W. Hackleman, displays a confident command of cinematic convention, and that confidence extends to blatantly flaunting those conventions at numerous points throughout. The style of the movie is at times reminiscent of anime, at others of traditional film, and toward the end there is a sequence that can only be described as an integrated music video. Yet through all this it retains its originality.

The original music also deserves mention, having been composed by the other half of the sibling pair responsible for the film, Clint Hackleman. In a form in which the majority of the music is borrowed, the quality of the score for *Super Snacks* is doubly impressive. The sound and visuals are woven so tightly as to create a fluent, propulsive motion, full of rhythmic shifts and tonal variations. The movie does not reject Hollywood style in the way that *Leeroy!!* seems to, but neither does it concern itself overly with mimicking that style. It appears polished and professional, while somehow eluding the cinematic standard.

What distinguishes *Super Snacks* is its ability to play freely with both style and content. It mixes elements of cinematic storytelling with elements not usually found in cinema or in the game itself, such as apparently handheld in-game footage and the final music video sequence, which goes so far as to include a caption providing the title of the music and details of where to get it. The movie contains many references to the game that are clearly aimed mostly at players, such as the familiar in-game quest-giving screen inserted at the point when one character gives another a task, and the image of the Murlocs (amphibious froglike creatures) worshiping a tank (while entertainingly cute to most, this has special resonance for a *World of Warcraft* player). Several scenes rely almost entirely on the knowledge of the viewer—gags will not come off; sequences will seem pointless; indeed, certain scenes will not make any sense unless the viewer is aware of some of the idiosyncrasies of the game. For instance, the scene in which the characters Rosi and Basutei arrive at their destination in Kalimdor ends on what could be a very confusing note. As Rosi becomes increasingly irritated by Basutei's preoccupation with a snack-vending machine, we jump from a shot of the interior of the watchtower (where they are) to a long shot from outside the tower. The second shot is accompanied by the sound of an animal snarling, and we see the vending machine pushed out of the top of the tower by some sort of large beast—to the uninitiated an incongruous match. This leap assumes some knowledge of Rosi's in-game character class (which she has previously mentioned): she is a shape-shifting druid, and can "go feral" like this when she chooses. This is game-specific at the level of content, but it manages to inform the style of the piece. The breakneck editing rockets along on the assumption that the audience requires only a certain amount of information to recognize what is happening.

Many sequences in *Super Snacks* are constructed out of extremely brief close-ups or medium shots. The montage moves rapidly, skillfully using the characters' built-in actions and dance routines in combination to produce a distinctive form of visual narrative. The greater structure of the piece also has a rapid pace, jumping from one location and time to another, indifferent to the conventions used to ease the audience between spatial and temporal sites in mainstream cinema. It sometimes feels a little like a series of cut-scenes without a game (I mean this in the best possible way).

As for a form language, *Super Snacks* might indicate a step toward a particular evolution of visual narrative. It certainly feels slightly foreign to a cinematic sensibility on first viewing, though with repeated viewings one comes to realize that it does have an order and logic all of its own. However, it might equally indicate a progression toward a freedom of form, a rejection of convention, and the will to produce for a small specific audience rather than a flattening of the stylistic possibilities in the hope that the work will appeal to as wide an audience as possible.

I hesitate to suggest a particular set of characteristics that might help to define this new form of language, as it would undoubtedly become inadequate within a short time. Yet there are certain tendencies that can be identified, such as the following:

1. An indifference to (though not necessarily an eschewal of) the conventions of visual storytelling originating in mainstream cinema
2. An orientation of content toward gamers, or at least an audience with a specialized knowledge (not just a tolerance for the whim of the artist)
3. A reliance on that specialized knowledge as a foundation on which to build a distinctive mode of representation

Conclusion

Contemporary machinima offers clear examples of both formal experiments and cinematic imitation. It is probably true, however, that examples of the latter far outweigh the former. We might suggest that the absence of a form language at machinima's inception called for the adoption of an already existing grammar. This, however, is no dark secret at the heart of machinima that I am exposing; likeness to cinema is for most machinima makers a measure of success, and the great volume of study already done on techniques of visual narrative has encouraged a rapid growth in the quality of production. *World of Warcraft* machinima displays both tendencies, yet the volume of story-based works consciously modeled on mainstream cinema and TV dwarfs those that attempt to break away from such influences. It remains to be seen whether that dissident element (and its audience) will gain enough momentum to succeed in determining a characteristic form language for machinima.

Notes

1. The hub of *World of Warcraft* machinima activity on the Internet is <http://www.warcraftmovies.com>. Here one can find the most complete collection of the works themselves, as well as download figures and viewer ratings.

2. While Griffith can be said to have popularized and consolidated the grammar of film language with *The Birth of a Nation*, the elements of this grammar can be identified in earlier works by Griffith and others.

3. Machinima LIVE! Web site, podcast downloads, <http://www.machinimalive.com/cms/index.php?option=com_content&task=view&id=61&Itemid=49>.

4. The music for this film, like that of most currently produced machinima, is borrowed, in this case from respected film composers such as Danny Elfman and Hans Zimmer.

5. Pals4Life World of Warcraft Guild. *Leeroy!!* (Pals4Life, 2005), 2 min., 51 sec.; <http:/www.warcraftmovies.com/movieview.php?id=1666>.

6. For an elaboration of the view that the primary creative force in filmmaking is that of the director on both the pro-filmic space and the manner of its recording, see Perkins 1981.

References

Balázs, Béla. 1970. *Theory of the Film*. New York: Dover Publications.

Bolter, Jay, and Richard Grusin. 1999. *Remediation: Understanding New Media*. Cambridge: MIT Press.

Mactavish, Andrew. 2002. Technological Pleasure: The Performance and Narrative of Technology in *Half-Life* and Other Hi-Tech Computer Games. In *Screenplay: Cinema/Videogames/Interfaces*, ed. Geoff King and Tanya Krzywinska, 33–50. London: Wallflower Press.

Manovich, Lev. 2001. *The Language of New Media*. Cambridge: MIT Press.

Perkins, V. F. 1981. Moments of Choice. *Movie* 58:1141–1145. <http://www.rouge.com.au/9/moments_choice.html>.

Van Sijll, Jennifer. 2005. *Cinematic Storytelling: The 100 Most Powerful Film Conventions Every Filmmaker Must Know*. Studio City, CA: Michael Wiese.

Software References

Half-Life. Sierra. 1998.

Half-Life 2. Valve Corporation. 2004.

Illegal Danish—Super Snacks. Dementia Myndflame. 2006.

The Lord of the Rings. New Line Cinema. 2001, 2002, 2003.

Model Viewer. WoW Model Viewer. 2005-10.

Return. Rufus Cubed Productions. 2005.

Rise of the Living Dead III. Sleeping Dogs Productions. 2006.

The Sims 2. Electronic Arts. 2004.

Teamspeak. Triton CI & Associates. 2003.

World of Warcraft. Blizzard Entertainment. 2004.

12 Machinimatic Realism: Capturing and Presenting the "Real World" of Video Games

Jeffrey Bardzell

Machinima videos are shot both inside of and using game worlds. That is, a machinima film from *Halo: Combat Evolved* (Microsoft Game Studios, 2001) not only is produced within the *Halo* fictional game world, it is also produced with the technical content authoring tools that *Halo* provides, and in particular its camera (though these tools are usually augmented with other tools). If these two facts establish that all machinima videos have a fundamental production relationship with the video games in which and with which they are made, they also suggest a likely relation between the meanings of machinima films and the meanings of their host games.

One can imagine a spectrum on which to map these relationships. At one extreme is an instrumental view and at the other is an immersive view. By instrumental view, I mean that one could imagine that the virtual world is merely an instrument, a neutral vessel, in which a machinimator is the source of content or meaning and the game world is simply and incidentally the space in which it unfolds. This view reflects a broader commonsense understanding of all language as a vessel that contains the meanings that we, as intentional and communicative beings, pour into it and transmit to others, a view critically explored in Lakoff and Johnson's seminal *Metaphors We Live By* (1980). This view is partly enabled by the practical reality that most machinima videos, unlike big-budget Hollywood films, are made by single directors operating under a single overarching vision. The concentrated creative agency of machinima videos positions them in a roughly analogous position to the auteurs, filmmakers such as French New Wave directors Truffaut and Godard, who stressed the importance of a single director writing the screenplay, doing the shooting, and so forth, to ensure that a film is the creative output of an individual who is skilled, has a distinctive voice, and has a special spirit whose relationship to the world is a source of art and meaning on film.[1]

One can also imagine an opposite extreme, what I refer to as an immersive view. According to this view, the game world *is* the real content, and a machinima video cannot have any meaning that is not bound up in it in some way. Because it is by means of the video game world that narrative or other video content is rendered available to our perceptions, and because this relationship thereby structures what viewers perceive and how it is understood, the world itself comes to dominate what is said (by circumscribing what can be said). This view echoes the perspective of Marshall McLuhan and his slogan "the medium is the message," which diminishes human authorial agency in meaning-making and places it instead in the medium itself (McLuhan 2003). This line of reasoning has been developed in the context of new media by Lev Manovich, who argues that software tools, such as *Adobe After Effects*, unleash visual languages that exceed the intentions or control of any professionals who work in them (Manovich 2001, 2007).

I characterize the instrumental and immersive views as the extreme positions on a spectrum because it is easy to imagine quite a bit of room between them. Thus, we can also imagine what might be called a mixed-reality view, which suggests that a machinima video is shaped by, and bears marks and traces of, its host game world, and at the same time it contains meanings external to that world. Such a view leaves room for meanings appearing in machinima films that are not only external to the game worlds but, more important, for which the game worlds are only incidental to the meaning. That is, a machinima video may contain meanings that are essentially *not* of the game world, though they can enter the game world's representational space through machinimatic means.

A purist's commitment to either of the two extreme positions seems hard to defend. The instrumental view suggests that the game world is in no significant way a part of the content of machinima, or if it is, it is because the machinimator wanted it to be that way; the game world's meanings can be voluntarily included or excluded. Yet it is hard to imagine any video where this is the case, and we can find some empirical confirmation of this skepticism of the fact that machinima communities themselves are overwhelmingly organized by game or world, though surely other organizational strategies are theoretically possible. The immersive view has the opposite problem, by suggesting that the "real world" is in no way a significant part of the content of the machinima except inasmuch as it has been integrated into the game universe. When so many machinima videos derive their meaning from the juxtaposition of worlds, such as *World of Warcraft 300*, an enormously popular machinima that represents key sequences in the film *300* (Snyder, 2006) using *World of Warcraft* (Blizzard Entertainment, 2004) images and video and *300*'s original audio, it is hard to accept the immersive view. More generally, the common machinima strategy of setting game visuals to real-world original or popular music sound tracks or original or imported voice acting suggests that the audio-video nature of machinima doubly increases the mixed-reality potential of the medium.

Let us proceed under the assumption, then, that the mixed-reality view is correct. This raises several issues for any theory of machinima.

• Virtual worlds offer backdrops, actors, visual styles, and narrative themes for machinima videos. How do these elements affect the contents of those videos?

• Virtual worlds offer the primary production and multimedia authoring technologies for machinima videos. How do these technologies affect the contents of those videos?

• What are the relationships among the machinimator's creative voice, the game, and the process of making machinima videos?

This essay seeks to explore these sorts of issues to contribute to an understanding of the ways that machinima captures and presents the reality of games and virtual worlds. I begin by examining ways in which film theory has engaged with the problem space of realism. Film theory offers a critical vocabulary, including sets of distinctions and a history of possibly useful examples, with which we can begin to think about machinimatic realism. I then try to situate this theory relative to machinima, whose "reality" is presumably distinct from the reality of cinematic film. The outcome of this exploration is to propose three stances that machinimators can take vis-à-vis the relationship between machinima and their host games. Next, I offer close readings of three machinima films from the *Halo* universe to apply and explore the critical ideas developed here. Finally, I identify some new difficulties and suggest additional refinements to this understanding of machinimatic realism.

Cinema and Reality

A major topic in film theory is the relationship between a film and the physical reality it represents. Production practices, in the hands of skilled filmmakers, shape the ways that reality is presented on the screen. For example, using wide shots is traditionally understood to help viewers perceive the context of an action, while close-ups are likewise traditionally understood to help viewers understand characters' emotional reactions. By building chains using shots that change the viewing distance, filmmakers are able to guide spectators' understanding and emotional identification. The use of handheld cameras, with their constantly moving, jerky nature, can create a sense of gritty presence that is often harder to communicate using stationary studio cameras. Film theorists, aestheticians, and philosophers have created conceptual vocabularies to describe the mechanisms by which film presents reality and, much more broadly, the aesthetic and ethical implications of the different choices. In this section I offer a summary of film theory that raises several major themes.

One highly influential account of cinematic relationships with reality is offered by Siegfried Kracauer's 1960 *Theory of Film* ([1960] 2004). In it, Kracauer returns to the origins of film in the 1890s, to identify two basic "tendencies" of film. The first tendency is represented by the brothers Auguste and Louis Lumière, whose work Kracauer refers to as "strict realist," because they simply "recorded the world about us for no other purpose than to present it" (Kracauer [1960] 2004, 146). The Lumières' films show workers leaving factories and trains arriving in stations, among other subjects, without any apparent artistic statement. In contrast to the Lumières' realism is an artistically stylized imaginative expressionism. The origin of this tendency, for Kracauer, is the "formative" tendency of Georges Méliès, who "gave free rein to his artistic imagination" to ignore "the workings of nature out of the artist's delight in sheer fantasy" (ibid., 145–148). Méliès's films are about fairy tales and dreams, such as *Voyage to the Moon* (1902).

From these two starting points, Kracauer elaborates the formal characteristics of both the realistic and formative tendencies. For example, in a realistic film, if action is shot on a set, then that set should be designed to convey reality faithfully; additionally, the movement that the camera captures is the objective movement of objects rather than inner or subjective movements. Formative or expressionist films have metaphorical sets that do not resemble a particular place but rather express the fears, hopes, or inner life of a character. Kracauer notes that good films should balance these two tendencies, but adds that they should do so in a way that the formative tendency follows the lead of the realistic tendency, because the realist tendency is closer to the "basic properties" of a photographic medium—"to record and reveal physical reality" (ibid., 151). One can trace the evolution of these two strands through the early decades of the twentieth century in silent film. Realism is the dominant strand in American silent film, including the work of Charlie Chaplin, Robert Flaherty, and Erich von Stroheim, who explored realist strategies such as deep focus and mise-en-scène (Monaco 2000). In Europe, where filmmaking was more closely associated with art, the formativist tradition is seen in the expressionist films of Robert Wiene, Friedrich Wilhelm Murnau, and Fritz Lang,[2] in which characters' internal psychological reactions were explicitly articulated on film using image distortion, exotic camera angles, sudden camera movements, lighting, and painterly sets.

Though the portions of Kracauer's argument cited champion realism on the grounds of its supposed connection to the basic properties of a photographic medium, much more is at stake than an aesthetic position. Much theorizing on the relationship between film and physical reality occurred as a response to fascist regimes'—in particular the Nazis'—use of propaganda. Films such as Leni Riefenstahl's 1935 Nazi propaganda film, *Triumph of the Will*, were successful as propaganda because they exploited the strengths of the film medium so well. Even today, *Triumph of the Will* remains troubling because of its juxtaposition of undeniable cinematic beauty with undeniable moral repugnance (Devereaux 1998). The German critic and artist Bertold Brecht (1898–1956) once characterized realism as "a major political, philosophical, and practical issue" (quoted in MacCabe 1986), a position he shared with Kracauer, whose earlier work focused on explicating how cinema became such an effective tool of fascism. For Kracauer, film lent itself to fascism precisely when it disengaged from reality to pursue fantasy, turning audiences' attention away from their social realities and into a dangerous form of escape. This line of reasoning clearly extends concerns about realism beyond aesthetics to philosophy and politics.

Building on this tradition is arguably the most important proponent of cinematic realism, the French critic André Bazin. A contemporary of Kracauer's, Bazin connects the value of cinematic realism to a range of specific cinematic techniques. Bazin advocated for getting the cinematic apparatus out of the way, so audiences can experience pro-filmic scenes as directly as possible, that is, so the emotional content of films would come from the filmed reality itself (Fabe 2004, 51). To achieve these goals, for Bazin, the film must be set in a recognizable, historical place and time, and each scene should be presented "in its physical entirety," rather than "analyzed bit by bit" (Bazin [1967] 2005, 35), so that filmed scenes are "based on a respect for the continuity of dramatic space and, of course, its duration" (ibid., 34). For Bazin—and here he seems to be invoking the neoclassical aesthetic theory of the three unities originally proposed in Aristotle's *Poetics* and quite influential in French aesthetic theory—reality is manifest in unified action that unfolds in a unified space and time, and it is this reality that the film must present.

Developing this idea, Bazin connects specific cinematic production techniques with the meaning of the film as it is experienced by the viewer. In a realist film, action unfolds in lengthy, deep focused, wide shots, that is, sequences that have few cuts, are equally in focus in both the foreground and the background, and take in whole scenes, as opposed to a reliance on close-ups. The benefit of composing events in such shots, for Bazin, is threefold: such composition "brings the spectator into a relationship with the image closer to that which he enjoys with reality"; such shots bring about in viewers "a more active mental attitude," because viewers have some choice as to which parts of the scene they attend to; and finally such shots introduce ambiguity into the film, because such filming techniques do not predetermine the meaning of the shot (ibid., 34–35).

Bazin develops these ideas in an essay titled "The Evolution of the Language of Cinema," which suggests that his purpose is to chronicle the emergence of cinema as an expressive language. Like Kracauer and Brecht, he was motivated in part by the value that films should bring audiences closer to reality, rather than directing them away from it into mere fantasy. Realism, for Bazin, is not simply recording reality as it unfolds as the Lumières had done; he once wrote in praise of Welles, "To anybody with eyes in his head, it is quite evident that the one-shot sequences used by Welles in *The Magnificent Ambersons* are in no sense the purely passive recording of an action shot" (ibid., 34). Rather, realism is found in constructing episodes in such a way that the artist can leverage the medium of film to make a scene "more realistic" by clarifying its own internal coherence (MacCabe 1986, 181).

Yet if realist film transcends the mere recording of reality, an accomplishment made possible, according to Bazin, by the filmmaker's clarification of an event to present it in the most real way, the problem remains that the director is still mediating the audience's relationship to reality. In other words, Bazin's neorealism may seem better disposed to produce a reality effect, that is, an experience that *feels as though* it's real, rather than reality itself. This is a position argued by Colin MacCabe, who writes in a critique of Bazin, "I argue that film does not reveal the real in a moment of transparency, but rather that film is constituted by a set of discourses which (in the positions allowed to subject and object) produce a certain reality" (ibid., 182). Realism is not, for MacCabe, a transparent mode of filmmaking that reveals reality but another *style* of film, that is, another type or genre of discourse.

This criticism has stood up over time and is echoed in more recent works on realism, including Stephen Prince's 1996 essay, "True Lies." Prince agrees that Bazin's realism is a rhetorical style, a discourse coded for transparency, but he also points out that Kracauer's original distinction between realism and formativism breaks down in today's digitally produced films. A film such as *Jurassic Park* (Spielberg, 1993) is neither realist nor formative, according to the traditional definitions, because much of what is filmed on-screen was never a part of the pro-filmic reality (there were no actual dinosaurs chasing the actors around), yet the film is seen as at least perceptually realistic, in contrast to films associated with expressionism.

To address neorealist theory's lack of applicability to contemporary digital filmmaking methods, Prince suggests replacing indexical notions of realism (i.e., that reality and film are in a causal relationship) with a correspondence-based notion, in which "realist" describes a film that "structurally corresponds to the viewer's audio-visual experience of three-dimensional space" (Prince 1996, 32). That is, instead of realism inhering in the relationship between reality and film, it inheres in a correspondence between two relationships, (a) reality and film and (b) reality and our perceptual experience, such that (a) and (b) are structurally similar. Prince's move from correspondence between reality and film to filmic representation-perceptual representation shifts concerns for realism away from reality itself and toward a relational analysis of modes of capturing and representing it.

In this section, I have developed five key premises of realism in film theory, which I present here in summary for clarity.

• A useful distinction can be made between films that seek to represent external reality in a more or less faithful way, and films that seek to present artistic visions of reality. These two tendencies have been named realism and expressionism or formativism, respectively. (Here I am summarizing Kracauer, as described above.)
• The question of realism extends beyond mere aesthetic preferences and engages much larger philosophical considerations of reality and epistemology, as well as ethical and political considerations. In other words, much more is at stake for realism than a taste for a certain kind of film. (This point summarizes the positions of Brecht and Kracauer.)

• Realism is, among other things, a practical achievement of certain production practices, including set design, uses of the camera, and editing techniques. (This was Bazin's contribution.)

• Realism, rather than an effect caused by reality, can instead be seen as a rhetorical or discursive effect. That is, realist film is not actually a transparent window on reality but rather a style that imitates or presents itself as such a window. (This position is argued by MacCabe, as summarized above.)

• Realism can be seen as inhering not in a causal relationship between reality and film but rather in a structured set of correspondences between a presentation of reality on film and the presentation of reality given to us by our perceptions as embodied subjects in a three-dimensional world. (This position was advocated by Prince in response to emerging digital filmmaking practices.)

The cinematic relationship to reality is clearly complex, entailing production techniques as well as philosophical positions on narrative appropriateness, film spectatorship, the ethics of film, and the aesthetics of the cinematic language.

From these theories of cinematic realism, it is possible to identify four dominant styles of reality portrayal. I do not take a position on whether any of these is more or less an example of realism; all I am seeking to do is identify discursive styles that describe how reality comes to be portrayed on film.

1. *Portraying reality as if it had been merely recorded*, associated with the Lumières.
2. *Presenting reality in a stylized way to facilitate fantasy and expression*, inaugurated by Méliès, prewar German expressionism, and described by Kracauer as formativism.
3. *Presenting reality by staging it in a clarifying yet truthful way*, associated with the films of Chaplin, Welles, and de Sica, and developed as a theory by André Bazin, now commonly referred to as neorealism.
4. *Presenting reality through a structural correspondence to viewers' phenomenological experience*, as developed by Prince to explain the perceptual realism of films such as *Jurassic Park*.

Each of these is today recognized as leading to different reality effects. In other words, each of these embodies a cinematic language, itself built out of directorial choices such as camera angles, set construction, editing, and choice of narrative, and yields a certain spectator experience of the reality shown.

Of these four styles, two can be described as oriented toward a relatively objective portrayal of reality (i.e., reality as it exists "out there") and the other two are oriented toward a much more subjective portrayal of reality (i.e., reality as it is experienced by subjects). Specifically, styles 1 and 3 are both objectively oriented in the sense that their meaning is understood to inhere in or derive from the reality filmed, and film is accordingly understood as a more or less transparent medium through which we see it. It is highly doubtful that these styles actually achieve objective transparency, of course, but objectivity serves as a goal toward which these styles are oriented, rather than a literal accomplishment. Styles 2 and 4 are fundamentally subjective in the sense that they emphasize reality as it is perceived, experienced, and lived by a subject. In the case of style 2 the subjectivity at stake is typically that of a depicted character, while in the case of style 4 the subjectivity that matters is that of the viewer.

Machinima and (Virtual) Reality

I noted at the outset that the video game has a unique relationship with machinima production in that it is simultaneously the world in which the action occurs and also the primary tool in the digital authoring toolset with which these videos are made. I then explored some key themes in cinematic realism because in that theory one finds the elaboration of a technical vocabulary that sheds light on the relationships between the production of film and its presentation of reality, which is the theme I want to explore in this essay with regard to machinima. Obviously, the reality that cinema reveals is not the same as the reality that machinima reveals, if indeed either reveals any reality at all; but my interest is not in reality per se but rather in how video production practices add up to discourses that present reality in certain stylized ways. In other words, the basis for using realist film theory for machinima is not on the grounds that both of their source realities are similar but rather on the grounds that both constitute video discourses that present something we experience as real.

The Reality of Video Games

To make additional progress, we need to develop an understanding of video game reality. Let us begin by including everything within its diegetic world. This includes the virtual physical world, including its landforms and buildings; its perceptual style, from the architectural styles of its buildings to the stylizations of the graphics (e.g., the gritty realism of *Gears of War* [Microsoft Games Studios, 2006] or the cartoony fantasy of *World of Warcraft*); its rule systems, including physics, gameplay rules, software features, and behavioral algorithms; its history, lore, and accompanying narratives; and its ideology (e.g., the construction of heroism, gender, romance, good and evil, and moral dilemmas). In addition to these static aspects of the diegetic worlds these game realities also include the actions or behaviors of inhabitants within them— what players can *do*.

   The diegetic approach to defining the reality of games fails to account for the ways games enter our physical, cultural, and political reality. *Halo* borrows codes and conventions from science fiction films and novels as well as from other action adventure games. *World of Warcraft* depends on the medieval fantasy visual and narrative themes of Tolkien and the majority of role-playing games. Games are cultural texts and subject to intertextual relations. Games also relate to nondiegetic reality in more pinpointed ways than the broad thematic codes just mentioned. For example, one quest in *World of Warcraft* begins with a man in a fedora hat named Harrison Jones, who refers to the player as "kid"; the quest itself is called "Dun-da-Dun-tah!" in a clear—and utterly anomalous—reference to the *Indiana Jones* movies. In-world designs—virtual architecture, virtual fashion, and virtual products—all clearly are made meaningful by the player's understanding of their real-life counterparts. For example, in a content analysis of hundreds of *Second Life* (Linden Labs, 2003–) fashion blog posts, my colleagues and I demonstrated that commentary on any given item of virtual fashion inevitably made reference to readers' knowledge and expectations of corresponding artifacts of real-life fashion, in terms of their functions, cultural meanings, and production processes (Bardzell et al. 2009).

More deeply, games embed the normative values of their designers; for example, Pace demonstrates the white, male, heterosexual bias built into the *World of Warcraft* character selection interface (Pace 2008). Players also understand games using real-world mental models and biases, as seen in the *Big Blue Dress* machinima video, in which a powerful mage in *World of Warcraft* humorously laments that he is forced to wear a dress, which makes him "look so gay." Nakamura has shown that real-life racist attitudes toward Asians have become a part of *World of Warcraft* player culture, including machinima, in discourses surrounding gold farming (Nakamura 2009).

Collectively, this exploration of the reality of games suggests a range of phenomena. It includes objective features of the game, such as the shape of a building; the cultural meanings of those shapes (e.g., the meaning of a building's shapes as they constitute recognizable architectural styles); and individual subjective responses to those features and meanings. These subjective responses are situated within social and cultural situations, from aesthetic preferences about avatar fashion to political phenomena, such as homophobia and racism.

Styles of Cinematic Realism

The reality of a video game is a hybrid, then, of the diegetic world as if it existed as an independent entity and also of the ways that our world—culturally, physically, and socially—is constitutive of the virtual world. Given such an understanding of a video game's reality, we can now consider what machinimatic realism might entail. We can consider four styles of machinimatic realism, corresponding roughly to styles of portraying reality described earlier:

1a. *Simply recording game play*, using screen capture software, a practice that may or may not include the UI (depending on whether diegetic vs. nondiegetic aspects of game play are important).

2a. *Stylizing the presentation of the game world to express internal psychological phenomena or fantasies*, that is, events that have no literal place in the diegetic world of the game or in the typical experience of playing it.

3a. *Presenting the game's reality in a truthful and clarifying way*, whether it is some aspect of the diegetic game lore or an aspect of nondiegetic gameplay.

4a. *Presenting game reality in a way that corresponds to our experience*, regardless of the means by which the finished video is actually constructed .

As analogs to the four styles of portraying reality in film described above, these four also inherit the respective objectifying or subjectifying tendencies of their analog styles.

The simplest style of machinimatic realism is simply recording the game, item 1a in the list above, because some aspect of the game or its play is understood to be interesting in one way or another. This is quite common in machinima. For instance, at the popular online portal for *World of Warcraft* machinima, warcraftmovies.com, one finds thousands of videos that simply show what happened during a play session or even play event. A typical example is *Disc/Rogue 2v2 Season 7 2200+ Disc PoV*,[3] whose title artlessly summarizes the video's contents. The video begins with a one-minute cinematic title montage, but after that it is a nine-minute reel of unadulterated, roughly minute-long combat clips with popular music playing in the background. In the video's accompanying description, the video is characterized as "clips from a few nights" of gameplay, and accompanying comments suggest that viewers are watching these machinima to study or comment on player-versus-player (PVP) play. Many of the comments are quite technical: one commenter asks, for example, "W T F Did it go wrong for that restoShammy/locl you throwed out a 5k HF? With a 3k smite onto?" While a few posters comment on the background music, the majority of the substantive comments are about the mechanics of the fights themselves. Aside from the title and the background music, this video is a collection of recordings of gameplay, and the community appreciates it as such. The reality foregrounded in this type of video is that of game play itself.

A more aesthetically ambitious style of portraying reality is the stylized presentation of reality as a mechanism to express fantasies or psychological states—item 2a in the list. Zimtower's *Kim Lukas—Cloud Nine*, a *World of Warcraft*-based machinima video of a song that is about "going to a place beyond imagination, reaching pure bliss and Cloud 9 itself," is an example of this style. Using original 3D animation applied to *World of Warcraft* avatar models, postproduction blurs and color effects, and even external 2D art, this video is at times hard to recognize as *World of Warcraft* at all; indeed, the machinimator who made it writes that it is "barely machinima." The video's description at warcraftmovies.com notes that no less than ten authoring tools (including *Lightwave*, *Photoshop*, and Sony *Vegas*) were used to make it. Certainly it does not represent *World of Warcraft* in any meaningful way, but the video does use the *World of Warcraft* world as a stage on which to construct a video about "going beyond imagination, reaching pure bliss." In a review of the video at WoW.com, Michael Gray uses the words "enthralled," "expressive," "soft glow," "ephemeral quality," and "sense of serenity and peace" to articulate the way that he connected to the protagonist's feeling of joy (Gray 2009). If it can be called realistic at all, *Kim Lukas—Cloud Nine* can only be deemed so on the basis of its convincing expression of a psychological state (i.e., joy), as expressed in the original Kim Lukas pop song, and not on the basis of its representation of *World of Warcraft*—as a fictional universe or as a video game.

A third style of portraying reality is the use the medium of video to present a game's pro-filmic reality in an artfully clarifying way—item 3a above. Thus, a video staged in such a way as to bring out certain essential characteristics of the game would constitute realism. In this regard, the controversial *Serenity Now Bombs a World of Warcraft Funeral* machinima is an example. The video depicts a raid (a large-scale, team-based attack) on a group of players mourning in-world the real-life death of a player. The virtual funeral was originally planned via public Web forums, and some users read the forums and subsequently planned the attack. The raiders planted one raid member in the funeral party to collect footage of the funeral, while the rest invaded the funeral en masse from a nearby zone. The raiders then killed all the funeral attendees, while mocking them. The video features a pair of musical tracks—Mozart's *Requiem* and the Misfits' "Where the Eagles Dare"—that respectively accompany footage of the funeral party and the raiding party, as parallel editing is used to introduce both parties and set up narrative tension. The video foregrounds the mixed-reality nature of *World of Warcraft*, staging a conflict between real-life social etiquette (i.e., respect for the dead and mourning) with in-game rules and practices (i.e., take-no-prisoners raiding). The conflict between game rules or practices and real-life social etiquette is a fundamental aspect of participating in massively multiplayer online games, such as *World of Warcraft*, and the *Serenity Now Bombs a World of Warcraft Funeral* machinima brings elegant (if troubling) clarity to this conflict.

The final style of presenting the reality of a game is to do so not by ensuring a tight relationship between what happens in-game and the video but rather by ensuring a tight relationship between the machinima's presentation of the game and the player's perceptual experience of the game. Fidelity, in other words, does not inhere in the relationship between the world and its representation but rather in the phenomenological experience of the world and the experience of its representation. An example of this style is arguably found in *The Craft of War: BLIND*, a custom-animated martial arts *World of Warcraft* music video, whose animation style is inspired by Hong Kong martial arts films but which is otherwise convincing as an action sequence animated in *World of Warcraft*. In fact, much of the video was produced using a community-made toolkit called *WoW Model Viewer*, which enables users to dress and animate characters in the game in front of a blue screen, facilitating subsequent compositing. It is easy to see that the video was painstakingly constructed, one animation at a time, and yet it seamlessly flows as an intense combat sequence. This sequence begins with an assassin, who looks rather like a high-level *World of Warcraft* player character, easily dispatching a series of faceless guards; later the battle continues between the assassin and another martial arts master who arrives on the scene. The faceless guards look like (indeed they are) nonplayer characters in *World of Warcraft*, the kinds of everyday "mobs" that players dispatch by the thousand as they work through the game. That the assassin meets her match in another fighter who, like her, looks like a player character analogously suggests the PVP experience, which is, both in-game and in the narrative of this video, a whole new level of combat. Thus, *The Craft of War: Blind* corresponds to the phenomenological experience of playing *World of Warcraft*, even though it has no indexical relationship with it: this video could never be confused with actual footage of PVP combat.

Production Techniques and Reality Effects

I've introduced four high-level styles of portraying reality in machinima, items 1a–4a. But as film theorists have demonstrated, realism is not an abstract aesthetic position but rather a practical accomplishment of production. That is, different styles of machinimatic realism can be achieved through the use of different production techniques. In this section, I explore production techniques that are commonly used to achieve the styles that are comparatively objective in their portrayal of reality (in the sense described in items 1a and 3a) and those that are comparatively subjective in their portrayal of reality (2a and 4a). Certain aspects of production construct differential reality effects, depending on how they are used. Here I explore the use of game assets, such as avatars and buildings; the use of a virtual camera to capture action; and the staging of events in which actions occur.

Game assets constitute much of the visuals and even audio of machinima films. Such assets include the land formations and buildings of the virtual world itself; character models and gestures; actions, such as running, shooting, climbing, and sitting; in-game sounds, such as nondiegetic scores, voice acting, and effects; and textures and graphics. As constituents of their native games, these assets are pre-endowed with meaning. Their use inevitably invokes the game's native meanings, including the game narrative and lore, visual style, and interactive functions.

In a more objective style (i.e., 1a or 3a), these meanings are preserved in the sense that their use in the machinima is similar to their use in the game; in this way, the machinima "faithfully" represents them and by extension the game itself. In both the *Serenity Now Bombs a World of Warcraft Funeral* and the *Disc/Rogue 2v2 Season 7 2200+ Disc PoV* machinima videos described earlier, environments, models, and user interface elements appear in the videos more or less as they appear in the game. In contrast, in a more subjective style (i.e., 2a or 4a), these assets are subject to appropriation, such that their meanings are subverted, distorted, or otherwise altered to produce a meaning that is not native to the game world. In *Kim Lukas—Cloud Nine*, a *World of Warcraft* avatar is shown to soar through the clouds singing a pop song and directing her gaze into the camera at the viewer, a feat made possible by the use of software, multimedia assets, and production techniques that are all external to *World of Warcraft*.

A second production feature whose use can lead to objective versus subjective reality effects is the virtual camera. This camera, like any other, frames reality, brings certain objects into focus, and emphasizes or marginalizes objects, directing our attention. Lev Manovich has observed that most video game cameras work in medium to wide shots, and that these shots can be very long in duration, that is, proceeding without any cuts (Manovich 2001). These defaults are practical for gameplay, because they allow players to see the world with which they are interacting, including their in-game characters' relationship to that world. Virtual cameras also tend to operate in deep focus; unlike in traditional photography, objects in the foreground and background are usually equally in focus and equally lit. This suggests that the typical video game camera is quite similar to the cinematography and editing style championed by Bazin as realistic. Thus, using the in-game camera can be realistic on two independent levels: using a game asset as it was intended, and the fact that the video game camera is already realist in its operation.

In both *Serenity Now Bombs a World of Warcraft Funeral* and *Disc/Rogue 2v2 Season 7 2200+ Disc PoV*, we see the game camera used in the way it is used for gameplay, revealing characters in their environments with deep focus and generally few cuts. Yet in the more subjective-style videos, *Kim Lukas—Cloud Nine* and *The Craft of War: BLIND*, we see much more variability in the distance between the camera and the principal characters. In both films the characters frequently exit to and enter from outside of the frame, which is impossible in the main game (the *World of Warcraft* character is always at the center of the screen in normal gameplay). Both of these videos—the action-oriented *Craft of War: BLIND* in particular—make use of frequent cuts, which again is quite uncharacteristic of gameplay.

A third way to produce objective versus subjective reality effects is to stage events that the game encourages or is intended to support. These include death matches, collaborations, timed accomplishments, special challenges, daring explorations, and so forth. A *Halo* video featuring a character driving a Warthog jeep quickly and elegantly through difficult situations is the kind of event the game was designed to support. A raid party in *World of Warcraft* taking down an epic boss is likewise exactly the sort of activity the game was designed to support. To build machinima out of such events is to work within a realist framework, and both *Serenity Now Bombs a World of Warcraft Funeral* and *Disc/Rogue 2v2 Season 7 2200+ Disc PoV* stage just such events. For if the *World of Warcraft* funeral raid was unorthodox in our social reality, the raid shown in the video, once exposed as a raid, is quite typical of large PVP-style raids. In contrast,

Kim Lukas—Cloud 9 stages the achievement of an affective state, joy, rather than a traditional game event. This state is achieved metaphorically through a basic narrative: a gnome is singing in a sunny field and then is shown soaring through the skies on the back of a hippogriff, before eventually skydiving and opening a parachute.

Many other production techniques not mentioned here operate in this way, including audio design, montage, and the use of recognized actors (e.g., Nhym, Cranius, and Summergale come to mind for *World of Warcraft*). Each of these techniques, like the others I have explored, come with meanings that can be accepted and used in the video in the same way they are used in the game, or they can be subverted or extended to generate meanings, a relationship I explore through close readings of three *Halo* videos.

Three Machinimatic Stances on Game Reality

I have presented the styles above as discursive languages, that is, as resources available to directors to negotiate the relationships between their intentions, their video, and the reality of virtual worlds. Of course, directors can use, ignore, and blend these styles. In this section, I propose three stances that directors can take with regard to the relationships between their videos and the game realities they portray or express. These are stances of acceptance, of resistance, and of extension.

In the *acceptance stance*, the reality of the game is accepted more or less as is. This includes the game's lore, its visual language, its gameplay and actions, and its ideology. This stance corresponds most closely to classical realism in film, because it seeks to present reality as it is, with minimal artistic intervention. Although many of the worst machinima films fall into this category (e.g., one-star reviewed machinima videos on popular sites), it is also possible that a video that portrays the game in straightforward and accepting ways can be quite appealing. In other work (Bardzell 2007), I argued that as far as amateur multimedia communities go, the usable is the message, that is, usable software features were used most, and there is much less evidence of the use of more difficult features, and consequently the meanings of amateur multimedia disproportionately bear the marks of easy-to-use features of authoring software. That seems to apply in this category as well, especially with regard to the use of the game camera to frame game reality, as I argue in my close readings below.

Finally, machinima is in general a highly intertextual form. For example, many machinima videos have sound tracks imported from popular culture. In the acceptance stance, intertextual references tend to support the dominant meanings of the game universe.

Machinima made in the *resistance stance* seeks to subvert the reality of the game or subordinate it to the vision or meanings that the machinimator seeks to express. This stance most closely resembles expressionism in film. Whereas in expressionist films the settings represent states of mind rather than streets and living rooms, so too in resistance machinima the game setting is used to express something other than what the game normally seems to deliver. For example, the supposedly fun, novel, and social first expansion pack of *World of Warcraft* is shown in the machinima *Jimmy: The World of Warcraft Story* to be boring, derivative, and friendship-destroying; likewise, the consequence-free action adventure universe of *Halo* is shown to have deeply personal, emotional consequences in the video *To Heaven* (Jamie98s, 2006) (analyzed below). To achieve these qualities, the resistance stance often relies on intertextual juxtapositions to help subvert dominant meanings; so for example in *Jimmy: The World of Warcraft Story*, the dominant meanings of the game world are subverted with an extensive comic narrative composed outside the game, delivered with outstanding voice acting, loaded up with pop cultural references (e.g., to the board game *Clue*), and parodying treatments of the game publisher Blizzard's customer service.

Finally, the *extension stance* seeks to go beyond the dominant meanings of the world without fundamentally subverting them. In this stance the expressive vocabulary of the game world is insufficient to support everything that the machinima video wants to tell, and so the machinimator innovates on that language to enhance its expressiveness. Often, extension happens through the intertextual intermingling of discourses from the game with those from outside, in a way that pushes the game to new expressive capabilities without actively subverting it, either. An example of this is *M.A.G.E.*, a *World of Warcraft* music video celebrating the mage character class. Attempting such a video in an acceptance stance, a machinimator might have shown clips of a mage dominating in PVP fights or against a difficult boss. But Nyhm, the machinimator of *M.A.G.E.*, instead rewrote the lyrics of and reperformed the song "P.I.M.P." by rapper 50 Cent. The original rap video features a swaggering confidence—a Bentley-driving, couture-wearing mansion owner surrounded by scantily clad, worshipping women—that has no analog in *World of Warcraft*. Nyhm's extension of *World of Warcraft*'s expressive language by fusing it with a popular rap song, and the visual swagger of its accompanying music video, enables him to express the superiority of the mage class in a way that extends *World of Warcraft*, celebrating more than subverting its dominant meanings.

In the remainder of this section I analyze each of these three stances as they are exemplified in three *Halo* videos. Specifically, I consider both the meanings and themes of *Halo*, and I also consider it as a machinima video production environment; both these perspectives come together to constitute the discursive stances that these three videos take vis-à-vis *Halo*.

Halo as a Machinima Authoring Platform

Halo: Combat Evolved is a first-person shooter (FPS) that takes place on a mysterious unnatural life-supporting ring that surrounds a distant planet. *Halo*'s rather minimal backstory is a science-fiction cliché: three intergalactic alliances, each divided from the others by race and language and enemies for no apparent reason, battle for supremacy. Players take the role of Master Chief, a massive cyborg warrior and ally of the humans; his face is obscured behind a mask and his person is largely unreadable as well. He has few gestures available to him that can be used to express his emotional responses to the events in which he finds himself.

The settings in which play occurs involve spaceships and strange, colorful lands with futuristic alien architecture, which vaguely resembles contemporary industrial sites, without the pollution or crowds. Exotic geological structures and vehicles contribute to the environment. Players have little ability to customize maps or import or position props. Even with available options, constructing sets is nontrivial, and most machinima films that we have seen do not significantly alter the look or feel of the *Halo* settings. Options to control sound and lighting are minimal, and custom lighting and sounds are not a significant part of *Halo* machinima.

A basic production setup in *Halo* is relatively easy for small groups, because they can access private multiplayer servers, choose a map, and begin video production. As an FPS, the camera is fixed inside the player's head; so in many *Halo* films, designated camera operators capture but do not participate in the action. Shots are therefore generally at eye level. Action occurs in real time, so shots must be carefully staged and executed or they come across like amateur video.

Prisoner of War: Accepting the Platform

Prisoner of War (Carter, 2006) is used as an example of a platform accepting form even though it has very low ratings on its source site, *halomovies.org*. In it, two Master Chief characters, one in white armor and one in black armor, encounter an alien Elite fighter after an invasion. At first they try to communicate with the Elite, but he screams gibberish back at them and attacks. A chase scene, set to a heavy metal sound track, follows, in which different areas of the map are shown. The black Master Chief is killed, leading to a showdown between the white one and the alien Elite. After a dramatized face-off, the alien charges and is killed by the white Master Chief. The tone of the video is a humorless action adventure, more or less like *Halo* itself. Likewise, this video recapitulates much of *Halo*'s other themes: the machinima film is set just after a military invasion and involves a clash between two races that can only be resolved in inarticulate violence. The fact that the black Master Chief is killed and the white Master Chief is victorious suggests some correspondence between the racially motivated violence in the game world and plays off subtle forms of color and race symbolism in the United States. The plot and mostly voiceless characters fit in with, without adding anything to, the existing *Halo* myth.

On the production side, the influence of *Halo* is also palpable. The credits list three actors and one filmmaker as participants in the project. That one of the participants was a camera operator is a common strategy for *Halo* machinima. However, whereas higher-quality *Halo* machinima uses Hollywood-style camera positions, master shots, cutaways, and a reliance on nonmoving shots to separate the camera operators from the action, the camera operator in *Prisoner of War* often inadvertently becomes part of the action. This is an important difference. When the operator is separate from the action, the illusion of a disembodied virtual camera is created and the viewer relates to the depicted action as a witness, but when the camera operator participates, his embodiment as a Master Chief and player becomes foregrounded, bringing the viewer into the action. In *Prisoner of War*, the camera operator's unwitting participation is visible in several instances: with the exception of a cinematic establishment shot at the beginning, every single shot is at eye level; the camera operator follows his actors around corners in long, jerky takes; in one shot that tracks across the set, the camera bounces up and down as the operator steps over virtual railroad tracks; most important, in the climactic confrontation between the hero and villain, the killing of the alien occurs off-screen because the operator gets too close to the action, loses the shot, and spends a few seconds looking around for the now vanquished alien. *Halo*'s placement of the camera in the head of the player, who is bound to the physics of the game, determines many of the shots taken in this video. The result is that the viewer sometimes relates to the action as a disembodied witness and sometimes as an embodied player, and the transitions back and forth are jarring.

This video throws into relief some of the issues that *Halo* filmmakers have to deal with if they are to do more than ape the platform's clichéd science fiction action theme (which is more excusable for a game than for a narrative film) as it blandly depict its faceless hero and burdens its "camera" with a humanoid body subject to physics.

To Heaven: Resisting the Platform

To Heaven is a music video with an artistic cinematographic touch and a theme of pensive sadness. The video depicts the violent death of a *Halo* Master Chief character through a frame tale; in the central main part of the video is a sequence in which the soldier walks among other people and places that vanish as he nears them. The sound track is a melancholic acoustic "In the Deep," sung by Kathleen (Bird) York. Thematically, rather than glorifying battle, this video explores the experience of death as the loss of all one's social contacts, one by one. In the final shot, as the broken body of the soldier lies on the ground and the song fades away, blue particles rise (figure 12.1), completing the promise of the title (*To Heaven*) and offering a pleasing, if melancholic, conclusion.

Perhaps even more interesting than its thematic resistance to *Halo*, this music video stands out in its visual resistance as well. While *Halo* is typically well lit and filled with bright, saturated colors, this video is shot on a campaign map, as opposed to the more commonly used multiplayer maps, possibly in part because it takes place at dusk. Most of the shots occur in the shadows, creating a soft light effect that also dulls the colors

Figure 12.1
In *To Heaven*'s final shot, blue particles (added in postproduction) rise from the body of the fallen soldier.

and supports its message. A subtle filter appears to have been added in postproduction, which gives the video a diffuse quality as well. In addition, while most of the shots are at the default *Halo* eye level, a number of the shots are taken looking down on the protagonist, diminishing him, while none of them is taken from below, which would suggest a more powerful positioning. This video is also one of the uncommon *Halo* machinima pieces—indeed, uncommon machinima of any variety—that include extreme close-ups and shots with soft focus, both of which express the affect of the protagonist, as do some creative gesture animations. In addition, the filmmaker added heavy motion blurs in postproduction to the framing (beginning and end) death sequences, making the violent crash dreamlike and distant. Pointing simultaneously to *Halo*, cinematic dream sequences, and fears of isolation, and taking the form of a music video with a nested narrative, *To Heaven* creates a symbolically sophisticated experience for the viewer.

Interestingly, this video was not initially embraced by its community. Six months after its first release, and despite a glowing introduction and recommendation from the site hosts, who gave it a five-star rating and praised its unique take on *Halo*, the site users had given it only three stars. Since then, its rating has increased, though its download count is hardly extraordinary. These numbers may reflect the semiotic inertia that Metz, following de Saussure, describes: no individual alone can change a language. Instead, to innovate, the artist must use the code cleverly (Metz [1974] 1991). Perhaps the filmmaker Jamie98's confrontation of the *Halo* platform was slightly ahead of its time, but now it is finding its audience.

Red vs. Blue: Episode 39: Extending the Platform

Among the earliest and most popular machinima works of all time, the *Red vs. Blue* series has completed at the time of this writing more than one hundred episodes. It carries many of the themes of *Halo*, including the military setting and action-orientedness, but it adds to *Halo* a complex comic story. *Halo*—especially multiplayer *Halo*—features endless combat, which, while fun to play in its own right, serves little narrative purpose. Gameplay rather than story rules *Halo*, a general point about video games made by several video game theorists (Frasca 2003; Aarseth 2004; Juul 2005). Instead of trying to retell a *Halo* action story, as many especially weaker *Halo* machinimas do, *Red vs. Blue* builds on the pointlessness of game combat to push it into a loving parody. Its opening episode features an existentialist discussion among a couple of its characters about why they are trapped in an exitless gulch locked in a death-battle with an unknown enemy. One reason the humor works so well is because it describes *Halo* quite accurately but it also surprisingly echoes our own condition (especially as described by existentialist philosophy [Camus 1955]), born without our consent into an absurd world of conflict. Another aspect of the humor is its self-referentiality. For example, *Red vs. Blue: Episode 39* (Rooster Teeth, 2005) features a play-within-a-play narrative structure in which two of the characters teleport into a random gulch and find another pair of red and blue teams battling it out, over and over. As the enactment parodies multiplayer battle scenes and their social interaction—from complaints about camping to players squabbling over kills, all spoken in leet-speak—the main characters witnessing the action fail to grasp that they reenact the same conflict in their own space. By extension, the episode makes its viewers wonder as they watch to what extent *Red vs. Blue* is an allegory of their own lives.

Red vs. Blue also exploits, rather than fall victim to, the facelessness of its protagonist. Instead of depicting their characters as stereotypically manly heroes, as do many less distinctive *Halo* videos, the writers make use of Master Chief's facelessness as a blank canvas on which to paint each character into a unique and largely comic personality. In the *Red vs. Blue* machinima series, characters are distinguished by their armor color and voice acting. Characters persist and develop across episodes, resulting in substantial (if silly) personal histories, which only deepen with further episodes.

From a production standpoint, *Red vs. Blue* successfully distances its camera operators from the action. It looks like a television sitcom filmed from invisible, disembodied cameras. Shots are taken from a variety of angles, suggesting that the camera operators climbed on top of props or squatted to get different-angled shots (figure 12.2). Shot-reverse shot and parallel editing is common, and camera movement is minimized, ensuring that each shot is well composed. Careful shot composition and editing lead to visual juxtapositions that often form the basis of *Red vs. Blue*'s humor. The *Halo* game camera, in the embodied participatory sense, has been suppressed (though in early episodes the telltale crosshair still appears, as seen in figure 12.2). It is replaced by a flexible camera that not only depicts the action and dialog, but also establishes viewers as witnesses of that to which the filmmakers direct their attention, helping to shape their responses to the events.

Figure 12.2
Red vs. Blue's carefully composed shots give no indication of the embodiment of the game camera.

Machinimatic Realism

Realism is a complex issue in cinema; applied to the mixed-reality medium of the contemporary video game, it becomes even more complex. Rather than committing to a position on whether a given film is or is not realistic, this essay has considered realism as an effect created by different discursive styles, themselves made up in large part by production techniques that are (more or less) intentionally chosen.

In the course of this essay I have introduced four styles of portraying reality in film and explored what these might mean for machinima. I subsequently explored three directorial stances, which can use these styles as resources to help achieve certain kinds of machinimatic meaning. And yet, while I gave examples of each of the four styles and three stances, the problem is that many machinima videos cannot be classified so easily. Where exactly is the boundary between neo-realist and correspondence-based realist film? What ultimately distinguishes between machinima videos that resist versus those that extend their host games? Additionally, different audiences may answer these questions in different ways.

Rather than seeing these stances as overall categories into which we must try to fit machinima videos, as if these stances were some kind of Procrustean beds, perhaps a more constructive way to think about it is to point to the way Carl Freedman under-stands genre in literature: as tendencies within a text. Freedman writes, "a genre is not a classification but an element or, better still, a *tendency* that, in combination with other relatively autonomous generic elements or tendencies, is active to a greater or lesser degree within a literary text that is itself understood as a complexly structured totality" (Freedman 2000, 20). My point is not to extend this study of machinimatic realism to questions of genre but only to borrow the notion of a machinima video as a text comprising many tendencies, some of which are more dominant than others. Applied to machinima stances, such a conceptualization of genre dispenses with any presumption that a video neatly exemplifies or falls under a single style or stance.

This conceptualization of styles and stances as a tendency within a machinima video in turn suggests that the unit of analysis for machinimatic realism is not the film as a whole but rather its constituent parts. Such a move leaves open the possibility of a video whose production bears all the marks of acceptance but that is ideologically subversive, or a video that extends the expressive language of a game world only to reinforce its dominant meanings. Perhaps we might understand machinimatic realism as a critical mass, or a *Gestalt*, of realistic tendencies in a text, adding up to a felt experience of game realism: imagine a viewer reacting, "That's exactly what Halo is like."

At any rate, I hope I have shown that the game-worldedness of machinima is more than merely incidental and that the relationship among a game world, the production of machinima videos, and the videos as finished products is deep and complex. This relationship is clearly the source of many of these videos' meanings.

Further, these relationships do not unfold in univocal ways. Machinimators have different options at their disposal to accept, resist, or extend the expressive language of game worlds. In many ways, these options were first pioneered in cinematic film, in its various phases of realism and expressionism. As machinimators appropriate and develop these tendencies in the context of presenting virtual worlds to video audiences, perhaps a new wave of realistic filmmaking is just around the corner.

Acknowledgments

The author gratefully acknowledges the lively discussions and critical feedback of Shaowen Bardzell, Erik Stolterman, Will Ryan, and Natalie DeWitt, as well as the constructive criticism (and patience!) of the co-editors of this volume, Michael Nitsche and Henry Lowood.

Notes

1. I am paraphrasing the three premises of auteur theory, according to Serris (1963).

2. See Monaco (2000, 290–291), but also Fabe (2004, 37–58).

3. See <http://www.warcraftmovies.com/movieview.php?id=134705> (accessed January 2, 2010); also here for comments of viewers.

References

Aarseth, Espen. 2004. Genre Trouble: Narrativism and the Art of Simulation Response. In *First Person: New Media as Story, Performance, and Game*, ed. Noah Wardrip-Fruin and Pat Harrigan, 45–55. Cambridge: MIT Press.

Bardzell, Jeffrey. 2007. Creativity and Amateur Multimedia. *Human Technology* 3 (1): 12–33.

Bardzell, Jeffrey, Tyler Pace, Laura Brunetti, Qian Huang, Nina Onesti Perry, and Hyewon Gim. 2009. Emerging Standards in Virtual Fashion: An Analysis of Critical Strategies Used in Virtual Fashion Blogs. In *Hawaii International Conference on System Sciences* (HICSS-42), 1–10. IEEE Computer Society Press.

Bazin, André. [1967] 2005. The Evolution of the Language of Cinema. In *What Is Cinema*, vol. 1. Berkeley and Los Angeles: University of California Press.

Camus, Albert. 1955. Myth of Sisyphus. In *Myth of Sisyphus and Other Essays*. New York: Vintage International.

Devereaux, Mary. 1998. Beauty and Evil: The Case of Leni Riefenstahl's *Triumph of the Will*. In *Aesthetics and Ethics: Essays at the Intersection*, ed. Jerrold Levinson, 227–256. Cambridge, UK: Cambridge University Press.

Fabe, Marilyn. 2004. *Closely Watched Films: An Introduction to the Art*. Berkeley and Los Angeles: University of California Press.

Frasca, Gonzalo. 2003. Simulation versus Narrative: Introduction to Ludology. In *The Video Game Theory Reader*, ed. Mark J. P. Wolf and Bernard Perron. New York: Routledge.

Freedman, Carl. 2000. *Critical Theory and Science Fiction*. Hanover, NH: University Press of New England.

Gray, Michael. 2009. *WoW Moviewatch: Cloud 9*, by ZimTower. Posted February 19. <http://www .wow.com/2009/02/19/wow-moviewatch-cloud-9-by-zimtower>.

Juul, Jesper. 2005. *Half-real: Video Games between Real Rules and Fictional Worlds*. Cambridge: MIT Press.

Kracauer, Siegfried. [1960] 2004. Basic Concepts. From *Theory of Film*, excerpted in *Film Theory and Criticism*, ed. Leo Braudy and Marshall Cohen, 143–153. Oxford: Oxford University Press.

Lakoff, George, and Mark Johnson. 1980. *Metaphors We Live By*. Chicago: University of Chicago Press.

MacCabe, Colin. 1986. Theory and Film: Principles of Realism and Pleasure. In *Narrative, Apparatus, Ideology*, ed. Philip Rosen, 179–197. New York: Columbia University Press.

Manovich, Lev. 2007. Velvet Revolution. *Artifact* 1 (2): 67–75.

Manovich, Lev. 2001. *Language of New Media*. Cambridge: MIT Press.

McLuhan, Marshall. 2003. *Understanding Media: The Extensions of Man, Critical Edition*. Berkeley, CA: Gingko Press.

Metz, Christian. [1974] 1991. *Film Language: A Semiotics of the Cinema*. Chicago: University of Chicago Press.

Monaco, James. 2000. *How to Read a Film: Movies, Media, Multimedia*, 3rd ed. Oxford: Oxford University Press.

Nakamura, Lisa. 2009. Don't Hate the Player, Hate the Game: The Racialization of Labor in *World of Warcraft*. *Critical Studies in Media Communication* 26 (2): 128–144.

Pace, Tyler. 2008. Can an Orc Catch a Cab in Stormwind? Cybertype Preference in the World of Warcraft Character Creation Interface. In *CHI '08 Extended Abstracts on Human Factors in Computing Systems*, 2493–2502. New York: Association of Computing Machinery.

Prince, Stephen. 1996. True Lies: Perceptual Realism, Digital Images and Film Theory. *Film Quarterly* 49 (3): 27–37.

Serris, Andrew. 1963. Auteur Theory and Film Evaluation. *Film Culture* 27 (1962/63): 1–8.

Software References

Gears of War. Microsoft Games Studios. 2006.

Halo: Combat Evolved. Microsoft Game Studios. 2001.

Second Life. Linden Labs. 2003–.

World of Warcraft. Blizzard Entertainment. 2004.

13   Undefining Machinima

Erik Champion

The grumpy gamers among us are still smarting over the important, challenging, and frustrating questions made famous by Roger Ebert and Steven Spielberg: whether games can be classified as artworks, and therefore capable of eliciting the nobler emotions, or whether they can even be spoken of in the same breath as cinema or literature. And if games cannot be art, how could machinima stake claims to being a form of art? Machinima may be created by game engines or by real-time rendering engines, but its content is often that of the games associated with the engines that it uses. On the other hand, even if the original games modified for machinima cannot be art, machinima does not have to refer back to its game-based origins. Yet if we consider machinima as art only whenever and if ever it creates cinema-standard work, how is it different from film? Some of the best or at least most recognized machinima, it can be argued, is irreverent to cinema, an established medium of techniques and conventions that machinima frequently borrows from and parodies.

A large part of the problem of determining machinima's status as art has to do with a mutable understanding of what art is. Generally, grand theories about what counts as art are based on extrapolating from media statements or from the theoretician's personal experience of specific works. Theories of art that attempt to be universal, always and everywhere applicable, tend nevertheless to have a direction, a hidden hierarchizing system, and to exhibit a situated sensitivity. We are historically thrown, physically constrained, and by nature or by training socially hierarchical.

Even if we try to avoid our own personal biases, in many of these grand theories masterpieces and only masterpieces are used as examples. Hence, when we create a grand and unifying theory, it typically suits only a few works of art (those that are of particular significance to us) or a few outstanding examples. In this regard, film directors and critics are likely to judge games and machinima either against canonical films or using specialized or localized criteria that are typically suited more to films than to other media. The *Myst* game series, for example, may seem closer to cinema than other games, but it is arguably not advancing the particular potential of games as a new form or mode of art. In gauging the value of a new medium, it seems unfair to judge its unique strengths or potential according to the conventions of what has preceded it. Rather than say art is exactly this or that, in this essay I propose a few strands that may explain why certain effects of machinima can induce us to consider them works of art even if their materials, processes, or traditions of construction, display, or involvement overlap with or separate them from more conventional works.

To avoid reviewing the entire history and theory of art, I offer a simplified and personal view of what a work of art can do. According to several dictionary definitions, work can be considered art when it reaches a high level of technical skill.[1] A work may be considered art when it is expressive and empathic, when the artist captures and conveys a moment, scene, or passage that we believe is innate, personal, or unique. A work may be considered art when it follows certain conventions, such as being accepted as art by a small section of the community, looking or acting like other pieces of art so considered, or being displayed, used, or purchased like other forms of art so considered. Art may also create an epiphany in the viewer or listener; it may be art when the experience of it challenges our previous perceptions and conceptions of the world, of our self, or of our relationship to the world.

The above thoughts are summarized from my readings of both art historians and philosophers of art, including such disparate figures as John Ruskin (Berg 1982), Wilhelm Worringer (Sorenson n.d.), Susanne K. Langer (1953), Arthur C. Danto (Carrier 1998), and Martin Heidegger (1971, 1977). These encapsulations of art may also rely on each other. It may require a high level of skill to capture a moment; it may (paradoxically) require considerable knowledge of the history of a certain artistic medium to transcend it.

There are, of course, problems with the above views of art. Attempting to create works that are solely examples of technical mastery may lead to works that are sterile, lack expression, or do not invoke a feeling of empathy. Art that simply follows the rules, canons, or expectations of artistic media in history, theory, or practice may also fail to inspire empathy or interest and may require expert knowledge to be considered art. Art as expression and empathy arousing is highly subjective and may be vulnerable to changing fashions and social mores. Similarly, art as epiphany may require a unique combination of participant, setting, and background context. It may be experienced by viewers or participants only once or not at all, and the "shock of the new" may slowly fade over time.

Does machinima, or certain works arising from it, fit any of the above views of what constitutes art? If machinima is not yet capable of producing art, might it one day create works worthy of art status? What kind of art would it be? To make matters even more complicated, even if we could agree on a definition of art, and agree on what counts as examples of art, it is quite possible that if machinima *could be* a potential art form, it could also be considered art in many diverse ways. With its catholic tastes in technology and its careening selection of parody, satire, cheeseball homage, or pathos, machinima as a cannibalistic genre oscillating between gameplay and cut-scene and film further exacerbates the problem of defining and prescribing boundaries, standards, and achievements.

Machinima may astound us as an author-controlled demonstration of an interactive game that conveys great skill or innovative exploration of a game genre. Machinima may approach art as a form of cinema (when we gain as great an aesthetic experience from it as if we were watching a great movie). However, the position I wish to advance is that machinima is fascinating because it combines different interactive and prerendered media in a way that causes us to question who we are, what we have experienced, and how we may have taken our past experiences for granted. For the paradox of machinima, that it uses real-time game engines to create prerendered content, may be leveraged creatively to challenge our preconceptions and behavioral triggers. Machinima could be a new hybrid form of reflection-provoking media.

Machinima as Technique: If It Uses A Game Engine, How Can It Be Art?

Does mastery of the techniques of animated filmmaking adequately cover mastery of machinima? Machinima is typically defined as a video produced using real-time, interactive (game) 3D engines, as a genre using these engines, or as emergent gameplay. Paul Marino (2004) declares that machinima could be explained as "animated filmmaking within a real-time virtual 3D environment." However, it is important to note that machinima here is defined by how it is made, not by what it is capable of. Marino and others are attracted to machinima as an accessible, cheap, and artistically unrestricted medium, at least in comparison to mainstream filmmaking. As an operational definition aimed at explaining to budding filmmakers the advantages of machinima as a tool, this makes sense. Yet in this essay I am interested in the value and potential of machinima as it is experienced, not as it is operated, and Marino's definition does not really explain the advantages of machinima to an end-user.

In 2005 the American film critic Roger Ebert wrote,

I did indeed consider video games inherently inferior to film and literature. There is a structural reason for that: Video games by their nature require player choices, which is the opposite of the strategy of serious film and literature, which requires authorial control. I am prepared to believe that video games can be elegant, subtle, sophisticated, challenging and visually wonderful. But I believe the nature of the medium prevents it from moving beyond craftsmanship to the stature of art.

Ebert seems to be suggesting that video games have fundamental and irresolvable limitations: video games can only be craft, as player choices cannot be predetermined or predicted by an author. In this case, interactivity does seem an essential part of games, but it does not necessarily follow that games are improved by containing as much interactivity as possible. And I don't believe that games could consist only of interaction, or that a game must be as interactive as possible to succeed artistically. The onus is to create interaction that appears thematic, immersive, meaningful, and innovative, not necessarily ubiquitous and ever-present. However, given that games are considered interactive entertainment, do we have to concede that interaction interferes with authorial control in a way that destroys the possibility of art?

Improvisational theater is based on the confluence of these two elements. Interestingly, as far back as 1967 there was interactive cinema, which reputedly was popular with the audience (Hales 2005). Modern literature, painting, and hypertext also challenge the notion of authorial control; perhaps Ebert is not a fan of Duchamp or Pollock. Films can also incorporate "happenings" or spontaneous dialog, narrative events, or emergent character change. The films *Casablanca* and *Apocalypse Now* come to mind as example of works that emerged from a combination of personality, unpredictable set conditions, and freak circumstances, not from tightly written and carefully followed scripts.

There is another aspect to gameplay that may not be obvious to less experienced gamers. Choreographers and composers consider themselves artists, but performers have some degree of individual expression when they dance or perform music created by others. Like music, dance, and improvisational theater, suggestive and coercive elements of gameplay can be stimulated, triggered, guided, and choreographed.

Ebert may have missed not only the creative potential of players but also the careful choreography and attempts at supporting emergent drama that are motivating game designers and game theorists (Adams and Rollings 2003; Salen and Zimmerman 2004; Jenkins 2007). In this respect, perhaps gameplay is closer to musical performance or theatrical performance (or even improv theater) than to cinema. For in these fields the players do matter.

Machinima as Convention: Function Laughing at Procedure

I am not sure if he would agree with my summation, but Ebert has criticized computer games (a new or emerging medium) for not having created works of art with artistic value discernible to film critics (who are critics of relatively established media). His criteria for what constitutes art are also very demanding, leading me to wonder if Ebert was comparing massively popular commercial games with the artistic highpoints of cinema rather than like with like. If games are structurally distinct from movies, as Ebert has claimed, should the canons and conventions of films even be applied to games and to machinima? On Roger Ebert's Web site, Jim Emerson remarked,

Ebert said he'd also been intrigued by *Myst*, but that he'd wished it had just played itself like a movie rather than as a game where the user was called upon to unlock parts of the riddle in order to move on to the next level of the game. . . . On the other hand, I've also watched friends play more simplistic, stimulus-response games such as Doom and, as a critic, that's where I draw the line. Sure, a lot of artistry and technical know-how goes into the creation of the game, but the experience of playing it is purely mechanical. . . . I look at it this way: Gamers are on the cutting edge of a new form of expression. I think a game like *Myst* qualifies as art, but any artwork can only be apprehended and evaluated one work at a time. So, even if games haven't achieved the highest levels of artistic expression yet, it's not up to them to conform to anyone's idea of what art is. They have the potential to expand the boundaries of what we consider art to be.[2]

If computer games (and by extension machinima) are only digital extensions of previous forms of artistic activity, and if originality is a fundamental requirement of art, then perhaps computer games cannot qualify as art. Acceptance of this argument does, however, raise the possibility that all products of popular media lose their potential value as great works of art as they become accepted and institutionalized. If this is the case, Chekov, Shakespeare, and Picasso may all be considered creators of great art, but only because they got in first. The only good artist, in this extreme view, is a dead artist.

While the above is a reductio ad absurdum, Ebert's argument does seem to be predicated on the belief that a new artistic medium will immediately produce geniuses who identify and communicate its value to the wider public. Unfortunately, history has birthed far too many trailblazers who died of loneliness and neglect. However, it is not clear how Ebert views civilization as distinct from culture. According to the author of *The Decline of the West*, Oswald Spengler (1932), there is an explicit distinction: one allows us to live together civilly, the other is related more to growth and cultivation. And this distinction raises a question: perhaps some forms of artistic output need large amounts of time, energy, and commitment to eventually result in works of genius. Genius is not necessarily ex nihilo; it is not necessarily recognized at the time of its conception; and specific works of art may not be immediately identified as part of a new style, movement, or philosophy. Because computer games are a branch of popular culture, it is not clear how work derived from them (such as machinima) could avoid reflecting the influence of the increasingly sensationalized and visceral focus of television, film, and theater.

I should mention in passing that the above comments relate to computer games; Ebert has been quoted as praising various examples of machinima on machinima.com:

An individual animator, working alone like a painter, a novelist, or a poet, makes a work of art. Intrigued, I looked at some examples. . . . *Ozymandias* . . . involves simply rendered landscapes and a sketchy human figure that traverses them. Very basic, but curiously effective, and the music establishes the mood. Another film, *The Kick*, is simply a game demo. These films represent two choices. One has an idea, but the other just recycles the exhausted clichés of games. Neither is realistic in appearance, but here's an important point: Animation does not need realism. . . .The means of production are here. It's the artist part that's tricky.[3]

If we view only the work itself, how could we really know for sure that *Ozymandias* was not in-game footage accidentally captured? And why is it that a game cannot be art but machinima can? Imagine a player using an in-game camera that was automatically filming an actual game. Imagine she or he then sent the video to a machinima festival. If the audience could not distinguish the recording from machinima, would that mean the work could be considered art? If in this hypothetical example we could not distinguish authorially controlled digital filmmaking from spontaneous real-time player-based camera views (which we mistakenly believe to be authorially controlled), the argument that cinematic art requires a cinematic director falls flat. Perhaps I should call this a machinamatic Turing test, for it raises the question of the importance of directorial intention.

In his book *Definitions of Art*, the philosopher Stephen Davies (1991) argues that definitions of art are typically functional or procedural. The functionalist view holds that an object is a work of art only if it performs a particular function (such as providing or affording a rewarding aesthetic experience). By contrast, the proceduralist view holds that something is an artwork only if it has been created according to certain rules and procedures.

Machinima works may be seen as more procedural than functional, and hence can be judged as digital filmmaking art, or they may be judged like film, as they often contain cinematic elements or film genre references, or are informed by cinematic technique. Yet while it is true that machinima *classics* tend to be mining other genres using a certain type of equipment in a certain way, they do so by subverting the intended procedure, such as the limitations and expectations we automatically assume when presented with what appear to be understood game genres. And at least part of our aesthetic experience of machinima, the functional aspect, is informed by this procedural subversion.

Game theorists have written how constraint *is* design (Dugan 2006), or even that constraints actually inspire creativity (Perlin 2005a), and of course this is not new to theater designers and playwrights. But machinima takes this further by reminding us of the diegetic illusions of games and how quickly and powerfully they can stimulate default player response. Machinima can also allude to our shallow treatment of the avatars' virtual bodies when we are in game mode, and juxtapose serious philosophical and social issues against the typical stock behavior of shoot-and-run videos. To parody one's own creator and the ludic teasing of that segment of the audience that is in on the jokes—that is, game players—is an interesting media development. Machinima reminds us of the diegetic bubble as it mocks its own cinematic ambitions and limitations.

This Spartan Life is an example of machinima as a live talk show available to *Halo* (Microsoft Game Studios, 2001) players and often mistaken by them as a computer game and not as a virtual show being filmed. This means that guests may be gunned down by players totally ignorant of what is going on, and who are acting purely in competitive game mode. I am not the only one to see this use of machinima as innovative. D'Arcy Norman (2005) has also written:

If you've seen *Red vs. Blue*, or some of the similar movies made using "in game" videography from some games like *Halo* or *Quake3*, you'll know what machinima is. But *This Spartan Life* takes it one step further—instead of being a scripted "in-game play" being acted out, it's a full-blown talk show. Complete with guests, interviews, cameramen and crew, perimeter security snipers, stray rocket fire from nearby newbies, and the Solid Gold Elite Dancers.

So, in a way machinima is similar to theater, as the software and hardware constraints can actually help create thematic design, and machinima can use those constraints in an imaginative and reflective fashion.

For example, the Achilles' heel of games masquerading as both interactive entertainment and as drama is inadequate facial expression and orientation, as well as a lack of gestural expressiveness or free-form body language (Perlin 2005b). The complexity of real-time human facial movement is just too difficult and demanding for mainstream computer games. Expressive actors (game avatars) are still a chimera, although new game editors such as Source are changing this.

The game *Halo* avoids the problem of dynamically embodied expression by confining the player to run, jump, and shoot, by using bulky robots and strange little creatures as protagonists, and by concealing the avatars' faces with helmets. *Red vs. Blue*, for example, constantly reminds us of the blank visage of a *Halo* avatar; the overly expressive voices are juxtaposed against the expressionless facades of the blank helmets. The dramatic conflict of the characters, the speed with which they can be antagonized by each other, and their ability to (apparently) see what others are looking at or facially expressing is a startling contrast to *Halo* the game, in which the expressive qualities of the face are unimportant.

This technique is both humorous and startling. We are reminded how we forget about other players as fully embodied expressive agents when we play a game, and we are asked to imagine that the avatars inhabit their own world, which has its own laws and motives that are independent of the game world we can see and interact with. Of course, there are many stories of toys that come alive at night when humans are asleep, toys or cartoon characters that appear to have their own secret lives. Yet machinima has an additional feature, which *This Spartan Life* partially exemplifies: machinima can be pre-scripted yet run as a real-time medium with spectator intervention or interaction.

Machinima as Emotional Affordance: Must Art Always Make Us Cry?

In September 2004, Anthony Breznican wrote that Steven Spielberg and Robert Zemeckis believed "video games are getting closer to a storytelling art form—but are not quite there yet." Spielberg sets down a benchmark for reaching this level:

I think the real indicator will be when somebody confesses that they cried at level 17. . . . It's important to emphasize story and emotion and character. This is one of the things that games don't do," Spielberg said. . . ."Is the player in charge of the story, or is the programmer in control of the story?" Spielberg asked. "How do you make those two things reconcile with each other? Audiences often don't want to be in control of a story. They want to be lost in your story. They come to hear you be the storyteller, but in gaming it's going to have to be a little bit of both, a little bit of give and take.

I partially agree with Spielberg that computer games will be hard-pressed to reach the expressive and controlled level of films. Game characters are simplified in form and movement; they have a limited range of animation. The typical plot is skimpy at best, for the player has to concentrate on surviving, as well as on what to do next. The camera is also limited, and lighting is limited, restricted, and reduced, to save on rendering time and processing power. The games that use game engines that in turn are used for machinima are also geared toward panic and hurry, not toward viewing picturesque scenes and contemplating the universe. So, game engines will have trouble approximating the emotional impact and aesthetic beauty of film; they simply lack the control and finesse in character expression, setting, and cinematic tools (cameras, filters, lighting). On the other hand, as Zemeckis admits, films have borrowed from game techniques (Breznican 2004): "In the '80s, cinema became influenced by the pace and style of television commercials. . . . I think the next decades are going to be influenced greatly by the digital world of gaming."

Roger Ebert appears to agree with Spielberg that games do not currently exert great emotional hold over us, but he goes farther in suggesting that by their very nature, games can not gain the status of art as that which is morally uplifting or has the ability to *enculturate* us:

To my knowledge, no one in or out of the field has ever been able to cite a game worthy of comparison with the great dramatists, poets, filmmakers, novelists and composers. That a game can aspire to artistic importance as a visual experience, I accept. But for most gamers, video games represent a loss of those precious hours we have available to make ourselves more cultured, civilized and empathetic.[4]

I wonder why Ebert mentions drama and not painting. In painting the eye is allowed to wander; direction can be coerced but it is not precisely predictable. Perhaps Ebert does not mention painting because the experience and perception of painting may stretch his notion of authorial control. Or perhaps the reason is related to Spielberg's point, that the weakest artistic component of games is typically the story element, and so games will typically fare badly in telling a story when compared with film and literature, but painting (and performance art) does not require this emphasis to be considered art.

Do the structural features of games preclude games from creating meaningful experiences and also prevent games from being considered great art? Jeremy Reimer (2005) believes that "a closer examination of Ebert's comments seems to indicate that he is critical of the artistic value of the games themselves, not their structure." I am not yet convinced by Reimer's suggestion. Yes, Ebert put forward the claim that "video games represent a loss of those precious hours we have available to make ourselves more cultured, civilized and empathetic." He also said that games couldn't be "worthy of comparison with the great dramatists, poets, filmmakers, novelists and composers." However, as I mentioned earlier, he also said, "There is a structural reason for that: Video games by their nature require player choices, which is the opposite of the strategy of serious film and literature, which requires authorial control."

Do the repetitive features of mainstream computer games preclude games from creating meaningful experiences or raising moral issues, and therefore exclude games from being considered to be great art? Quite often aesthetic theories rely on the premise that because an activity contains a significant amount of X, therefore X is an integral, essential feature of this activity. This is not necessarily true, however much it would help simplify definitions of art. To make universal claims about the evils inherent in computer games, these critics must not only prove that games currently have these flaws, but also that these flaws are inescapable.

Ebert does not explain why player choices are the opposite of authorial control. My assumption is that he means a player will not choose an option with as much mastery or skillful long-term vision, but perhaps he means something else (such as there needing to be a foreign or almost uncanny agency, such as direction by an outside director, not by the player, for it to be art). Second, Ebert is saying that *current* games have these flaws, and assuming (not proving) that therefore *all* games must (as a collective genre) have these flaws. This does not necessarily follow.

Ebert criticized games as being antisocial or of questionable moral value, yet films can be as well, even artistic ones of the caliber of *Clockwork Orange*. I can see his underlying point here, for a typical computer game does not allow reflection and contemplation during playing, but that does not mean reflection on moral or social issues cannot be induced by the game after the gameplay has finished. Interestingly, Ebert himself has severely criticized the famous Kubrick version of *Clockwork Orange* for being too immoral and supportive of the main character (Ebert 1972). Kubrick's version is based on the U.S. version of the book, which is missing a chapter found in the UK version. In that final, twenty-first chapter, the main character realizes the error of his ways. So, one can say the film version is less reflective and has less moral balance than the original book. Curiously, there are also many stage productions of the book. One, a theatrical multimedia production of *Clockwork Orange*, featured various video streams and the main character prerecorded as a narrator while the same character is on the stage (*L.A. Weekly* 2004). It has been nominated for several awards, and one wonders whether in this case at least, interaction can help rather than hinder.

Apart from the above example (where Kubrick's version could be said to be too immoral and tangential to the book precisely because it lacks interaction, choice, and decision making), the statement that video games are artistically hindered by player choice and by the sacrifice of authorial control is fascinating. If you take the left passage rather than the right one in a game, has the designer any less control? Or if you fail to see that the first sentence of *Steppenwolf* continues up from the last sentence of the book, have you missed the artistic value of Hesse's masterpiece? If several directors take turns shooting a film, one after another, is it then ruined? If a film becomes famous as a studio cut version rather than as the director's version, is the director an inferior artist? If a master artist is asked to play a sandbox-type game, could he or she *not* be able to produce something worthy of the status of art?

The question facing us now is, does interactive entertainment lower the ability of the work to transfer and inspire? Boris Johnson (2006) described computer gamers as "blinking lizards," and demanded the destruction of games and game consoles in homes. The logic is not immediately apparent to me. If games cannot be structurally similar to films, and if this feature precludes them from being art, I can see they cannot result in great art. If that is the case, why even attempt to compare them to works of art? However, Ebert seems to be saying rather that the activity of playing games cannot lead us to be "cultured, civilized and empathetic." Hence their inability to be considered art relates to their content, not to their intrinsic structure.

Strangely, television no longer raises the same complaints, even if television can be as mundane, addictive, and meaningless, without the benefits of strategic decision making, player choice, and player action. Critics and gamers against the regressive and mind-numbing commercial games churned out by the larger companies can also point out films that just as easily (and inadvertently) induce in viewers a zombie-like state. And to suggest that games and game-related content lack reflective, nonviolent, or morally edifying content when compared with film or literature sounds good on the face of it, but a more accurate statement would be that in their nascent state, few new forms of media have polished form or culturally accomplished content. And of course, games have far fewer examples to choose from than do established media.

Art as Epiphany

In the nineteenth century Konrad Fiedler argued that art is an immersion in the study of perception by the individual. Fiedler believed that people are too quick to turn their perceptions into feelings, or into concepts. In order to be artists they must instead be able to hold on to and explore their perceptual knowledge without relegating (i.e., binding) perception to either abstract knowledge or emotion. In other words, art works as a portal to self-discovery and expansion of our understanding of how we perceive or the outside world as long as we don't automatically categorize and compartmentalize it.

Fiedler believed that only by exploring the world as an infinite and ever-changing interplay of perceptual knowledge does the artist become an artist. Art is thus a process of discovery, a questioning. We see effects that don't explain the origin of the work of art, but, according to Fiedler (1978, 17), we ask the following question:

[H]ow can it emerge out of the artistic consciousness? At that very moment the work of art attains true life for us. Immediately we see ourselves drawn into the activity of the creating artist and we grasp the result as a living, growing one.

Thus the appreciation of art involves the notion of recreating artistic activity. In viewing a work as a work of art, we in turn explore questions and expand our perceptual knowledge of the world. In the viewing of art we in turn become artists. For Fiedler, art differs from nature in that it is essentially an intentional activity and the creative purpose is the only essential aspect of art. But that does not mean that the public determines what art is. Fiedler in fact believed that the more people view a work of art, the more likely it is to be misinterpreted and misunderstood.

Fiedler argued that art is not art because people attempt to put it into a historical framework, for knowledge of historical form does not necessarily lead to a deep and vivid knowledge of the worth of individual works of art. Fiedler also deemed it impossible to know art via the role of the connoisseur: the range of art is too huge for any one individual to know. If a connoisseur becomes a collector of rarities and peculiarities, that does not mean that the connoisseur has become knowledgeable about art, only that he or she has become knowledgeable about the rarities and strange trivia found in art as a classification system.

Another method of appreciating art, in terms of how we can classify it, Fiedler rejected as also being peripheral to an experience of art. His argument was that knowing the history of an artwork is not the same as an appreciation of the work itself. The above approaches to art, Fiedler (1978, 28) argued, are in fact approaches to the appreciation of artistic effects, and do not lead to the appreciation of art itself. If we are to appreciate art, we must, like artists,

grasp its [art's] very existence, and they [artists] feel the object as a whole even before they break up this general feeling into many separate sensations.

In order to further explain art as epiphany, I feel compelled to refer to the writings of a mid-twentieth-century philosopher, Martin Heidegger (1971, 26). He argued that the notion of art couldn't be merely the response to sensations:

Much closer to us than all sensations are the things themselves. We hear the door shut in the house and never hear acoustical sensations or even mere sounds. In order to hear a bare sound we have to listen away from things, divert our ear from them, i.e., listen abstractly.

Heidegger argued that we hear sounds, not acoustic sensations, and thus by implication all aesthetic phenomena (i.e., those sensations that the brain responds to) are actually distillations of past experiences, codified and responded to as the outcomes of deliberate, intentional activity. There is thus, Heidegger argued, something to works of art, the "thingly character," which is not encompassed or created by the perception of mere sensations.

A work of art brings out the unique, significant aspects of an object, and these aspects reveal the object as a distinct thing. The revealing of such distinctness is part of the encountering of a work of art. When we encounter art, we are experiencing it as a thing, and we are experiencing our relation to it as a thing, as if our eyes were opened for the very first time. Hence our encounter with art can sometimes be seen as an epiphany.

Machinations So Far: Interstitial Media as Procedural Subversion

We may further extend the argument to suggest there is an aspect of "thingness" to our perception of our world that should be considered in designing virtual environments in general, and games and machinima in particular. And Heidegger's argument has recently been bolstered by experiments in virtual environments. Researchers have suggested that there is indeed a "toolness" quality to certain objects in virtual environments in that certain objects have an especially compelling feature or attachment that induces us to pick them up and use them for no apparent reason (Handy et al. 2003).

In a *Gamasutra* article, John Hopson has also mentioned how the computer game is a behavioral Skinner box, a reward system consisting of *reinforcers*, *contingencies*, and *responses* (Hopson 2001). Because machinima often uses or evokes images and associations with playing a game, and because these resources are such powerful triggering mechanisms, the game player as spectator is caught between viewing the machinima as film and reaching for a keyboard mouse or joystick to shoot the bad guys, strafe to avoid danger, rotate the camera view, or run toward a portal. Computer games have their own acquired language of perceived affordances (Norman 1990), and reacting to these perceived affordances becomes second nature to the experienced gamer (van Vugt et al. 2006).

Machinima pieces are typically created from the camera functions of game engines. However, they are also typically made from resources associated with the game engine, and hence they carry genre attachments. The repetitive nature of games conditions us to automatically respond by enacting game-behaviors, dodging, shooting, running, strafing, and so on. So there are triggers, but there are also "things" that stimulate the player vocabulary. Another *Gamasutra* article explains how game-level designers deliberately develop a "player vocabulary" so that the game player acts instinctively: "As designers, we can carefully build a vocabulary of game mechanics and shape what the player knows about the environment, and when they know it" (Johnson 2001).

To say that the power of machinima is derived from its refocusing on what we have previously taken for granted, or previously adopted without reflection, relies on previous gaming knowledge. Yes, my interpretation of machinima as an art form may rely on creating a reflection on what some hardened critics of games consider a zombie-like or "blinking lizards" state when playing, but, like Stephen Johnson (2005), I believe that the way in which games are designed to trigger and overload certain cognitive processes is deliberate, intricate, and difficult. To trigger behavioral responses while at the same time causing the player or observer to reflect on them and still stay engaged is sophisticated and skillful. For example, it would not be easy to play on our Pavlov-like tendency to reach for a shiny gun a *Halo* character is toying with while he recounts how he survived severe teenage acne and a dominating mother.

And yes, I understand that this perspective means that machinima may not appeal to or be widely understood by a nongaming public. Yet machinima is not alone in this regard; cinema, architecture, and even painting can be self-referential or disparaging of other media, and in so doing may require from the spectator knowledge of the other work they are targeting or to which they pay homage. The primary experience is still dependent on the immediacy of the connections. Machinima doesn't gain its distinctive power from simply linking different media and genres but from the thoughts provoked by the synthesizing of these links.

I suggest that the uneasy and unfaithful alliance between machinima as aesthetic experience and machinima as an accidental offspring of game replays should be teased out still further. If there are no hard-and-fast rules, machinima could potentially be partially or entirely real time (just as the early demo recordings of games were) rather than fully prerendered. Audience interaction and participation can influence the development and or the contextual infill or backstory of the work. Bots could be controlled by actors or by script or alternate between the two. Off-scene dynamic data or even audience biofeedback could be fed into the scene or affect the environmental conditions, provide motivatioal triggers for the characters, and change story pathways. Even in the final presentation or exhibition, designers could layer machinima between real-time user-controlled artifacts with script triggers or commands and traditional film clips, allowing viewers to explore and play with what is interactive and what is not.

Research into Procedural Subversion

While there is current research to incorporate and improve on localized rather than walkie-talkie-style voice chat in games (Wadley, Gibbs, and Benda 2005), machinima could also use a form of indirect audience interaction (triggered by anything from heat, stress, movement, gesture, light, or shadow to voice) to emphasize key cinematic elements, navigate between different filmed scenes, or influence prescribed characters to forgo certain lines of programming.

If the machinima was actually prerendered in the foreground of live and dynamic content, ambient audience interaction could also be utilized. For example, I supervised

Figure 13.1
Car racing in a tent. Courtesy of Jonathan Barrett and Bonnii Weeks.

a group of students (Bonnii Weeks and Jonathan Barrett) who built an ambient form of audience interaction, initially inspired by an interpretation of *MechWarrior*. In their game installation the player sits on a hydraulic chair with gameplay-driven force feedback, surrounded by the game environment projected via a curved mirror (Bourke 2005) onto the inside of a dome or tent.

In another project, Andrew Dekker examined how biofeedback could enhance gameplay (figure 13.2). Using a cheap commercial biosensor interface, and with access to the software development kit, he incorporated the player's biofeedback at regular intervals into the game level. For example, as the galvanic skin response of the player increased, the shaders of the game would change, to white or red (or whatever the designer thought cinematically related to increased or decreased stress levels), and the higher the readings, the higher the rate of spawning of monsters.

For the biofeedback project, we were very keen to test the psychological gameplay possibilities of multiplayer biofeedback. The survey found that music was a more powerful atmospheric trigger than interactive graphic shaders. In the future we hope to discover whether players see their opponents' biofeedback, and try to discover and set phobic triggers that cause their opponents to experience stress and decrease their game performance.

These two research projects were only initial investigations, but aspects of them could also be incorporated into a layered combination of machinima and gameplay.

Figure 13.2
Biofeedback is incorporated into gameplay, changing the shaders and the NPCS. Courtesy of Andrew Dekker.

That is, the audience and the player could share some amount of interaction, directly, or indirectly, but they may not exactly know what is prerendered and what is interactive, or who is consciously, accidentally, or subconsciously controlling the interaction. Variable authorial control is but one aspect of this form of transmedia; biofeedback and improvements in facial tracking could see real-time facial and bodily expressions in games, which could also open up new dramatic possibilities in machinima and related media.

Conclusion: Are There Essential Features of Machinima?

Machinima, even if it is an uneasy offspring of computer games (for the moment, let us equate them with Ebert's video games), can have elements of authorial control and embodied expression. This does not mean that machinima is art, for Ebert's criteria conflict with each other and are not necessary and sufficient conditions to determine what art is. However, we are surely right to question whether machinima wants to be classified by institutions as a form of art, as then it may lose its subversive power. This subversive power or appeal may be due to many different creative possibilities. I have suggested some of the possible features are reflective game genre and impulse criticism, and aesthetic provocation and puzzlement around what is interactive and what is not, around what appears to be scripted, emergent, or chaotic, real or virtual, or even around levels of sentience, from automated through preprogrammed intelligence, to human intelligence.

Defining the boundaries may satisfy the academics (or least give them more ammunition to argue with each other), but it may also limit a creative future aspect of machinima not currently envisaged. These possibilities may never be tested if we see machinima in an essentialist light, an auteur in-game FPS video capture, or a poor if disrespectful cousin to cinema. To separate activities or objects through classification may describe these activities or objects, but it often leads to an essentialism based on easily perceivable differences without actually meaningfully explaining why the creation of one is more intrinsically valuable than the other. And while Davies' bifurcation of theories of art into functionalist or proceduralist is an initially interesting approach, it does not really highlight the more interesting features of machinima, for part of the appeal of machinima is that it is not so easily bifurcated and even deliberately confuses the two.

The current operational definitions of machinima do not interest designers; they already understand the advantages of machinima as a filmmaking tool. For theorists, exploring essentialist definitions of machinima is an interesting exercise as long as such definitions both highlight important features and reveal the blindness or indifference of their proponents to other features. For the public, for the spectator or end-user (and hopefully the former is merging into the latter), to enjoy experiencing a self-reflective jolt when the gaming impulses or genre-detection facilities are provoked, challenged, or questioned by machinima is surely a worthy (if difficult) challenge. And interactive media have a long way to go to achieve this.

Machinima as epiphany has implications for teaching; machinima can act as a catalyst for students to question their own opinions and conventions. Their tacit acceptance of game conventions becomes self-evident, for example, when they are asked to create or to reflectively critique and challenge media or genres that their compatriots value. Allowing students to use their favorite game engines and game genres does not necessarily encourage them to build fresh and innovative new games. However, encouraging their ambitions of a cinematic-quality experience in such a way that they are confronted with the practical limitations of current machinima, and in particular of game engines, could prove to be a far more valuable experience. Although students are often attracted to the latest and most advanced game engines, the constraints of earlier (and probably more stable and accessible) game engines can actually aid creativity rather than stymie it.

This observation leads me to suggest that machinima can be viewed as a design procedure. It is possible to say it is machinima if one uses certain tools in creating it. Yet machinima may also be an experience that either reminds or hides from the end-user its origins as a fairly primitive virtual camera in a game engine attempting to provide a cinematic experience. For example, the way in which early machinima either downplayed or emphasized the limited field of view as it was using the limited camera functions of early shooter games is technically interesting to experts but unlikely to be noticed by an infrequent gamer.

Machinima may also be a reflective and aesthetically directed re-experience of gameplay, game genre, and game-level resources that gains impact from its new take on cinematic conventions. Innocuous games like *The Sims* or machinima like Rooster Teeth's *The Strangerhood* could be used to parody the homogeneity and shocking plot devices of, say, a television soap opera. But a more powerful interpretation is to consider machinima as an interpretively amorphous vehicle that questions and challenges our understanding of what is static, dynamic, alive, sentient, responsive, or automated, and what is not.

Heidegger viewed art (well, great art) as a portal between what we suddenly see of our own relation to our past and a glance at and glimmer of a potential future. He posed the following question about appreciating art: "[Can] wonder open what is locked?" (Heidegger 1996, 55–56.). His answer is yes, initially, and no, not continually. Wonder is needed, for art is extraordinary, but it also needs safeguarding, for "the issue is keeping meditative thinking alive." Heidegger was not thinking of machinima when he wrote these comments, but I am. For the purpose of this essay was not to define machinima. In its messy vitality, machinima has the potential to redefine us.

Notes

1. "Art (first definition)," Oxford Dictionaries, <http://www.askoxford.com:80/concise_oed/art_1?view=uk>. Also, "Art," Encyclopædia Britannica, <http://www.britannica.com/EBchecked/topic/630806/art>.

2. Jim Emerson, "Video Games: The Epic Debate," comment posted April 18 2006, <http://rogerebert.suntimes.com/apps/pbcs.dll/article?AID=/20060418/SCANNERS/60418001>.

3. Roger Ebert, quoted in machinima.com post "Roger Ebert on Machinima" on May 15 2000, <http://www.machinima.com/news/view&id=395>.

4. Roger Ebert, "Why did the chicken cross the genders?" comment posted November 27, 2005, <http://rogerebert.suntimes.com/apps/pbcs.dll/section?category=ANSWERMAN&date=20051127>.

References

Adams, Ernest, and Andrew Rollings. 2003. *Andrew Rollings and Ernest Adams on Game Design*. Indianapolis: New Riders.

Berg, M. 1982. John Ruskin's Definition of D. G.Rossetti's Art. *Victorian Poetry* 20 (3–4): 103–112.

Bourke, Paul. 2005. Using a spherical Mirror for Projection into Immersive Environments. In *Proceedings of the 3rd International Conference on Computer Graphics and Interactive Techniques in Australasia and South East Asia*, 281–284. New York: ACM Press.

Breznican, Anthony. 2004. Spielberg, Zemeckis Say Video Games, Films Could Become One. Associated Press, September 4. <http://legacy.signonsandiego.com/news/features/20040915-1336-ca-games-spielberg-zemeckis.html>.

Carrier, D., ed. 1998. *Danto and His Critics: Art History, Historiography and After the End of Art*. Middletown, CT: Wesleyan University Press.

Davies, Stephen. 1991. *Definitions of Art*. Ithaca, NY: Cornell University Press.

Dugan, Patrick. 2006. Constraint Is Design: Katherine Isbister and Nicole Lazzaro on Intimate Relations. Gamasutra.com. <http://gamasutra.com/features/20060714/dugan_01.shtml>.

Ebert, Roger. 2005. Why Did the Chicken Cross the Genders? <http://rogerebert.suntimes.com/apps/pbcs.dll/section?category=answerman&date=2005112http://rogerebert.com>.

Ebert, Roger. 1972. A Clockwork Orange. <http://rogerebert.suntimes.com/apps/pbcs.dll/article?AID=/19720211/REVIEWS/202110301/1023>.

Fiedler, Konrad. 1978. *On Judging Works of Visual Art*. Berkeley and Los Angeles: University of California Press.

Hales, Chris. 2005. Cinematic Interaction: From Kinoautomat to Cause and Effect. *Digital Creativity* 16 (1): 54–64.

Handy, Todd C., Scott Grafton, Neha Shroff, Sarah Ketay, and Michael Gazzaniga. 2003. Graspable Objects Grab Attention When the Potential for Action Is Recognized. *Nature Neuroscience* 6:421–427. <http://www.nature.com/neuro/journal/v6/n4/abs/nn1031.html>.

Heidegger, Martin. 1996. *Discourse on Thinking*. New York: Harper and Row.

Heidegger, Martin. 1977. *The Question Concerning Technology and Other Essays*. New York: Harper and Row.

Heidegger, Martin. 1971. *Poetry, Language, Thought*. New York: Harper and Row.

Hopson, John. 2001. Behavioral Game Design. *Gamasutra*. <http://www.gamasutra.com/view/feature/3085/behavioral_game_design.php?page=1>.

Jenkins, Henry. 2007. Game Design as Narrative Architecture. *Electronic Book Review*. <http://www.electronicbookreview.com/thread/firstperson/lazzi-fair>.

Johnson, Boris. 2006. The Writing Is on the Wall: Computer Games Rot the Brain. *Telegraph* (London), December 28. <http://www.telegraph.co.uk/opinion/main.jhtml>?xml=/opinion/2006/12/28/do2801.xml>.

Johnson, Brett. 2001. Great Expectations: Building a Player Vocabulary. Gamasutra.com. <http://www.gamasutra.com/resource_guide/20010716/johnson_01.htm>.

Johnson, Stephen. 2005. *Everything Bad Is Good for You: How Popular Culture Is Making Us Smarter.* London: Allen Lane.

L.A. Weekly. 2004. The 25th Annual *LA Weekly* Theater Award Nominees. <http://www.laweekly.com/ink/04/12/theater-awards.php>.

Langer, Susanne K. 1953. *Feeling and Form: A Theory of Art.* London: Routledge & Kegan Paul.

Marino, Paul. 2004. *3d Game-Based Filmmaking: The Art of Machinima.* Scottsdale, AZ: Paraglyph Press.

Norman, D'Arcy. 2005. This Spartan Life: Machinima Talk Show. *D'ArcyNorman.net.* <http://www.darcynorman.net/2005/08/19/this-spartan-life-machinima-talk-show>.

Norman, Donald. 1990. *The Design of Everyday Things.* New York: Doubleday.

Perlin, Ken. 2005a. A Riposte to: Ken Perlin. *Electronic Book Review.* <http://www.electronicbookreview.com/thread/firstperson/perlinr2>.

Perlin, Ken. 2005b. Between a Game and a Story? *Electronic Book Review* (original post May 1, 2004; last activity July 26, 2005). <http://www.electronicbookreview.com/thread/firstperson/formal>.

Reimer, Jeremy. 2005. Roger Ebert Says Games Will Never Be as Worthy as Movies. ArsTechnica.com. <http://arstechnica.com/news.ars/post/20051130-5657.html>.

Salen, Katie, and Eric Zimmerman. 2003. *Rules of Play: Game Design Fundamentals.* Cambridge: MIT Press.

Sorenson, L. n.d. Worringer, Wilhelm. *Dictionary of Art Historians* (online). <http://www.dictionaryofarthistorians.org/worringerw.htm>.

Spengler, Oswald, and Charles Francis Atkinson. 1932. *The Decline of the West.* London: Allen & Unwin.

van Vugt, H. C., J. F. Hoorn, E. A. Konijn, and A. Dimitriadou. 2006. Affective Affordances: Improving Interface Character Engagement through Interaction. *International Journal of Human-Computer Studies* 64 (9): 874–888.

Wadley, Greg, Martin Gibbs, and Peter Benda. 2005. Towards a Framework for Designing Speech-Based Player Interaction in Multiplayer Online Games. In *Proceedings of the Second Australasian Conference on Interactive Entertainment*, 223–226. Sydney, Australia: Creativity & Cognition Studios Press.

Software References

Halo. Bungie; Microsoft Game Studios. 2001.

MechWarrior. Activision. 1989.

MechWarrior IV. FASA Interactive. Microsoft Game Studios. 2000.

Myst. Cyan Worlds. Brøderbund Software. 1993.

Sims. Maxis. Electronic Arts. 2000.

Sims 2. Maxis. Electronic Arts. 2004.

V Pedagogy

Bernhard Drax, dir., *Your California Legacy:* Dickens in Camp, *by Bret Harte* (2009).

14   Everything I Need to Know about Filmmaking I Learned from Playing Video Games: The Educational Promise of Machinima

Matthew Thomas Payne

Teachers, education policy professionals, and politicians have long lamented the fact that we are encumbered with "an education system based on an agricultural calendar and organized after an Industrial Age model [that must now] transform itself to provide a 21st century education that prepares students for the Information Age" (Patrick 2004).[1] Retrofitting our educational system to accommodate the communication tools of the twenty-first century demands numerous adjustments—economic, technical, administrative, political, and, not least, pedagogical. The difficulty of introducing and using new media texts and information and communication technologies in most classrooms is not simply a resource allocation dilemma (the most obvious type of digital divide) or a question of appropriate application. There is the additional need to assure and persuade educators that these new digital texts and tools do in fact present pedagogical opportunities and are not simply distractions from, or threats to, valued educational goals. The digital divide problem is thus twofold: first, educators must deliver and situate information and communication technologies and new media texts in classrooms, thereby creating a semblance of technological parity between schools and other social spaces; and second, as media literacy scholar Kathleen Tyner (2003, 6) observes, "pre-digital definitions of school success [should not continue to] require young people to park their media skills and cultures at the schoolhouse door."

Over its relatively short life as a formal discipline, media education has readily adopted different media texts and technologies as prospective learning tools. This technology-friendly attitude made media literacy classes and programs vanguard sites for assessing how information and communication technologies might aid educators. The "digital natives," those who have grown up around such technologies and interactive media, are familiar not just with older media (e.g., radio, television, film) but also very frequently with contemporary convergence culture,[2] the user-centric practices that combine and remix existing media to create original expressions that are played on and across various communication devices and platforms (e.g., iPods, PCs, mobile phones, online social networks). Convergence culture is represented by an ever-growing list of expressive forms, including mashups, blogs, vlogs, viral videos, and machinima (a portmanteau word formed from "machine" and "cinema"). This essay's goal is to explore how media education might harness machinima as a creative fusion of digital storytelling and video gameplay to teach digital analysis and practice in collaborative learning spaces.

Machinima has unique formal characteristics that make it especially well-suited for media education. First, the art form bridges common student-teacher interest areas and profits from shared popular cultural references, such as video game culture and online fandom. Machinima-making platforms and programs also offer budding video directors the virtual equivalents of the creative tools used by real-world production companies—camera, lighting, props—and at a fraction of the price of any live-action equivalent. Furthermore, producing digital narratives in this manner entails the creative processes of worldly film and video production. In fact, the two are so coterminous at a decision-making level that media educators could use machinima to teach film and video preproduction, production, and postproduction skills to students who are already conversant with popular visual culture and basic computer technologies.

Using machine cinema in the classroom will likely lead to two interdependent goals valued by nearly all media literacy programs—increased media production and analysis competences. Story creation, shot composition, transitions, art design, image capturing, audio recording, nonlinear video editing, and performance directing are not only vital logistical and creative skills advocated by film and video production curricula but also indispensable tools for making compelling machinima works. Learning transferable and potentially employable production skills might be a positive outcome of creative work in a virtual environment, but machinima making need not be justified or legitimated only by referencing some live-action equivalent. After all, machine cinema is not a farm league for worldly moviemaking, and it is categorically not pseudo-filmmaking. Teaching students how to craft original digital narratives from repurposed game content begets increasingly sophisticated machinima, which ought to be deemed an artistic and educational good in its own right. And because reading machinima-made texts requires a working literacy of the same visual and narrative rules employed in contemporary moving image culture writ large, this emergent art form invites students to engage in "practical criticisms and critical practices" whereby they can become increasingly sophisticated media critic-producers (Eddie Dick, quoted in Tyner 1998, 156). Media teachers can also track student learning by observing the production choices that are exercised over the course of making these virtual stories, and then compare these decisions with an assessment rubric listing the conceptual feats deemed central to achieving media literacy for a given group of learners.

This essay does not focus on the breadth of machine cinema expressions but instead examines how media education can leverage one game to support its twin goals of cultivating media production and analysis competencies. To make this argument, the essay begins by reviewing how twenty-first-century media literacy has been defined and framed. Next, the essay demonstrates how the process of machinima making is strongly compatible with constructivist learning theory. Finally, it argues that *The Sims* is a game primed for educational application because it easily doubles as a virtual film school, providing a clear framework and workflow for students wanting to learn both production-related skills, such as screen aesthetics and editing, and analytic skills, such as media criticism and narrative strategies.

The ideas about machinima and digital storytelling explored herein are largely applicable to K–12 and post-secondary education students, though it is ultimately outside this essay's purview to outline specific blueprints for curriculum development.[3] Instead, the essay aims to begin a conversation about how machine cinema might be mobilized to aid media educators wishing to teach critical moving image production *and* analysis skills.

Machinima and Twenty-first-Century Media Literacy

To frame machinima and machinima-making as a twenty-first-century media literacy is to enter into a longstanding debate concerning what constitutes media literacy in particular, and basic literacy in general. Designating this pop art, moving image form of expression as an emergent literacy is potentially controversial because by linking machinima with literacy, one implies that machine cinema is capable of making educational inroads for better understanding media, culture, and language. A variety of challenges can be anticipated to this claim. For example, despite (or perhaps owing to) the popularity of electronic games among youth and the technology's growing social presence (e.g., in cars, hotels, cell phones), video and electronic games are still popularly perceived as anathema to educators.[4] Meanwhile, the institutional appropriateness and educational value of hands-on media production in K–12 classrooms is still roundly debated, most vociferously in the United States (Tyner 1998, chap. 10). And as school budgets are slashed and teachers are encouraged to "teach to the test," it becomes increasingly difficult to justify the allocation of already limited resources to teaching an unpiloted and trendy, fan-centric moving image practice. Yet none of these probable challenges to introducing machinima into the classroom disqualifies it as a valuable resource for media literacy programs. Before exploring how machinima might contribute to media education by mobilizing popular culture and play for educational ends, it is worth reviewing how the creative processes that animate machine cinema complement media education.

Media education, with its primary goal of media literacy, is, like other academic disciplines, rife with differing basic conceptualizations. Complicating matters is that media education should also, according to its key critics, be interested in fostering a range of literacies, including information literacy, technology literacy, and visual literacy, to name but a few (ibid., chap. 4). For the purposes of this essay, I understand media education as "the process through which one learns to become media literate," and I define media literacy as the ability to critically analyze, use, and produce contemporary media texts (Center for Media Literacy n.d., Question 1). Teaching others to decode and create their own media is undergirded by a set of core, shared ethical imperatives. Andrew Hart (2001, 3) characterizes media education's moral modus operandi generally, stating,

> Media education is unavoidably concerned with learning about values. It involves a search for meaning and purpose in relation to challenging life experiences; the growth of self-awareness and responsibility for one's own experience and identity; the development of self-respect; recognition of the worth of others and the importance of relationships; the importance of compassion, of imaginative engagement with experience and creative activity.

Media educator Bob Ferguson (2001, 21) echoes Hart's position, noting that "the idea that the media student can or could be a dispassionate observer of societies' foibles is neither productive nor responsible. Media students and researchers, like other intellectuals, are implicated in the societies of which they are a part." Media analysis, even insightful readings of media texts, processes, and the culture industries, represents only one part of media education's holistic mission. The other half is to inculcate ethically informed media production practices built on artifacts and techniques co-opted from popular culture.

Media education students are not only positioned as active participants in their own education (in both formal and informal learning venues), they are encouraged to draw analytic insights and creative inspiration from their peers and extant media environments. And because the endgame of media education is to become functionally, if not superlatively, media literate, the discipline is unapologetically interdisciplinary. The field's objects of study are drawn from popular culture, a birthplace that is still maligned by well-ensconced and elitist traditions. This means that unlike other educational curricula, media literacy welcomes nontraditional, emergent, and popular artifacts; after all, media education has no privileged canon to defend. The discipline purposefully recognizes the significance of everyday cultural goods in the lives of media users, and the need to track how social power circulates through mass media. In a brief but illuminating write-up of their 2005 21st Century Literacy Summit, the New Media Consortium's conference attendees underscored the importance of popular media to media education:

> Media and the arts are the vanguard in this world, out in front, breaking new ground. Creative people are inventing new forms of expression, experimenting with them, and disseminating them. Not all new forms are adopted, of course, but the drive to explore and create is fueled by artists, musicians, and popular culture. Researchers have begun to think about these new forms of expression in the same way they might a new language. Using the very language forms they are studying, researchers work collaboratively to discover and describe the nature of 21st century literacy. (Ibid., 7)

Machinima, then, is only one of the convergent forms of expression in our constantly growing new media lexicon.

Culture and technology critics mine cutting-edge media tools and texts (e.g., video games, vlogs, machinima, social networking sites) to uncover latent and manifest social meanings. But the onus typically is on teachers and education scholars to best mobilize these digital wares for educational ends.[5] In *Teaching Youth Media*, Steven Goodman (2003, 35–36) rightly contends that "Educators must apply a broad knowledge of language, media, technology, and culture to their teaching since their students use multiple literacies to make sense of these various media—literacies that are constructed by variables such as race, class, ethnicity, gender and age." Media education's interdisciplinary nature, in concert with the seemingly exponential growth of new media, begs the question, how should popular media be used for educational ends? After all, just because certain media are popular with students does not de facto mean that they are, or might become, viable candidates for classroom application. Media literacy educators often look for two basic criteria when evaluating whether popular media can serve their pedagogical needs: first, can the text(s) be analyzed and produced, and second, can these dual tasks be performed collaboratively?

Media education places considerable importance on shared learning and praxis because learning *about* media *through* media in a collaborative setting agrees with what Kathleen Tyner calls the "analysis-learning formula." According to Tyner (1998, 200), this reciprocity of tasks engenders "a spiral of success: analysis informs production, which in turn informs analysis." Eddie Dick advocates a similar but more forceful analysis-production linkage for media education, saying,

An aim of media education is to close the gap between analysis and practice, between criticism and doing. Only those who have engaged in practice are in the "correct" position to criticize; practice without critical awareness is blind, "commonsensical" and sterile. The media are best understood as sets of processes (e.g., technical, professional, aesthetic, ideological, economical, political) whose purposes include the social generation of meanings. In the context of that view, production work and the simulation of professional production are of vital importance. However, Media Studies is not in the business of training technicians or of merely informing armchair critics but . . . encouraging practical criticisms and critical practices. (Quoted in ibid., 156)

This impassioned endorsement of classroom media production supports experiential learning, a pedagogical strategy more commonly known as learning by doing. When media education employs this technique, students are asked to interpret and evaluate their peers' works as media consumers (readers) and build their own narratives with visual tools and pop culture elements as media bricoleurs (writers), opening themselves up for critique. With the right time, equipment, and instruction, machine cinema can meet both of these "reading" and "writing" requirements, thereby achieving a "reprisal of the symbiotic relationship between alphabetic reading and writing" (ibid., 200). Moreover, when media educators lead these criticism-production activities in the classroom, the shared experience of interpreting and making student-centered media together begets better analyses and better productions.

As Dick's observation cited earlier suggests, there is an often overlooked problem concerning the expectations of hands-on learning exercises. While there is an overtly pragmatic, almost refreshingly romantic good in producing do-it-yourself media texts in supervised learning settings (a goal that is sometimes neglected in media analysis-only classes), these spaces should not be framed mainly as vocational training grounds.

The goal of student production is not creative self-expression, nor vocational "job readiness" for future jobs in media industries, although these may be important by-products of production in the classroom. Media educators realize that although some of their students will go on to become artists, producers and media workers, most will not. Even so, all students are ardent consumers of media. Therefore, the primary emphasis of hands-on production is to inform analysis of the information produced by others. In turn, students analyze their own products and other media products in order to create more satisfying productions, thus strengthening their knowledge of media codes and conventions. (Tyner 1998, 200)

The goal of putting machinima in classrooms is not to churn out virtual copies of Steven Spielberg, Ingmar Bergman, or Orson Welles; the goal of putting machinima in classrooms is to help students recognize, analyze, and replicate the poetics of a Spielberg, Bergman, or Welles before gaining the confidence and cognitive acuity to manufacture their own signature style, while becoming sharper consumers and citizens.

As Henry Lowood (2005) and others in this book observe, machinima's recombinant mix of play, performance, and pop culture resonates especially powerfully with today's youth.[6] Machinima is a potentially rich resource for media educators principally because the very act of making these digital stories demands a working literacy of the visual and narrative rules (e.g., continuity editing, framing conventions, styles and genres) of film and television while simultaneously profiting from the cultural capital particular to video gameplay and fandom. The analytic operations and creative decisions needed to successfully construct these digital stories agree especially well with pedagogical models of learning by doing, and with cognitive theories that privilege multipronged student-centric heuristics and processes of self-discovery over repetitive, standardized, and didactic instructional programs. The next section looks at one open-ended theory of learning that privileges play as an essential ingredient for cognitive growth, underscoring the case for machinima's untapped educational potential.

Machinima as Constructive Play

When teaching production techniques, instructors in film schools tend to stress technical proficiency, a strict adherence to protocols (e.g., crew hierarchies, set operations), and expediency and efficiency. This no-nonsense working environment is stressed because film and video shoots are usually expensive and arduous undertakings.

Aspiring writers, directors, producers, and assorted crew learn that there is typically little room for on-set improvisation and experimentation. Machine cinema, by contrast, offers many of these same decision-making opportunities at the preproduction, production, and postproduction stages, but it does so outside the most onerous real-world financial and logistical pressures. Like video gameplay, in which the gravity of decision making has been temporarily suspended, machinima offers a relatively risk-free environment in which video game players-cum-directors, actors, cinematographers, and so on can experiment with the narrative structure, performances, camera angles, and sound design of their digital projects and can rest assured that their successes and failures are relatively inexpensive and low-stakes learning opportunities. Machinima makers are not just learning by doing, they are learning by playing—a freedom that is rarely if ever seen on a real-world movie set.

Storytelling's open-ended nature challenges many instructors' curricula and authority because student-centric moviemaking is a classroom event that destabilizes the one-sided power dynamic enjoyed by those using instructionist teaching models. Teachers committed to constructivist media educational programs, by contrast, are more likely to embrace the always unpredictable nature of story creation, trusting that this openness will lead to student self-discovery and knowledge construction.

The idea that students can learn in open educational fora is based largely on the groundbreaking work of developmental psychologist Jean Piaget. His constructivist learning theory posits that knowledge is constructed through a process of accommodation and assimilation whereby life experiences either conform to or differ from an individual's expectations and mental representations of reality. Life experiences build on one another so that, over time, they constitute the foundation of an individual's knowledge base. Educators embracing Piaget's theory are generally open to using a range of methods to facilitate student-centric knowledge production, "including hands-on, learner-centered, interdisciplinary, collaborative and inquiry-based processes" (Tyner 1998, 198).[7]

One of Piaget's most enduring concepts, and one that is of great value to this essay, is his concept of constructive play. In *The Handbook of Child Psychology*, the constructive play entry reads, in part:

...Piaget suggested that "constructive games" occupied a position halfway between play and adaptive intelligence. For example, Piaget . . . wrote: Making a house with plasticine or bricks involves both sensory-motor skill and symbolic representation, and, like drawing a house, is a move away from play in the strict sense, towards work, or at least towards spontaneous intelligent activity. (Rubin et al. 1983, 726)

Piaget's productive synthesis of play and cognitive growth had a formative impact on Seymour Papert, perhaps Piaget's most famous protégé. Papert, a reputable computer scientist, educator, and theorist in his own right, subsequently developed constructionism as a way of expanding Piaget's notion of constructive play by injecting learning technologies (namely computers) and popular culture into the educational setting.[8] Like other constructivists, Papert contended that learning comes easiest when people focus on a common project that is built sequentially and collectively (putting the construction in constructionism).[9] New media tools, popular culture, and team productions emerge as three distinct elements in Papert's constructionism. These three elements are also readily apparent in the art of machinima making: the game technology provides the primary screen elements, popular culture imbues these screen elements (avatars, fictional worlds) with extratextual social meanings, and the basic creative process of making machine cinema reprises a century-old film production process.

Machinima has the added benefits of being inexpensively produced and available to students as disposable media projects. This is not to suggest that the creative impulse at the heart of student productions is somehow less valuable for machine cinema than for film or video. Rather, by positioning these projects as a series of one-offs, the work does not become overly prized by students, and so an obstacle to subsequent experimentation. Like the video games it is appropriated from, machinima invites us to learn from our mistakes, and to enjoy small successes before advancing to the next level.

Machinima as a Virtual Film School

Halo 2 (Microsoft, 2004), *Unreal Tournament* (Atari, 2003), *Counter-Strike* (Sierra, 2000), and *The Movies* (Lionhead Studios, 2005) are but a few of the games that have been used to create diverse digital narratives for an equally diverse range of genres, including melodramas, talk shows, westerns, music videos, and even how-to videos on machinima making.[10] One of the preeminent titles among this growing list of machine cinema-friendly games is *The Sims 2* (EA Games, 2004). Originally a PC title, *The Sims 2* is the sequel to the most successful "virtual life" strategy game of all time, Maxis's *The Sims* (2000); both games have been ported to nearly all video game platforms, including Sony's PS2 and PSP, Nintendo's Game Cube and DS, and Microsoft's Xbox. Like the original title, *The Sims 2*'s gameplay focuses on creating virtual characters and micromanaging the lives of the seemingly autonomous personalities that work, explore, fight, love, and procreate in their virtual communities.

The Sims 2 is a popular platform for gamer-auteurs because of its open-ended gameplay design, its wealth of prepackaged assets, and its cinema-like image-capturing tools. In fact, *The Sims 2* has been used to create some of the Web's most faithful film and video reimaginings. One of the more popular machinima recreations is of R. Kelley's *Trapped in the Closet* (2005) epic, which meticulously and humorously parrots the video's (already comic) poetics. There are also less faithful but no less inspired *Sims*-based machinima versions of the TV series *The Family Guy*, the feature film (and video game icon) *Lara Croft: Tomb Raider* (Eidos, 1996), and music videos of songs by the bands Garbage and Good Charlotte (to name a few), as well as tribute videos made to the audio tracks of the now famous arcade game, *Dance, Dance Revolution* (Konami, 1998). Rooster Teeth Productions, the creators behind the wildly popular *Halo*-based serial comedy *Red vs. Blue* (2003), also commercially released a DVD of their own *Sims*-based "melodrama," *The Strangerhood: Season One* (2006). While these examples hint at *The Sims 2*'s viability as a virtual filmmaking platform, the question remains, why should this game be used as a virtual film school?

The Sims 2 is better equipped than most games to teach machinima and digital storytelling, for three reasons. First, its signature gameplay style encourages players to custom build their own virtual communities and avatars from expansive asset libraries, thereby providing considerable latitude for personalized choice. Next, the game's editing mode can be positioned to complement filmmaking's three basic creative stages of preproduction, production, and postproduction, enabling *The Sims 2* to be used as an incremental scaffolding tool for leading students through the process of assembling digital narratives. And third, the game (and also machinima making in general) allows learners to establish and grow cognitive apprenticeships with those already skilled in specific film and video production tasks, be they fellow students or adult facilitators.

Technology

Beginning in the 1970s, educators looked to consumer-grade video cameras as a means for achieving a variety of media educational goals. Media instructors saw video's affordability, easy of use, and immediate feedback as offering clear advantages over film. Indeed, "Compared to film and digital reproduction, low-end consumer video provides relatively low cost and ease of use for students, factors that explain video's popularity as the medium of choice for hands-on student production in the K–12 classroom" (Tyner 1998, 184). And computer-generated animation, like celluloid-based filmmaking before it, has been a valued practice that has similarly been beset by medium-specific hurdles—a steep learning curve, high equipment costs, and protracted image generation times—that make it impractical for most media education projects. Enter machine cinema. Not only do the prefabricated environments, game elements, and robust 3D engines of today's video games make image rendering a moot point, but the low cost of most off-the-shelf games and basic video editing software, in concert with digital natives' familiarity with digital programs of all ilk, ameliorates many of the fiscal and technical challenges that beset the creation of student-made computer animation.

With respect to the game itself, *The Sims 2* comes loaded with a variety of character "skins" (or avatar bodies) and animations, a wide assortment of easily modifiable environmental props, and a virtual image-capturing tool that mimics the optical functions of a standard motion picture camera. The game's flexibility of design contrasts noticeably with other popular machinima platforms but most especially with those games belonging to the first-person shooter (FPS) genre. For example, while much of the humor of the *Halo*-based narratives is born out of the fact that all the actors are clones of the Master Chief (the game's hero in different-colored armor), gamer auteurs are powerless to alter the game's lead character or his sci-fi world. Master Chief's animations and poses are similarly restricted to movements that make sense in the FPS genre (e.g., jumping, ducking, aiming, firing weapons) and do not enjoy any conventional "dramatic" range. Again, this is not to say that FPS-based (e.g., *Doom* [id Software, 1995], *Counter-Strike, Unreal Tournament*) machinima works are inherently flawed per se, as they are created and enjoyed as much as any *Sims*-based machinima. The point, rather, is that *The Sims 2* grants students wider freedoms to choose how their actors perform (laughing, crying, flirting), how they appear (age, size, race), and how they are characterized (wardrobe and props). Gamer auteurs are also comparatively free to construct their sets from scratch and do not have to rely on the dungeons, space bases, and extraterrestrial landscapes common to FPS and action adventure games. Admittedly, *The Sims 2* is similarly limited insofar as its prepackaged building materials revolve around domestic structures and props, but still, the game editor's relative openness underscores the fact that art direction is not something that just happens in filmmaking but is as creative and conscious a choice as directing performances and cinematography.

The game's sophisticated image-capturing tool is yet another of *The Sims 2*'s most notable features. The game's camera can record action from a wide variety of places, angles, and focal lengths. Unlike the comparatively limited "cameras" in other games, gamer auteurs can easily pan, track, and even rack focus to get the coverage they want without compromising on perspective or focal length. All of these technological freedoms mean very little for students and teachers, however, if the game cannot be adequately situated within a useful educational framework. Fortunately, machinima making can be presented to students in a tiered fashion to familiarize them with narrative filmmaking's linear creative process while also exposing them to the challenges inherent to game-based moviemaking.

A Scaffolded Approach

Presenting machinima as a creative process composed of discrete steps with sequential tasks and responsibilities encourages students to see the value of their own creative input and their interdependent role within a larger creative system; it gives them a wider cultural appreciation for how film and TV programs are assembled. The creative and logistical steps for making machine cinema with *The Sims 2* are similar enough to the considerations of worldly moving image production, and a brief outline of how this process might unfold provides evidence for the potential of machinima's educational praxis.

Our hypothetical *Sims*-based project begins in the preproduction stage, during which students engage in scriptwriting and casting, and participate in discussions about art direction, camera coverage, and storyboarding. The preproduction stage also has students studying the script to generate the necessary props, avatars, and sets. After they finish prepping the game for production, the production crew (which might be the same student group) controls and records its in-game performances. Once the crew has recorded all the takes, from all the necessary angles, these clips are exported to a digital editor for postproduction, where they are sutured to voice performances and edited into a fine cut. The preproduction, production, and postproduction stages of virtual filmmaking have many of the same cognitive, creative, and procedural needs as any live-action production or high-end computer animation project, making machinima a feasible virtual production proxy for applied media education.

A quick word about machinima's postproduction stage is needed before discussing the third reason for using *The Sims 2*. Whereas the preproduction and production phases are about planning and performance, respectively, the postproduction stage most clearly foregrounds the meaning-making power of shot assembly and audio design. This important fact is evident in Julian Sefton-Green and David Parker's report, *Edit Play: How Children use Edutainment Software to Tell Stories* (2000). Sefton-Green and Parker find that editing is much more than a mere technical competence, being an essential skill encompassing "all-round creative capabilities" for those living in a visual culture (ibid., 8). Their findings reinforce many of the ideas behind Papert's constructionism and give credence to this essay's belief that using machine cinema in the classroom reprises the classic writing-reading literacy dialectic in a new media form. The researchers deftly note that

editing lies at the heart of competence in any moving image language because it is the central process in possible meaning-making activities. Editing allows "writers" of moving image media to manipulate at both the syntactical level and in terms of larger units of sense. Understanding how editing creates meaning is crucial in interpreting moving image narratives. In practical terms, most editing now takes place in digital environments, on computers. At a technical level, digital editing allows unprecedented experimentation and flexibility, so it also seems to bring the editing process closer to the idea of learning to write. (Ibid, 8–9)

Machinima is obviously not the only new media creative process that permits writing with moving images and sound. However, machine cinema is one of the few ways in which students can cheaply and collectively produce digital narratives in virtual environments with relatively few restrictions—limitations that would often be too great in traditional moving image productions.

Cognitive Apprenticeships

The third pedagogical advantage of using machinima is its easy compatibility with cognitive apprenticeships. In conventional apprenticeships, specialists model replicable skills, manufacturing processes, and produce material goods to educate their trainees. A cognitive apprenticeship, conversely, is an immersive educational method from the constructivist paradigm of learning that enculturates students in productive processes through which students produce certain symbolic goods, and bolster their cognitive abilities in the process.

Over the last one hundred-plus years, worldly filmmaking has been a mix of craft and art, technique and aesthetics. And as in so many other industrial arts, on-the-job training has been the norm for the motion picture and television industries. When cognitive apprenticeships are combined with machinima making, this synthesis replicates the apprenticeship model of a motion picture arts education on a virtual set. The apprenticeship model facilitates the strengthening and monitoring of valued competencies by forging relationships between learners and their peers and between learners and their instructors in goal-oriented scenarios that unfold in the sequential and scaffolded filmmaking steps discussed above. Student teams (e.g., camera and audio groups, art team) work closely with their mentors to produce their specialty products, which are later pieced together in post (by the editing team) to deliver the group's final product. It is important to understand that teachers and experienced peers are not authority figures in this constructivist framework but rather are collaborators who lead by example and demonstrate what is conventional, what is possible, and what is aspirational for machine cinema.

Cultivating and refining transferable skills is not the lone justification for teaching students how to express themselves through machinima. As media education scholar Kathleen Tyner recognizes, there is yet another, more personal benefit to media production work. Fortunately, the personal good that results from student-made video productions is equally at play in machinima. Tyner (1998, 179) discusses the value of forming one's personal and creative identity, saying,

In addition to improving students' abilities to make sense of information created by others, culturally based cognitive apprenticeships have implications for student media productions of stories that they generate on their own. Through scaffolding that provides incremental interventions and feedback, students can bring metacognitive awareness to bear as they explore rhetorical devices, discursive styles, and figurative language. In particular, students can use the concept of voice to "try on" their evolving public and private personas. The skill of representing themselves, instead of being represented by others, is particularly crucial for students whose cultures may be underrepresented, or misrepresented in mainstream, commercial mass media.

If positioned properly, machine cinema gives educators a new media production pathway that not only allows students to find their own artistic voices while becoming increasingly well versed in the representational strategies, storytelling techniques, and formal aesthetic devices of narrative film and television (one of the goals of media literacy) but also foregrounds the political value of crafting one's own vision by repurposing co-opted material from popular culture.

Machinima as Educational and Political Power

In years past, media educators tended to overestimate and oversell the empowering effects that media education programs would play in the lives of its students. And while the desire to engender positive cognitive and behavioral changes in students' engagement with, and consumption of, popular media remains vigilant, most media education scholars have since toned down their pedagogical rhetoric. According to David Buckingham, Pete Fraser, and Julian Sefton-Green (2000, 133): "Broadly speaking, the sense of burning political mission that characterized media education in the 1970s and early 1980s has given way to a more neutral emphasis on developing students' critical understanding of—*and participation in*—the media cultures that surround them." What has not waned over this time is the discipline's steadfast commitment to educating others in how to deconstruct their media products' codes and conventions before responding to these products with their own self-fashioned media. Fortunately for us, authoring, distributing, and exhibiting DIY moving images have become increasingly easier, thanks to the proliferation and interoperability of affordable information and communication technologies, user-friendly software, and faster Internet connectivity. Digital natives are comfortable with an assortment of these consumer-grade digital technologies and texts, and they enter today's classrooms ready to utilize their digital know-how. And unlike more conservative disciplines, media education has matured alongside many of these technological innovations and has petitioned our educational system not to quarantine students from popular culture and new media lest they be isolated from contemporary and emergent media literacies.

Machine cinema is only one new media expression in our complex and convergent twenty-first-century mediascape. It is a uniquely constituted media form that may be deconstructed and analyzed as a narrative text, and operated as a moving image writer. *The Sims 2* in particular grants its would-be auteurs considerable creative freedoms typically absent from most games. However, nearly any video game *could* be reconfigured to produce some novel expression; and gamer auteurs need only reassemble the available screen elements into new syntactic orders to do so. It is this simple fact that makes machinima such a politically vibrant new media convergence. In *Recycled Images: The Art and Politics of Found Footage Films* (1993), William Wees discusses the personal volition needed to reimagine image and sound that have already taken material form. Although his comments are about film, they are equally applicable to the political intervention that is machine cinema. Wees states,

it is not the splicer that makes a collage film. It is the decision to invest found footage with meanings unintended by its original makers and unrecognized in its original contexts of presentation and reception. In its most comprehensive sense, then, a collage film could be anything a filmmaker finds and decides to show in the form he or she found it: the filmic equivalent of a Duchamp "ready made." But found footage films based on a montage of disparate and incongruous images are . . . more likely to challenge the media's power to make ideologically loaded images seem like unmediated representations of reality. (48)

Machine cinema, like found-footage films, can be used by media educators to encourage students to see their media and entertainment products as formal constructions that can be dismantled with critical analysis and reassembled with their production skills as *they* see fit. Machine cinema is no self-contained technological panacea, however, and its educational promise will remain dormant until it wins support from key proponents. Machine cinema has the potential of changing formal and informal media education spaces only after media literacy projects are shored up by progressive educational policies, after machinima gains the support of education professionals who value constructivist learning environments, and, most important, after machine cinema is used by students who see, or are taught to see, the meaningfulness of their repurposed gameplay.

Notes

1. This is a common criticism that has been leveled by a number of prominent officials and groups, including Secretary of State and former New York senator Hillary Clinton, Secretary of Homeland Security and former Arizona governor Janet Napolitano, former U.S. Secretary of Education Dr. Rod Paige, and the Michigan State Board of Education, among others.

2. Marc Prensky is an advocate of game-based learning programs and is credited with coining the controversial term "digital natives" in 2001. See Henry Jenkins's *Convergence Culture* (2006) for more on the general technosocial contours of participatory media culture.

3. Each media classroom's potential machinima uses should be informed by a host of needs particular to that class's situation (e.g., available technology, learning goals, student level, student-to-technology ratio) and not be guided chiefly by the generalized educational theory discussed herein.

4. This situation exists despite excellent scholarship and ongoing projects on the educational potential of video games, most notably the recent work of James Paul Gee (2003) and MIT's Education Arcade project, led by Henry Jenkins, which are summarized in Payne (2005). James Newman (2004) also offers reasonable speculation as to why video games are generally decried as artifacts unbefitting academic and educational research.

5. Think tanks and research initiatives such as the New Media Consortium, MIT's Education Arcade, and University of Wisconsin's Academic Advanced Distributed Learning Co-Lab are interested in answering this formidable question.

6. See the New Media Consortium's report, *A Global Imperative* (2005, 12).

7. It is important to note that Piaget's cognitive theory (constructivism) is not the same as the pedagogies that bear its name. For example, constructivist and experiential educational programs are programmatic attempts to apply Piaget's learning theory. Piaget's cognitive theory is epistemological; attempts to leverage his findings are pedagogical.

8. See Papert and Harel (1991) for a collection of works dealing with constructionism and education.

9. Papert's most famous educational project to date is his computer language, Logo. He developed it while working with children at the MIT Media Lab. See his seminal work, *Mindstorms* (1980).

10. There is a growing list of good machine cinema sites on the Web, including: <http://www.halomovies.org>, <http://www.machinima.com>, <http://www.machinima.org>, <http://www.selectparks.net>, and <http://www.sims99.com>.

References

Buckingham, David, Pete Fraser, and Julian Sefton-Green. 2000. Making the Grade: Evaluating Student Production in Media Studies. In *Evaluating Creativity: Making and Learning by Young People*, ed. Julian Sefton-Green and Rebecca Sinker. New York: Routledge.

Center for Media Literacy. FAQ: Best Practices. <http://www.medialit.org/faq_best.html> (accessed July 25, 2006).

Ferguson, Bob. 2001. In Defense of Media Education. *International Journal of Media Education* 1:7–22.

Gee, James Paul. 2003. *What Video Games Have to Teach Us about Learning and Literacy*. New York: Palgrave Macmillan.

Goodman, Steven. 2003. *Teaching Youth Media: A Critical Guide to Literacy, Video Production, and Social Change*. New York: Teachers College Press.

Hart, Andrew. 2001. Editorial. *International Journal of Media Education* 1:2–4.

Jenkins, Henry. 2006. *Convergence Culture: Where Old and New Media Collide*. New York: New York University Press.

Lowood, Henry 2005. Real-Time Performance: Machinima and Game Studies. *International Digital Media Arts Association Journal* 2 (1): 10–17.

New Media Consortium. 2005. *A Global Imperative: The Report on the 21st Century Literacy Summit*. Austin, TX: New Media Consortium.

Newman, James. 2004. *Videogames*. New York: Routledge.

Papert, Seymour. 1980. *Mindstorms: Children, Computers, and Powerful Ideas*. New York: Basic Books.

Papert, Seymour, and Idit Harel. 1991. *Constructionism: Research Reports and Essays, 1985–1990 by the Epistemology & Learning Research Group*. Norwood, NJ: Ablex.

Patrick, Susan. 2004. Children, Schools, Computers, and the Internet: The Impact of Continued Investment in Educational Technology under NCLB. *Education Statistics Quarterly* 5.4. <http://nces.ed.gov/programs/quarterly/vol_5/5_4/2_4.asp> (accessed July 25, 2006).

Payne, Matthew Thomas. 2005. The Digital Divide and Its Discontents. *Currents in Electronic Literacy* 9. <http://www.cwrl.utexas.edu/currents/fall05/payne.html> (accessed July 25, 2006).

Rubin, Kenneth H., Greta G. Fein, and Brian Vanderberg. 1983. Play. In *The Handbook of Child Psychology: Formerly Carmichael's Manual of Child Psychology*, volume IV: Socialization, Personality, and Social Development, 4th ed., ed. Paul H. Mussen, volume ed. E. Mavis Hetherington. New York: John Wiley & Sons.

Sefton-Green, Julian, and David Parker. 2000. *Edit Play: How Children use Edutainment Software to Tell Stories*. London: British Film Institute.

Tyner, Kathleen. 2003. Introduction: Mapping the Field of Youth Media. In *A Closer Look: Media Arts 2003*. San Francisco, CA: National Alliance for Media Arts and Culture. <http://www.namac.org/article.cfm?id=2&cid=4& aid=326&monly=0> (assessed July 25, 2006).

Tyner, Kathleen. 1998. *Literacy in a Digital World: Teaching and Learning in the Age of Information*. Mahwah, NJ: Erlbaum.

Wees, William. 1993. *Recycled Images: The Art and Politics of Found Footage Films*. New York: Anthology Film Archives.

Software References

Counter Strike. Sierra Entertainment. 2000.

Dance, Dance Revolution. Konami. 1998.

Doom. id Software. 1995.

Halo 2. Microsoft Game Studios/Bungie Software. 2004.

The Movies. Lionhead Studios; Activision. 2005.

The Sims. Maxis. 2000.

The Sims 2. Maxis. 2004.

Tomb Raider. Core Design Ltd.; Eidos Interactive. 1996.

Unreal Tournament 2004. Epic Games; Atari. 2004.

Machinima References

Red vs. Blue. Rooster Teeth Productions. 2003.

The Strangerhood: Season One. Rooster Teeth Productions. 2006.

Trapped in the Closet (Parts 1–5). Kendra Flemons aka Showho1234. (2005).

15 Machinima and Modding: Pedagogic Means for Enhancing Computer Game Literacy

Danny Kringiel

Pedagogy and the Digital Games Boom

Playing games is an important part of children's lives as well as an integral component of their learning processes. Since the end of the eighteenth century, academic studies concerned with child development have shown a growing interest in explorating forms of play and games common among children and juveniles. In the works of scientists like Friedrich Froebel, Sigmund Freud, or Jean Piaget, strong connections between infantile learning and children's play have been established. Around 1970, a separate branch of research concerned exclusively with child's play began to form within education sciences: play pedagogy.

Even today, however, one area of the ludic culture of children and youth has hardly caught pedagogic attention—digital games. This seems odd, since it is exactly this form of game playing that has experienced the most dramatic boom in recent years. Since their early days in the seventies, when these new arcade attractions offered little more than a few minutes of fun through simple gameplay and even simpler block graphics (not to mention nonexistent story lines) in exchange for a few coins, computer games have undergone a number of drastic changes. Today they are a highly complex game-media hybrid phenomenon on the verge of surpassing the cinema in popularity. U.S. video game and gaming hardware sales hit an all-time high of $10.5 billion in 2005 (CNN 2006), while U.S. cinema box-office sales reached only $8.8 billion (MPAA 2008, 2). According to these sales figures, playing games has obviously gained new importance in Western popular culture. Despite the growing popularity of digital games, however, until now pedagogic scholars have largely ignored the whole phenomenon. Skepticism toward the new medium and alarm concerning its allegedly harmful effects on minors are the dominant reactions. Instead of asking how this new kind of game might best be understood, many educational researchers are asking how the spread of digital games might be prevented most efficiently. Although the academic field of game studies has been growing since the late 1990s, almost no pedagogic intervention in this multidisciplinary debate has taken place.

Pedagogical tendencies toward tabooing video games are embedded in a similar bias in current public and political debates over the dangers of digital gaming, debates that, ironically, themselves depend strongly on mass media and the principles of media effectiveness. Again and again, tragedies such as those at Columbine High School, Colorado, in 1999, or Erfurt, Germany, in 2002, after having been edited and presented in dramatic ways by mass media, set the stage for allocations of blame stating that only depictions of violence in digital games could be held responsible for the mass murders by teenagers running amok.

Accordingly, legal media protection for children and young persons in many nations has centered on prohibitive measures. One current example is the Family Entertainment Protection Act, co-sponsored by senators Hillary Clinton, Joseph Lieberman, Tim Johnson, and Evan Bayh. One of the main goals of this act is to transform the Entertainment Software Rating Board's (ESRB) age guidelines into binding ratings supervised by the U.S. government. Abroad, binding rating systems are already enforced in Australia and Germany, where institutions such as the Australian Office of Film and Literature Classification (OFLC) or the German Unterhaltungssoftware Selbstkontrolle (USK) and Bundesprüfstelle für jugendgefährdende Medien (BPjM) try to keep children and adolescents away from video games that have not been approved as suitable for their age category, or to ban games that have been determined to be harmful to minors.

Unfortunately, this prohibitive approach brings two major problems: First, any attempt to keep video games away from children and youth by trying to block legal chains of distribution is doomed to fail because, to a great extent, video games spread through illegal chains of distribution. These may be the circulation of self-burned copies on schoolyards or, more important, file-sharing clients such as "eMule" or "BitTorrent," which are used to spread pirated copies more or less anonymously on the Internet. The Entertainment Software Association (ESA) rated the financial loss done to the U.S. gaming industry by software piracy at $3 billion, a figure that does not include the Internet-based spreading of illegal copies.[1] In accordance with the annual German *JIM-Studie* published by the Medienpädagogischer Forschungsverbund Südwest, in 2005, only about 9 percent of German youths considered it "difficult" to obtain digital games not rated suitable for their age group by the USK and the BPjM, even though in Germany these age restrictions are binding (MPFS 2005, 34). On the other hand, 76 percent of the interviewees considered it to be "easy" or "very easy" to avoid such legal measures and get their games by other means. This result suggests that most young people who cannot buy the game of their choice at the local Wal-Mart because of an age rating might play the game anyway, obtaining a copy by means of Internet file-sharing clients or simply by asking a friend for an illegal copy of the game. Quite clearly, prohibitive measures inevitably fail here.

Second, locking up allegedly problematic video game content as strictly as possible and shutting digital games off from minors as effectively as possible means eliminating the possibility of learning how to deal with such problematic media content in critical, self-determined, and responsible ways as well. How can we assume that young people automatically acquire the knowledge and skills necessary to understand and withstand the effects of problematic video games simply by reaching the age of consent, when they have been kept away from such games all their life by legally enforced taboos? Of course, this argument should not be construed as a call for confronting children regardless of their age with even the most shocking depictions of violence. Still, if we wish to help young people deal with digital games responsibly, we would be well advised not to treat contact with those games as a taboo. Only through contact with an entertainment medium can they learn to question and use it in self-determined ways instead of being manipulated by it. In short, only thus can they develop a literacy for computer games.

The Concept of Multiple Literacies

"Literacy" in the traditional and narrow sense of the word—that is, the ability to decipher and derive meaning from written language and to use it to convey one's own messages by producing written texts—is not natural. Literacy is acquired culturally, most often in schools. It is here that still more or less illiterate children are usually first introduced to the basic elements of written language, and to the communicative results that arise from the possible combinations of these basic elements. While literate adults often take these skills for granted, learning them is quite a challenge; many years of practice have to pass before newcomers to literacy have fully developed an understanding of which visual symbol is linked to which sound, which variation of the syntactic arrangement of single words causes which shift in meaning, or what wondrous phenomena may hide behind terms like "metaphor," "alliteration," or "onomatopoeia," let alone how to use them to convey their own messages. Still, it is worthwhile for a society to pay teachers to teach pupils how to read and write, because literacy offers a number of enormous advantages.

Written language not only helps us unburden our memory every day by allowing us to note down important events and tasks in shopping lists and the like. It also makes it possible for us to conserve messages over time, for instance by leaving a note for someone to read hours or even days after we have left it there. Not least, the spread of literacy has catalyzed the democratization of communication processes and knowledge acquisition. As a consequence of the invention of the printing press by Johannes Gutenberg during the fifteenth century, education and knowledge became accessible to the general public for the first time. Printed books could conserve and spread the knowledge of scholars and bring it to those unable to afford private tutors—if they could read. Suddenly, it became possible for many more authors to communicate their thoughts and ideas to a growing readership. This in turn multiplied the diversity of contents and viewpoints, concepts and worldviews communicated through books. Thanks to printing technology, the benefits of reproducing written documents—and thus of culturally shared knowledge—were no longer restricted to a few scribes and copyists.

What is obvious in the reception of written language—that it is necessary to be literate to fully comprehend its media content and use it for one's own communication purposes—is valid beyond written texts as well. The concept of *visual literacy*, first introduced by John Debes (1970), proceeds on the assumption that visual communication (e.g., painting or viewing an image) also requires a specific form of literacy. To be able to "read" in this context means to be able to identify and distinguish between basic elements of visual communication such as dots, lines, shapes, colors, and movements, and to understand their syntax as precisely as possible. Training in visual literacy aims at broadening our communicative possibilities when dealing with visual elements. It aims at making people who "read" visual messages capable of understanding them in a more differentiated way, which is expected to increase their pleasure in visual communication as well as strengthen their resistance to visual manipulation. For people who "write" visual messages, training in visual literacy aims at making them capable of using the basic elements of visual communication more precisely, efficiently, and purposefully.

Literacy in this broader sense is not exclusively differentiated by modes of perception, as is the case with visual literacy. Other literacies allow us to understand and apply communicative elements specific to certain types of media. Like languages, movies and television shows fall back on principles and elements that their recipients have to learn to decipher in order to understand the messages conveyed by the respective medium. This kind of *media literacy*, according to Stanley Baran, includes "the ability to effectively and efficiently comprehend and utilize mass media content" and aims at assisting "the skilled, beneficial use of media technologies" (Baran 2006, 35, 29). Like visual literacy, media literacy enables users of language-like communication systems to deal with them in a more self-determined and efficient manner. We usually acquire the basic competencies necessary to understand the messages communicated in movies or TV newscasts more or less unconsciously by repeatedly using these media, whereas we are taught how to use written language systematically by our parents, teachers, and schoolbooks. Still, just because everybody has already fully developed all visual or media literacy skills relevant for modern mass communication doesn't mean that it is unnecessary to teach these other kinds of literacy systematically.

According to Paul Messaris, the basic set of literacy skills of moviegoers that allows them to identify objects on the screen, to comprehend shifts in time and space, or to make sense of film montage "is something the typical viewer appears to acquire quite readily," while he claims that "skills required for the perception of intentionality" behind such medial constructs rely "on exceptional experience or explicit training"

(Messaris 1994, 164). Thus, it is exactly those literacy skills that are necessary for developing critical faculties and for analyzing and questioning media messages that require explicit and systematic instruction. Baran underlines this necessity: "media literacy is a skill we take for granted, but like all skills, it can be improved. And if we consider how important the mass media are in creating [. . .] the culture that helps define us [. . .] it is a skill that *must* be improved" (Baran 2006, 34). The more each user of media is literate, "the more we can be equal partners with media professionals in meaning making" (ibid., 40).

Over the years, the concept of media literacy has been divided into further subliteracies such as cine-literacy or TV literacy. Yet if it is possible to train people to "read" a movie or a TV newscast as one would read a book, and to "write" one's own content via productive use of media, and if by doing so we can help users of these media to become more emancipated from the influence of the media industry, then everyone concerned about harmful influences of computer games would be well advised to think about promoting a new kind of literacy: computer game literacy.

What Is Computer Game Literacy?

Few attempts have been made to adapt the concept of literacy to computer games. The most prominent so far has been James Paul Gee's model of literacies corresponding to the genre-specific "semiotic domains" (Gee 2004, 18–19) of digital games. But in contrast to Gee's linguistically motivated concept, the term "computer game literacy" as used here relates more strongly to the concept of media literacy. whereas Gee takes an interest in the learning principles of well-designed digital games that initiate learning beyond the game itself, this essay focuses on a kind of literacy that helps to facilitate a more self-determined, critical, and analytical usage of the medium. Gee analyzes learning processes that are initiated more or less automatically through the use of video games, whereas I will try to show ways in which computer game literacy can be extended beyond the skills that are achieved just by playing toward the skills that allow the perception of intentionality behind the medium's messages, but need to be trained explicitly.

My use of the term "computer game literacy" refers to a new submedia literacy occupied with learning how to "read" and "write" digital games by understanding their basic communicative elements, their syntax and aesthetic conventions, as well as their cultural, social, and economic dimensions. Based on the basic elements of media literacy as coined by Silverblatt (1995, 2–3) and supplemented by Baran (2006, 35–38), the seven constitutive elements of computer game literacy can be described as follows:

1. An awareness of the impact of digital games on our lives.
2. An understanding of the components of the process of game-related mass communication.

3. The development of strategies for analyzing and discussing messages conveyed by digital games.

4. An understanding of how computer games shape our understanding of and insight into our culture.

5. Cultivation of the ability to enjoy, understand, and appreciate computer game content (including the ability to use multiple points of access to approach the content to derive from it multiple levels of meaning).

6. An understanding of the ethical and moral obligations of the producers of computer games.

7. The development of appropriate and effective production skills to be able to create useful media messages via making one's own video game content (learning to "write").

Following Baran again (2006, 38–40), the seven essential skills necessary for a literate usage of digital games would be the following:

1. The ability and willingness to make an effort to understand computer game content, to pay attention, and to filter out noise.

2. An understanding of and respect for the power of messages conveyed by digital games, for the influence they can exert.

3. The ability to distinguish emotional from reasoned reactions when responding to computer game content and to act accordingly.

4. The development of heightened expectations of computer game content.

5. Knowledge of the genre conventions of digital games and the ability to recognize when they are being mixed.

6. The ability to think critically about messages conveyed by digital games, no matter how credible their sources.

7. Knowledge of the internal language of computer games and their grammar, and the ability to understand its complex effects.

Computer game literacy cannot be distinguished from other submedia literacies without any intersections. These intersections lead back to the ability of media to "remediate" (Bolter and Grusin 1999) elements and syntactic principles from semiotic systems of older media, that is, to assimilate, recycle, and transform these semiotic fractions (e.g., by displaying text in a video game). Consequently, computer game literacy always includes parts of submedia literacies referring to older media—elements of cine-literacy, for instance, when a game confronts us with cinematic conventions during its cut-scenes.

But is the concept of media literacy applicable to digital games at all? Are these games a new *medium*? Because of the growing complexity of the mimetic worlds they are able to create, they must at least be considered game-media-hybrid phenomena. They can be used to tell complex stories or to communicate complex worldviews. In this respect, they differ significantly from traditional games such as chess, poker, or backgammon. Even though such precomputer games may convey rudimentary messages (e.g., religious worldviews such as the Buddhist cycle of birth, death, and reincarnation and the final arrival in nirvana that show through in the games Ludo and Parcheesi), computer games have new representational layers, which allow them to communicate much more complex stories and ideas. Computer games don't have to fall back on an abstract world painted on cardboard and abstract pieces that are moved around in this symbolic world. Most often, modern video games stage elaborate fictional worlds in which gameplay is embedded. *Max Payne 2* is not only a digital game in which the player has to dodge enemy gunfire, it is also a narration of lethargy, loss, and a search for new will to live. *Beyond Good & Evil* is not only a third-person-view action adventure but also the critical commentary of a French development team on the *Gleichschaltung* of American mass media during the war on terrorism. Of course, despite all this, computer games are still games, not *only* a medium, not *only* a means of communication. But at the very least they are a medium *too*.

In the following discussion, the term "computer game literacy" is preferred over "game literacy" because the literacy examined here specifically refers to computer games, while excluding more traditional games such as checkers or football. The term game literacy would falsely suggest an inclusion of such noncomputer games.

On the other hand, the term video game literacy is avoided because it points too strongly to the perceptive mode of seeing. This would make it difficult to distinguish it from visual literacy. Also, to be able to "read" a digital game, it is not sufficient to understand only its basic visual elements and their relations. The acoustic (sound, music), haptic (force feedback), and kinetic (controlling devices) dimensions and strategic aspects of digital games are important elements of computer game–specific mass communication as well.

By using the term computer game literacy, I refer to the technological basis of these games. While the visual mode of perception is not common to all video games (e.g., audio games), all video games are based on computer technology, regardless of whether they are played on PCs, video game consoles, or handheld devices. With computer game literacy now defined, a question arises: How can such literacy be achieved?

Enhancing Computer Game Literacy through Machinima and Mods

Machinima and modding are special cases of the use of digital games. When turned into a machinima film or a mod, games are diverted from their original purpose; the player no longer follows the developer's carefully prefabricated gameplay structures. Instead, she empowers herself to transform the game, to play creatively with its underlying structures, rules, and mimetic elements. This transformation may involve turning the MMORPG—or massively multiplayer online role-playing game—*World of Warcraft* into a coarsely humorous musical featuring a female Tauren and a male troll singing about Internet pornography. Or it may involve turning the first-person shooter (FPS) *Unreal Tournament 2004* into a futuristic soccer game in which players use off-road vehicles to guide an oversized ball into the goal.

It is exactly through this principle of deconstructing and rearranging the basic elements of video games that machinima and modding qualify as means for enhancing computer game literacy. In the following, I will differentiate and exemplify several ways in which these practices are suited for enhancing the basic elements or skills of computer game literacy mentioned earlier.

Development of Production Skills to Create Media Messages

In her reflection on a preliminary model of game literacy, Caroline Pelletier points out the importance not only of analyzing games to increase literacy skills but also of *making* one's own games: "making games [. . .] involves more open-ended and calculated manipulation of game-based semiotic resources than is achieved through play" (Pelletier 2005, 3). It has often been emphasized that playing video games itself already is a productive act. Still, this does not prove Pelletier's point wrong.

To understand why, we have to examine the difference between interpretative and ergodic interactivity. Espen Aarseth (1997, 1) coined the term "ergodic" to describe how users of certain media (such as digital games) are not only interactively involved in the interpretative act of meaning-making but are also involved in physically configuring the media text and trying to find a path through it. In an adventure game, for instance, the player must successfully solve puzzles to find a path that leads farther through the game. Only under these preconditions will he be granted access to subsequent sections of the media text and thereby be able to interpret them. Still, the amount of freedom offered by this ergodic interaction is restricted to the number of alternative paths the developers of the game have created.

Producing video game content, on the other hand, offers a much higher degree of interactive freedom. The maker of a machinima film or a mod has a wider variety of possible media messages to send than a player deciding to take one out of four different dialog options in an adventure game or deciding on a certain sequence of swift movements in an online shooter.

If it is important for developing literacy, how can pupils learn to create game content? While Pelletier aims at creating stand-alone game-editing software that allows pupils to produce video game content, an alternative approach might be the production of machinima movies and mods, which offers various possibilities to produce game elements (through partial conversion mods), new games (through total conversion mods), or game-based movies (through machinima) without having to program the content from scratch. Moreover, in recent years the growing modding and machinima communities have brought forth a wide range of increasingly easy-to-use editing tools.

By taking a closer look at one of the most popular machinima productions ever, *Red vs. Blue*,[2] it becomes obvious that producing machinima does not necessarily involve complicated technical skills. After the script for a particular episode of *Red vs. Blue* is written, the spoken dialog is recorded. The movie scenes are acted out by players controlling their avatars on a set of four Xbox consoles connected via a local network. The avatars are used like in-game puppets, thereby becoming virtual actors who follow stage directions and act out the story line in real time and synchronously with the prerecorded audio. Their actions are recorded through another player's first-person perspective, which is recorded by a PC connected to his Xbox, making him the virtual cameraman. Finally, video-editing software is used for montage and to join video and audio data.[3] In this way, without a budget of millions of dollars, a weekly comedy series with more than seventy episodes was created that at its height attracted between 650,000 and one million spectators each week (Delaney 2004).

Further simplification of the machinima production process can be achieved by using in-game editing tools like those of the game *The Movies*. This game is almost a machinima production kit. Although making movies is embedded in its rather conventional gameplay, essentially a film industry simulation, it is possible to enter a "sandbox mode" that leaves all conventional gameplay elements aside. Here, players can choose virtual actors, costumes, movie sets, special effects, and so on, then shoot and edit their footage. Afterward, the movie can be published on the game's Web site for others to watch and rate. Although *The Movies* may be a special case, there are other examples of games offering such in-game machinima tools. The *Driver* series not only features action-packed gameplay built around shooting and driving missions but also a tool to record and edit replays of missions. These data can then be saved and sent to other gamers.

The effort necessary to produce a mod tends to be higher than that required to make machinima, but it depends on the extent of modification. The construction of virtual architecture, for instance, which is called mapping, is often made relatively manageable by comprehensible in-game level editing tools. These can even be integrated into the game itself, as is the case with the racing game *Trackmania Sunrise* or the skateboarding game *Tony Hawk's Underground*, which offer easy-to-use WYSIWYG editors for building one's own racing course or skate park.

Since the gaming industry has begun to realize that mods can contribute to the longevity of their product—the *Half-Life* mod *Counter-Strike* set an important precedent—more and more easily accessible editing tools that allow complex modifications are included with commercial video games. *The Elder Scrolls Construction Set* for the role-playing games *Morrowind* and *Oblivion*, for instance, not only offers a clear working environment for the almost Lego-like construction of virtual architecture but also makes it possible to create avatars and nonplayer characters, to manipulate artificial intelligence (AI) behavior, etc. Using simple script commands, it is also possible to control complex chains of events inside the game world without any programming skills. Since *The Elder Scrolls Construction Set* has been used in the creation of *Morrowind* and *Oblivion*, the amount of freedom it offers to modders approximates that of the original developers.

Such enhancement of the production skills of video game users can also contribute to a democratization of the game-medium hybrid itself. Being able to produce video game content offers (not only) minors the chance to get involved in the process of meaning-making through digital games more strongly, beyond mere interpretative involvement. Someone able to construct machinima or mods is no longer confined to the consuming, receiving use of computer games. She can use the medium to conceive and send her own media messages. As a result of changing structures of distribution in the gaming industry—one prominent example being Valve's online platform *Steam,* through which games can be bought and downloaded—unconventional amateur mod projects like *The Ship* or *Garry's Mod* are being noticed by the industry and turned into commercial products, thereby slowly blurring the line between modders and professional game makers. Online distribution diminishes financial risks for publishers and raises their will to promote and publish mods as stand-alone games. Consequently, mods and their (often unusual) gaming concepts are gaining growing influence over the structures of commercial video games.

A similar convergence of amateur and industrial content is emerging in the machinima community as well. Rooster Teeth Productions, the makers of *Red vs. Blue*, have been assigned by software giant Electronic Arts to make advertising machinima spots for EA Sports games. So far, two short advertisements for *NCAA Football 07* have been completed and aired on television. They have also made a series of machinima pieces called *P.A.N.I.C.S.*, based on the FPS *F.E.A.R.*, in cooperation with its developer, Monolith; the first of these pieces has been exclusively published as part of the game's *Director's Edition* DVD. In these examples, the communicative balance of power between industry and users has been shifted through a creative and productive use of the medium.

With this in mind, one might at least hope that the expansion of machinima and modding subcultures might have a similar impact on computer games as letterpress technology had on written language: the democratization of mass communication and an increase in the variety of messages communicated through the medium. Judging from the examples discussed thus far, machinima and modding can indeed help us approach the goal of educational media production set by Pelletier (2005, 5): "to enable people [to] participate in and contribute to media culture in ways which enable some manipulation of its semiotic, institutional and economic structures."

Development of Strategies for Analyzing and Discussing Messages Conveyed by Digital Games

To develop the production skills necessary to make a good mod or machinima movie, the producer has to understand how the medium of the computer game, including the cut-scenes, usually conveys meaning. What she needs is knowledge of the internal language of computer games and their grammar. To communicate meaning to viewers of a machinima piece, its director has to become familiar with the "language" of in-game movies. She has to analyze the communicative elements of those movies closely enough to make competent decisions about camera angles, shot sizes, camera movements, mise-en-scène situations, and so forth. In doing so, she acquires knowledge of just those areas of cine-literacy that form intersections with computer game literacy. To put it more exactly, she does not actually acquire knowledge of cinematic conventions but knowledge of those fractions of cinematic conventions that have been remediated in video games. She doesn't have to know too much about casting actors or applying for filming permits, but she must understand how to accomplish elaborate tracking shots or extravagant stage settings, which are easier to implement in and therefore more common in computer game cut-scenes and machinima than in real movies. But she doesn't only have to learn these production principles, she also most likely will have to learn how to discuss them with other members of her machinima team, for most often, machinima movies are not produced by individuals but cooperatively; the team must agree on a basic core concept about how it wants its machinima piece to look.

In a similar way, modders must familiarize themselves with the basic communicative structures of video games. They have to understand how games structure their tasks, gameplay, and story lines. To make a high-quality mod, they cannot simply treat enemy NPCs as mere cannon fodder, as they might while *playing* a game. A modder working with *The Elder Scrolls Construction Set*, for instance, has to carefully consider a multitude of details that can be overlooked completely when playing. What does he want his NPCs to look like? Do they fit in their environment? Why are they where they are? Does it make sense to let them fight alone, or can they be combined with a horde of other enemy characters? In which way is their AI meant to behave? How, according to the AI, are the NPCs supposed to act toward the player's avatar? Which consequences are which player's interactions with which NPCs meant to have? Instead of perceiving virtual characters as a player would—say, as the frightening Orc that suddenly rounds the corner of a dimly lit dungeon and has to be killed immediately— modders have to look at how that virtual agent is integrated into the whole game. They have to examine its ludic, artistic, and narrative *functions*. To an even greater extent, modders are forced to discuss these functional aspects with others. Almost without exception, bigger mods are created by modding teams, so discussing design principles is a vital part of the modding process itself.

This enhancement of analytical skills is significant for the development of other game literacy skills mentioned earlier, too: as a consequence of being able to analyze how games convey their messages, the player's ability to think critically about messages conveyed by computer games is improved. These same analytical skills make it easier to understand how computer games shape our understanding of and insight into our culture.

Cultivation of the Ability to Enjoy, Understand, and Appreciate Computer Game Content

One of the logical consequences of a growing insight into the "producedness" of video games is an augmentation of the ability to recognize well-made games, as well as to understand and appreciate them. Having experienced in their own machinima editing how much work has to be put into a decent script, how difficult it is to achieve certain effects by manipulation of the lighting or how a well-made sound design can subtly contribute to a game's or cut-scene's atmosphere, game players are much more likely to realize when these elements are applied masterfully. Accordingly, they will experience heightened enjoyment of the medium. The literate gamer thus experiences the deeper joys of connoisseurship.

The same applies to the producers of mods. Someone who had to pay particular attention to achieving proper gameplay balancing through sensible AI calibration and allocation of hit points and damage points will also be able to identify and appreciate such elaborate balancing measures when playing commercial games. His productive experience enables him to not only vaguely like or dislike a game but to point out exactly the reasons for his reaction. Someone who has designed game characters, events, and levels will be attentive to details of elegant game design that he failed to notice previously. Modding production experiences have increased his ability to enjoy well-made games.

Moreover, game connoisseurs who have produced mods or machinima movies have exploited additional points of access to the medium, allowing them to derive multiple levels of meaning from the game's communicative content. They may access an FPS from the access point of a normal gamer, experiencing it as a stunning adventure in which they have to hold their ground against a hostile environment. On the other hand, they may access it from the position of a machinima maker, perceiving the shooter as a more or less artfully executed sequence of cut-scenes. From this perspective, certain elaborate cinematic techniques may be the primary source of enjoyment. Third, they can access the game from the position of a modder, for whom the center of interest and enjoyment might be elegant and inventive game design solutions. Regardless of whether the player wins or loses the game or if its cut-scenes are all that interesting, from this access point the joy of the player could stem from the well-made architectural balancing of an asymmetric capture-the-flag map, for example. Through these additional points of access, the player develops a more differentiated and multifaceted concept of the game. Also, the player experiences how strongly the meaning derived from the game may depend on the points of access chosen by its players.

Development of Heightened Expectations of Computer Game Content

Alongside the development of analytical skills and the ability to achieve additional enjoyment through insights into the composition of machinima and mods, the expectations of gamers are raised. Someone able to distinguish a well-made from an unimaginative cut-scene will be able to point out exactly in which respect a game is satisfying and in which respect it is not. Consequently, the gamer will no longer be satisfied with average-quality games.

Game players whose ability to distinguish inventive design details from useless ones has been enhanced through their modding experience will detect poorly made pathfinding, trivial map design, or awkwardly implemented script events much more easily than average players. Obviously, players who have learned to identify design flaws in interactive sections or cut-scenes of digital games, because they had to eradicate them in their own constructive work, will be less likely to be satisfied with any games featuring such flaws, and will therefore develop heightened expectations for video games.

The Ability to Filter Out Noise

As mentioned earlier, computer games differ from most other media in that they are ergodic. The users of this medium not only receive a media message, they also must find a path through the "text," the game. By having to perceive and interpret as well as deal with ergodic interaction at the same time, game players cope with doubled interactive efforts compared with users of nonergodic media.

Even during nonergodic sequences such as cut-scenes, gamers are not released completely from this mode of involvement, because most often cut-scenes represent rather short transitions between separate interactive parts of the game. They sum up the events of the preceding level and their consequences while at the same time introducing the tasks awaiting the player in the upcoming level and preparing the player for them. The player gets only a small amount of time to lean back and relax during the cut-scene. He still has to pay attention to important clues for the next section of the game, and also must expect to be thrown back into the ergodic mode at any moment. In this respect, his receptive situation is not identical to that of a movie viewer, whose only interactive task consists in interpreting media messages.

With this in mind, we could conceptualize the ergodic involvement of gamers as a sort of signal noise complicating certain parts of the communication process. A typical symptom of the existence of this noise is the inability, after having played through a whole game featuring a rather complex story line, to recall its story—even though the game has been completed in the ludic sense.

However, when watching a machinima piece based on a computer game, the user enters a purely interpretative mode of interaction in which he can observe the basic communicative elements of the game without having to take any ergodic obligations into consideration. This difference in effect may have been one of the reasons why Jake Hughes, one of the developers of the sci-fi role-playing game *Anachronox*, decided to edit together all of the cut-scenes in the game and create a full-length machinima movie from them, which tells the story of the game in the manner of a motion picture. Although the game was published before the release of *Anachronox: The Movie*—suggesting that quite a number of players were already familiar with its story—it became one of the most popular machinima movies ever. At the Machinima Film Festival 2002, *Anachronox: The Movie* won first-place prizes in five categories: best picture, best writing, best technical achievement, best visual design, and best editing. This movie's success confirms that filtering out the communicative noise of ergodic gameplay can be quite an interesting and enjoyable experience.

Knowledge of Genre Conventions and the Ability to Recognize When They Are Being Mixed

It is quite common among mods to cross the genre conventions of the underlying original game. Popular examples include the *QPong* mod, which changes the gameplay of the FPS *Quake* into that of the old table tennis game Pong, or *International Online Soccer*, which turns the shooter *Half-Life* into a multiplayer soccer tournament to be played on the Internet. *Garry's Mod* turns the dystopian shooter *Half-Life 2* into a kind of virtual sandbox. Crossing the genre borders of the original game by changing its gameplay elements, such mods turn the modder's attention particularly to these genre-defining elements. For example, when we compare the changes the mod *Shantytown* made to its original game *Half-Life 2*, it becomes obvious what characterizes the former as a point-and-click adventure game and the latter as an FPS. *Shantytown* puts more stress on dialog and features a player inventory in which objects can be stored; its avatar is not controlled directly (as in *Half-Life 2*) but indirectly through moving and clicking a cursor; and the gameplay centers on solving puzzles, while shooting actions, though essential for *Half-Life 2*, are left out in the mod. But because *Shantytown* is clearly built out of the same basic material as *Half-Life 2*, the genre-defining importance of each of these single design decisions becomes apparent.

Machinima movies cannot be classified in terms of video game genres since they are not games but movies. Nevertheless, they can be quite useful in pointing out the game design conventions of combining certain game genres with specific movie genres. Though these are separate genre systems, affinities do exist: shooters, for instance, quite often use action movie elements, while adventure games frequently fall back on whodunit clichés. A notable example of how a machinima movie arouses attention by breaking with such conventions is, again, the *Red vs. Blue* series. Though their machinima work was based on the sci-fi FPS *Halo*, the makers of *Red vs. Blue* decided to create a sitcom crowded with quirky characters instead of an action movie. They achieved an even more radical break with conventions in another machinima series, *P.A.N.I.C.S.*, which turns the horror shooter *F.E.A.R.* into an absurd comedy series. The humor of both these series is quite often fueled by the tensions achieved through this rather unusual combination of game and movie genres. It is through such violation of expectations that the conventions of genre combination and their effects become apparent.

Outlook

Creative work with machinima movies and mods looks promising as a means for developing a number of the basic skills of computer game literacy. It opens up a variety of possibilities, especially for the acquisition of production skills and the development of analytical skills, and should therefore be taken more seriously by those who work in media pedagogy.

Already, thousands of young people devote themselves to these fields of creative media work without the slightest intervention of pedagogues. They form multinational workgroups communicating over the Internet and working for months or even years on mods. Or they create full-length in-game movies simply by means of a commercial video game, a PC, and the help of a couple of friends. Modding and machinima are gaming phenomena of growing popularity. More and more commercial games are being shipped with more and more efficient editing tools encouraging such creative use of the medium. Machinima works like *Red vs. Blue* are reviewed in (nongaming) magazines and newspapers and published for sale on DVDs. Countless young gamers are already seeking empowerment over their games through modding and machinima making. Many more could follow, should pedagogy grab the chance and add these creative practices to its agenda.

Notes

1. See Entertainment Software Association, "Anti-Piracy FAQ," <http://www.theesa.com/policy/antipiracy_faq.asp>.

2. *Red vs Blue* is a hugely successful machinima sitcom series based on the popular sci-fi shooter *Halo*.

3. See *Red vs. Blue: Season 5 Preview*, which aired May 24, 2006 (<http://www.bungie.net/News/content.aspx?cid=8233>).

References

Aarseth, Espen. 1997. *Cybertext: Perspectives on Ergodic Literature*. Baltimore, MD: Johns Hopkins University Press.

Baran, Stanley J. 2006. *Introduction to Mass Communication: Media Literacy and Culture*. Boston: McGraw-Hill.

Bolter, Jay David, and Richard Grusin. 1999. *Remediation: Understanding New Media*. Cambridge: MIT Press.

CNN. 2006. Video Game Set Sales Record in 2005. CNN.com. January 14. <http://money.cnn .com/2006/01/13/technology/personaltech/gamesales/index.htm>.

Debes, John. 1970. The Loom of Visual Literacy: An Overview. In *Proceedings: First National Conference on Visual Literacy*, ed. C. M. Williams and J. L. Debes, 1–16. New York: Pitman.

Delaney, Kevin J. 2004. When Art Imitates Videogames, You Have "Red vs. Blue": Mr. Burns Makes Little Movies Internet Fans Clamor For; Shades of Samuel Beckett. *Wall Street Journal Online*, April 9. <http://nikon.bungie.org/pressscans/wsj.040904/red_vs_blue_wsj.pdf>.

Gee, James Paul. 2004. *What Videogames Have to Teach Us about Learning and Literacy*. New York: Palgrave Macmillan.

Messaris, Paul A. 1994. *Visual Literacy: Image, Mind & Reality*. Boulder, CO: Westview.

MPAA (Motion Picture Association of America). 2008. Theatrical Market Statistics 2008. <http:// www.mpaa.org/2008%20MPAA%20Theatrical%20Market%20Statistics.pdf>.

MPFS (Medienpädagogischer Forschungsverbund Südwest). 2005. JIM 2005. Jugend, Information, (Multi-)Media: Basisstudie zum Medienumgang 12- bis 19jähriger in Deutschland. Stuttgart: Medienpädagogischer Forschungsverbund Südwest. <http://www.mpfs.de/fileadmin/Studien/ JIM2005.pdf>.

Pelletier, Caroline. 2005. Studying Games in School: A Framework for Media Education. <http:// www.digra.org/dl/db/06278.32248.pdf >.

Silverblatt, Art. 1995. *Media Literacy*. Westport, CT: Praeger.

Software References

Anachronox. Ion Storm. 2001

Beyond Good & Evil. Ubisoft. 2003.

Counter-Strike. Valve Corporation. 1999.

Driver (series). Reflections Interactive. 1999–2004.

The Elder Scrolls III: Morrowind. Bethesda Softworks. 2002.

The Elder Scrolls IV: Oblivion. Bethesda Softworks. 2006.

F.E.A.R. Monolith Productions. 2005.

Garry's Mod. Team Garry. 2005.

Half-Life. Valve Corporation. 1998.

Half-Life 2. Valve Corporation. 2004.

Halo: Combat Evolved. Bungie Studios. 2001.

Max Payne 2. Remedy Entertainment. 2003.

The Movies. Lionhead Studios. 2005.

NCAA Football 07. Electronic Arts Tiburon. 2006.

Quake. id Software. 1996.

The Ship: Murder Party. Outerlight. 2006.

Tony Hawk's Underground. Neversoft. 2003.

Unreal Tournament 2004. Epic Games. 2004.

World of Warcraft. Blizzard Entertainment. 2004.

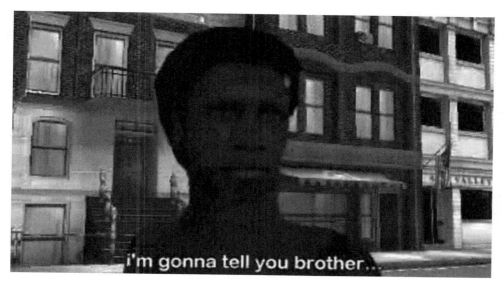

Alex "Koulamata" Chan, dir., *The French Democracy* (2005).

16 Pink vs. Blue: The Emergence of Women in Machinima

Robert Jones

As machinima moves forward as a growing medium and cultural phenomenon we must examine its place within not just the history of art but the history of technology as well. As is true of most histories of technology, the issue of gender warrants a central part in the discussion. Though the literature on women in video gaming is far from comprehensive, it has increased steadily in the years following Cassell and Jenkins's definitive volume.[1] This essay attempts to contribute to the growing body of work by tackling the issue of gender as it plays out in machinima. Although much of what has been written about machinima celebrates it as a democratizing force in the ever-changing landscape of consumer-produced media, little has been said about it as a contested space where points of access are far from equal. To be clear, machinima is viewed here not as a technology per se but as a medium made possible by the relatively new technology of video game engines. As was true for traditional filmmaking, making machinima requires access to the technologies that make it possible. Drawing on the historical examples of amateur radio and the personal computer, I illustrate a historical trajectory that shows how access to new technologies gets determined in large part by the gender inscriptions imposed by the dominant culture. Therefore, any claims that might be made about machinima's emancipatory storytelling capacity must be tempered by the material conditions that implicate machinima as the medium of a select group.

Like the pioneering hobbyists from the early days of both radio and the personal computer, the creators of machinima adapted a technology and appropriated it for their own purposes. The history of radio and the history of the PC parallel that of machinima in other ways as well, providing a better understanding of this growing phenomenon. The historical absence of a female presence in the early days of the three technologies may serve as a starting point in an investigation of the relationship between gender and technology. Only by situating machinima in the history of communication technology can we fully grasp the breadth of this phenomenon and determine where it falls in the larger historical context of women in technology.

Donna Haraway's work on the masculine bias in scientific culture and her subsequent work on cyborgs forms the backbone of a number of feminist theories regarding technology. Arguing against an essentialist explanation for the existence of patriarchy, Haraway finds that such narratives have commonly excluded women who did not fit comfortably in a victimization role (Haraway 1991). Cyberfeminists like Sadie Plant (1997) continue in this line of thought, invoking the figure of Ada Lovelace, who played a vital role in the development of the computer yet has often been placed outside that history. Plant goes so far as to define cyberspace as a feminine space because of its fluidity and undefined nature. At the core of this particular approach, then, cyberfeminists try to reappropriate spaces and technologies where women have always existed but have been excluded from the discourses surrounding them. Nina Wakeford, who does research on the presence of women Web designers online, says that Plant reminds us "of the necessity of being alert to writing which ignores alternative discourses of women's experiences in on-line life, and unthinkingly mirrors the 'moral panics' of widespread media publicity" (Wakeford 1997, 53). This approach celebrates the existing voices of women in the history of technology rather than lamenting the silenced ones. Along those lines, Jennifer Terry and Melodie Calvert insist that "technologies do not simply control and victimize their users, even though they often produce and reinforce hierarchical social relations" (1997, 4). Instead, women are historically seen as always having had access to power, and focusing on the ones who have succeeded creates the potential for future success.

Not all feminists who deal with the issue of technology, however, agree with this position. Sara Diamond, for example, finds optimistic cyberfemmes like Plant to be excessively utopian in their understanding of electronic technologies. Citing the example of Canadian clerical workers, she notes that although laptops may have made it possible for women to explore online spaces in the privacy of their homes, the introduction of this technology into the home also had the adverse effect of importing office work into the home. Rather than celebrating access to this supposedly liberating technology, Diamond unveils it as an extension of a wage labor regime that adheres to the work efficiencies of Taylorism (Diamond 1997, 83). Also not inclined to embrace cyberfeminism's optimism is Jennifer Light, who wrote a detailed account of the "computer girls" of the ENIAC project during World War II. In this history, she points to the important role that women played in the development of the computer during the war and their simultaneous absence from the discourses surrounding them. As a cautionary example, she presents a photograph published by the *New York Times* in a story on ENIAC, featuring a man working on a mainframe computer and two women in the background also working on machines, and contrasts it with the same photograph as it was used in an ad in *Popular Science Monthly*, where the two women were cropped out of the image (Light 2003, 310–311). This example graphically underscores that women have always had a presence in technology, but how they are framed by the dominant culture perpetuates the social hierarchies that situate men as the controllers of technology. The histories of the amateur radio and PC presented here follow a similar tack as these last two examples, delving into the way the discourses surrounding technology can prohibit access. By examining how technology gets inscribed with certain gender identities, we are in better position to understand that the current technological innovation continues to carry a gendered baggage that we must unpack, and acknowledge that gender is a contested space even within something as seemingly democratizing as machinima.

The history of machinima follows in the same vein as other twentieth-century technologies, lacking any strong presence of women in its development. Other than trailblazers such as Katie Salen and Katherine Anna Kang, very few women have either won an award for their machinima work or become household names in the machinima community.[2] Moreover, machinima originated with first-person shooter (FPS) games like *Doom* and *Quake,* whose fan base consisted of young men. With their militaristic narratives and warrior aesthetic, these shooters create what Henry Jenkins calls a gendered play space that mostly appeals to males (Jenkins 1998, 265). The most popular and commercially successful machinima series is *Red vs. Blue* (figure 16.1), which is based on *Halo,* the space-marine shooter. Because the majority of machinima pieces are made with shooters, the lack of women producers of machinima makes sense.

This situation, however, changed with the introduction of *The Sims 2.* Maxis noted the popularity of a photo album function in the original *Sims* game that allowed players to use the in-game screenshot function to document the lives and stories of their characters. For the sequel, Maxis created an interface that allowed players to record their gameplay and easily manipulate the camera in the 3D environment, in

Figure 16.1
Red vs. Blue. Courtesy of Rooster Teeth Productions.

effect turning the game into a machinima studio. In addition, Maxis marketed the moviemaking functionality through a Web site created for players to upload and share their movies, and it also sponsored several competitions.[3] The result was a tremendous increase in the number of women making machinima.[4]

Jenkins would explain this as a difference in the play space: "In the case of *The Sims*, the default set of characters are, indeed, 'everyday people,' [the] setting is domestic, and the challenges confronted are familiar ones" (Jenkins 2003, 250). *The Sims*, unlike most shooters, has no violent element. Instead, it is about building and maintaining virtual relationships. I certainly agree with Jenkins that the difference in the game's content plays an important part in its popularity, and by extension in machinima produced by women; however, I want to argue that *The Sims 2* increased the production of machinima by women by making the interface more user-friendly and thereby accessible to women. This by no means implies an innate technological inability on the part of women, as many stereotypes suggest. Instead, it belongs to a long history of gendering technology as exclusively male. Dating back to early radio, the discourse around technology situated it as something to be mastered by men and merely used by women (Douglas 1999, 70). Making machinima has always required some sort of technical ability, whether it be simply getting the game footage in an editable video form or completely repurposing an engine. The technical skills necessary thus posed a barrier to women, who have had the message driven home that this technology is not theirs to master. By situating machinima in a larger gendered history of technology as a contested space where access is the central issue of power, I hope to provide a better sense of where it comes from so that we can determine where it is going. Moreover, viewing how women create machinima within the larger historical context of gender and technology offers deeper insights into the accessibility to power women now have. As historian Nina Lerman warns,

Ideas and ideologies about technology demand no less scrutiny than the traditional categories examined by social history. To treat technology as a social product is to recognize that technology in our society has reflected, reinforced, and been built into the social boundaries we construct and reconstruct. (Lerman 2003, 144)

Examining how the current emergence of women creating machinima parallels previous moments in history can possibly help us better understand how technology will continue as a contested, gendered space into the twenty-first century. Reviewing the history of the earlier technologies reveals that despite the efforts of women to overcome the status quo, men have maintained hierarchies of power through technology. Although today's social landscape hardly resembles that of a hundred years ago, hierarchies still prevail, and issues of power in relation to technology must be interrogated. To begin, I go back to a technological subculture bearing many similarities to the machinimator subculture: amateur radio operators.

Boy Inventor-Heroes

The gendering of technology as a realm of mastery reserved primarily for boys and men predates machinima. Cultural barriers that have stood in the way of women pursuing computer technologies existed with prior technologies, such as radio. Emerging at the turn of the twentieth century, radio offered a new means of exploration for a culture that had largely traded in its heritage of adventurous expansionism for the cool urbanity of modernism. Cities grew and frontiers vanished, while life became more mechanized, and people lost their old ways of connecting with one another. Whereas young men could at one time demonstrate their "manliness" through rugged living in the wide-open spaces and on frontiers, they now found themselves cooped up in the domestic confines previously occupied mostly by women and the infirm.[5] Radio offered young men the means both to discover a new frontier and to recapture the sense of power that mastery over uncharted territory can provide. Access to this new technology, however, was limited to a small population, a trait echoed in the early days of machinima. In fact, the first amateur radio organization, formed in 1909 in New York City, consisted of five boys (Walker 2001, 13). Run by an eleven-year-old, this elite group represented the core demographic of the amateur operators, who came to be known as "hams," a term likely derived from the slang for a "show-off"[6]: white, middle-class males in urban areas. Part of what made hams such an exclusive group was the prohibitive cost of the equipment. Batteries, transmitters, and radio wave–sensitive crystals were expensive items. Moreover, the technical skill necessary to get all the components to work in concert required some sort of training or the time and patience to tinker with them to find the voices of others hovering in the ether. As historian Susan Douglas notes,

Working-class boys with neither the time nor the money to tinker with wireless could not participate as easily. Nether could girls or young women, for whom technical tinkering was considered a distinctly inappropriate pastime and technical mastery a distinctly unacceptable goal. This fraternity, whether self-consciously or accidentally, brought together roughly similar men in a region uninhabited by those so different from them: women, immigrants, blacks, and boys ignorant about electrical technology. (Douglas 1987, 205)

Like so many previous and subsequent technologies steeped in discourse about their democratizing potential, radio reaffirmed that mastery over technology was a boys' club. In the case of machinima, the developments in interface design that allowed greater access to the video game engine and the affordability of computers able to run such powerful engines have certainly made machinima more available than in its fledgling years. However, access is hardly universally available to all, and in the beginning, access was limited to a select few, for the same reasons that access to amateur radio was limited.

Compared to the blistering speed and increasing bandwidth of wireless technology we now benefit from today, the radio seems rather primitive. However, radio in its early days did not resemble the modern terrestrial radio. The technology roughly functions on the same principles, but radio is now used primarily as a unidirectional broadcast medium. Prior to government regulation of the bandwidth and the development of radio as a lucrative commercial industry, wireless sets could send as well as receive. Another parallel emerges here with the pioneers of machinima in their similar use of a technology to produce, even though its commercial viability was based on a model of consumption.[7] The simple task of dialing in a station on the car radio is made easy by technological improvements that the early hams did not have access to. Instead, they engaged in an active process of exploratory listening, constantly adjusting the apparatus for maximum efficiency, sending out their call sign in hopes of making a connection (Douglas 1987, 307–308). The metaphor of fishing was often used to describe the process, each ham casting out his line, trying to reel in a far-off signal. Analogous to the performances that hackers display through their mastery over information systems,[8] these young men prided themselves on seeing how far they could hear, a pursuit known as "DXing." The hackers of the demoscene, who were really the precursors to machinimators, paralleled the hams' spirit of competitive performance.[9] Attaching graphical tags at the beginning of a piece of cracked software to indicate who had cracked it served as an announcement of the hacker's prowess. In both cases the ability to harness a new technology and demonstrate a mastery that surpassed one's peers' became an overt expression of masculine dominance. In fact, the competition to dominate certain frequencies often led to a public image of hams resembling how hackers are viewed by mainstream culture. As Michelle Hilmes points out, "However, at other times their activities could be cast in a more negative light; like today's computer hackers, these boys could also disrupt official transmissions, spread false information, and create havoc and disharmony in the airwaves" (Hilmes 1997, 38). This move toward articulating manhood through technological mastery rather than physical strength and mastery of the physical universe marked a key turn in the way technology became gendered as a male pursuit. Young girls found themselves being told that the wireless radio was meant for young men, both by their families and by the media messages accompanying this new phenomenon.

Perhaps one of the largest contributors to the discourse that cast amateur radio as an exclusively male enterprise was the popular press. In 1907, the *New York Times Magazine* ran a featured story about Walter J. Willenborg entitled "New Wonders with 'Wireless'— And by a Boy!" (Douglas 1987, 187–191). Apparently an ordinary young man, he embodied the archetype of the inventor-hero, gaining power and notoriety through his mastery of this new technology. With a wireless set powerful enough to dominate most of the operators in his area, Willenborg became a "hero" to every boy who lacked physical prowess and desired the ability to control something. Similar short stories emerged in popular magazines, telling tales of young men saving peoples' lives and impressing girls through their radio operating skills. The surge in popularity of amateur radio over the course of the next decade owed much to the figure of the boy inventor-hero. In fact, from 1913 to 1916, the number of licensed amateurs grew from 322 to 10,279 (ibid., 293). With science and technological progress becoming entrenched parts of the national identity, radio provided young American males an opportunity to demonstrate their patriotism. Drawing on the insatiable curiosity of the scientific imagination, the exploratory listening of the hams sought to conquer new frontiers. More and more, young men sought to discover this new and wondrous technology. Diagrams and how-to guides found their way into children's books, magazines, and the Boy Scouts manual. The *New York Times* even went so far as to say, "If every boy does not possess a receiving outfit, it is because he lacks imagination or money" (quoted in Douglas 1987, 303). Meanwhile, women found themselves on the sidelines, witnesses to this growing phenomenon without any real potential of trying it out for themselves. That was the situation until the commercial potential of a mass broadcasting system changed the nature of the medium and led to the formation of an entire new industry.

During the boom of amateur radio operators in the early 1920s, Harry P. Davis, vice president of Westinghouse Electric & Manufacturing Company, understood that radio had a far greater potential than the relatively small niche market of hobbyists. Rather than seeing hams as the primary market, Davis thought these "amateurs were simply the forerunners of a much larger market of radio receivers" (ibid., 300). Once realized as a medium of distribution on a mass scale, radio drastically changed from the two-way means of exploratory listening that had made it popular among young men to a fixed signal designed to deliver content to a quickly growing consumer audience consisting largely of women. But before this could happen, manufacturers such as Westinghouse had to retool the design of receivers to make them user-friendly: "This meant, first and foremost, making tuning easier, upgrading the appearance of receivers, and improving sound amplification and fidelity" (Douglas 1999, 77). Whereas the radio had previously offered status to the amateur because of its complexity and the skills necessary to control it, the newly designed receivers made the technology available to everyone.

The discourse surrounding the inventor-hero type provided a necessary form of masculine identity when young men found themselves trapped in the domestic settings that marked urban living. Finding refuge in the garage or backyard sheds, they were able to explore new spaces with their wireless transmitters. But once the economic potential of this technology became too great to ignore, it was time for those transmitters to become receivers. More important, it was time to move the radio out of the garage and into the living room so that it could serve as a vital tool to commerce. This gendering of technology as masculine during its infancy in order to

maintain a power hierarchy and shifting to incorporate women only when the economic potential was fully realized is a common trajectory in the history of technology.
It happened later with the home computer, and I want to suggest that a similar process
has occurred with machinima.

When discussing the relationship of gender technology, as in the case of amateur
radio, it is important not to fall into the trap of biological determinism. Gender is
understood here as a social construct, culminating in an attitude toward technology
that limits access. The technologies of the amateur radio and the PC are hardly masculine; rather, the discourses around them inscribe them as such. The overwhelming
number of young men operating wireless sets derived not from innate technological
proficiency but rather from the social discourse that constructed that as part of their
masculine identity. Conversely, young girls internalized the narrative from both peers
and the media that the inventor-hero archetype was exclusively male. A young woman
who sought to pursue amateur radio operating faced numerous hurdles because of the
way ham radio was framed as a male endeavor. There exists evidence of female amateur
operators, but they do not have a prominent place in radio's history. As Hilmes writes,
"Their exclusion from the dominant representation points to the need to "control"
this phenomenon discursively in a way that least threatened the established social
hierarchies" (Hilmes 1997, 39).[10] Thus, the history of ham radio demonstrates that
females are often granted less of a choice in relation to their interests. Instead, they
find themselves on the receiving end of an exteriorly formed identity that relegates
their power within the culture. Radio was one of the most powerful technologies of
its time, and of its use overwhelmingly by men illustrates a larger social imbalance.
Only through the close investigation of these historical moments and learning from
previous injustices can we hope to move forward and form relationships with technology that are far more egalitarian.

Girls and Computers

Similar to the adoption of wireless radio, the personal home computer designates yet
another historical instance where the cultural expectations and surrounding discourse
of mastery over technology situate young men as the "natural" operators of these
devices. Young women, on the other hand, develop a relationship that is often anxiety
inducing. Sherry Turkle suggests that children cope with the social upheaval of adolescence by constructing "microworlds" of, for example, literature, dance, or mathematical expertise. These safe havens provide a space where they feel control when
their lives are otherwise filled with elements they cannot control. She goes on to say,

It is during adolescence that the "hacker culture" becomes born in elementary schools and junior
high schools as predominately male—because in our society men are more likely than women
to master anxieties about people by turning to the world of things and formal systems. (Turkle
1986, 40)

The anxiety that young women feel about the computer, however, derives not from a genetic predisposition but from a cultural narrative they internalize that prohibits them from achieving the same level of comfort enjoyed by boys. Joel Cooper and Kimberlee Weaver indicate that under certain conditions, girls are as competent as boys in their computing skills (Cooper and Weaver 2003, 6). But as girls grow older, they maintain these anxieties, which may even intensify, creating a self-identity that is antithetical to having mastery over computers. One effect of this situation is a tremendous imbalance in the field of computer science, with women making up less than 20 percent of computer science graduates, even though women and men surf the Web in equal numbers.[11]

Though the reasons why girls internalize the computer as a "boy" technology span numerous possibilities, developmental psychology offers some useful hypotheses. Before age five or six, children do not demonstrate a permanent notion of their gender (Kohlberg 1996). For example, a young boy who puts on a wig with long hair could be asked if he were now a girl and answer yes without any sort of disruption in his identity. Only once children have fully internalized their gendered identity do they exhibit gender constancy, after which notions of gender become fixed, as do the cultural associations of what it means to be a girl or a boy. Therefore, the exposure to gendered stereotypes has a stronger impact after the stage of gender constancy is reached. To test this, Bronsan conducted a survey drawing connections between psychological gender and computer attitudes (Brosnan 1998, 63–78). He found that boys with more masculine identities had stronger positive feelings about the computer, while boys with less masculine identities had weaker feelings. Similarly, the girls who had the most negative feelings toward computers were those who had the most feminine gender role orientations. This result suggests that independent of biological sex, gendered identities play a large role in the development of attitudes toward technology.

Another possible contributor to the disparity between men and women in computing has to do with the social aspect of computing as an act of performance. Like the hams who flexed their technical muscles, "DXing" across great distances, hackers prove themselves through acts of information manipulation. Status is won or lost according to how quickly codes can be cracked. Controlling such powerful technologies, framed as expressions of "manliness" by the cultural discourse, then leads to competition. The push for mastery at these high levels has a trickle-down effect so that anyone who sits at a keyboard gets judged on his or her ability to operate it. The end result is a high-pressure situation that inevitably leads to poor performance. And in a phenomenon known as social facilitation, the presence of others causes a change in performance. Michaels et al. tested this concept on pool players and found that good players were socially facilitated by an audience and improved their game, while poor players fell short due to the lack of confidence in their skills (Michaels et al. 1984,

21–21). Cooper and Weaver insist that "social facilitation is one of the social psycho-logical factors that contribute to the gender difference," and "when the social context of technological learning includes groups of children, the performance of girls is likely to suffer" (Cooper and Weaver 2003, 43). Both the coding of the demoscene and creation of machinima can be seen largely as isolated endeavors, and would thus seem to be outside the influence of social facilitation. However, if we understand that both hacking and machinima creation are derived from general computing skills a young person acquires in school or by practicing at home—that is, in front of mom and dad or a sibling—the issue of anxiety remains prohibitive on the level of overall access to the technology for young women.

Building on the notion of performance anxiety as an inhibiting force, Margaret Morse frames the relationship between women and technology in terms of what she labels *unwill*:

Unwill is thus a hazy mixture of vegetative corporeality and an ineptitude that amounts to cul-turally inscribed hysteria. As a woman in a male-oriented technological world that devalues the flesh, my struggle is thus against myself embodied as a woman—albeit a culturally constructed one. (Morse 1997, 26)

Invoking Michel Foucault's explanation of power as "infinitesimal mechanisms" oper-ating on the body, Morse drives home the point that the experiences of anxiety that women feel toward technology, though socially constructed, have actual physiological impacts. That is to say, it is not just a general sense of unease so much as a physical tension that is brought on by the stark fear of failure. Whereas to will something draws on the connotations of deeply entrenched desire that manifests almost as a physical demand, unwill reflects a repulsion of almost equal intensity. Sherry Turkle in *The Second Self* similarly draws on the notion of will to explain what she labels "hard masters":

Hard mastery is the imposition of will over the machine through the implementation of a plan. A program is the instrument of premeditated control. Getting the program to work is more like getting "to say one's piece" than allowing ideas to emerge in the give-and-take of conversation. (Turkle 1984, 104)

Describing children learning to program in the LOGO language, Turkle contrasts them with "soft" masters who use a more organic approach to programming that more resembles the way painters create their art. The obvious cultural connotations divide these concepts along gendered lines, with "hard" embodying the masculine and the "soft" the feminine. The microworlds of computers represents a way of imposing order on the world. Unlike human interactions, however, which are marked by uncertainty, programmers' relationship to technology is one of absolute control. Though soft masters operate unfettered by the rigidity that confines their counterparts, they still demonstrate a mastery over technology on par with that of the amateur radio operator. Edwards clarifies that the hacker subculture, by this definition, would consist primarily of soft masters, owing to their intuitive nature and resistance to structure, thus complicating the hard versus soft binary (Edwards 2003, 185). So, while Turkle's distinction offers some insight into different approaches to mastering technology and the possible ways the different approaches might illustrate differences in how gender is manifested in computer programming, the labels work best as flexible identities not bound precisely by a gender division. For machinima, the hard/soft binary divides along the lines of how the engines are being used. In its inception, the kind of machinima being made represented a soft mastery over the engine in its appropriation on the part of the gamer to use for something other than the purpose for which it was designed, such as the use of *Quake* to create *Diary of a Camper.* More recent interfaces, such as that of *The Movies* or *The Sims 2,* which integrate recording functions and camera control as part of their design to facilitate the creation of machinima, embody hard mastery because they create a structure for the machinimator to work within.

Girl Gamers

The face of gaming has transformed in many ways since Justine Cassell and Henry Jenkins published their definitive collection of essays on gender and computer games in 1998. The girls' games movement, led by women such as Brenda Laurel of Purple Moon and Heather Kelly of Girl Games, never found its place in the market; Jenkins observes this outcome was largely due to the fact that these were new media companies in the age of the dot-com explosion that were not making the same return on investment that Internet companies were making (Jenkins 2003, 248). Yet despite these setbacks, women have made their presence felt in the gaming market, accounting for nearly 40 percent of the total game players in the United States, with the proportion of women over eighteen (30 percent) surpassing the proportion of boys aged seventeen and younger (23 percent).[12] Even gaming industry giant Nintendo has responded to this changing landscape by revamping the way that it markets its technology. For example, upon introducing its new handheld console the DS, Nintendo found and pursued new markets that seemed to be excluded by the previously male-targeted Game Boy. Similarly, the choice to change the name of their current-generation console from the rather masculine Revolution to what many hard-core gamers (read: young males) have complained is a "weak" name,[13] the Wii, demonstrates that the days of *Barbie Fashion Designer*[14] as the only option for girls may be behind us.

Much of the criticism from feminists in regard to the girls' game movement was directed toward its tendency to cater to market demands to the point that it simply recreated the gender stereotypes that situate girls on the outside of these technologies. Often called "pink software," after Brenda Laurel declared she would ship her games in pink boxes if the market research suggested girls would respond to them better, these games tried to turn young girls on to video games by appealing to what they liked about other forms of media, such as children's books (Laurel 1998). Taking a critical stance against pink software, Suzanne De Castell and Mary Bryson posed the question,

How will retooling technologies in conformity with the conceptions and desires of girls ever reverse girls' apparent lack of interest in things technological, given what girls themselves appear to believe and to value—specifically, as market research indicates, clothes, make-up, boys and shopping? (De Castell and Bryson 1998, 251)

Comparable to the concerns articulated in Angela McRobbie's work regarding the way popular magazines assume that girls of all ages are united by stereotypical "girly" interests while boys are divided by a myriad of niche interests, their question underscores what still keeps video games from moving into a place that is more inviting to girls without condescending to them. Similarly, the integration of user-friendly interfaces in both *The Movies* and *The Sims 2* to better facilitate the creation of machinima could be seen as condescending. In one respect, lowering the learning curve for the software so that entry-level new machinimators increase is a smart marketing strategy, given that both of these games have utilized film competitions in the promotion of the games. However, that these games target female gamers more than shooters like *Unreal Tournament 2004* shows how the same gendered stereotypes regarding women and technology that existed with the ham radio and the PC reappear in the design of game interfaces. So, while machinima holds tremendous potential for democratizing animated filmmaking, it is important to understand that it is a contested space when it comes to the issue of gender.

I want to clarify here that the history of computer technologies has had a strong female presence. The problem is that this presence tends not to survive the dominant discourses that insist on situating computers as a masculine technology. From pioneers like Ada Lovelace to the women who worked as "computers" during World War II, calculating ballistic trajectories, to the cyberfeminists of the 1990s, women have carved out a space in that history.[15] Unfortunately, computer programming in general and video game design in particular remain a "boys' club." Despite a few exemplary cases of overcoming stereotypes, gender roles in computing persist. For example, in one study, when given the opportunity to create their own games, many young girls created games that diverged drastically from those created by boys; however, their designs tended to recreate the sorts of play that have long been gendered as female (Kafai 1999). As demonstrated by the girls' game movement, the influence of girls (at the marketing research level) often recreates gendered stereotypes. And the tremendous success of Mattel's *Barbie Fashion Designer* suggests that young girls will continue to respond to and consume these gendered identities in regard to technology. Along these lines, Brenda Laurel talks about how they intentionally slowed down the gameplay of *Secret Paths in the Forest* because they found that girls preferred it (Jenkins 1998,

284). While I understand that she was working within a commercial structure that required her to sell games—and I certainly do not want to contribute to the criticism of her efforts—I do want to point out that a similar pattern existed with radio: technologies traditionally associated with boys and men get defined in terms of complexity as a means of maintaining existing power hierarchies. Though video game software categorized as "slow" is not necessarily less complex, the desire for slowness implies an aversion to what would be considered "fast" games. My concern is that the cultural reading of video game software as either slow or fast carries with it connotations that might perpetuate the idea that most computer technologies are too complicated for young girls. When the marketing research conducted by Purple Moon discovers a desire for slowness in its customers, can this be read as girls simply responding to a societally preconstructed relationship with technology in which they are clearly not masters? I believe it does. Moreover, the attempts by Purple Moon to accommodate this penchant echo the attempts by Westinghouse to make the radio more user-friendly so that it could tap into a previously unexploited female market. This is not to suggest that Laurel was simply trying to sell games so much as responding to a market cultivated by a fixed notion of gender and technology. Despite her failed attempts, Laurel had the overall interest of women in mind when she created Purple Moon. She understood that video games serve as a gateway to computer literacy, and wanted to open that to girls. The growing dependency on computers requires increasingly sophisticated computer literacy skills for everyone who hopes to have an opportunity in this competitive world. Laurel insisted that "true computer literacy means that we start to own this technology as individuals and as a gender when we see it as an empowering device that makes representations" (Laurel 298, 133). Machinima illustrates precisely how mastery over a computer technology provides access to this power of representation. And the increase in machinima created by women demonstrates an important step toward women owning this technology in the same way as men do. However, the access granted to women in the case of machinima seems to be facilitated by again making the technology more user-friendly for the sake of expanding the market, as is the case in both *The Movies* and *The Sims 2*. On the one hand, the wider availability could be read as an overall empowering move in machinima's short history; on the other, the simplification involved in making a video game engine more user-friendly can be read as limiting the possibilities of what can be achieved with that software, thus reinforcing to women that they are merely the users of computer technologies while men remain technology's masters.

The Sims 2 vs. Unreal Tournament 2004

To illustrate how just the difference in content of a game, which defines what sort of gendered play space it is, does not solely result in the exclusion of women in the creation of machinima, I want to look at two very different games, *The Sims 2* and *Unreal Tournament 2004*. Released in the same year, these games stand at opposite ends of video game genres. As a shooter, *Unreal Tournament 2004* demands excellent hand-eye coordination and involves fast-paced action requiring quick responses, all of which give the game a high learning curve, especially since it is played against other players online who spend many hours honing their twitch skills. By comparison, *The Sims 2* moves at a much slower pace and consists primarily of resource management, as is often the case in simulation games. Though the game is far from simple, its intuitive Heads Up Display (HUD) provides an entry level that is far more inclusive than that of *Unreal Tournament 2004* or any other shooter. And given that shooters make up a relatively small portion of the entire video game market, consisting largely of males, and *The Sims* is the largest-selling PC game series of all time, which includes a heavy percentage of women, it would make sense that few machinima pieces are made by women using the *Unreal* engine while most of those made with *The Sims* are by women. These games do, however, share a unique quality in that they were shipped with toolkits designed to assist in making machinima, and both launched marketing campaigns to sell this aspect. The content of these games certainly predicts the overall user demographic. However, a closer examination of the toolkits and of how their interface design builds on gendered stereotypes suggests that any potential power machinima may have as a means of expression still adheres to social hierarchies that stretch back to the early days of radio.

Before I delve into the particulars of each of these games' toolkits, I want to talk briefly about the impact of machinima on selling games. Designers have long understood that play as a design-guiding concept works best as a malleable rather than a fixed notion. Salen and Zimmerman talk extensively about the various ways play gets defined and how these definitions carry cultural implications. They introduce the concept of transformative play to illustrate precisely how phenomena such as mods and machinima differ from traditional forms of play. Whereas play is defined as "the free movement within a more rigid structure," in transformative play "the free movement of play alters the more rigid structure in which it takes shape."[16] In the case of machinima, simply playing the game within its confined boundaries no longer satisfies the player. As with mods, where the player seeks to alter the game in either appearance or gameplay, machinima extends the life of a game beyond what the initial designers may have anticipated. The *Red vs. Blue* series is one of the best examples of how through a machinima series, a game (*Halo* in this case) benefits from a constant presence online and more traditional film forums. Although many *Red vs Blue* fans were *Halo* fans prior to the series, a number of fans discovered the game through the machinima series, particularly at the film festivals where *Red vs Blue* premiered, which do not typically boast of a gamer demographic. With machinima becoming better known in gaming communities, it made sense for both Epic Games (*Unreal*) and Maxis

(*The Sims*) to develop toolkits as part of the original design to accommodate this budding interest and extend the lifetime of their products. This was not a huge departure for either developer; both had procedural game design components in their earlier releases that allowed players to create game content. In the case of *Unreal*, Epic simply followed in the tradition of shooter pioneers at id Software, who provided level editors as part of the release to allow players to design their own maps.[17] For *The Sims*, Will Wright has always been interested in procedural game design that allows the bulk of game content to be user-created; *Spore* was developed with the goal of making that part of the primary gameplay.[18]

The inclusion of toolkits in games like *The Sims* has recently demonstrated that offering an "open innovation gateway" to customers contributes to a game's success. Prügl and Schreier found that the most beneficial component of these toolkits was that they allowed users to share with other users, providing a variety beyond what Maxis could produce or the user could on his or her own (Prügl and Schreier 2006). One of the ways they discuss these toolkits is by level of complexity. High-end toolkits were described as requiring more expert ability to create content for the game (i.e., *SimsBlender*).[19] Often created by players with knowledge of game design, these player-created toolkits illustrate the type of transformative play that exists in gaming communities. Low-end toolkits, usually the ones provided as part of the game, offer detailed customization but not the power for entire transformation. One way to contrast the difference between *Unreal* and *The Sims*, then, is to examine how their toolkits differ, revealing the target demographic and hence the cultural assumptions they are making about gender and technology.

As a basic element of filmmaking, mise-en-scène plays a crucial part in the process of storytelling. Simply using the assets that come with a game would limit the narrative possibilities. The amount of control machinimators have over the assets in the game is determined by the game they choose and which technique they choose to use. Kelland, Morris, and Lloyd outline four techniques used to create machinima: AI, puppeteering, recamming, and scripting (Kelland, Morris, and Lloyd 2005, 80–96). Each involves different levels of control and complexity, resulting in machinima that varies in its quality of production value. Making machinima with *The Sims 2* offers great control of the camera, navigable anywhere in the 3D environment; however, controlling the characters is limited to prompting them into certain moods so that the AI induces a desired reaction. Although there are far too many differences between these techniques to detail here, the most relevant to the analysis of *Unreal* and *The Sims* regards the correlation between level of control over the mise-en-scène and the complexity of the interface. As the histories of the radio and PC imply, as access to these technologies increases, users tend to have less control over them. The toolkits that come with *The Sims 2* allow rather detailed customization; however, creating content is restricted by the menu choices in the game. Using just the toolkits provided

Figure 16.2
The Sims 2. Courtesy of Maxis.

with the game, users perform more of a "catalog shopping" form of design to change the buildings and surrounding neighborhood (figure 16.2). Even within these limitations, the game offers a myriad of possibilities, with expansion packs available to extend that variability further. Maxis's decision to limit the possibilities in order to create a user-friendly, menu-based interface is a strategy similar to that employed by Westinghouse to capture an unexploited female market. Therefore, the gendering of *The Sims 2* as a game trying to target women occurs both at the design level of content, as Jenkins suggest, and at the level of interface design. Similar to the strategies of Purple Moon, simplifying the interface tries to overcome the possible anxieties women users may have when encountering a daunting screen filled with complex menus and toolbars. So, while this tactic may appear to provide greater access for women, inviting them into the new subculture within gaming, it simultaneously reinforces cultural stereotypes about women and technology.

The *Unreal Tournament* level editor, *UnrealEd*, now in its third version, exemplifies the increasing demand of hard-core gamers for control over the code. As one of the most powerful toolkits available from a developer, this scripting software allows modifications ranging from simple skin swapping to full conversions of the game. In addition, this version also contains another toolkit designed specifically for making machinima, Matinee. Scripting offers the most precise control of all the techniques,

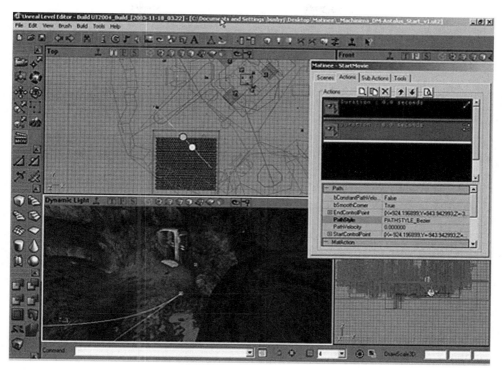

Figure 16.3
UnrealEd and Matinee. Courtesy of Epic Games.

which is why it is used to create the cut-scenes in most video games. Matinee affords gamers the ability to create virtual cameras within the 3D environment to document events and actions of characters that are scripted out, using the game's assets or ones designed specifically by the user. Like most powerful software, *UnrealEd* consists of a complicated interface requiring a steep learning curve (figure 16.3). Despite Epic's attempts to simplify scripting by designing a more user-friendly interface with toolbar and menu systems that try to make modding intuitive, the screen can be daunting to even a seasoned gamer. The Editor's Choice version of the game came with an additional DVD filled with hours of tutorials on the program to help ease gamers into it. However, when placed next to *The Sims'* interface, *UnrealEd* clearly appears to be targeting a different type of gamer, one who has had a rather long relationship with computers and has a mastery of them. Unfortunately, these users have historically not been female.

Shortly after both releases, the developers used contests to promote the toolkits as a way of providing an incentive to create machinima. For Maxis, this was simply a way to market the game and introduce the concept of machinima to an audience beyond the players from the first version who used the photo album function to create narratives. The contest was created in conjunction with University of Southern California's film school and offered a top prize of $5,000. Of the four top films, three were made by women. On the other hand, Epic's Make Something Unreal contest challenged not just machinimators to use the Matinee software to make a film but modders to completely transform the game with *UnrealEd*. Winning the grand prize of $25,000 for best film, Friedrich Kirschner's *The Journey* revealed just how powerful the *Unreal* toolkits were, creating a world that looked nothing remotely like the game. Several other prizes were awarded for different types of modifications made to the game. The contest generated a fair amount of buzz about the *Unreal* engine and what it could do, and provided aspiring designers a venue for showing off their abilities in hopes of seeking employment. Having witnessed how Valve Software capitalized on a user-created mod that eventually became one of their best-known games, *Counter-Strike*, and then hired those modders as part of the design team, Epic found it made business sense to promote *Unreal Tournament* this way. Holding contests as a means to uncover talent predates digital technologies, going back to 1931, when the Fisher Body Craftsman's Guild began their model building contests. In her analysis of the history of the contest, Ruth Oldenziel notes that the primary goal was to start young men thinking about engineering, specifically designing automobile bodies, because the Fisher company was the sole body manufacturer for General Motors (Oldenziel 2003). The discourse surrounding the Fisher contests, from the ads to the connection with the Boy Scouts, continuously put forth the message that mastery over technology was for boys only. Though the Epic contest hardly makes such claims, the implicit message that women have internalized about computer technologies played out in the results of the contest, which had no female winners.

Machinima stands to be a medium with a long future, and as the commercial potentials are realized that longevity will only be extended. But what makes machinima most significant in this particular moment is that it has opened up the art of animated film-making to such a great number of people. The power of storytelling carries tremendous possibility, and those who have access to it at least have the opportunity to be heard. Therefore, machinima should be understood as as a contested space about access and power, a space where the inscription of gendered identities draws on long histories that preceded current media. Even as the technology improves, allowing newer and more user-friendly interfaces like that of *The Sims 2*, more advanced technologies like that of *UnrealEd* get more powerful as well, which helps maintain a hierarchy. So, even though the greater number of women now making machinima may offer hope that issues of inequality and gendered technology have solutions, the history of the early radio and the PC suggests that the implicit narrative that women merely use technology while men control it will continue forward into real-time 3D virtual realms.

Notes

1. For more on gender and video gaming, see Hayes (2007), Taylor (2003, 2006), Graner Ray (2004), and Krotoski (2004).

2. The machinima communities that have grown up around *The Sims* offers a counterexample, but this happened at a much later stage in machinima's history.

3. For more on *Sims* machinima, see <http://www.sim-movies.com>. For more on the competitions, see <http://thesims2.ea.com/contests/index.php?pid=Community_contests>.

4. Part of the challenge in examining the role of gender in a relatively new phenomenon like machinima is that there is little in the way of reliable demographic data. I am basing the argument that women have had little representation in the making of machinima on the fact that the games used to make the majority of machinima pieces reflect a demographic that is heavily male. For the purpose of this essay I conducted a content analysis of the two major Web sites devoted to *Sims* machinima (<http://www.sims-movies.com> and <http://www.sims99.com>) to try to determine the demographic of the users. Several criteria were used to determine the gender of the machinimator. First, each Web site has an option to create a Web page for promoting the user's films. This page often provided the user's full name in addition to the chosen screen name used by the Web site to catalog the films. Each page also had a *Sim* avatar at the top that the user designed that served as the clearest indication of gender. However, not all machinimators created these Web pages. If no page was available, the screen name was used to determine gender in cases where there was no doubt (e.g., skatergirl22). If the screen name gave no strong indication, the machinima film was scanned for credits providing a name other than the screen name. Gender was only determined by names that clearly indicate female (e.g., Mary, Alice) or male (e.g., David, Mike). If no gender could be reliably determined, the user was marked as "unknown." Given these criteria, sim-movies.com revealed that female users made up 51 percent of machinimators while males accounted for only 30 percent, with 19 percent of users not being clearly identifiable to gender. The sims99.com showed similar results: 50 percent female, 27 percent male, and 23 percent unknown. Though more data are needed (particularly demographic information on the machinima community as a whole), these results indicate a pattern of increased machinima creation on the part of women. (I am greatly indebted to my research assistant, Naomi Geller, for undertaking the tedious task of compiling the data.).

5. Henry Jenkins (1998) discusses this aspect of boy culture.

6. Though there is no consensus as to the etymology of the term "ham," many have come to accept the connection to the slang term for "show-off," in that it accurately portrays the one-upmanship that seemed to be part of the character of these young men. This is also the origin accepted by one of the largest amateur radio organizations, the American Radio Relay League. For more information on this term or modern amateur radio operation, see <http://www.arrl.org>.

7. It should be made clear here that video games are understood as a product of consumption despite any definitions of interactivity. That is to say, any video game allows the "creation" of

audio-video images by virtue of the player playing the game. Machinima transforms that process in a fundamental way that ends with a product that can be distributed. Normal gameplay and the financial models based on video games do not necessarily account for this application. Except for games like *The Movies*, which adopt the use of the game engine to make machinima a core part of their gameplay, including the distribution of the created films through an established network, gamers typically consume rather than produce in the traditional sense.

8. For a general discussion on the character traits of hackers, see Thomas 2005.

9. For more on the demoscene, see Tasajärvi (2004). For more on the history of machinima, see Marino (2004) and Kelland, Morris, and Lloyd (2005).

10. For a similar instance of women's role in technology being underrepresented in history, see Light (2003).

11. For more on women in computing, see Margolis and Fisher (2002, 2). For more on women Internet usage, see <http://www.pewinternet.org/PPF/r/171/report_display.asp>.

12. For this and more information on the computer game industry, see the Entertainment Software Association Web site, <http://www.theESA.com>.

13. The point here is not to reinscribe gendered stereotypes about gamers. The presence of females in the hard-core gamers demographic is well documented by Taylor. However, young males still make up the majority of that population, and this sentiment can be garnered from any number of the fan boy online forums like <http://forums.nintendo.com/Nintendo>.

14. For a detailed discussion of *Barbie Fashion Designer* and its place in the girls' game movement, see Subrahmanyam and Greenfield (1998).

15. For a detailed history of Ada Lovelace, see Plant (1997). For more on how women were an important part of the ENIAC project during World War II, see Light (2003). For a detailed account of the cyberfeminist movement of the nineties, see Galloway (2004).

16. For a detailed of discussion on play and transformative play, see Salen and Zimmerman (2004, 301–310). For a specific analysis on transformative play within machinima, see Jones (2006).

17. For more on id Software's contribution to gaming history, see Kushner (2004).

18. To see the video of Will Wright's presentation at the 2005 Game Developers Conference on *Spore* and procedural game design, go to <http://www.gdconf.com>.

19. For Simsblender and other Sims toolkits, go to <http://modthesims2.com>.

References

Brosnan, Mark. 1998. The Impact of Psychological Gender, Gender-Related Perceptions, Significant Others, and the Introducer of Technology upon Computer Anxiety in Students. *Journal of Educational Computing Research* 18:63–78.

Brunner, Cornelia, Dorothy Bennet, and Margaret Honey. 1998. Girl Games and Technological Desire. In *From Barbie to Mortal Kombat: Gender and Computer Games*, ed. J. Cassell and H. Jenkins, 72–89. Cambridge: MIT Press.

Cassell, Justine, and Henry Jenkins. 1998. Chess for Girls? Feminism and Computer Games. In *From Barbie to Mortal Kombat: Gender and Computer Games*, ed. Justine Cassell and Henry Jenkins, 2–45. Cambridge: MIT Press.

Cooper, Joel, and Kimberlee D. Weaver. 2003. *Gender and Computers: Understanding the Digital Divide*. Mahwah, NJ: Erlbaum.

Coppa, Francesca. 2006. A Brief History of Media Fandom. In *Fan Fiction and Fan Communities in the Age of the Internet: New Essays*, ed. K. Hellekson and K. Busse. Jefferson, NC: McFarland.

De Castell, Suzanne, and Mary Bryson. 1998. Retooling Play: Dystopia, Dysphoria, and Difference. In *From Barbie to Mortal Kombat: Gender and Computer Games*, ed. Justine Cassell and Henry Jenkins, 232–261. Cambridge: MIT Press.

Diamond, Sara. 1997. Taylor's Way: Women, Cultures, and Technology. In *Processed Lives: Gender and Technology in Everyday Life*, ed. J. Terry and M. Calvert. New York: Routledge.

Douglas, Susan. 1999. *Listening In: Radio and the American Imagination*. New York: Times Books.

Douglas, Susan. 1987. *Inventing American Broadcasting, 1899–1922*. Baltimore, MD: Johns Hopkins University Press.

Edwards, Paul N. 2003. Industrial Genders: Soft/Hard. In *Gender & Technology: A Reader*, ed. N. E. Lerman, R. Oldenziel, and A. P. Mohan. Baltimore, MD: Johns Hopkins University Press.

Galloway, Alexander R. 2004. *Protocol: How Control Exists after Decentralization*. Cambridge: MIT Press.

Graner Ray, Sheri. 2004. *Gender Inclusive Game Design: Expanding the Market*. Hingham, MA: Charles River Media.

Haraway, Donna. 1991. *Simians, Cyborgs, and Women: The Reinvention of Nature*. London: Free Association Books.

Hayes, Elisabeth. 2007. Gendered Identities at Play: Case Studies of Two Women Playing *Morrowind*. *Games and Culture: A Journal of Interactive Media* 2 (1): 23–48.

Hilmes, Michelle. 1997. *Radio Voices: American Brodcasting, 1922–1952*. Minneapolis: University of Minnesota Press.

Jenkins, Henry. 2003. From Barbie to Mortal Kombat: Further Reflections. In *New Media: Theories and Practices*, ed. A. Everett and J. T. Caldwell, 243–254. New York: Routledge.

Jenkins, Henry. 1998. Complete Freedom of Movement: Video Games as Gendered Play Spaces. In *From Barbie to Mortal Kombat: Gender and Computer Games*, ed. Justine Cassell and Henry Jenkins. Cambridge: MIT Press.

Jones, Robert. 2006. From Shooting Monsters to Shooting Movies: Machinima and the Transformative Play of Video Game Fan Culture. In *Fan Fiction and Fan Communities in the Age of the Internet: New Essays*, ed. K. Hellekson and K. Busse. Jefferson, NC: McFarland.

Kafai, Yasmin. 1999. Video Game Designs by Girls and Boys: Variability and Consistency of Gender Differences. In *Kid's Media Culture*, ed. M. Kinder. Durham, NC: Duke University Press.

Kelland, Matt, Dave Morris, and Dave Lloyd. 2005. *Machinima: Making Animated Movies in 3D Virtual Environments*. Boston: Thompson Course Technology.

Kohlberg, Laurence. 1996. A Cognitive-Developmental Analysis of Children's Sex-Role Concepts and Attitudes. In *The Development of Sex Differences*, ed. E. E. MacCoby. Stanford, CA: Stanford University. Press.

Krotoski, Aleks. 2004. *Chicks and Joysticks: An Exploration of Women in Gaming*. London: Entertainment & Leisure Software Publishers Association.

Kushner, David. 2004. *Masters of Doom: How Two Guys Created an Empire and Transformed Pop Culture*. New York: Random House.

Laurel, Brenda. 1998. An Interview with Brenda Laurel (Purple Moon). In *From Barbie to Mortal Kombat: Gender and Computer Games*, ed. J. Cassell and H. Jenkins. Cambridge: MIT Press.

Lerman, Nina E. 2003. Industrial Genders: Constructing Boundaries. In *Gender & Technology: A Reader*, ed. N. E. Lerman, R. Oldenziel, and A. P. Mohan. Baltimore, MD: Johns Hopkins University Press.

Light, Jennifer. 2003. Programming. In *Gender & Technology: A Reader*, ed. N. E. Lerman, R. Oldenziel, and A. P. Mohan. Baltimore, MD: Johns Hopkins University Press.

Margolis, Jane, and Allan Fisher. 2002. *Unlocking the Clubhouse: Women in Computing*. Cambridge: MIT Press.

Marino, Paul. 2004. *3D Game-Based Filmmaking: The Art of Machinima*. Scottsdale, AZ: Paraglyph.

McGaw, Judith A. 2003. Why Feminine Technologies Matter. In *Gender & Technology: A Reader*, ed. N. E. Lerman, R. Oldenziel, and A. P. Mohan. Baltimore, MD: Johns Hopkins University Press.

McRobbie, Angela. 1991. *Feminism and Youth Culture: From Jackie to Just Seventeen*. London: Macmillan.

Michaels, J. W., J. M. Blommel, R. M. Brocato, R. A. Linkous, and J. S. Rowe. 1984. Social Facilitation and Inhibition in a Natural Setting. *Replications in Social Psychology* 2:21–24.

Morse, Margaret. 1997. Virtually Female. In *Processed Lives: Gender and Technology in Everyday Life*, ed. J. Terry and M. Calvert. New York: Routledge.

Oldenziel, Ruth. 2003. Why Masculine Technologies Matter. In *Gender & Technology: A Reader*, ed. N. E. Lerman, R. Oldenziel, and A. P. Mohan. Baltimore, MD: Johns Hopkins University Press.

Plant, Sadie. 1997. *Zeros + Ones: Digital Women + The New Technoculture*. New York: Doubleday.

Prügl, Reinhard, and Martin Schreier. 2006. Learning From Leading-Edge Customers at *The Sims*: Opening Up To Innovation Process Using Toolkits. *R & D Management* 36:237–250.

Salen, Katie, and Eric Zimmerman. 2004. *Rules of Play: Game Design Fundamentals*. Cambridge: MIT Press.

Subrahmanyam, Kaveri, and Patricia M. Greenfield. 1998. Computer Games for Girls: What Makes Them Play? In *From Barbie to Mortal Kombat: Gender and Computer Games*, ed. J. Cassell and H. Jenkins, 46–71. Cambridge: MIT Press.

Tasajärvi, Lassi. 2004. A Brief History of the Demoscene. In *Demoscene: The Art of Real-Time*, ed. L. Tasajärvi. Helsinki: Even Lake Studios.

Taylor, T. L. 2006. *Play between Worlds: Exploring Online Game Culture*. Cambridge: MIT Press.

Taylor, T. L. 2003. Multiple Pleasures: Women and Online Gaming. *Convergence* 9 (1): 21–46.

Terry, Jennifer, and Melodie Calvert. 1997. Machines/Lives. In *Processed Lives: Gender and Technology in Everyday Life*, ed. J. Terry and M. Calvert. New York: Routledge.

Thomas, Douglas. 2005. *Hacker Culture*. Minneapolis: University. of Minnesota Press.

Thompson, Clive. 2005. The Xbox Auteurs. *New York Times*, August 7.

Turkle, Sherry. 1986. Computational Reticence: Why Women Fear the Intimate Machines. In *Technology and Women's Voices: Keeping in Touch*. New York: Pergamon Press.

Turkle, Sherry. 1984. *The Second Self: The Computer and the Human Spirit*. New York: Simon & Schuster.

Wakeford, Nina. 1997. Networking Women and Grrrls with Information/Communication Technology: Surfing Tales of the World Wide Web. In *Processed Lives: Gender and Technology in Everyday Life*, ed. J. Terry and M. Calvert. New York: Routledge.

Walker, Jesse. 2001. *Rebels on the Air: An Alternative History of Radio in America*. New York: New York University Press.

Software References

Barbie Fashion Designer. Mattel. 1996.

Counter-Strike (modification of *Half-Life*). Minh Le/Jess Cliffe. 1999.

Doom. id Software. 1993.

Halo: Combat Evolved. Bungie Studios. 2001.

The Movies. Lionhead Studios. 2005.

Quake. id Software. 1996.

Secret Paths in the Forest. Purple Moon. 1997.

The Sims 2. Electronic Arts. 2004.

Spore. Electronic Arts. 2008.

Unreal Tournament 2004. Atari. 2004.

17 Participatory Fan Culture and *Half-Life 2* Machinima: A Dialogue among Ethnography, Culture, and Space

Gareth Schott and Bevin Yeatman

Irrespective of the growing call for the legitimization and commercialization of machinima as a mode of digital filmmaking, this essay upholds an interest in the emergent play practices of gamers rather than filmmakers, not only embracing the curiosity and discovery exhibited within the fluid peripheries of the virtual worlds they inhabit but also delving into open-source 3D engines of games such as *Half-Life* (Sierra, 1998). It is this kind of playful exploration that was responsible not only for the initial emergence of machinima but also for its continued and increasingly popular application as a key mode of articulating game fandom and the pleasures of play. We therefore examine the novel contribution of machinima to the existing multiple media channels adopted and utilized by participatory cultures that form around specific texts. Such communities are characterized not only by a shared practice (game playing) and heightened levels of appreciation but also by the execution of creative practices that enunciate and define their specific tastes, while also transforming game texts to serve their alternative interests. Such practices are indicative of a contemporary fan base that is no longer content with singular media experiences.

Over the past fifteen years, sporadic academic accounts of fandom have presented compelling arguments for treating fans as more than just avid, loyal consumers of the mass-produced commodities of popular culture and instead as audiences that possess active critical and productive relationships with popular texts. In line with the broader subculture of fan communities (see Brooker's 2002 account of the *Star Wars* fans), game players also perform a broad range of practices in communication of their fandom, including the more traditional composition of fan fiction and the creation of fan art, often rooted in a desire to expand fictional worlds and deepen accounts of character motivation and game ecology (see Schott and Burn 2004 and McGeady and Schott 2008 for accounts of fandom practice directly spurred by game texts). In doing so, stand-alone game titles, yet to receive a high-profile Hollywood adaptation, attain fan-generated cross-modal representation through the re-mediation of game content within other complementary media such as film or graphic novels (print media that also offer readers a heightened sense of spatial dynamics). Such practices serve to further integrate the distinctive aesthetic, physics, and possibilities offered by game worlds with other media,[1] an increasingly popular strategy among more mainstream narratives such as the hypertext, artificial reality–inspired *Matrix*, whose cross-media convergence was transversely played out across live action, animation, and games formats. The affordances connected to different representational media are regularly being exploited to offer audiences different entry points and experiential engagement with the same narrative form.

In games, the significance usually given to an "authoritative original" or "primary" text by cultural and media studies appears to be eroding and giving way to what Aumont (1997) has referred to as "stratified time in which we move through different levels simultaneously, present, past(s), future(s)" (ibid., 129–130). For players and fans, time (and space) surrounding this popular media artifact is collapsing, allowing its different elements and treatments to casually coexist. Indeed, a spatial conception of the networks of representations connected to a particular game such as *Half-Life* would only serve to undermine the fluidity of the processes of connection and disconnection that operate in and around the different depictions of *Half-Life*'s universe and characters across different media. In creative practices such as player-created machinima (or gamics such as *Apostasy*), it is possible to locate the presence of multiple interpretations of characters' identities, personalities, temperaments, and motivations that do not imply a convergent stability or an end-point of unification but the normal state of a continual *process* in which moments of convergence are matched by moments of divergence.

Unlike traditional accounts of fandom and its practices, such as Lewis's (1992) early proclamation that "We all know who fans are. They're the ones who wear the colors of their favorite team. . . . Fans are, in fact, the most visible and identifiable of audiences" (ibid., 1), those that explore game media technologies as a source and means of filmic expression mobilize a different form of fandom. In Fiske's (1992) account of fans as those who engage in a broader range of "producerly activity" than conventional audiences we find a more faithful prediction of the rise of digital subcultures characterized by a "consciousness of difference" (Hebdige 1997) with regard to the nature of production, ownership, agency, and authorship, a consciousness that very quickly led to the initial subversion of game software to produce alternatively animated films using game engines and continues to define players' treatment of game texts as objects that are revered by players and fans not just for what they are but for what they enable. Understanding machinima as displays of interest, affection, and attachment so often associated with fandom is not adequately rationalized as a similar kind of response to celebrity or stardom that has seen fans attributed a sense of passivity. Instead, the way fandom is manifested in digital cultures demands an alternative account from those previously framed by the relationship of audience to an object of fandom. Machinima practices arise from and exist within a game culture propagated by the hybridization of players and authors and in which the act of playing itself constitutes "presence" or virtual embodiment within a gamescape (King and Krzywinska 2003), thus granting players the capacity to effect change by activating, producing, and reworking assemblages of "narratemes" (Cubitt 2006).

Even before machinima began pushing into public awareness, Henry Jenkins (1992) had been arguing that fans were characterized almost exclusively in terms of their relationship with consumption rather than production. Attempts to aim similar charges at video game culture and its players are quite easily dismissed because of the distinct media experience that game texts *offer* (rather than deliver). The distance between player and screen-mediated objects of fascination is collapsed by players' acceptance of the presentational truth on offer (van Leeuwen 1999), leading them to assume responsibility for the interactive unfolding of plot (rather than story) in which the "simple conflicts of survival, prosperity and progress" (Lindley 2003, 4) are realized. Such immersive qualities function to place the player unselfconsciously within a performance that reduces the need for the same levels of "slavish" forms of consumption in order to achieve a quantitative sense of immediacy with the objects of fandom that generates devotion.

Shifting the Educational Landscape

Cultural hierarchy may traditionally separate the practices of fandom from more valued cultural artifacts such as high art or literature. Yet Joli Jenson's (1992) is one voice that has been eager to question the boundaries and practices that separate aficionados (such as scholars) from fans, arguing that devotion and loyalties to high cultural forms (as opposed to the popular, inexpensive, and widely available) are not that qualitatively different in terms of levels of knowledge, expertise, research, and time investment. When it comes to the value of machinima, such distinctions are collapsed further not just by the existence of academic volumes such as this one but also by Matt Hanson's *The End of Celluloid* (2004) and general "game studies" research (e.g., Carroll and Cameron 2005). Indeed, among the contributors to this collection the boundaries between and among fans, players, scholars, and filmmakers are consistently blurred (e.g., the contribution of machinima filmmaker Friedrich Kirschner). An outcome of this hybridization, which Copier (2003) originally introduced in relation to players, designers, and scholars, is the expansion of media and film production practices to include the themes of technoludic cinema (Bittanti 2002) and game-mediated film techniques (e.g., the teaching practice of *C-Level's* Brody Condon). Thus, the generative and productive cultures of gaming are not simply being subjected to Aristotle's contemplative ideal within academic accounts but are actively transforming and generating new forms of creative practice and research methods.

Another form of intersection that illustrates the transformative qualities of machinima is its move out of shadow cultural economies (Fiske 1992) into the creative industries, evident in the exploitation of its source and techniques by high-profile media organizations such as *Industrial Light and Magic* (which used *Unreal Tournament 2004* [Atari, 2004] to storyboard the recent *Star Wars* prequels), *The History Channel* (which used *Rome: Total War* [Activision, 2004] to recreate scenes for *Time Commanders and Decisive Battles*), and *MTV*, with its machinima program *Video Mods*. The argument that this form of fan practice can be singled out as an inane distraction when compared with the more worthy practice of furthering knowledge associated with, say, academia is less convincing when it is the outcome of spontaneous learning within "communities of practice" (Lave and Wenger 1991), not just the scrutinizing of "prestige conferring objects" (Jenson 1992) that now guides the content and coverage of scholarly pursuits and industry practice.

Players Operating as Digital Ethnographers

The legitimacy and authenticity given to time spent immersed in virtual locations by players are evident in players' desire to capture and share significant aspects of their everyday practices either in real-time action or as a scripted performance. In the case of massively multiplayer online games, or MMOGs, the evolving sociocultural practices among large populations are increasingly subjected to an array of documentation practices that allow players to relive key moments (such as leveling up) or social events (such as successful raids, or even unsuccessful raids, as captured in the *World of Warcraft* [Blizzard, 2004] film *Leeroy*). While online configurations of *Half-Life* have produced machinima documentary works such as the instigation of political protest of *Velvet Strike* (Anne-Marie Schleiner's infiltration of *Half-Life* mod *Counter-Strike* [Minh Le/Jess Cliffe, 1999]), even the player-to-game experiences of a text like *Half-Life* produce equivalent levels of player appropriation, active negotiation, and reconfiguration of its material resources.

The active culture surrounding the game text is defined in part by the practice of assembling and producing machinima artifacts that communicate the different pleasures of the particular space of *Half-Life* and the possible manifestation(s) within it (e.g., *Raining Men Half-Life 2*, Baron Von Fuchenstein Productions, 2005). Machinima works such as the Barney-as-cyborg recital of Edgar Alan Poe's poem "A Dream Within a Dream" (Tom Jantol, 2005), *The Life of Raphael Carter* (Ride The Emu Productions, 2006), and *Fight* (Andy12343, 2005) illustrate the possibilities for broadening developers' creations (which themselves can be understood in terms of their provenance, that is, the use of existing semiotic resources by developers in the construction of their text; see Kress and van Leeuwen 2001) in a way that does not compromise their principal state but instead develops and examines the robust nature of the original gaming context.

Fan-generated machinima also functions to obscure the boundaries between game media and other media spaces, such as enactments of song narratives as found in *Stacy's Mom*, by Fountains of Wayne (Nick Powell, 2006), the mock chat show *Select Start: Episode 1* (Select Start, 2006), which features an interview with *Doom III* (Activision, 2004) creator John Carmack, and *Duct Tape Infomercial* (Teckno Studios, 2006). Such works present reconfigurations of and addenda to the game's presentational context. In doing so, players engage in the construction of an anthropology of "themselves," reminiscent of the UK mass observation movement devoted to researching everyday life in real-world settings. The key difference is how the creative practices of *Half-Life* players reflect and express their media intake and preferences, as well as media literacy. This is particularly evident in the production of the cross-media narrative assemblage of *A Few Good G Men* (Glass, 2006), a *Half-Life 2* (Sierra, 2004) reenactment of the court scene between Jack Nicholson and Tom Cruise that gives heightened narrative and textual structure to familiar game characters via the technological agency of the player-director.

As a source of fan and player fascination, the game text of *Half-Life* constitutes a popular groundbreaking first-person shooter (FPS) series that generates fan-created machinima reflecting players' affinity with the mise-en-scène of the game environment, their desire to extend, reflect on, and find humor in the narrative context of the game, as well as celebrate the source responsible for its digital exchanges. Following the first installment of *Half-Life* in 1998, the second *Half-Life* game utilizes the suspense, challenge, and visceral charge of the original's real-time gameplay, with players again gazing at the crowbar-wielding arms of embodied research scientist Gordon Freeman as they make their way through an alien-infested Earth. New levels of player immersion are achieved in the second game through an increased array of human emotions possessed by in-game nonplayer characters that enable greater levels of responsiveness to the player. Likewise, material objects in the game environment (from water to steel) respond as expected in relation to each other, as they obey the laws of mass, friction, gravity, and buoyancy.

Beyond the inventive application of machinima by players and fans to extend the boundaries and deepen understanding of the *Half-Life* game, a common practice among fan subcultures, *Half-Life 2* players produce an interesting brand of machinima that demands a different kind of explanation and theorization. A key aspect that makes fan-expression surrounding *Half-Life* interesting is how a great number of the available audiovisual and still image works utilize the outcome of another fan product, *Garry's Mod* (or *G-Mod*), a popular "sandbox" modification that enables gamers to appropriate and apply the contents of *Half-Life* for their own pleasures.[2] One of its defining features as a modification platform, ragdoll posing, arose from *paidea* (Caillois 1958) linked to modification practices while engaging in constructing new configurations from preexisting objects. The account given on the *Garry's Mod* Web site outlines the process:

I decided that it would be cool to pause one object in mid air while you welded it to something else. I programmed this in and it worked great. Then I did it on a ragdoll. I was amazed, I could put them in any position. I felt a hot throbbing on the back of my head—I realised how big this was going to be for people taking screenshots as soon as I did it. The first pose was Alyx and Kleiner having sex. The second was Alyx holding Kliener [*sic*] above her head. As soon as I did this I rushed to the forums to post my results. No-one could believe it.

This account of the first application of *Garry's Mod* ragdoll tool is significant for the excitement derived from the tool's potential contribution to the community and the poster's immediate desire to share the outcome of play. Indeed, this process of discovery and sharing plays a role in pushing the degrees of freedom given to players to construct their own configurations (or set constructions), including the representational motivations more readily associated with, and limited to, the construction of avatars in MMOGs (Carr et al. 2006). For example, with the *Half-Life 2* tool *Face Poser*, players are given the autonomy to change facial features by adding drooping eyelids or wrinkles around the mouth or changing the height of the eyebrows. The representational motivations of playing in these spaces are not confined to characters, as it is possible to alter the color or transparency of any object or apply a material quality (flowing water, stained glass, swirling energy fields) to any object. Inanimate objects are also given a more dynamic quality as they become easily attachable through welding, rope, springy elastics, ball-and-socket joints, and pulley systems and can be set in motion by means of keypad-controlled thrusters and wheels of different varieties. In an age of ubiquitous creativity, these tools reflect the catalytic nature of the game developers' innovation as well as an ethnographic articulation of a new sense of spatial (dis)order in these new cultural domains. Thus, the everyday machinima practices of fans utilizing these tools not only articulate and embody the social experience in the *Half-Life 2* gamescape but also form a dialog between and among ethnography, culture, and space.

Transforming Spatial Practices into Cartographic Tales

Paul Marino's definition of machinima as "animated filmmaking within a real-time virtual 3D environment" (2004, 1) cleverly suggests the importance of what it means to engage with virtual spaces and how the process of play shapes our understanding of what occurs when the virtual becomes actualized in an animated film. The definition implies that the multiplicity of choices potentially generated through interaction in a virtual environment become contained as a singular and repeatable trajectory of actual choices made by the producer of machinima as a final outcome. Using Cubitt (1998) as platform, Shields (2003) states that virtual environments are characterized by four elements:

• The primacy of navigation and movement
• Smoothness or unity of the digital environment, including a computer-generated character or avatar representing the user

• A single point of view that represents the user's position and outlook on the virtual environment

• Implied off-screen spaces (Shields 2003, 60–61)

These elements are utilized by fans as the producers of machinima in a process that sees the openness of choice, connected to spatial practices within *Half-Life*'s game space or Valve's modification interface, displaced by a map of *particular choices* channeled into an animated film. It is this displacement of possibilities within the virtual environment and its capture as a sequential film that has become the celebrated outcome of machinima production. Yet an understanding of machinima as a communication channel for fans and players of *Half-Life* seems to require an examination of the spatial practices involved in producing machinima.

Laurie Taylor (2005) is known for her examination of spatial practices in video games, carving out an essential conceptual avenue for understanding the experience of video games and implicitly for our own engagement with machinima. Her argument is inspired by the spatial theorizing of Henry Lefebvre[3] but is also driven by Espen Aarseth's belief that "the representation of space is the defining factor in video game play" (Aarseth 2001, 1). Taylor acknowledges that

games are created by mathematical programming code and that they are thus created with a necessarily logical and systematic language. This means that all video game spaces can be represented as geometrical spaces: spaces defined by the programmatic ordering of space according to a predetermined logic of its boundaries. Yet to equate video game spaces with only their geometrical equivalent is to ignore the broader context and significance of the spatial logic and experience of gaming. (2005, 1)

Her discussion of FPS-style games, the basis of *Half-Life* machinima, is fascinating. She does not believe that representational spaces are present, for she argues "there is no emotional, social, or personal significance to any of the rooms, hallways, or corridors in these games insofar as the narrative or player is concerned," stating further that "even their geometric space is skewed by having the screen act as the player's viewpoint, forcing the player outside the game world and requiring inaccurate spatial reasoning within that skewed perspective" (ibid., 3).

Our own encounter with *Half-Life* machinima and the potency of its spatialities takes a slightly different track, and consequently we have some disagreement with Taylor's take on the nature of FPS games and their spatiality in the context of machinima. Certainly the spatial focus in cultural theory evident in Lefebvre and continued in Edward Soja (1996) provides a potent framework for understanding the experiences of the virtual environments presented in machinima, and we agree with Taylor that the understanding of gaming through the examination of spaces, however those spaces might be articulated, is a powerful analytical tool. The question we ask is whether or not this is the most useful approach for understanding the relationships between the producer of machinima, the player engaged in the potentialities of the virtual environments in the game world, and the cultural contexts they are embedded in as players and fans.

Bryan Reynolds and Joseph Fitzpatrick's (1999) discussion of de Certeau's conceptualization of space and spatial practice suggests that for de Certeau, space was "the product of the subject's interaction with the existing environment" (ibid., 2), and further, that stories themselves are treatments of space in that they "spatialize by enumerating possibilities, by demarcating the boundaries of what is possible within a given place" (ibid., 6). These ideas offer clues to a slightly different take on the spatial practices that generate the production of *Half-Life* machinima. Machinima can be understood as reflecting the actual spatial practices generated through the choices made in the virtual environment of the game. These practices reflect the explorations and demarcations of possibilities within these environments as different stories or strategies are constructed to develop different approaches to machinima. These stories and strategies are shaped by the agendas and intentions of those producer players and fans who express their own pleasures as part of a gaming community. From this it follows that spatial practices, although an essential part of machinima production, need to be considered in the context not only of the virtual environments of the games used as a basis for machinima but also in the context of the cultures of play and production that the strategies of spatial practices are influenced by.

It seems useful to understand fan production of machinima as a reflection of a process of performance that is shaped not only by actions in various spaces but also by other dimensions of experience stemming from the culture of gaming. We strongly disagree that FPS spaces are not and cannot be affective spaces contributing to the emotional resonances of a game-playing experience. This is even more the case in machinima when the environment itself is foregrounded, for instance, in the multitude of domino Rube Goldberg–style machinima works, in which the environment makes its own contribution to the feel of the work. Environments, however they are constructed, actively affect the experience of viewing in numerous ways, especially for players who have an investment in the particular game engines used to produce machinima.

Although machinima registers a process of performance, both the performances of creation and the performances of viewing when the work is actualized as final product, it is not the same performance space as in an interactive game, where different combinations of actions and different trajectories can be developed each time. The myriad of possibilities open to production choices is contained by the final decisions made to establish the finished product. Machinima, so far in its evolution, is more like a film than a game, but that might not always be the case as new techniques, new tactics of presentation, and a stronger experimental aesthetic begin to question the structures of the single pathway mapped by current machinima practice. Machinima is a spatial production but currently a spatial production that seeks to confirm a particular and fixed spatiality allowing a particular and fixed performance for viewing. These spatial practices will change as new conceptions of the possibilities for machinima are created. These possibilities might come from outside the domain of gaming culture, from practitioners who are not so caught up in the expression of their particular pleasure with the games world and its community of fans.

The production of machinima can therefore be viewed as a cartographic practice, that is, a mapping of particular actions that trace out particular desires, including those of narrative, technical prowess, and expressions of pleasure. This perspective is useful, for it continues to acknowledge the importance of the spatial but also points to the concept that machinima production is a registration of particular performances symptomatic of the desires that are shaped by the conditions of previous game experience and the producers' investment in particular cultural practices. Machinima maps these cultural practices of game players as expressions of their experiences and pleasures in their own productions of machinima. Furthermore, there is an exchange of these maps in relation to other players and viewers within the gaming culture, an exchange that suggests particular readings and interactions with these maps, allowing an appreciation of shared knowledge and pleasures, as well as the display of skills that signals the conditions of production implied by the mapping process.

What might this mean then when we attempt an actual analysis of the types of machinima produced specifically on *Half-Life* platforms? How might we classify and analyze *Half-Life* machinima and make some sense of these new and vibrant practices that have appeared since the late nineties? Spatial production has a role, but, more important, in light of this essay's focus on the cultural practices of players, authors, and filmmakers, it is crucial to recognize the pleasures of these practices and how they manifest in the strategies and conditions of production that have arisen so far.

One approach that seems to reflect similar strategies of earlier machinima and earlier platforms is the speedplay of such works as *Half-Life Completado en 45 min* (Phase Zero, 2003), *HL2Done Quick* (HL2QQ, 2006), and *Half-Life 2 Runthrough in 3 Hours* (Not Me, 2006). In these examples the mapping is one of the display of skill as part of an earlier investment and development of knowledge in the game; it is a display of how the player has been through the game enough times to be able to navigate with considerable speed and presumably, as part of a competitive agenda, to get through the game as fastest player. This display and its implicit competitive attitude are characteristic of another approach previously cited that seems to be obsessively interested in the domino effect. Here the machinima is a mapping of skill, which has its own competitive streak, the display of technique coming from investment in *Garry's Mod* and its manipulative possibilities. The machinima pieces *HL2 Rube Goldberg Device: Reloaded* (Deans, 2005) and *Asskicking Device* (Matthias Seidel, 2005) are two excellent examples of this approach. The strategy based on the idea of dominos tumbling against each other, but broadened to explore connective possibilities in the *Garry's Mod* environment, maps both the imaginative and the technical skills of the producers, coupled with a wonderful display of humor, a dimension apparent in many machinima works. For example, in *Asskicking Device*, exploding drums connect with intricate pulley systems, rocket-propelled sleds, rolling drums, and metallic sheets in a trajectory marked by explosions and debris that finally operates a swinging arm with a boot on the end kicking Breen, a prominent character in the *Half-Life* environment, in the backside.

These works display sophistication in manipulation that becomes part of the pleasure of display, and this sophistication-pleasure connection is evident in similar displays of manipulative skill grounded in the *Garry's Mod* repertoire. Examples of such works include *Garry's Mod—The Catapult Part 1* (Digital Pimps Video, 2006), *Garry's Mod—Building Catapults* (Digital Pimps Video, 2006), and *Garry's Mod—Thruster Man* (Digital Pimps Video, 2006), with the last exploring the possibilities of reconfiguring the physics and gravity of the *Garry's Mod* environment. This process is extended to displays of construction and the creation of different machines, which are shown for their multiple add-ons established through the component choices of *Garry's Mod*. *Garry's Mod—The Kill Car . . .* (Digital Pimps Video, 2006) is a typical example of this common approach. The justification from the designer is that it was made to "look badass. It isn't the best performer but it does look cool," and this reinforces the particular strategies of display and shared pleasures we are exploring.

Another pleasure is mapped in stunts performed in the environment, as well as in the actual pleasure of shooting and destroying things, a simple and real pleasure that all gamers experience in the *Half-Life* environments. Here we have a pleasure of spectacle rather than any narrative agendas, and what is mapped is the shared and exhilarating experiences of exploiting the possibilities of the physics engine and, more often, the possibilities of shooting other characters in the game world. Examples of this are numerous, but a few examples include *Stunts of Garry's Mod 3 Remix* (Stunt Finland Product, 2006), *Half-Life Enhanced* (Ryan Bloom, 2006), and *Bargaining with Larry* (Slight Miscalculation, 2000).

Bargaining with Men also signals another approach to machinima: that of imitating previously established genres, including music video, drama, parody, and fantasy. Again, *A Few Good G-Men* (Randall Glass, 2006) is a famous and sophisticated version of this type of display, in which the skills displayed are those necessary to simulate a scene from the film *A Few Good Men* (Reiner, 1992) by using the possibilities afforded by the game engine. *Half-Life 2: The Matrix Reloaded* (Unknown, 2005) is similarly inspired by cinema, but in this case, rather than a direct simulation, it is a capturing of some of the aesthetics and unique techniques of the film in terms of bullet time and the acrobatic, gravity-defying movements of the characters. Other genres adapted and often parodied include commercials such as *Nike Basketball Spoof—Half-Life 2*

(Unknown, 2006), music videos, *Half-Life 2 Session* (Monkey Junkey, 2006), and numerous trailers anticipating the *Half-Life* experience. *Half-Life 2: Unofficial Trailer* (Crepuscular, 2005) is an example of this latter genre adaptation that, given the format, is another example of the display of pleasure and aesthetics that the producer or player celebrates.

The trailer production also shows a strong sense of an independent feature while utilizing the experience of the virtual environments of games, as well as the conventions and codes of the cinematic experience. For example, *The Last Trailer* (Unknown, 2006) anticipates a forty-minute feature released on July 15, 2006, while the trailer *The Life of Raphael Carter Trailer* (Ride the Emu, 2006) similarly announces the production of another machinima series also based on the *Half-Life 2* game engine.

Machinima is still heavily bound to the pleasures of the game-playing and fan experience, but there are growing indications, evident in the investment in features, for instance, that suggest this link is porous and open to new possibilities. The potential for new directions and even an escape from the model of conventional cinema as a basis for machinima production is growing, and as new energies are invested, possibly from sources outside the game world itself, the characteristics and energies of machinima will also change. One new direction can be anticipated from the introduction of the portal tool that is packaged with *Half-Life 2: Episode 2* (Buka Entertainment, 2007), which offers a new relationship to dimensionality ("where the impossible is easy": Valve) and therefore challenges the assumptions of the three-dimensionality of the virtual environment. The portal tool allows movement through walls, floors, and ceilings, breaking boundaries and offering new possibilities for trajectories that until now have not been explorable. This tool suggests new approaches to spatiality and new approaches to understanding what machinima might become as it evolves through the multiple investments of players, designers, programmers, and above all the fans who feed the desire to celebrate and explore game worlds in all their manifestations.

Conclusion

This essay has begun to conceptualize the dialog that exists between creative exchanges of fans and players that have been shown to emanate from ethnographic practices in game spaces. Fans of *Half-Life 2* have constructed a body of work that reveals the spatial pleasures that initially arise from "everyday" experiences in gameplay but are elucidated in the cartographic practice of machinima production, through the mapping of particular actions that reflect particular desires and pleasures enclosed within the representational spaces of *Half-Life*. By examining a particular group of machinima producers, such as *Half-Life* fans, we have sought to uncover the practices that shape their particular modes of filmic expression. Along the way, we have seen how machinima contributes to the articulation of a shared community of game-player interests and investments. In opening up its software for player manipulation, *Half-Life 2*'s developers have enabled fans and players to absorb and translate game-playing practices into another form of cultural activity, namely, the production of machinima works that combine emergent digital authorship with cultural appropriation in a manner that seamlessly and effectively integrates and absorbs other texts. Even the level of the environmental journeying of players in virtual Rube Goldberg works suggests a complex combination of self-reflexive referencing that acknowledges and combines the experiences of the gamer and more universal, accessible, and interpretable forms of expression. Machinima has therefore effortlessly developed into a key mode of communication contributing to the social nature and interpretive and cultural activities of game players.

Notes

1. According to the *Half-Life* Web site, Source's shader-based renderer operates much like the one used at Pixar to create movies such as *Toy Story* and *Monsters, Inc.*, thus contributing to one of the most realistic environments ever seen in a video game.

2. G-Mod's ragdoll capacity has been used to create still image narratives such as *Lamar's Big Day*, a children's picture-book narrative parody that presents an anthropomorphic "day-in-the-life" portrayal of a deadly zombifying parasitic *Half Life 2* Head-crab as a lovable petlike character.

3. Lefebvre (2004) discusses three types of interconnected approaches to spatiality—perceptual space, representation of spaces, and representational spaces.

References

Aarseth, Espen. 2001. Allegories of Space: The Question of Spatiality in Computer Games. In *CyberText Yearbook 2000*, ed. M. Eskelinen and R. Koskimaa, 000–000. Jyväskylä, Finland: Research Centre for Contemporary Culture, University of Jyväskylä.

Aumont, Jacques. 1997. *The Image*. London: British Film Institute.

Bittanti, Matteo. 2002. The Technoludic Film: Images of Videogames in Films (1973–2001). *Gamasutra*. <http://www.gamasutra.com/education/ theses/20020501/bittanti_01.shtml>.

Brooker, Will. 2002. *Using the Force: Creativity, Community and Star Wars Fans*. London: Continuum.

Caillois, Roger. 1958. *Man, Play and Games*, trans. Meyer Barash. Paris: Libraririe Gallimard.

Carr, Diane, David Buckingham, Andrew Burn, and Gareth Schott. 2006. *Computer Games: Text, Narrative and Play*. London: Polity Press.

Carroll, John, and David Cameron. 2005. Machinima: Digital Performance and Emergent Authorship. In *Changing Views: Worlds in Play. Proceedings of the 2005 DiGRA Conference*, ed. S. de Castell and J. Jenson. <http://www.gamesconference.org/digra2005>.

Copier, Marinka. 2003. The Other Game Researcher: Participating in and Watching the Construction of Boundaries in Game Studies. In *Level Up*, ed. M. and J. Raessens. Utrecht: Utrecht University Press.

Cubitt, Sean. 2006. *EcoMedia*. Amsterdam: Rodopi.

Cubitt, Sean. 1998. *Digital Aesthetics*. London: Sage.

Fiske, John. 1992. The Cultural Economy of Fandom. In *Adoring Audience: Fan Culture and Popular Media*, ed. L. Lewis. London: Routledge.

Hanson, Matt. 2004. *The End of Celluloid: Film Futures in the Digital Age*. Mies, Switzerland: Rotovision.

Hebdige, Dick. 1997. Subculture: The Meaning of Style. In *The Subcultures Reader*, ed. K. Gelder and S. Thornton. London: Routledge.

Jenkins, Henry. 1992. *Textual Poachers: Television Fans and Participatory Culture*. London: Routledge.

Jenson, Joli. 1992. Fandom as Pathology: The Consequences of Characterisation. In *Adoring Audience: Fan Culture and Popular Media*, ed. L. Lewis. London: Routledge.

King, Geoff, and Tanya Krzywinska. 2003. Gamescapes: Exploration and Virtual Presence in Game-worlds. In *Level Up*, ed. M. and J. Raessens. Utrecht: Utrecht University Press.

Kress, Gunther, and Theo van Leeuwen. 2001. *Multimodal Discourse: The Modes and Media of Contemporary Communication*. London: Arnold.

Lave, Jean, and Etienne Wenger. 1991. *Situated Learning: Legitimate Peripheral Participation*. Cambridge, UK: Cambridge University Press.

Lefebvre, Henry. 2004. *The Production of Space*, trans. D. Nicholson-Smith. Oxford: Blackwell.

Lewis, Lisa. 1992. *Adoring Audience: Fan Culture and Popular Media*. London: Routledge.

Lindley, Craig. 2003. The Gameplay Gestalt: Narrative and Interactive Storytelling. In *Level Up*, ed. M. and J. Raessens. Utrecht: Utrecht University Press.

Marino, Paul. 2004. *3D Game-Based Filmmaking: The Art of Machinima*. Arizona: Paraglyph Press.

McGeady, Mark, and Gareth Schott. 2008. De-territorializing Nature: An Analysis of Social and Spatial Change in Videogames. In *Playing with Mother Nature: Video Games, Space, and Ecology*, ed. S. Dobrin, C. Martin, and L. N. Taylor.

Reynolds, Bryan, and Joseph Fitzpatrick. 1999. The Transversality of Michel de Certeau: Foucault's Panoptic Discourse and the Cartographic Impulse. *Diacritics* 29 (3): 63–80.

Schott, G., and A. Burn. 2004. Art (Re)production as an Expression of Collective Agency within Online Fan Culture. In *Capitalizing on Play: The Politics of Computer Ga*ming, ed. Ken McAllister and Ryan Moeller, special issue. *Works and Days 43/44,* 22 (1–2): 251–274.

Shields, Rob. 2003. *The Virtual.* London: Routledge.

Soja, Edward. 1996. *Thirdspace: Journeys to Los Angeles and Other Real-and-Imagined Places.* Cambridge, UK: Blackwell.

Taylor, Laurie. 2005. Toward a Spatial Practice in Video Games. <http://www.gameology.org/node/809/print>.

van Leeuwen, Theo. 1999. *Speech, Music, Sound.* London: St. Martin's Press.

Software References

Counter-Strike (modification of *Half-Life*). Minh Le/Jess Cliffe. 1999.

Doom III. Activision. 2004.

Garry's Mod (modification of *Half-Life 2*). Garry Newman. 2004.

Half-Life. Sierra. 1998.

Half-Life 2. Sierra. 2004.

Half-Life 2: Episode 2. Buka Entertainment. 2007.

Rome: Total War. Activision. 2004.

Unreal Tournament 2004. Atari. 2004.

World of Warcraft. Blizzard Entertainment. 2004.

18   Don't Mess with *The Warriors*: The Politics of Machinima

Matteo Bittanti

In the absence of aesthetic value, the history of art is just an enormous storehouse of works whose chronologic sequence carries no meaning. And conversely: it is only within the context of an art's historical evolution that aesthetic value can be seen. (Kundera 2007, 5)

The focus of this essay is an apparently negligible episode in the history of machinima, the self-censorship of Dave Beck's *The Highest Score*, a controversial school art project based on Rockstar Games' video game *The Warriors* (2005). My interest in this artwork is twofold. First, *The Highest Score* belongs to the relatively small body of artistic machinima, that is, game-related videos created outside fans communities with the explicit intention of commenting on issues that are often extrinsic to the ludic domain. Although this practice has a long tradition in art, it is relatively atypical in the communities that revolve around gaming. Unlike the canonical view, which sees machinima as a quintessential example of player-created practices (Lowood 2005, 2007) and thus endogenous to game culture, I locate the roots of this medium in early artistic experimentations such as Miltos Manetas's Videos after Videogame (1996–2006),[1] a series of videos created by recording users' activities in digital environments, from flight simulators (F18 Hornet) to 3D platform games (Mario 64). Since the mid-nineties, Manetas's Game Art projects have been exhibited in art galleries across Europe and the United States. For instance, *Miracle*, a short video that exploits a glitch in F18 Hornet, was first shown at the exhibition Joint Ventures, curated by Nicolas Bourriaud, at Basilico Gallery, New York, in 1996, around the time that the ILL Clan was tinkering with the *Quake* engine to produce its first movie.

Second, *The Highest Score*, and especially the online debate that followed its removal from public view, is indicative of game communities' reluctance to explore the political and artistic potential of machinima. This comes as no surprise, insofar as the vast majority of user-created machinima pieces often operate as promotional rather than critical texts; they tend to be self-referential, juvenile, and apolitical. When an author dares to embed resistant meanings in his or her production, the reaction from the game community is often derisive and contemptuous. The comments made by online gamers to Dave Beck's online installation show that cultural appropriations[2] of video games by artists that oppose the game industry's dominant ideology are often seen as questionable and misinformed, if not despicable.[3] To fully understand machinima, therefore, it is necessary to go beyond the mere texts and take into consideration the broader contexts in which machinima is consumed, evaluated, and accepted or rejected. In other words: texts are never produced and consumed in a vacuum; the discourses that surround them are equally important, if not more so.

I begin my investigation by briefly describing two "toy stories," seminal interventions in which two artists, Todd Haynes and Zbigniew Libera, appropriated specific ludic artifacts—Barbie dolls and Lego building blocks, respectively—to make a commentary on society. I then move to illustrate Dave Beck's artwork and its repercussions in the blogosphere. The key questions I try to answer in this essay are: What happens when ludic artifacts—dolls, construction blocks, and videogames—are used for artistic interventions? And, perhaps more important, What do we *really* talk about when we talk about machinima?

Level 1: Haynes and Barbie Dolls

In 1987, American film director Todd Haynes produced and released *Superstar: The Karen Carpenter Story*, a forty-three-minute 16mm film reconstructing the life and death of Karen Carpenter, the pop vocalist of the band The Carpenters. Instead of recruiting real actors, Haynes used Barbie dolls. The result was—and remains—startling: a bizarre mix between a school art project and an episode of *Thunderbirds*. To detail the Karen's physical deterioration caused by anorexia, for instance, the director finely whittled away the face and arms of the "Karen" Barbie doll. The movie takes places in various locales, including recording studios, restaurants, the Carpenters' residence in Downey, California, and Karen's apartment in Century City, and all the sets were designed properly scaled to the dolls. Shortly after its release, two things happened. *Superstar* became a minor art house hit but was hastily withdrawn from circulation. Richard Carpenter, Karen's brother and musical collaborator, sued Haynes for copyright violation—the director never sought clearance for the Carpenters' music used in the film—and won. It is also widely believed that toy maker Mattel would have sued Haynes as well, based on his unauthorized use of Barbie dolls. As a result of the lawsuit, all copies of *Superstar: The Karen Carpenter Story* have been recalled and destroyed. Nonetheless, numerous bootleg copies survive and are available on various Internet sites.[4] The Museum of Modern Art also retains a copy of this film but has agreed with the Carpenter estate not to exhibit it to the public (Wyatt 1993).

Level 2: Libera and LEGO

In 1996, Polish artist Zbigniew Libera unveiled LEGO, the latest piece of his ongoing Correcting Devices[5] series, which comprised seven limited-edition LEGO kits that include all the elements necessary to build one section of a Nazi concentration camp. "Libera created his piece by assembling Lego blocks into replicas of death camp facilities, photographing them and then using the photos to adorn authentic-looking Lego cardboard packages, complete with the disassembled pieces, the company logo and multi-language safety warnings" (Murphy 1997). As Laura Bien observed, "The resulting tableaux shown on the boxes' cover photos include martial uniformed Lego men dragging white skeletons from homes, beating them, administering electroshock, and committing other violent acts" (Bien 2006, 4).

Interestingly, all the pieces used by Libera came from existing LEGO sets. The black prison guards, for instance, originally belonged to the policemen kits, while the white skeleton figures representing the captives were originally used in the pirate sets; the inmates came from LEGO medical or hospital sets. The outer box looks like a normal LEGO box except in the upper left corner, where instead of the "system number" is the inscription, "This work of Zbigniew Libera has been sponsored by LEGO." Murphy further elaborates: "The display is so unsettling in its playful simplicity that the Lego Group, which sponsors Lego art contests and donates thousands of plastic pieces to artists around the world, tried to persuade Libera to withdraw it from public view. Only when lawyers became involved did the company give up" (Murphy 1997, 12). As Stephen C. Feinstein recalls:

The LEGO Group from Copenhagen at first tried to stop Libera by bringing a lawsuit against him. However, the three sets of the LEGO Concentration Camp had already been sold, making a retraction even more difficult. On top of this, European copyright law, unlike that in the United States, permits use of corporate logos for artistic purposes. Thus, the lawsuit was soon dropped, although LEGO still goes through pains to ensure that museum viewers who now see Libera's work understand that it is not their product. (Feinstein 2000, 13)

Level 3: Beck and *The Warriors*

In 2006 Dave Beck, at the time an art student at the University of Madison–Wisconsin, created *The Highest Score*, a Flash-based Web site that displayed a short sequence from *The Warriors*, a video game produced by Rockstar Games and released in October 2005 for the Sony PlayStation 2, and subsequently for Microsoft Xbox and Sony PSP. The game is a faithful adaptation of Walter Hill's 1979 movie of the same title. On his Web site and in his artist's statement, he described *The Highest Score* as a "five second video of myself playing." Specifically, the video depicts a game character

Figure 18.1
Dave Beck, dir., *The Highest Score* (2006).

stomping on the body of a downed and presumably dead woman. Beck then looped the clip "to play continuously and randomly," and subsequently added a counter in the top right-hand corner of the display to add the scoring element. Hence the somehow ironic title.

Kristian Knutsen (2006a) reported that a few days before launching his project, Beck sent a viral email to several media outlets describing his initiative, hoping to reach a wider audience. In his epistolary statement, Beck illustrated the rationale behind *The Highest Score*. For reasons that will become clear, I cite Beck's message in its entirety:

1. I've always been interested and fascinated with video games, but not until recently did I become intrigued enough to analyze it with my own work. I feel that video games as a medium are perhaps one of the final frontiers where sexism and graphic violence exist, to a certain point, unchecked and DEFINITELY encouraged. If you look at movies or books for instance, things such as rape, murder, graphic sex, etc. do in fact exist, but they usually carry the weight of some "message or lesson" to be learned in a broader story. If they do not carry this factor, it is often thought of as some sort of pornography or "NC–17" rated film/book. In the case of video games, what is depicted on my website is something that occurs in the game, but does not help you solve puzzles or learn lessons—it exists for pure entertainment. In the *Grand Theft Auto* game for

instance, you can actually pay a prostitute for sexual intercourse, participate in that action, and then kill her and steal the money you paid her. That act not only awards you extra points, but gives you extra "energy" or "life" in the game as well. The saddest part concerning this "entertainment" approach to these issues is that while these games are rated for certain age groups, it is a common fact that video game rental stores and many other stores that actually sell the game do not check the purchaser's age at the time of the sale (just as this website does not). When I worked as a kindergarten assistant a few years ago, I had 6 year old kids telling me about how they "watch their older brother play *Grand Theft Auto* and its cool cuz you can just run around and shoot people and run away from the cops." So as far as this point is concerned, it is more of a critique of our culture's situation at the moment.

2. Secondly, I'm very interested in the concept that our postmodern world has dealt with for the past 20 years, namely, the desensitivization of violent images on one's mind. The fact that this video clip is occurring at a constant sound beat and motion, and it is paired with a numeric value, I'm interested in the idea of this image becoming less and less hard to look at with every second that passes, due to the hypnotic rhythm that exists within the site.

3. Paired with that, I wanted to point out how America seems to be so obsessed with large numbers (hence, thehighestscore.com) lately—whether it be money, church congregation populations in megachurches, myspace friends, or even deaths in Iraq, I truly believe things have changed in our society from being concerned with what the number means (ramifications, the goods, the bads, etc) to focusing more on how high it can get period. That is why I put a counter in the top left corner of the video, tracking the number of times the man has kicked the woman. I'm essentially conducting an experiment, as i am curious as to whether people will begin to lose their focus on how brutal the image is and begin to become obsessed with the number's growth. (Essentially, people will begin to focus on the number, and not the atrocity). I'm able to track how many people have visited www.thehighestscore.com, as well as how many people have returned a second time—thus proving that people are curious as to whether the number has climbed to a larger height, or perhaps something has happened in the clip itself, and there is something new to look at.

4. Finally, and least importantly, i wanted to experiment with the idea of public art via the internet—where it is absolutely free (as all public art is ideally supposed to be) and accessible by anyone, anytime, anywhere (which is not the case for public art in its physical form).

This artist's statement is extremely interesting for a variety of reasons. After linking his fascination for games to his artistic practice, Beck boldly suggests that the medium's true meaning has been largely ignored, misunderstood, or overlooked by critics. Specifically, Beck states that "graphic violence" and "sexism" are not simply tolerated but "DEFINITELY" encouraged in games, presumably by the producers or publishers themselves. Thus, *The Warriors* is not significantly different from another controversial Rockstar Games' title, *Grand Theft Auto*. What Beck seems to find problematic is that the procedural and configurative nature of digital games—that is, the ability that players have to actively shape the "narrative" of the game instead of consuming a prepackaged story—has a dark side: games are amoral, devoid of any "message or a lesson." That is, unlike other forms of narrative, videogames lack ethical principles.

Beck suggests that the graphic violence of *The Warriors* is not a means to an end but rather an end in itself. Finally, the artist is concerned that games intended for mature audiences are easily accessible to minors.

Beck expressed his concerns not in essay form or in a "letter to the editor" but with "an online art installation" remixing a few seconds of footage from the game. His intervention brings the viewers' attention to three factors: *desensitization* (the numbing effect produced by the continuous consumption of violent media content), a *fascination* with *statistical data* (America's obsession "with large numbers"), and the *need for art to be freely accessible* ("all public art is ideally supposed to be" free). Beck's message is both a statement of intentions and a critique or interpretation.

Interestingly, Beck felt it necessary to express his admiration for *The Warriors*. "I want to put out there that I'm an avid video game player. [. . .] *The Warriors* is a great game and I'm not going to deny that," he told Knutsen (2006a). It is not uncommon for artists experimenting with video games to openly communicate their "love and hate" relationship with the medium. One is reminded of Anne-Marie Schleiner's appreciation for *Counter-Strike*, a game that she deliberately subverted with the classic hack, *Velvet-Strike* (2002). In an essay titled "*Velvet–Strike*: War Times and Reality Games (War Times from a Gamer Perspective)," she wrote: "I must also confess to enjoying many aspects of the game—I have actually always enjoyed shooters" (Schleiner 2002, 4).[6] At the same time, one cannot but wonder if these message were also intended as a *captatio benevolentiae*[7] directed to the game community, a rhetorical artifice meant to prevent, or assuage, the predictable backlash. If that was the case, it did not work.

The Highest Score was officially launched at 7 p.m. on Saturday, February 4, 2006. The counter increased methodically by one point per click: the visitors, therefore, became assistants (or accomplices) in Beck's experiment. This makes *The Highest Score* a collective artwork whose value relies heavily on the power of networks. In less than five days, the "score" reached approximately 300,000 points. Beck's original intention was to keep the Web site operating "for as long as [possible] without intervention" (Knutsen 2006a). But like the fire of a matchstick that burns brightly before being killed by a sudden, forceful blow, the life span of *The Highest Score* was short. The cause and manner of death were not "natural." Beck's previous disclaimer was not enough for the game publisher, which threatened him with legal action. A few days after launching his online project, Beck suddenly replaced the looped video on his Web site with the following message:

On February 9th, 2006, I received a cease-and-desist letter from Morrison Cohen LLP of New York, New York, ordering me to immediately remove all screen shots and video displays taken from the video game "The Warriors." If I were to ignore these orders, I would be subject to a trial in the United States District Court, where they would "seek preliminary and permanent injunctive relief," as well as "compensatory and punitive damages, attorneys fees and costs." (Knutsen 2006b)

The letter was signed by Fred H. Perkins, a lawyer who "handles a wide range of intellectual property matters, including trademark, copyright, unfair competition, trade secrets, patent, antitrust, licensing, Internet and software related disputes," as described on the Morrison Cohen Web site.[8] According to Perkins, *The Highest Score* "constitutes *unequivocal* copyright infringement under 17 U.S.C. § 501" because Beck "copied and [is] continuously displaying Take-Two's copyrighted material without its authorization. As a result, Take-Two is entitled to enjoin [Beck's] continuing copyright violation and recover damages, costs and attorneys fees because of enjoin [Beck's] *unlawful* activity" (Knutsen 2006b, emphasis added). Unwilling to confront Perkins in a court of law because of economic constraints, Beck complied with the demands—as Todd Haynes did with *The Karen Carpenter's Story* before—and withdrew his work.

Yet the game was not over for *The Highest Score*. It respawned elsewhere. In a sense, the authoritarian response from the publisher extended rather than suppressed its life span. Shortly after Beck's online installation vanished from public view, an intense debate took place on GamePolitics.com, a popular Web site that "explores the complex (and often controversial) relationships between the world of politics and videogames." In just a few days, 309 comments written by users explored issues relating to intellectual property rights, copyright, and trademark law. Similarly to Haynes and Libera, Beck's artwork had ignited a controversy, although his performance went mostly unnoticed outside the confines of the game domain.

I tried to reconstruct the lengthy conversation that took place on GamePolitics .com. For reasons of fidelity, I decided to transcribe the users' comments with minimal or no editing, even though they often contain misspellings, grammatical mistakes, and profanities. Like it or not, the debate is exemplary of the kinds of conversations that take place in online forums, and I feel it is necessary to maintain the original style, format, and content. Like email, online forums are an asynchronous means of communication, but they differ from email in many ways. As Harasim et al. (1995) have noted, forums offer a unique setting in which textual messages represent the connecting line between the participants and the knowledge that is being built. Participants read or write the comments at their convenience. All epistolary correspondence is saved and maintained in one shared space. The messages are arranged by threads according to the different discussion groups or according to different topics in the same discussion. Ravid and Rafaeli have remarked that

The existence of common message storage, the option every forum participant has to read and to write to any other participant, and a communication topology based on messages and knowledge as the main connecting axes, are the characteristics that separate discussion groups from e-mail communication. Differences in the attributes of interaction and the topology of the technology create a social structure of special interest. (2004, 11)

When the debate took place, GamePolitics was hosted on LiveJournal, a popular virtual community that allows users to keep a blog, journal or diary. GamePolitics combines journalistic content on videogame–related controversies with user-generated comments. It is important to clarify that LiveJournal differs from other blogging platforms because, especially in its early days (its origins can be traced back to 1999), it was more like a self-contained community than a collection of loosely connected sites. Moreover, it offered—and still does, at the time of writing—several social networking features that subsequently became a mainstay on such sites as Friendster, MySpace, and Facebook. Each journal entry has its own web page, which includes the comments written by other users. In addition, each user maintains a journal page, which shows all of his or her most recent entries, along with links to the comment pages. The most distinctive feature of LiveJournal is the "friends list," a feature that can be found in most—if not all—social network sites. Each user has a "friends" page, which collects the most recent journal entries written by contacts on his or her friends list. This function has been examined by, among others, Fono and Raynes-Goldie (2006).[9]

Interlude: A Top-Down View

For the sake of completeness, I should add that I have discussed Beck's case elsewhere (Bittanti and Quaranta 2006). It seemed to me a textbook example of the ongoing struggle between the "popular forces" and the "power bloc," a struggle described by Stuart Hall in his seminal essay, "Notes on Deconstructing the Popular" (1981). Hall suggests that popular culture is informed by an opposition between these factions. Popular forces are defined as "a diverse and dispersed set of social allegiances constantly formed and reformed among the formations of the subordinate" (230), whereas the power bloc is "a relatively unified, relatively stable alliance of social forces" whose influence has economic, legal, moral, and aesthetic implications. To explain this dichotomy, Hall uses a series of analogies—such as "homogeneity vs. heterogeneity," "occupying army vs. guerrilla fighters," and "center vs. the circumference"—all based on notions of confrontation and conflict. Based on this premise, *The Highest Score* can be considered an exercise in semiotic resistance in the form of a "remixed" artifact. Beck wanted to beat "dominant capitalism" (as represented by the game industry) at its own game, "hacking" a popular culture text to create a new, antagonistic, meaning to that intended by the creators. As John Fiske writes in *Reading the Popular*,

The basic power of the dominant in capitalism may be economic, but this economic power is both underpinned and exceeded by semiotic power, that is, the power to make meanings. So semiotic resistance not only refuses the dominant meanings but constructs oppositional ones that serve the interests of the subordinate is as vital a base for the redistribution of power as is evasion" (9–10).

In his artistic intervention, Beck was acting in an "adversarial" mode. As Lionel Trilling writes in *Beyond Culture*, "A primary function of art and thought is to liberate the individual from the tyranny of his culture and to permit him to stand beyond it in an autonomy of perception and judgment" (Trilling 1966, 63).[10] Beck subverted a popular video game to transcend his subordinate position. As Fiske argues,

Popular culture is made by subordinate peoples in their own interests out of resources that also, contradictorily, serve the economic interests of the dominant. . . . Popular culture is made from within and below, not imposed from without or above as mass cultural theorists would have it. . . . Popular culture is always a culture of conflict, it always involves the struggle to make social meanings that are in the interests of the subordinate and that are not those preferred by the dominant ideology, . . . The victories, however fleeting or limited, in this struggle produce popular pleasure, for popular pleasure is always social and political. (Fiske 1989, 2)

The practice of appropriation has been used in the art world since the 1960s and is very common in game art. Martin Pichlmair notes that

Appropriation art sought the de-contextualisation of consumerism's symbols: brands, advertisements and logos. The digital hijacking of mass-produced products and the succeeding abduction of digital content is a recent phenomenon. Artists working with games as raw material, adapting its code include Cory Arcangel, who solders his own cartridges and the artist-duo jodi3, who stripped *Wolfenstein 3D* from all its colours and most of its textures. [. . .] Appropriating a game means meta-playing. It means playing *with* the game (as coded possibilities) rather than playing the game. (Pichlmair 2006, 2–6)

Clearly, Dave Beck was silenced for using copyrighted work in his performance. "I just intended to make a statement about the situation our culture (I believe) happens to be in," he told a journalist, "and by making that statement, I was punished by higher powers" (quoted in Knutsen 2006b).

This case exemplifies an ongoing paradox. It is obvious that the game industry benefits from the massive labor generated by enthusiasts from all over the world, to the point that the boundaries between appreciation and exploitation have become blurred (Sotamaa 2007). At the same time, the game industry rejects remixes of "their" intellectual properties for purposes other than pure celebration. The same applies to the gaming community. On February 15, 2006, Dennis McCauley published a short entry on his Web site, GamePolitics.com, eloquently titled "Rockstar's Legal Gang Beats Down Online Art Installation." McCauley linked the aforementioned article written by Knutsen (2006a) describing Dave Beck's case (here erroneously referred to as "Dave Berg"), and added a few personal comments. To foster reader comments, McCauley did not explicitly state his position on the matter. His strategy proved successful. It did not take long for the first comment to materialize.

At 4:22 a.m., less than three hours after McCauley's original entry, a user named "featherspy" wrote, "I find it really interesting to see someone using video games as an artistic medium, rather than having the game itself being the medium. I am interested to see some more of this fellow's work."[11] A second comment, written by "lampbane," appeared fifteen minutes later, at 4:37 a.m.. It was equally concise, if

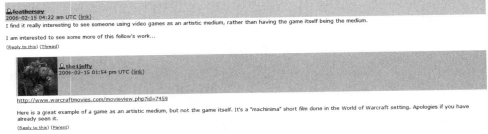

Figure 18.2
LiveJournal thread discussing the artistic potential of digital games, <http://gamepolitics
.livejournal.com/207696.html>.

vastly different in content and tone: "What a pretentious asshat. This screams publicity stunt to me."

The two messages started an intense debate that took place over the next few days
on GamePolitics.com. The initial two postings were soon followed by 307 more comments that built on and expanded these initial positions. According to Rheingold
(1993), online discussion forums can evolve into vibrant communities, virtual spaces
where users share valuable information, provide mutual support, and experience a
sense of belonging. Others, however, have observed that the relative anonymity, the
absence of a moderator, and fragmentation can often lead to nihilistic rather than
productive exchanges. (Ess 1996; King 1996) In my analysis of this particular conversation, I encountered both productive and disruptive moments. While this case shows
that forums can be a powerful tool for convivial, informal learning, it also proves that
the often invoked "collective intelligence" (Levy 1999; Lanier 2010) can be marginal-
ized by the wrath of the crowds.

"Rockstar's Legal Gangs Beats Down Online Art Installation": The Debate on GamePolitics

Analysis of the GamePolitics Discussion

As previously mentioned, my primary goal is to document the reaction from the users
of an online community originally hosted on the LiveJournal site GamePolitics to
Dave Beck's installation *The Highest Score* and its abrupt removal from his Web site
due to alleged copyright infringement. To this end, I collected and analyzed the

multiple threads posted on GamePolitics between February 15, 2006, and February 18, 2006, by seventy-eight users, most in their early twenties, as indicated by their visible profile.[12] Overall, 309 comments were posted below McCauley's story. Rather than selecting a specific thread, I decided to analyze the entire body of the discussion. After collecting the data (comments, user profiles, additional contextual information), I applied grounded theory methods (Glaser and Strauss 1967; Strauss and Corbin 1990) to develop a coding scheme for the types of behavior exhibited in the threads. I chose grounded theory over other approaches because of its emergent nature. Grounded theory does not test hypotheses but rather examines specific situations in order to identify interesting phenomena. Grounded theory aims at discovering the theory implicit in the data (Glaser and Strauss 1967). On a practical level, applying grounded theory to my research situation meant reviewing and revising my coding strategy after a first pass through the data. I also used qualitative content analysis to examine the body of comments. That allowed me to identify patterns in terms of related themes. I subsequently coded all the members' posts accordingly and went through the data several times to extract the examples used in this essay. Both the coding process and the analysis drew on past experiences with online forums and an intimate knowledge of the issues discussed by LiveJournal users.

Findings

The data showed several interesting phenomena and trends. First, as mentioned earlier, users built on and expanded the original two comments, often repeating the same adjectives used by the earliest commentors. For instance, the word "asshat,"used by lampbane, recurs in at least three separate posts. A user named "the1jeffy" describes Beck in these terms: "He's acting like a pretentious asshat, but that's what young art students do" (February 15, 2006, 6:27 p.m.). "Mharpol8" describes his initiative as "jackassery" (February 15, 1006, 4:57 a.m.). Another user, "akbarthegreat," implicitly refers to Beck by saying, "It's my (naturally cynical/fairly young) point of view that people are always, by and large, asshats" (February 15, 2006, 12:58 p,m.).

Second, the users sorted themselves into two factions, Beck's "supporters" and "denigrators." Actually, aside from a couple of users, nobody openly defended Beck or his artwork. Even among the defenders, the vast majority were adamant in stating their dislike for *The Highest Score*. What they "defended" was Beck's right to express his ideas by using *The Warriors* as a vessel. Example: "I think his 'art' is questionable. Personally, I think it's dumb. I'll fight to the death to defend his right to display it, but I think it's dumb" ("mnememth2230," February 15, 2006, 3:29 p.m.).

Third, two diverging tendencies emerged among all posts: a constructive movement and a destructive one. By constructive I mean that the contributors tried to advance, enhance, and enrich the conversation, linking to other sources to support their thesis and citing examples from their personal and professional experience. Many, however, displayed a destructive tendency, using invectives to condemn both Beck and other contributors and attempting to suppress the conversation.

Example of a constructive post 1: After stating that he studies law, "cjovalle" (February 15, 2006, 1:54 p.m.) explains some aspects of copyright law to the other users:

You can make that assertion, but there are certainly counter arguments. In the US, fair use is defined in 17 USC 107. There are four factors to consider. The overall use needs to pass the four factors—not each one separately, but taken together in considering of the specific act. The four factors are the amount used, the purpose of the use, the nature of the original materials, and the effect on the marketplace. Historically art, criticism, and commentary have a much stronger chance of being fair than other uses. While I don't agree with Berg's points, I have some serious doubt that his work is infringing. I believe Rock Star's use of DMCA provisions to block his work in this manner is somewhat hypocritical, given their own battles with censorship. Of course, ultimately only a judge can determine whether or not any given use is fair in a legal case of that particular situation. (February 15, 2006, 7:33 p.m.)

Example of a constructive post 2: In one of the longest threads in the debate, "mharpold8" explains the meaning of fair use by inserting an entire paragraph from Wikipedia. The following passage is particularly relevant to the conversation, as it quotes another case involving an artist using a popular toy for artistic purposes:

The first factor questions whether the use under consideration helps fulfill the intention of copyright law to stimulate creativity for the enrichment of the general public, or whether it aims to only "supersede the objects" of the original for reasons of, say, personal profit. In order to justify the use as fair, one must demonstrate how it either advances knowledge or the progress of the arts through the addition of something new. A key consideration is the extent to which the use is interpreted as transformative, opposed to as merely derivative. When Tom Forsythe appropriated Barbie dolls for his photography project "Food Chain Barbie," Mattel lost its claims of copyright and trademark infringement against him because his work effectively parodies Barbie and the values she represents (cf. the 2003 9th Circuit case Mattel Inc. v. Walking Mountain Productions). However, when Jeff Koons tried to justify his appropriation of Art Rogers' photograph "Puppies" in his sculpture "String of Puppies" with the same "parody" defense, he lost because his work was not presented as a parody of Rogers' photograph in particular, but of society at large, which was deemed insufficiently justificatory (see Art Rogers v. Jeff Koons, 960 F.2d 301). Thus, even if a secondary work proves transformative, it must be appropriately so. (February 15, 2006, 11:45 a.m.)

Example of a constructive post 3: User "the1jeffy" provides an external link in order to validate the previous user's comment: "Here is [hyperlink] a great example of a game as an artistic medium, but not the game itself. It's a 'machinima' short film done in the *World of Warcraft* setting. Apologies if you have already seen it" (February 15, 2006, 1:54 p.m.; contains hyperlink).

Example of a destructive post 1: Verbal abuse of another poster: "Oh yeah, in case you didn't get the message, FUCK YOU for that Vietnam comment" ("jerico6," February 18, 2006, 2:23 a.m.).

Example of a destructive post 2: The recurrent, disapproving one-liner slur: "Wow, that guy is a pretentious asshole" ("echoesandwaves," February 15, 2006, 9:19 p.m.).

A ludic tendency can easily be seen both in the exchanges and in the tactics adopted by the users. Interestingly, Xin and Feenberg (2006) have compared online discussions to games and sports:

Like a game with alternating moves, dialogic inquiry generated intrinsic motives for participation. [. . .] The players aim at a goal external to the play such as winning, but at each round of play, their moves are provoked by and provoke responses for intrinsic reasons such as the excitement of taking the ball away from an adversary. The game consists in the back and forth of move and counter-move with winning as the horizon under which the interactions take place. In reality, dialog resembles relaxed volleying rather than a serious match. One wants one's volleys returned, and the aim is not winning, but improving one's game. Similarly, each message in educational dialog fulfills a double goal: to communicate a content and to evoke further response. The true pleasure of playing at online discussion consists in making moves that keep others playing. (Xin and Feenberg 2006, 417)

The gamelike nature of conversation, especially online conversation, is reinforced by the use of such utterances as "You win!" (the1jeffy, February 15, 2006, 1:57 p.m.) or "You are SO friended. ;)" ("kingnat," February 15, 2006, 9:17 p.m.). In the latter case the practice of "friending," that is, adding a user to one's friends list in online social networks, becomes a rhetorical strategy. Although Xin and Feenberg's analogy is clearly correct, when dealing with conversations like this one, the "game" can indeed become a bit rough. Unpleasant language is very common in many online forums, and this case is no exception. Luckily, flaming and trolling, that is, the posting of deliberately hostile and inflammatory messages on the Internet in order to provoke a vehement response from other users, were actively discouraged throughout this discussion. Those who indulged in such intentionally disrupting behaviors were invited to stop.

We can draw two conclusions from these exchanges. First, even in the absence of a visible moderator, users were able to informally regulate the discussion through practices of metacommenting.[13] Second, the rules of online conversations—the forum etiquette—were constantly discussed, negotiated, and articulated, thus enabling new users to quickly become fully integrated in the conversation. And those who knowingly violated the rules were openly disciplined, again, to reestablish the validity of the unwritten rules. As Xin and Feenberg (2006) note, "Online discussion is paradoxical. It consists in a flow of relatively disorganized improvisational exchanges that somehow achieve highly goal-directed, rational course agendas. Despite the apparent incoherence of online talk, participants have established norms that regain the coherence and personal character of conversational interaction" (2).

Nonetheless, the users' reaction against Beck was vehemently antagonistic, if not exceptionally aggressive. Beck's project was vilified and described as "shock treatment," "garbage," "dumb," "piece of crap," and "pathetic exploitation." The artist himself was labeled "an asshole," "a jackass," "immature," "a hack," "an art GEEK," and "a damnable artsy ignoramus." (I find the latter insult remarkable). There's more: "I read that guy's comments and my translation of it is 'I'm a pretencious jackass of an artist who uses simple things, add big words, and boast on how I am the best artist ever depsite my lack of research into what I am presenting as art. Anyone who disagrees is a low class buffoon. Love me'" ("revengeofthezio," February 15, 2006, 4:51 a.m.); "The guy just seems to enjoy the notion of flaunting an immature sense of art and sensationalism. I definitely see the same tones of egotism and pretentious arrogance, as though he's already decided he's original and brilliant for his display. Sure, Rockstar could have gone a little easier on him, but he's not going to get much sympathy with his attitude. I almost support Rockstar if they can knock this jackass down a peg or two" ("sprngpilot," February 15, 2006 5:22 a.m.); "So many pretty words . . . So little thought behind them. Experiment my ass. How was he supposed to get feedback?" ("froggersrevenge," February 15, 2006, 4:59 a.m.); "You can make anything seem bad when you take it out of context, now can't you?" ("goopgod," February 15, 2006, 5:17 a.m.); and many others like them. In short, none of the gamers involved in the conversation seemed to believe that the practice of manipulating a videogame could have artistic implications. As one of the participants implies, machinima is acceptable *only* for promotional, celebratory, and self-referential purposes.

Moreover, the participants were sharply divided between those who believed that Beck had clearly infringed Rockstar Games' copyright and deserved an exemplary punishment and those who argued that the student's work was protected under the terms set by fair use law. Among the latter was mharpold8, who wrote, "While I'm not exactly a subscriber of Berg's thesis here, hopefully he gets some legal representation and tells Rockstar to go park it rectally. Art always wins" (February 15, 2006, 4:50 a.m.). The vast majority of commentators, however, sided with Rockstar. Consider the following examples: "Rockstar is within their rights. . . . The warrior's belong to rockstar and it's within their right to say how screen shots and video of it can and can not be used . . . its something that all art students learn while they are in college. . . . An artist must either create all the media that is part of their art piece or they must have permission to use the media that he uses. . . . Even if the artist gives credit to the original creator, if the artist does not have permission from the creator then the creator has the full right to tell them to stop using it. . . . The laws that will defend rockstar in this case are the same laws that protect all artists from getting their work stolen" ("monte924," February 15, 2006, 5:30 a.m.), or "Rockstar are the people who complained, they created the game, and that means it's entirely justifiable for them to care about other people using it toward their own ends. Personally I don't give a shit whether what he's doing is art or not. But as a simple matter of whether he should use other peoples work without their permission he's in the wrong on this one" ("e_w_spiral," February 15, 2006, 10:23 a.m.).

I found surprising that many young users, including those who labeled themselves as art students, felt dismayed by Beck's artwork and message. Camaraderie was definitely not evident. I was equally puzzled by the fact that the majority of commentators not only supported Rockstar Games' authoritarian reaction but argued that, in this case, censorship was not sufficient as a countermeasure. My perplexity was shared by user leeny_me, "I find it kinda of hilarious that all of us in the gaming community are so quick to scream first amendment to protect the rights of expression of video game makers, but when someone creates something that we disagree with, we pounce all over them, and pat Take Two on the back for pursuing litigation. now, i'm not saying that i agree with his idea, that i like his work or even that it doesn't infringe on copyright, but if freedom of expression is so important we need to protect the rights of everyone, even those we disagree with in order to protect our own" ("leeny_me," February 15, 2006, 6:49 a.m.), or "I think we're in serious trouble when we start defending the rights a huge corporation over that of an individual. that was sort of the point i was trying to make that seemed to be missed. not to mention i think he would have a good case in fair use as copyrighted material is used in art all the time to criticize and analyze" (leeny_me, February 16, 2006, 7:30 a.m.).

It became clear that a significant portion of the commentators perceived Beck as an outsider who launched an a priori attack on video games. In many posts, Beck was compared to or associated with Jack Thompson, an American lawyer, who has repeatedly expressed his harshly critical views on video games, especially Rockstar Games' titles. Thompson was often mentioned on the pages of GamePolitics and in other game-related Web sites and had become a true nemesis of the game community. Thus, Beck's use of a video game to express his denunciation was considered the ultimate form of mockery. Users felt Beck deserved castigation, and some even mentioned the possibility of "gamer-driven social actions against him," as in "Its this guy's right to tell the world we're murderous automatons, and its our right and duty to tell him he's an asshole. The difference in 'first amendment' issues between us and Jack Thompson is that we won't litigate or censor stuff like this. We fight our own battles" ("semperar," February 15, 2006, 7:13 a.m.), or "I am bothered that it came down to Rockstar taking legal action, I admit. I would love to have seen gamer-driven social actions against him instead" (semperar, February 15, 2006, 8:09 a.m.).

Interestingly, the discussion around Beck's artwork quickly evolved into a broader conversation about the notion of art itself as understood within the game community. As the following examples show, many gamers dismiss the idea that video games could be a form of art or even that they could express complex ideas (besides killing and shooting, that is). Henry Jenkins has written about the problematic concept of art for gamers (and game designers), a concept that they often perceive as a "burden":

To be sure, some gamers and game designers still want to deny that video games can be art because of the low (or lofty, depending on your perspective) reputation art has in contemporary culture. How can something this engaging possibly be discussed alongside the usual forced march through the local art museum? Does anyone want their favorite recreation to be taken over by stuffy art historians, pompous society matrons, and mumbling docents? Gamers and game designers should think long and hard before taking the burden of art, if only because it may decrease sales and frighten the children. This says more about what some historians have called the sacredization of art acress the late-nineteenth and twentieth centuries than it does about the merits of this particular medium. (Jenkins, quoted in Kelman 2005, 11–12)

Some users argued indeed that using images or sequences from games cannot possibly have any artistic implications: "Make societal commentary using a scene from a video game HARDLY constitutes art" ("skemodan," February 15, 2006, 11:51 a.m.). According to some contributors, art requires exceptional, uncommon skills; the "if I can do it in less than thirty minutes, then it is not art" argument recurs in many posts (e.g.: "I wouldn't classify looping images and screenshots from The Warriors plastered onto a web page as 'art' to begin with. If it's something I can accomplish in under 30 minutes, it most certainly is not 'art,'" stated "dog_welde," February 15, 2006, 6:01 p.m.). Moreover, many commentors questioned the artist's true intentions. "This art student is claiming it, as a whole, is his work of art and is trying to use it for notoriety and profit" ("nate_oo," February 15, 2006, 5:55 a.m.).

For some users, "art is content." Others argued, tautologically, that "art is art." What follows is a selection of examples. Notice the sheer variety of positions:

"Art is whatever the creator/performer/enactor says is art. It's just a question of whether or not it's worthy of the time you give to it" ("kingnat," February 15, 2006, 8:24 p.m.). "Just because the creator says it's art doesn't make it art in the eyes of everyone else. Art, like opinions, is subjective. Everyone's got their own definition of art and good taste and all that stuff, so while I say that it's not art and you say it is, that doesn't make either of us right" ("alacron," February 15, 2006, 8:40 p.m.). "Without content all you have is illustration, or animation, not art. Marcel Duchamp dubbed a urinal (that he didn't even make) as art. Now that urinal is a famous art piece. Sounds silly, but the idea behind it was to make us think in a way we hadn't considered . . . his intention was to be a controversial 'anti-artist.' So there you go. It doesn't matter who made the object, if you place it in a circumstance that gives it a whole new meaning, you're something of an artist" ("heimdal00," February 15, 2006, 9:08 a.m.). "Content. The one thing that's been made clear by the statements of every artist, and every art prof I've ever heard has been that content is what makes something Art rather than just craft or illustration. If the animation was communicating it's point as clearly as a commercial or ad, using big bold lettering and such, it may not be art at all. However, it's not doing that, it's leaving us to infer all it's meaning on our own. That's what makes it enter the realm of art" (heimdal00, February 16,

2006, 6:16 p.m.). "Just because something lacks solid content doesn't stop it being art. It just merely means that it's inconsequential, or the artist has less to say than they might like to believe. To be honest though, all the artists I know would have to admit to themselves that a lot of their commercial work isn't so much art as the craft" ("kingnat," February 17, 2006, 12:12 a.m.); "Art is art. Its not for anyone to contest that fact. You don't like it. Ok, congrats, move on. But it doesnt make it _not_ art" ("deviancy," February 15, 2006, 8:06 a.m.).

Checkpoint: What's the Final Score?

The work of art, for those who use it, is an activity of unframing, of rupturing sense, of baroque proliferation or extreme impoverishment, which leads to a recreation and a reinvention of the subject itself.
—Felix Guattari, *Chaosmosis* (1995, 130)

On the Internet, if it doesn't look like a dog wearing raver pants or a kawaii anime catgirl, it's not art.
—LiveJournals post by "sngingcircusdog," February 15, 2006

What should we make of this debate? On one level, Beck, like Todd Haynes and Zbigniew Libera before him, achieved his goals. In just a few days *The Highest Score*'s website was visited by thousands of visitors and generated more than three hundred posts on GamePolitics.com. As one user commented, "I see a hundred-odd outraged messages by gamers on a blog, an inflammatory cease and desiat order by Rockstar, and some actual discussion about violence in games, all started by this thing. Seems like he made it work to me" (mharpold8). Another user agreed: "One purpose of art is to make people think. This piece of art (or, at least the notion of it, since I haven't been able to see it) made me think, so I consider it a succes" ("carl_foust,"). More important, this case illustrates how users construct meanings in free-flowing online conversations. Now, if the metric of success of this form of communication is reaching a full consensus among the users, the GamePolitics debate reads like a debacle. Somehow disparagingly, the last entry, published on February 18 at 2:23 a.m., reads, "Oh yeah, in case you didn't get the message, FUCK YOU for that Vietnam comment" (jerico6). If convergence "requires the sharing of common and different views, the negotiation of varying levels of understating, visiting and revisiting various horizons and the gradual fusion of them all" (Gadamer 1982, 273–274), then the debate instigated by "Rockstar's Legal Gang Beats Down Online Art Installation" ended with utmost divergence.

However, the lack of consensus and the frequent use of abusive language should not keep us from recognizing the potential of online discussions per se and the possibility of engaging in constructive discussion about the role of videogame practices in redefining the notion of art (and vice versa). The role played by several contributors, including kingnat, cjovalle, funnydale, and mharpold8, was instrumental in broadening the scope of the conversation. By directly quoting passages from Wikipedia and other Web sites, or simply by citing other artists, they were able to give an additional layer of meaning to the case. Although a significant number of contributions were intellectually thin—many users posted a single derogatory comment, an inflamed or sarcastic one-liner—others constructed complex arguments, rationally criticizing other views, applying concepts, using appropriate examples, and so on. A small portion of users acted as leaders, guiding the conversation. These users contributed with posts that generated several responses and, possibly unconsciously, shaped a collaborative learning process through dialog.

Although this debate does not qualify as a form of "engaged collaborative discourse" in the terms set forth by Xin and Feenberg ("a group dialogue in pursuit of shared understanding and convergence"), it confirms that users from different backgrounds and interests can actively interact with each other around substantial issues. Although the vast majority of users who took part in the discussion were Americans, contributors from Canada, the UK, and Germany freely shared their knowledge, formed temporary allegiances, learned from each other, and, hopefully, achieved a better understanding of the case. As naive and idealistic as this might sound today, a cease-and-desist letter does not prevent a collective process of sense-making. It can, paradoxically, be a catalyst.

As *The Highest Score* demonstrates, when we talk about machinima, we are really talking about self-expression, culture, and art.

Game on.

Appendix

The nicknames of the LiveJournal users who participated in the debate are Featherspy, the1jeffy, goodrobotus, shadowkatamari, phantompvp, burntouttech, beardoggx, lampbane, mharpold8, heimdal00, nangke, semperar, monte924, kingnat, cjovalle, revengeofthezio, sprngpilot, froggersrevenge, stormewolfe, goopgod, jerico6, the_new_1, riffraff1138, e_w_spiral, acroamatis, alacron, prickvixen, das_banjo, dudelovenext, kurisu7885, braindead1, timed95, bluejoshi, revotruthinary, jdmdsp911, howdoyouplead, lecherousoldman, carl_foust, leeny_me, andrew_eisen, dog_welder, kharne83, mnementh2230, deviancy, bustermanzero, jeremykpierce, dachande18, the_attorney, kyhwana, sqlrob, mofo_x, akbarthegreat, imahori, anticron, skemodan, Pahsons, nate_oo, kail_murushi, EnmityWithin, silver_derstin, snakemeister, tollwutig, dagrak, vaminion, tsknf, nightwng2000, larpguide, suigin_kou, mrbrightcoco, barfo, jabrwock, irrevilent, echoesandwaves, exis, hilaryduffgta, expert_gamer, so_sorry810, funnydale. The most prolific poster was mharpold8, with sixty-one posts, followed by kingnat (twenty-five) and jerico6 (eighteen). For thirty-five of these users, the date and location of birth are clearly indicated in their profiles. Although the vast majority of users indicated the United States as their current location, a significant number of participants were from Europe and Australia. The comment of an additional poster was removed from the site and replaced with a note that says "removed comment from suspended user."

Acknowledgments

This article went through several iterations since I became fascinated with Dave Beck's case. I would like to thank Sonja Baumer and Michael Carter for their vital comments and suggestions.

Notes

1. The entire series can be seen at <http://www.manetas.com/art/videoaftervideogames/index .html>.

2. The term "appropriation" is traditionally defined as the practice of taking something for oneself without consent. In cultural studies, the expression "cultural appropriation" is used to indicate the practice of "borrowing" and changing the meaning of cultural products (including video games), images, slogans, and the like.

3. Another paradigmatic example is the incensed reaction—by both the media and the game community—to Douglas Edric Stanley's *Space Invader* installation at the Leipzig Convention in 2008. *Space Invader* is an homage to Taito's classic arcade games that incorporates themes related to the 2001 terrorist attacks on the Twin Towers. Additional information can be found at Stanley's Web site, <http://www.abstractmachine.net>.

4. For additional information, see Hilderbrand's excellent chapter, "Grainy Days and Mondays: *Superstar* and Bootleg Aesthetics" (Hilderbrand 2009, 161–190).

5. According to the author, *Correcting Devices* was meant to illustrate the gap between the ideal world marketed to children and the real one created by adults. Other pieces include Barbies with bulging tummies and unflattering thighs, and an infant doll with hairy legs and armpits.

6. Additional comments on the allure of first-person shooters can be found in an interview of Anne-Marie Schleiner by Pedro Soler for SonarOnline at <http://www.opensorcery.net/ interviewp.html>. The essay is available at <http://www.opensorcery.net/aboutvs.html>.

7. *Captatio benevolentiae* is any literary or oral device that seeks to secure the goodwill of the recipient or hearer, as in a letter or in a discussion.

8. From Fred Perkins's profile, available online at <http://www.morrisoncohen.com/new_bios/ perkins.php>.

9. Scholarly analyses of LiveJournals include wide-ranging descriptions (Boyd and Ellison 2007), a friendship classification scheme (Hsu et al. 2007), motivations to contribute in online communities (Backstrom et al. 2006), and the role of displaying preferences relating to cultural artifacts such as films, books, and albums in creating a parallel network structure (Liu 2007). For additional resources, see Boyd and Ellison (2007). There is also is a significant body of scholarly analyses relating to online discussion groups that may be relevant, considering the hybrid nature of LiveJournal. As Anne-Laur Fayard and Geraldine DeSanctis (2005) tell us, researchers such as Rheingold (1993) have investigated member contribution patterns, churn, sustainability, and motivations for contributing, while Smith and Kollock (1999) discuss issues relating to social control. Finholt and Sproull (1990) studied how work-oriented groups differ in their contribution patterns from more entertainment-oriented groups. As Fayard and DeSanctis (2005) write, "Collectively, the research to date shows that intimate relationships and development of community are possible online, and that online forums can be productive and sustainable." The research produced contradicting results regarding the efficacy of online forums for sharing information. Some of the reasons advanced for lack of efficacy included lack of familiarity among individuals, distinctive thought worlds, disparities in verbal skill, differing cultures, status differences, and challenges associated with physical distance (Bechky 1999, 2003; Smith 1999; Gruenfeld et al. 1996).

10. For more information on the concept of an adversary culture in art, see Julian Stallabrass, *High Art Lite* (London: Verso, 2000).

11. For the sake of clarity, I quote entire comments (or excerpted comments) that appeared on LiveJournal. I indicate the user's nickname and the date and time of posting. The complete list of participants is provided in the appendix to this essay.

12. See the appendix.

13. As Xin and Feenberg note, "meta-comments include remarks directed as such things as the context, norms, or agenda of the forum; or at solving problems such as the lack of clarity, irrelevance, and information overload. Meta-comments play an important role in maintaining the conditions of successful communication" (Xin and Feenberg 2006, 20).

References

Backstrom, L., D. Huttenlocher, J. Kleinberg, and X. Lan. 2006. Group Formation in Large Social Networks: Membership, Growth, and Evolution. In *Proceedings of 12th International Conference on Knowledge Discovery in Data Mining*, 44–45. New York: ACM Press.

Bechky, B. A. 1999. "Creating Shared Meaning across Occupational Communities: An Ethnographic Study of a Production Floor." Paper presented at the annual meeting of the Academy of Management, Chicago, August 6–11.

Bechky, B. A. 2003. Sharing Meaning across Occupational Communities: The Transformation of Understanding on a Production Floor. *Organization Science* 14 (3): 312–330.

Berger, J., B. Cohen, and M. Zelditch. 1972. Status Characteristics and Social Interaction. *American Sociological Review* 37 (3): 241–255.

Bien, L. 2006. Controversial Toys. <http://www.arborweb.com/reviews/0601.libera–review.html>.

Bittanti, M., and D. Quaranta. 2006. *Gamescenes: Art in the Age of Videogames.* Milan: Johan & Levi.

Boyd, D. M., and N. B. Ellison. 2007. Social Network Sites: Definition, History, and Scholarship. *Journal of Computer-Mediated Communication* 13 (1): 11. <http://jcmc.indiana.edu/vol13/issue1/boyd.ellison.html>.

Ess, Charles. 1996. The Political Computer: Democracy, CMC, and Habermas. In *Philosophical Perspectives on Computer-Mediated Communication*, ed. Charles Ess, 197–230. Albany: State University of New York Press.

Fayard, A.-L., and G. DeSanctis. 2005. Evolution of an Online Forum for Knowledge Management Professionals: A Language Game Analysis. *Journal of Computer-Mediated Communication* 10 (4): article 2. <http://jcmc.indiana.edu/vol10/issue4/fayard.html>.

Feinstein, S. C. 2000. C. Zbigniew Libera's Lego Concentration Camp: Iconoclasm in Conceptual Art about the Shoah. Other Voices 2 (1).

Finholt, T., and L. Sproull. 1990. Electronic Groups at Work. *Organization Science* 1 (1): 41–64.

Fiske, John. 1989. *Reading the Popular*, 1–12. London: Routledge.

Fono, D., and K. Raynes-Goldie. 2006. Hyperfriendship and Beyond: Friends and Social Norms on LiveJournal. In *Internet Research Annual, vol. 4: Selected Papers from the AOIR Conference*, ed. M. Consalvo and C. Haythornthwaite, 91–103. New York: Peter Lang.

Gadamer, H.-G. 1982. *Truth and Method.* New York: Crossroads.

Glaser, B. G., and A. L. Strauss. 1967. *The Discovery of Grounded Theory: Strategies for Qualitative Research.* New York: Aldine.

Gruenfeld, D. H., E. A. Mannix, K. Y. Williams, and M. A. Neale. 1996. Group Composition and Decision Making: How Member Familiarity and Information Distribution Affect Process and Performance. *Organizational Behavior and Human Decision Processes* 67 (1): 1–15.

Guattari, Felix. 1995. *Chaosmosis: An Ethico-Aesthetic Paradigm.* Bloomington: Indiana University Press.

Hall, S. 1981. Notes on Deconstructing the Popular. In *People's History and Socialist Theory*, 227–249. London: Routledge.

Harasim, Linda, Starr Roxanne Hiltz, Murray Turoff, and Lucio Teles. 1995. *Learning Networks: A Field Guide to Teaching and Learning Online.* Cambridge: MIT Press.

Hilderbrand, L. 2009. *Inherent Vice: Bootleg Histories of Videotape and Copyright.* Durham, NC: Duke University Press.

Kelman, N. 2005. *Video Game Art*. New York: Assouline.

King, Storm. 1996. Researching Internet Communities: Proposed Ethical Guidelines for the Reporting of Results. *Information Society* 12:119–127.

Knutsen, K. 2006a. A Warrior's Highest Score. *ISTHMUS's The Daily Page*, February 7. <www .isthmus.com/daily/node/908>.

Knutsen, K. 2006b. Rockstar Legal Warriors Squash Online Installation. *ISTHMUS's The Daily Page*, February 14. <http://sentra.ischool.utexas.edu/~i312co/blog/wp-trackback.php?p=90>.

Kundera, M. 2007. *The Curtain: An Essay in Seven Parts*. New York: HarperCollins.

Lampel, J., and A. Bhalla. 2007. The Role of Status Seeking in Online Communities: Giving the Gift of Experience. *Journal of Computer-Mediated Communication* 12 (2): article 5. <http://jcmc .indiana.edu/vol12/issue2/lampel.html>.

Lanier, Jaron. 2010. *You're Not a Gadget: A Manifesto*. New York: Knopf.

Levy, Pierre. 1999. *Collective Intelligence: Mankind's Emerging World in Cyberspace*. New York: Basic Books.

Lowood, Henry. 2007. High-Performance Play: The Making of Machinima. In *Videogames and Art: Intersections and Interactions,* ed. Andy Clarke and Grethe Mitchell, 59–79. London: Intellect Books; Chicago: University of Chicago Press.

Lowood, Henry. 2005. Real-Time Performance: Machinima and Game Studies. *International Digital Media and Arts Association Journal* 1 (3):10–17.

Liu, H. 2007. Social Network Profiles as Taste Performances. *Journal of Computer-Mediated Communication* 13 (1): 13. <http://jcmc.indiana.edu/vol13/issue1/liu.html>.

McCauley, D. 2006. Rockstar's Legal Gang Beats Down Online Art Installation. Posted February 15 on GamePolitics.com. <http://gamepolitics.livejournal.com/207696.html>.

Murphy, E. Dean. 1997. An Artist's Volatile Toy Story. *Los Angeles Times*, May 19. <http://articles .latimes.com/1997-05-19/news/mn-60350_1_lego-toys/2>

Pichlmair, Martin. 2006. Pwned: Ten Tales of Appropriation. Paper presented at the Mediaterra conference, Athens, October 4–10.

Ravid, Gilad, and Sheizaf Rafaeli. 2004. Asynchronous Discussion Groups as Small World and Scale Free Networks. *First Monday* 9 (9). <http://131.193.153.231/www/issues/issue9_9/ravid/ index.html>.

Rheingold, H. 1993. *The Virtual Community: Homesteading on the Electric Frontier*. New York: Addison-Wesley.

Schleiner, Anne-Marie. 2002. Velvet-Strike: War Times and Reality Games (War Times from a Gamer Perspective). <http://www.opensorcery.net/aboutvs.html>.

Sotamaa, Olli. 2007. Let Me Take You to The Movies™: Productive Players, Commodification, and Transformative Play. *Convergence* 13:4.

Strauss, A., and J. Corbin. 1990. *Basics of Qualitative Research: Grounded Theory Procedures and Techniques*. London: Sage.

Trilling, L. 1966. *Beyond Culture*. New York: Penguin.

Wyatt, J. 1993. Cinematic/Sexual Transgression: An Interview with Todd Haynes. *Film Quarterly* 46 (3): 2–8.

Xin, C., and A. Feenberg. 2006. Pedagogy in Cyberspace: The Dynamics of Online Discourse. Journal of Distance Education 21 (2): 1–25.

Software Reference

The Warriors. Rockstar Games. 2005.

Contributors

Jeffrey Bardzell
Assistant professor of HCI design and new media, Indiana University, Bloomington

Matteo Bittanti
Associate researcher, Stanford Humanities Lab, Stanford University, California

David Cameron
Lecturer at the School of Communication, Charles Strut University, Bathurst, Australia

John Carroll
Professor of communication research, Charles Strut University, Bathurst, Australia

Erik Champion
Associate professor, Auckland School of Design, Massey University, New Zealand

Ricard Gras
Director, Inter-Activa, Leicester, UK

Robert Jones
Vice president of gaming programming, machinima.com

Matt Kelland
Creative director and founder, Short Fuze/Moviestorm Ltd., Cambridge, UK

Friedrich Kirschner
Artist, Berlin, Germany

Peter Krapp
Associate professor of film and media studies, University of California, Irvine

Danny Kringiel
Journalist, Hamburg, Germany

Henry Lowood
Curator of History of Science and Technology Collections and Film and Media Collections, Stanford University, California

Lev Manovich
Professor, Visual Arts Department, University of California, San Diego

Ali Mazalek
Assistant professor, School of Literature, Communication and Culture, Georgia Institute of Technology, Atlanta

Michael Nitsche
Associate professor, School of Literature, Communication and Culture, Georgia Institute of Technology, Atlanta

Matthew Thomas Payne
Instructor, Department of Radio, TV, Film, University of Austin, Texas

Michael Pigott
Lecturer, film and television studies, University of Warwick, UK

Dan Pinchbeck
Senior lecturer, School of Creative Technologies, University of Portsmouth, UK

Katie Salen
Associate professor, Design and Technology Program, and executive director, Institute of Play, New York

Gareth Schott
Senior lecturer, screen and media studies, University of Waikato, New Zealand

Bevin Yeatman
Senior lecturer, screen and media studies, University of Waikato, New Zealand

Index